JOHN RANDOLPH OF ROANOKE

A STUDY IN AMERICAN POLITICS

By Russell Kirk

John Randolph of Roanoke is unique in American political history. Only twenty-six when first elected to Congress in 1799, he easily became its most forceful figure. An incomparable orator, he was also, in the words of historian Dumas Malone, "a merciless castigator of iniquity." Booted and spurred, he commanded attention as he swaggered about Congress, whip in hand. But it is Randolph's convictions that take on new significance in our time.

With the exception of Jefferson's first term, Randolph's public career was as a leader of the opposition—to both Jeffersonians and Federalists. He was, says Kirk, "devoted to state rights, the agricultural interest, economy in government, and freedom from foreign entanglements." Above all things he cherished personal liberty. "I am an aristocrat," Randolph declared. "I love liberty, I hate equality."

Dr. Kirk's masterful study is not a biography, but rather a portrait of the exceptionally agile and brilliant mind of one of America's best, but least-known, political thinkers. His examination of Randolph is at once an essay in political theory and a sound contribution to American history.

Incorporated into this third edition of *John Randolph of Roanoke* are appendices containing several of Randolph's most important speeches and a representative selection of his letters.

RUSSELL KIRK, historian, critic, essayist and novelist, is the author of (at last count) twenty books, among them *The Conservative Mind* and *The Roots of American Order*.

I would not live under King Numbers. I would
not be his steward, nor make him my taskmaster. I would
obey the principle of self-preservation, a principle we find
even in the brute creation, in flying from this mischief.

John Randolph of Roanoke
at the Virginia Convention, 1829

A STUDY IN AMERICAN POLITICS
with Selected Speeches and Letters

John Randolph
of Roanoke

Russell Kirk

LibertyPress

Indianapolis

Liberty*Press* is a publishing imprint of Liberty Fund, Inc., a foundation established to encourage study of the ideal of a society of free and responsible individuals.

The cuneiform inscription that serves as the design motif of our endpapers is the earliest known written appearance of the word "freedom" (*ama-gi*), or liberty. It is taken from a clay document written about 2300 B.C. in the Sumerian city-state of Lagash.

Frontispiece art courtesy of Louis Mercier.

Library of Congress Cataloging in Publication Data
Kirk, Russell.
   John Randolph of Roanoke.
   Bibliography: p. 571.
   Includes index.
   1. Randolph, John, 1773–1833.   2. Legislators—United States—Biography.   3. United States—Politics and government—1783–1865.
I. Title.
E302.6.R2K5   1978   973.4′092′4   78–8659
ISBN 0–913966–40–1

To Rosemary

Contents

Prefatory Note

This new edition of my book on Randolph's political ideas is a modest improvement, and a considerable enlargement, of the version published twelve years ago. The principal additions are an appendix containing several of Randolph's more important speeches—hitherto available only in the document- and newspaper-stacks of a few university and public libraries—and a briefer appendix consisting of representative letters by him (some of them not printed before).

Mr. Kenneth Shorey read the proofs of this new edition; Mr. W. C. McCann, those of the original. At the University of Virginia, where are to be found the largest collections of Randolph's papers, Dr. James P. McClellan gave me much help. The advice of the late Charles Sydnor, of Duke University, aided me more than two decades ago, with the first draft of this study.

The libraries of the University of Virginia, Duke University, the University of North Carolina, and the state of Virginia kindly permit me to print passages, or whole letters, from manuscripts in their collections, as does the North Carolina State Department of Archives and History.

During the past twelve years, the political questions that vexed Randolph have increased, rather than diminished, in their relevance to the concerns of twentieth-century American society. Some suggestion of this may be found in my essay "The Prospects for Territorial Democracy in America," printed in a volume edited by Dr. Robert Goldwin, *A Nation of States* (Chicago, 1963).

—RUSSELL KIRK

Piety Hill
Mecosta, Michigan
May 1963

Afterword

This new printing of 1978 contains some small improvements, additions, and corrections to the previous edition. Mr. David Schock and Mr. Stanley Common helped me with the proofs and the index of this third edition.—R. K.

John Randolph of Roanoke

Chapter One

Randolph
and This Age

This book is an account of the lively mind of a radical man who became the most eloquent of American conservatives. John Randolph, the enemy of Jefferson and of the Adams family, has been the subject of several biographies—though as yet none entirely satisfactory has appeared. I do not propose in these pages to describe Randolph's life—except summarily in this chapter—but rather to describe his opinions and to suggest their influence.

Of Randolph's alternating ferocity and compassion, his duels, his beautiful letters, his entrancing extemporaneous eloquence, his fits of madness, his sardonic wit, his outbursts of prophecy and his visions of devils, his brandy and his opium, his passionate Christianity, his lonely plantation life, his quixotic opposition to the great political and economic powers of the day—everyone who reads American history knows something. Randolph would have done credit to the pages of Byron or Disraeli.

But also he was a man possessed of a genius literary and political. Few remember that he was a master of English style, and a strong influence upon conservative thought. A recent history of American literature, got up on a grand scale, has kind words for some obscure literary hacks, but does not mention Randolph even in the index; and Randolph has not fared much better in histories of American political thought. As a pious act, then, I summon up John Randolph from among the shades.

Almost in a fit of absence of mind, America has become in this day the chief protector of the patrimony of civilization: the great conservative power. So it is that Americans are reexamining political theory, in the hope of maintaining order and justice and freedom. Calhoun's ideas, for instance, now receive the attention they have long deserved. Randolph was the preceptor of Calhoun, a champion of the South and of prescription while Calhoun himself still was an innovator. But Randolph also deserves study in his own right.

This volume is an analysis of Randolph's principles, dealt with topically, not chronologically. The following bald brief account of his career (a most lively political life, yet not so interesting as his labyrinthine personality), together with the chronology at the end of this book, may help to bind together the several chapters concerned with his political ideas.

John Randolph was born three years before the Declaration of Independence, and he died during the great Nullification controversy. No man's life displays more clearly the chain of events which linked the proclamations of 1776 and of 1832. Jefferson, whose early follower Randolph was, belonged to an earlier generation of natural-rights optimists; Calhoun—who, in considerable degree, was the disciple of Randolph—belonged to the later generation which put its faith in legal logic. At both, Randolph sneered; he fought the administration of John Adams, and slashed at the administration of Jefferson, and harried every other President of his time. In Randolph's speeches, one finds at work the forces that brought on the events of 1832 and of 1861.

The heir to one of the greatest of Virginian aristocratic families, John Randolph was born near the mouth of the Appomattox, on the eve of revolution. His life was turbulent from the first. Proud, acutely sensitive, and animated by a darting passion, he was a natural champion of perilous causes. Though he was irregularly educated at Princeton and Columbia, his delight in humane letters soon made him the most eloquent man of his time.

About his nineteenth year, his character was given its tragic bent by a series of mysterious events. He contracted some disease, and by disease he was racked for the rest of his life. He may have been made impotent by scarlet fever, though this is not certain. Mr. William E. Stokes conjectures, from certain letters and traditions, that Randolph probably was the victim of syphilis, perhaps contracted in a quixotic youthful liaison (by which, apparently, he was endeavoring to rescue a friend from the clutches of an adventuress).[1] However that may be, the young man was altered, outwardly and inwardly. In appearance, he long remained a kind of boy preserved in amber, youthful of face, lean and lank to the point of grotesqueness. Suffering shook his reason, so that for two or three short periods during his life he was next door to madness; yet even during those times he preserved not only his eloquence, but a sardonic political realism.

---

[1] William E. Stokes, Jr., "The Early Career of John Randolph of Roanoke" (unpublished thesis, Alderman Library, University of Virginia, 1955).

What with his physical disaster, his engagement to marry a young beauty, Maria Ward, was broken off. Worse, his brother Richard and his cousin Nancy Randolph almost certainly were involved in incest and infanticide, leading to the early death of his brother in 1796. Thereafter, Randolph's appalling solitude admitted only a few close friends —and those had their patience sorely tried. His young kinsman Theodore Dudley, very shortly after Randolph's death, wrote of this complex being:

> The truth and beauty of the eastern allegory, of the man endowed with two souls, was never more forcibly exemplified than in his case. In his dark days, when the evil genius predominated, the austere vindictiveness of his feelings toward those that a distempered fancy pictured as enemies, or as delinquent in truth or honor, was horribly severe and remorseless.
>
> Under such circumstances of mental alienation, I sincerely believe (if it may not appear irreverent) that had our blessed Savior, accompanied by his Holy Mother, condescended to become again incarnate, revisited the earth, and been domiciliated with him one week, he would have imagined the former a rogue, and the latter no better than she should be.
>
> On the contrary, when the benevolent genius had the ascendant, no one ever knew better how to feel and express the tenderest kindness, or to evince, in countenance and manner, gentler benevolence of heart.[2]

Even in his years of success, this shadow lay heavy upon Randolph. Yet at first, defying all handicaps, he mounted very high, as the world reckons achievement. In 1799 he debated the aged Patrick Henry; and his brilliance of mind and his mordant tongue carried him into Congress. At the age of twenty-six, he was a hard hater of the Federalists,

---

[2] Theodore Dudley, ed., *Letters of John Randolph to a Young Relative,* p. 203.

a partisan of revolutionary France. He smote the administration of John Adams hip and thigh.

With the inauguration of Jefferson, picturesque Jack Randolph became the majority leader of the House of Representatives: in the mediocre House of Jefferson's two terms he had no near rivals in talent. Perhaps already emulating Burke, he endeavored to convict the Federalist Justice Chase of misconduct on the bench, much as Burke had impeached Hastings; but, like Burke's, his prosecution failed. This was the first of a series of reverses of fortune that dogged Randolph throughout his congressional career—and to which, so far as a passionate man might, he became inured with the passing of the years.

Congenitally suspicious of executive power, and uneasy at the tendencies of the Jeffersonians, Randolph began to break with Jefferson, Madison, and the other principal leaders of the Republicans in 1805. There were two immediate causes of the breach: the Yazoo controversy, and the attempt of Jefferson and Madison to acquire Spanish Florida.

The Yazoo lands of the state of Georgia had been acquired by speculators, through bribery of the Georgia legislature. An indignant public elected new legislators, who proceeded to repudiate the corrupt bargain. But the Yazoo land companies appealed to the federal government for compensation for their loss, pleading that the claims had passed already from the original speculators to innocent purchasers in good faith.

Madison and Gallatin, backed by President Jefferson, advocated a compromise by which the Yazoo claimants would be paid some compensation from the federal Treasury— though only a fraction of the sums they desired. Randolph set his face—successfully, until he was defeated temporarily in the congressional contests of 1813—against any payment. Outraged at such circumventing of the will of a sovereign state, John Randolph never forgave the other Republican leaders for their dallying with the "Yazoo men."

Also in 1805, the complex affair of Jefferson's and Madison's attempt to purchase Florida, through a secret appropriation of two million dollars, became the second cause of Randolph's schism. Though he had supported the Louisiana Purchase, Randolph opposed with all his force the scheme to acquire Florida from the Spanish government. In effect, said Randolph, this would have been paying blackmail to Napoleon, for whom the Spanish regime was a mask. Mr. Irving Brant attributes this unyielding stand to Randolph's dislike of Madison, and to his private frustrations.[3]

But the reasons for Randolph's attitude lie deeper far. As a champion of personal liberty, well before 1806 Randolph was disillusioned with the French Revolution. Napoleon he detested and feared. Only for a brief while had he been a Gallophile; his real sympathies, all his life, lay with England. And England, in 1806, was in grave peril. As much as any of the Federalists he condemned, Randolph took English society and culture for models. The abortive Florida purchase would have strengthened Napoleon: so Randolph went into opposition, his ties with the Jeffersonians already being greatly weakened.

Randolph had denounced the Yazoo scandals in January 1805; he quarreled with Jefferson and Madison over the Florida scheme in December of that year. On March 6, 1806, he spoke against Gregg's Resolution, which was intended to cut off commerce with Britain—here siding with

---

[3] Irving Brant, *James Madison*, IV, chap. xxiii.

the Federalists, though not joining them. By August 15, his alienation from Jefferson was complete; and he formed the faction of the Tertium Quids, which little band of Southerners he led most of the rest of his life.

So he forfeited the leadership of the House. And as the War Hawks—Calhoun, Clay, Grundy, and the rest—gained ascendancy over Congress, Randolph fought a rear-guard action, foretelling ruin from war with Britain. Yet the War of 1812 came; and, unpopular for opposing it, Randolph lost his congressional seat in 1813. To Roanoke he retired, there meditating on Christian doctrine, lamenting the evils of the times, and losing himself in his library. As Virginia suffered from embargo and war, however, Randolph's influence with his constituency revived, so that he was elected in 1815 to the Fourteenth Congress.

Ill health, capped by an interval of madness, made him decline reelection in 1817; but, better by 1819, he resumed his Southside seat. In the House he remained until the end of 1825, when he served a little more than a year in the Senate. He and his friends had tried to make Monroe president in 1808; but with Monroe in power they were bitterly disappointed; and they thought John Quincy Adams worse still. In 1828, Randolph came out for Jackson's candidacy—which later he was to regret.

In both House and Senate, John Randolph led an embittered group—chiefly Virginians and North Carolinians—of members devoted to state rights, the agricultural interest, economy in government, and freedom from foreign entanglements. He fought the drift toward war in 1811, the Bank of the United States in 1816, the Missouri Compromise in 1820, internal improvements at federal expense in 1824, increases of the tariff at all times, the Panama Mission proposal in 1826—and almost every other principal measure recommended by Jefferson, Madison, Monroe, and Adams. Occasionally he succeeded in blocking one scheme or another: but in most matters, as he said, Randolph "was beaten down, horse, foot, and dragoons."

Throughout these years in the political wilderness, Randolph's health spiraled downward, though now and again, to the astonishment of friends and enemies, his powers would return to him, almost miraculously. By 1829, when he retired from Congress, he wore the aspect of a corpse, and was in pain almost constantly. "His constitution was a wreck," J. G. Baldwin writes. "His mind had lost much of its strength and coherence. His speeches had deteriorated. They had become more rambling, desultory, disjointed, eccentric, extravagant . . . often deformed by coarse vituperation, and weakened by repetitions and prolixity."[4]

And yet this strange man was not altogether undone. Late in 1829, the Virginia Constitutional Convention convened, and Randolph attended as a delegate—to denounce the whole concept of a new constitution. Confronted by this challenge, his brain reasserted its endowments of wit, logic, and fancy. At the Convention, Randolph's speeches were the equal of his best thirty years earlier—perhaps better. Having raised his voice in warning against neoterism, he accepted Jackson's offer of the post of minister to Russia.

St. Petersburg's cold and damp promptly brought him low. He retreated to England, which he knew and loved well, and by the autumn of 1831 was back at Roanoke in his lonely cabin, surrounded by his hundreds of slaves. Calhoun and South Carolina were approaching their collision

---

[4] Joseph Glover Baldwin, *Party Leaders*, p. 251.

with President Jackson. Nullification was nonsense, the realist Randolph declared; but Jackson's resort to force against South Carolina roused him to a final burst of fury, and at Charlotte Courthouse—in February, 1833—he poured his molten metal upon the head of Andrew Jackson.

"Dying, sir, dying," had been his reply, for decades, when men asked him how he did. Political passion alone had kept vigor in his skeleton frame; and now that fire was flickering out. He commenced a fifth trip to England; but in a Philadelphia hotel, consumption mastered him at last. "Remorse, remorse!" he cried from the bed; and then he was gone into the mystery from which he had emerged sixty years before. Love and hatred, between which that wild strong personality had been torn since childhood, were spent.

It had been a career, if you will, of negation. Yet the eloquence remains, and the love of liberty, and the tragic sense of life which so few Americans of Randolph's time apprehended. Clay and Webster are only textbook names, now; Madison and Monroe are not much more; but John Randolph, even in his torment, lives for us still. Sometimes ghostly enough while alive, he assumes a curious vitality when long dead. Though this book cannot explore his soul, it is possible to suggest the quality of his genius by examining a mass of speeches and letters.

Randolph's pattern of politics, though formed in an age of flux, was internally consistent. It was an appeal to tradition, against the god Whirl, and it has its disciples yet. John Randolph contended against the world of his day, and three decades after his death his beloved country of Virginia rendered to Randolph's principles the last full measure of devotion.

Although Randolph and the other Old Republicans—Nathaniel Macon, Spencer Roane, Taylor of Caroline, Richard Stanford, and the rest—failed in their day to halt the political and economic tendencies they dreaded, and at no time could command a majority in the nation or even in the South, they were to triumph in the thirty years which preceded the Civil War. Randolph lived long enough to see the beginning of that fleeting victory. No one would maintain that Randolph's voice alone caused this alteration in Southern thought; nevertheless, Randolph exerted over the minds of the generation which followed his a force accorded to few parliamentary leaders.

For it was Randolph that Hayne quoted against Webster; it was Randolph to whom Calhoun listened, pondering, from his presiding chair in the Senate; it was Randolph of whom Beverley Tucker wrote to Hammond and his colleagues. The remnant of the Tertium Quids, the Old Republicans, split during Jackson's administration: some, like Benjamin Watkins Leigh, became Whigs; some found their places among Calhoun's Democrats; some went over to the Jacksonians; some set their hands against every man's. And yet a measure of the aristocratic, freedom-asserting politics of Randolph was retained by all these men, and their Southern factions were to find themselves united in 1861.

Concerning Old Republican political thought, little has been written. In recent years something has been made, with justice, of John Taylor of Caroline, an ally of Randolph's faction. Taylor's egalitarian principles, however, scarcely were identical with Randolph's. The Roanoke planter's speeches, which so astounded his contemporaries by virtue of their evocative character and their flaming wit, their unpremeditated splendor and their flashes of prophetic intuition, never have been collected; nor have his numerous letters. We can read Taylor's and Thomas Cooper's and Calhoun's books today, but Randolph wrote for publication nothing except a few revisions of his longer speeches and a few letters to the newspapers. Despising hard-and-fast expositions of political abstraction, perhaps he would not have written *Construction Construed* or *A Disquisition on Government* even had time and health permitted; in this, if in nothing more, Randolph resembled Jefferson.

Even hostile critics of Randolph—among them William P. Trent and Henry Adams—concede that the Virginian possessed a remarkable—perhaps a unique—consistency in a time of political inconstancy. Wisely or not, Randolph would not bend before the demands of the hour, as did Jefferson; nor would he alter his convictions, as did Calhoun. From 1803 to 1833 his course was inflexible. Yet it was not unchanging: he grew more intense in his beliefs and more biting in their expression.

Randolph was not a democrat, not a nationalist, not a liberal. (He did believe ardently in equality of civil rights, in his country, and in liberty.) Unlike Webster and Clay, he did not speak grandiloquently of the tremendous future of the Union. It may be that he struggled against the stars in their courses. Surely his principles are out of fashion nowadays.

And still Randolph's concepts of political honesty and of personal and local liberty remain valid. Randolph's speech on Gregg's Resolution (March, 1806), for instance, means more in these times of American incertitude than ever it did before; and Randolph's despair at the transience of social institutions never was better illustrated than by this present reign of King Whirl.

Though the course of his life was as fantastic as any romantic novel, the great merit of Randolph's political utterance is its merciless realism. For cant and slogan he reserved his most overwhelming scorn. Never equivocating, he spoke with a corrosive power unequaled in the history of American politics. In this time when the United States no longer can avoid hard and irrevocable decisions, the imaginative candor of John Randolph of Roanoke deserves rescue from obscurity.

Chapter Two

The Education
of a Republican

1

When John Randolph was three years old, the Virginian
legislature, influenced by Thomas Jefferson, abolished
entail; in the same year, Virginia adopted her liberal constitution—a constitution far less democratic, however, than
the reformed one Randolph was to denounce in 1829 (which
latter document would be impossibly conservative today).
When he was sixteen, he witnessed the inauguration of the
new national government, "with poison under its wings."
This revolutionary age won the youthful devotion of Randolph, but it did not fix him to the principle of perpetual
revolution; indeed, he was to advocate watering the tree of
liberty as infrequently as possible. Revolt against foreign
dominion was one matter, revolt against old ways another.
The Randolphs, Blands, and Tuckers, those great Virginian
families with which John Randolph was connected, were
American patriots, not Tories; reformers, not reactionaries.
They were, nevertheless, American gentlefolk of the English
pattern, great proprietors of lower Virginia, lovers of liberty
more than lovers of democracy. Randolph was to believe,
in later years, that the abolition of entail was the death
warrant of such families—as the new state constitution

meant the rule of new classes, and as the federal government threatened the states with subordination. Yet his youth experienced the workings of these innovations only slowly, and the optimistic predictions of Jefferson could convince even the independent mind of John Randolph.

All Virginia was in debt to England in those days—tied, indeed, by many another bond, economic and cultural, to old England, bonds which Randolph, unlike his kinsman Jefferson, never desired to sever. Whatever the influence of obligations to the English upon the motives of the Revolutionists, the Virginian planters did not escape debt. Randolph himself complained not of the creditors but of those in his family who had contracted the obligations; he lived in a two-room cabin and struggled with his nine thousand acres the whole of his life until, just before his mission to Russia, he paid the last penny.

A Virginian planter did not allow his debts to alarm him overmuch, however, as Randolph was to complain of his order. Prodigality of a sort existed, but it did not infect Randolph; he was to oppose extravagance so sternly as to be charged with avarice. As for the other aspects of that Virginian life, they have been described often (in Beveridge's *Marshall,* for instance)—the rurality, the pride, the freedom coupled with Negro servility, the plantation houses that were great assembly rooms below and great barracks above. Henry Adams perhaps exaggerates the roughness of Randolph's Virginia,[1] but there were in it elements of license and folly. Still, not the nature of the life so much as the nature of the boy made the man and his political ideas.

Contemporary descriptions of this youthful Virginian sug-

---

[1] Henry Adams, *John Randolph,* chap. 1.

gest that Randolph was not likely to have been other than he became, even had he been born in another land or age. Perhaps it is true, as Parrington says,[2] that in no other country or time could such a man have had such a political career; but, even had he not been the fierce leader of the opposition, at heart Randolph could have been nothing but an implacable defender of his liberties and a critic of his era and his nation. One reads of his painfully sensitive body and mind, further irritated by the disease which seemed to dog all the Randolphs of his branch and by the eccentricity peculiar to the family; of his early intensity in love and hate; of his precocious genius. How could such a being ever develop into a democrat, ever sympathize with or endure the masses, ever lower his wit or his patience to their level? He was meant for a St. Michael, as his bitterest critic calls him,[3] and, when one remembers that with this nature he combined an inheritance and environment of pride and affluence, it seems amazing that such a man ever could become as much a popular power in politics as Randolph became, even in his day of a limited electoral franchise.

So it is that we should not attribute to Randolph's education any very great degree of influence upon his career. Even from infancy, he seems to have been unique John Randolph, with the sparkle and the torment of eccentricity. It seems probable that Randolph's reading, schooling, and experience of the world served chiefly to confirm and intensify the inclinations of his boyhood. Those deep-seated political prejudices which even the complacency of modern psychology has generally shied away from analyzing, those mysterious

[2] V. L. Parrington, *The Romantic Revolution in America,* p. 9.
[3] Henry Adams, *History of the United States,* IV, 107.

proclivities of character toward conservation or innovation, all tended in Randolph toward a veneration of the old order of things; and his solitary life, his perpetual sickness, and the probably consequent sexual impotence with which his enemies had the callousness to taunt him—these influences acerbated his temper and augmented his dislike of novelty.

2

Unlike his most formidable opponents in Congress— Webster, Clay, Calhoun—John Randolph came of a family possessing wealth and education. A library of respectable dimensions was at his childhood home, "Matoax," near Petersburg. To his inheritance of great names was added that of the Tuckers, when, in 1788, his widowed mother married St. George Tucker, poet, jurist, soldier, and statesman— and also the American editor of Blackstone's *Commentaries* and the writer of *A Dissertation on Slavery,* in which he attacked negro bondage on the grounds of natural right and economic expediency. This latter book probably influenced Randolph's opposition to slavery; and Tucker's edition of Blackstone was the Bible of every Virginian lawyer. Tucker's annotations are a good exposition of natural-rights doctrine. Although after Randolph's break with the Judge, he sneered at the Blackstone, in his youth he appears to have thought highly of it.[4] This was before he fell under the influence of an immensely greater legal thinker, Burke.

Yet it was from his mother that Randolph received the direction of his reading and the greater part of his early

---

[4] Randolph to Tucker, September 20, 1802 (John Randolph MSS, Duke University).

education. Doubtless he learned more from her, who he loved with all that passion which sometimes overmastered him, than from his schoolmasters. A lady who knew her said of Frances Bland Tucker: "She was a woman, not only of superior personal attractions, but who excelled all others of her day in strength of intellect, for which she was so justly celebrated."[5] Randolph, long later, wrote of her: "Only one human being ever knew me. *She* only knew me."[6] She nourished his oratorical talents: "My mother once expressed a wish to me, that I might one day or other be as great a speaker as Jerman Baker or Edmund Randolph! That gave the bent to my disposition."[7] And it was she, too, who told the boy, as they rode together over the red fields, "Keep your land and your land will keep you."[8] The lonely man of Roanoke never disobeyed that injunction and all his life added field to field with an eagerness resembling agrarian avarice.

Randolph suffered from a violent distaste for formal schooling—at no time in his proud life could he bear restraint—and one notes his recurring denunciations of institutions of learning. This defiance of the powers that were, which ran all through Randolph's career, became evident in his early years. Ordinary schools were not for such as Randolph; as he said, he "acquired all his knowledge from his library at Roanoke, and by intercourse with the world."[9]

What were the books of his early years? Randolph has listed many of them, particularly in his letters to Theodore

---

[5] Hugh Garland, *Randolph of Roanoke*, I, 11.

[6] *Ibid.*, p. 25.

[7] *Ibid.*, p. 23.

[8] *Ibid.*, p. 18.

[9] R. T. Craighill, *The Virginia "Peerage,"* p. 290.

Dudley and to his niece, Elizabeth Coalter. Best known is
the letter of February 16, 1817, to Dudley, in which he
praises *Orlando Furioso,* and adds:

> If from my life were to be taken the pleasure derived from
> that faculty, very little would remain. Shakespeare, and Milton,
> and Chaucer, and Spenser, and Plutarch, and the Arabian Nights'
> Entertainments, and Don Quixote, and Gil Blas, and Robinson
> Crusoe, and "the tale of Troy divine," have made up more than
> half of my wordly enjoyment. To these ought to be added
> Ovid's Metamorphoses, Ariosto, Dryden, Beaumont and
> Fletcher, Southern, Otway, Congreve, Pope's Rape and Eliosa,
> Sheridan, Addison, Young, Thomson, Gay, Goldsmith, Gray,
> Collins, Cowper, Byron, Aesop, La Fontaine, Voltaire (Charles
> XII, Mahomed, and Zaire), Rousseau (Julie), Schiller, Ma-
> dame de Stael—but, above all, Burke.
>
> One of the first books I ever read was Voltaire's Charles XII;
> about the same time, 1780–1, I read the Spectator; and used
> to steal away to the closet containing them. The letters from
> his correspondents were my favorites. I read Humphrey Clinker,
> also; that is Win's and Tabby's letters, with great delight, for
> I could spell at that age, pretty correctly. Reynard, the Fox, came
> next, I think; then tales of the Genii and Arabian Nights. This
> last, and Shakespeare, were my idols. I had read them with Don
> Quixote, Gil Blas, Quintus Curtius, Plutarch, Pope's Homer,
> Robinson Crusoe, Gulliver, Tom Jones, Orlando Furioso, and
> Thomson's Seasons, before I was eleven years; also, Goldsmith's
> Roman History, 2 vols., 8 vo., and an old history of Braddock's
> war. . . .[10]

Elsewhere, he mentions reading Xenophon, Demos-
thenes, Sallust, Cicero, Lucian, Virgil, Horace, Chatham,
and Fox. He early became acquainted with other Greek and
Roman classics and frequently commended them to his
young relatives. He knew his Greek, Latin, and French,

---

[10] Dudley, *Letters of John Randolph to a Young Relative,* pp. 190–91.

although he sneered at those who taught him. A brief and miserable attendance at Walker Maury's grammar school in Virginia, a year at Princeton, nearly two years at Columbia, and a few weeks at William and Mary constituted his regular schooling; it was his custom to depreciate his accomplishments at school. His complaints of these institutions were much like Jefferson's criticism of William and Mary College, and very probably academies and colleges were not for the precocious Randolph, recognized even by such gifted classmates as Littleton Waller Tazewell as the superior of his companions.[11]

For three years, 1790–93, Randolph nominally studied law under his uncle, Edmund Randolph, the attorney general; the law was not for his impatient youth, and he thought his kinsman hardly a fit preceptor. On the flyleaf of his copy of Hume's *Treatise* he wrote: "This book was the first he put into my hands, telling me that he had planned a system of study for me and wished me to go through a course of metaphysical reasoning. After I returned the book, he gave me Shakespeare to read; then Beattie on *Truth*. After that Kames' *Elements of Criticism,* and fifthly Gilies' *History of Greece.* What an admirable system of study! What a complete course of metaphysics! Risum teneatis?"[12]

But what Randolph considered the insufficiency of his formal education was balanced by his private reading, some of which he later considered baneful. He found writers who deeply influenced the religious beliefs of his youth as well as the political faith of a lifetime. Writing, long afterward, to

---

[11] H. B. Grigsby, *Discourse on Tazewell,* p. 14.
[12] Grigsby, "Randolph's Library," *Southern Literary Messenger,* XX, 79.

his intimate friend Brockenbrough, after he had turned from his former skepticism to devout Anglican belief, he stated that he had been

> bred up in the school of Hobbes and Bayle, and Shaftesbury and Bolingbroke, and Hume and Voltaire and Gibbon; who have cultivated the skeptical philosophy of my vainglorious boyhood —I might almost say childhood—and who have felt all that unutterable disgust which hypocrisy and cant and fanaticism never fail to excite in men of education and refinement, super-added to our natural repugnance to Christianity. I am not, even now, insensible to this impression.[13]

When his house at Bizarre burned in 1813, he wrote, half ironically, "I have lost a valuable collection of books. In it a whole body of infidelity, the Encyclopedia of Diderot and D'Alembert, Voltaire's works, seventy volumes, Rousseau, thirteen quartos, Hume, etc."[14]

A very different author, some biographers assert, exerted over the youthful Randolph an influence greater than that of any other writer: Edmund Burke. In later life Randolph mentioned Burke as foremost among his favorites. But when did the great Whig become his exemplar? One of Randolph's earlier biographers, Hugh Garland, insists repeatedly upon Burke's early influence, and another writer, J. G. Baldwin, contends that "very seasonably, Burke's pamphlet on the French Revolution came into his hands, and made a power-ful, and, in the end, a controlling impression upon his mind."[15] Yet Beverley Tucker, Randolph's half-brother, in a review of Garland's *Life of Randolph,* demolished this hypothesis. John Randolph indeed had read the *Reflections*

---

[13] Garland, *op. cit.,* II, 100.

[14] *Ibid.,* pp. 9–10.

[15] J. G. Baldwin, *Party Leaders,* p. 143.

when it first appeared, Tucker remarked, but he considered Mackintosh's reply a masterly refutation. Randolph adopted the French calendar and used it almost until the end of the century. Though he was disgusted with Paine's coarseness, he admired his talents and dissented very little from Paine's opinions. Not until the latter four years of Jefferson's administration was Randolph

> led to suspect that there may be something in the enjoyment of liberty, which soon disqualifies a people for that self-government, which is but another name for freedom. "It is ordained," said Burke, "in the eternal constitution of things, that men of intemperate minds cannot be free. Their passions forge their fetters." We very much doubt whether Mr. Randolph ever had his mind awakened to this great truth until the time we speak of.[16]

Like Southey and Coleridge and Wordsworth, it appears, in Randolph an early generous enthusiasm for French visions gave way to a conversion to Burke's solemnly noble conservatism. "He is the Newton of political philosophy," Randolph wrote of Burke, in 1814, from his Roanoke retirement.[17]

So much, then, for the reading of Randolph's youth and its influence upon him. If we compare it with Jefferson's, we find Randolph more catholic in taste, except for scientific studies, in which the impatient Roanoke planter had small interest. We find it broader, too, than that of John Quincy Adams, as described in Adams' youthful letters. Randolph's fondness for the English novelists and dramatists is interesting—a

---

[16] Nathaniel Beverley Tucker, "Garland's Life of Randolph," *Southern Quarterly Review*, IV (new ser.; July 1851), 41–46.

[17] Randolph to Harmanus Bleeker, April 14, 1814 (Bleeker letterbook, Randolph MSS, Alderman Library, University of Virginia).

taste extending, indeed, to the older English poets and to
any book treating of English social life. We do not find this
preference in the earnest Jefferson—Fielding and Smollett
were not names frequent on his lips. Randolph seldom mentioned those juridical writers admired by Jefferson—no
Kames, no Coke, though he must have examined their works
during his legal studies. Nor is there evidence that he ever
investigated, like Jefferson, Anglo-Saxon institutions; he
cared nothing for what Henry Adams calls the futilities of
sac and *soc*. In time Randolph was to refer caustically to
Jefferson, with his historical approach to natural rights, as
"the philosopher." Randolph read his Locke, of course, and
Bolingbroke, Hobbes, and other English political writers;
and though Randolph referred to these authors now and
again, none of them seems to have affected his opinions profoundly. But boyhood education is not all, and it is worth-
while to glance at Randolph's reading during his maturity.

3

Some critics of Randolph's character have attempted to
link Randolph with the Romantic movement in literature
and to find some bond between literary nostalgia and
southern political thought. A thorough survey of Randolph's
reading defeats such an effort. The Virginian had, certainly,
a lively interest in the writers of his day, but his admiration
for the Romantics was strictly qualified, as his correspondence with Francis Walker Gilmer, Brockenbrough, Francis
Scott Key, and Josiah Quincy shows. He admired Scott's
best novels and condemned his poorer productions; his
preference for tales of British life and tradition like *The
Antiquary, Old Mortality,* and *Waverly* contrasts strongly

with his strictures upon Scott's medieval romances. He praised Byron's poetry but deplored Byron's character. He announced his determination never to read the Lake poets. Maria Edgeworth was his favorite contemporary novelist; this liking doubtless is evidence of his strong social interests, for the parallel between landlordism in Ireland and in Virginia was strong, though in Virginia's favor, Randolph thought. "I never could abide an Irish Tory."[18]

With the possible exception of Byron, Randolph's favorite poet among his contemporaries was Thomas Moore, but he liked Moore's satires, not his sentimental verses. "Tom Crib's Memorial to Congress" delighted him. To Henry Middleton Rutledge he wrote: "Tom you must know is my Aristophanes—he stands next to Shakespeare."[19] The verses addressing the American legislators as

> Most Holy, and High, and Legitimate *squad,*
> First *Swells* of the world, since *Bony's* in quod,

held no offense for Randolph, who replied to a critic of his oratory that congressmen should not be addressed as rational beings[20]—one of the many instances, by the way, in which his repartee was inspired, unconsciously or (like Mirabeau's) deliberately, by his reading of Burke. That famous flaying of his interrupters with the contemptuous ejaculation, "The little dogs and all, . . . see, they bark at me," is drawn from *Lear,* of course; but Burke had employed it in precisely similar circumstances in St. Stephen's.

---

[18] Jacob Harvey, "Randolphiana," *Richmond Enquirer,* July 25, 1833.

[19] Randolph to Rutledge, March 20, 1820 (Randolph MSS, Duke University).

[20] R. B. Davis, *Francis Walker Gilmer,* p. 169.

No, Randolph was not an enthusiast for the Romantics. His favorite authors were those quoted repeatedly by him in his speeches and letters—Milton, Shakespeare, Cervantes, Fielding, Smollett, Butler, Pope, Dryden, and Livy, to name a few. These are not the tastes of "morbid sentimentalism," which charge W. P. Trent brings against Randolph.[21] It is impossible to define in a single phrase Randolph's literary inclinations, particularly since he lived in an age of literary transition. A prominent Virginian thought Randolph's Roanoke library the best collection in Virginia, finding it deficient only in the sciences.[22] Among the political works included in a manuscript list of Randolph's books, one notes those of Aristotle, Machiavelli, More, Sidney, Harrington, Hobbes, Grotius, Locke, Bolingbroke, Burke, Chatham, Blackstone, Say, John Taylor, and lesser men, as well as a file of the *Anti-Jacobin Review*. Even Randolph's enemy Richard Rush, who prefaced his pamphlet satire on Randolph with the lines,

> The Fiend is long, and lean, and lank,
> And moves upon a spindle shank,

spoke of Randolph's great knowledge of books and of how his conversations were filled with "sayings and mottoes from other tongues and books—from the Whole Duty of Man, from Tom Jones, Dr. Faustus, Shakespeare, Rochester, the Bible, Racine, Pope, Sancho, Vicar of Wakefield, Virgil, Caleb Quotem, Patrick Henry, Juvenal, Jack Robinson, everybody; all this with various additional infusions of classi-

---

[21] William P. Trent, *Southern Statesmen of the Old Regime,* chap. 4.
[22] Grigsby, "Randolph's Library," *op. cit.*

cal, topographical, and genealogical erudition, the genealogy comprehending man and beast, king, peer, and race horse."[23]

A man of literary tastes so broad cannot be confined within any corral of literary generalization. So far as we may draw parallels with safety, we may say his tastes were in accord with those of the old English gentlemen, tempered by a vigorous interest in contemporaries. "Thank God," he said, when he came in sight of the English coast, "that I have lived to behold the land of Shakespeare, of Milton, of my forefathers!"[24] Randolph condemned Fielding as a coarse and licentious writer—"but his age deserved him." Still, it was to Fielding he turned for an allusion which was to put a bullet from Clay's pistol through Randolph's wrapper. The British mastiff quality in Smollett and Fielding summoned his admiration; the Gallic touch of Sterne—and yet Randolph, unwittingly, had something of that tinge—called forth his reproaches. In so far as he could make it so, his life was that of an English country gentleman; and his politics were nearly those of a Rockingham Whig adapted to the Southside.

This was the education of the man who reflected in his speeches "a degree of classical culture that is without parallel in American parliamentary history."[25] In regard to Randolph's political thought, perhaps the most significant conclusion to be drawn from all this is that there was little of the radical to be discerned. Such might be the taste of a Virginian Republican, but it certainly was not that of a Jacobin.

---

[23] Richard Rush, *John Randolph at Home and Abroad,* p. 5.

[24] Jacob Harvey, quoted by Garland, *op. cit.,* II, 175.

[25] P. A. Bruce, *John Randolph* ("Library of Southern Literature," vol. X), p. 4430.

Whether the man determined the tastes or the tastes the man, here was no spirit of leveling, no love of innovation, no admiration of the *philosophes*—or, at least, such inclinations died early. One may find the influence of Puritanism and parliamentarianism but not the egalitarian spirit.

Randolph's literary opinions, like his political convictions, grew more pronounced as the years passed. If social radicalism ever should touch such a man, it could not cling to him long.

Chapter Three

The Basis
of Authority

Of all those vexed questions in what Coleridge called "the holy jungle of metaphysics," perhaps none has been more hotly debated than that concerning the basis for authority in government. Votaries of the monarch's divine right or of the people's natural prerogative, of Leviathan or of civil disobedience, of social contract or of law of sword, have waged the battle long, and its end is not yet. Although today many regular students of politics—including some given to scoffing at Bentham and Mill—have adopted the viewpoint of the utilitarians, the mass of people in this country, when they reflect at all upon such questions, probably adhere to a vague natural-rights doctrine. But most writers and scholars have abandoned the cause of Locke and of Jefferson (although perhaps we are living at the beginning of a revival of natural-rights principle) and maintain that, so far as natural obligation or divine injunction is concerned, we have but one natural political law:

> Because the good old rule
> Sufficeth them, the simple plan
> That they should take, who have the power,
> And they should keep who can.

Not that this state of society is impossible to modify by political order; but this rule of might, most modern thinkers seem to hold, is the only *natural* order. Society alone confers rights and privileges. This opinion is far removed from Lockian theory, and in England the abandonment of natural-rights doctrine commenced more than a century and a half ago.[1]

In America, however, the adoption of new systems of political thought lagged behind British speculation. Jefferson's theory of the rights of governments and men, so often discussed, depended upon a juristic concept of natural rights. John Dewey would have us believe that we need only substitute "moral right" for "natural right" in Jefferson's expressions, and we will have modernized Jefferson and made him, indeed, a sort of Deweyite;[2] but Jefferson often used the term "moral" in our sense and preferred to speak of *natural* rights. The juristic social-compact theory was reinforced in his system by the argument that American liberties were rights inherited from the free Anglo-Saxons, before the Norman Conquest, and never forfeited; as Gilbert Chinard writes, "The Jeffersonian philosophy was born under the sign of Hengist and Horsa, not of the Goddess Reason."[3] In John Adams' works we find elements of natural-rights theory; and although John Taylor of Caroline did not follow Jefferson strictly, he stated that there exist two natural rights: the right of conscience and the right of labor.[4] It is in the speeches of Randolph of Roanoke that we first en-

---

[1] See H. V. S. Ogden, "The State of Nature and the Decline of Lockian Political Theory in England," *American Historical Review*, XLVI, 31–44.

[2] John Dewey, *The Living Thoughts of Jefferson*, p. 6.

[3] Gilbert Chinard, *Jefferson*, p. 87.

[4] John Taylor, *Construction Construed*, p. 204.

counter a thorough expression, in America, of opposition to the assumptions of the Declaration of Independence.[5] Randolph was not alone, it is true; by the time of the Virginia Convention of 1829, the new system of thought—or, perhaps, the revived old system of thought, long dormant—was strong in lower Virginia and developing in power elsewhere; but Randolph was the ablest spokesman of this opposition.

To call Randolph "the American Burke" is no great exaggeration. Randolph's character was more like that of the elder Pitt, with "his intractable, incalculable nature, his genius tinged with madness."[6] But Burke's theory of indivisible sovereignty, his contempt for abstract harmony in government, his impatience with questions of legal "right," and his advocacy of "expediency tempered by prescription and tradition,"[7] accompanied by his reverence for the experience of mankind—all these were the principles of Randolph. The Virginian statesman did not share Burke's admiration for the party system and lacked Burke's veneration of the state; we see more of the Jeffersonian "necessary evil" spirit in Randolph. But Randolph agreed that it is the duty of an aristocracy, as Burke put it, "to enlighten and protect the weaker, the less knowing, and the less provided with the goods of fortune";[8] and Burke's cautious sounding the lead, his devotion to prudence, was also Randolph's. The influence of

---

[5] Dumas Malone states that Thomas Cooper was the first southerner to express dissent from Jeffersonian theories; but Cooper's *Lectures on Political Economy* were published in 1828, years after Randolph had commenced his attacks (see Malone, *The Public Life of Cooper,* p. 290).

[6] L. P. Namier, *England in the Age of the American Revolution,* p. 181.

[7] Ogden, *op. cit.,* p. 27.

[8] Edmund Burke, "Appeal from the New to the Old Whigs," *Works,* III, 85–86.

Burke's works upon the Virginian grew stronger as his experience of practical politics increased. An admirer of Randolph wrote, not long after the death of the Old Republican,
concerning Burke and Randolph: "There is a volume of
Burke now in the library of Congress, which contains
copious notes in the handwriting of Mr. Randolph, evincing
how closely he has studied and copied his great exemplar."[9]

Although Burke and Randolph might denounce the
natural-right theories of Rousseau and evade the natural-
right theories of Locke, they were not the men to deny that
laws of nature exist—laws, that is, derived from the spiritual
character of man and demonstrated in the pages of history.
Liberty was no absolute and abstract "Right of Man," immutable and imprescriptible; but it was a privilege conferred
upon men who obeyed the intent of God by placing a check
upon will and appetite. As Burke's Tory friend Samuel Johnson appealed in the arts to Aristotelian nature, so ran the
political appeal of Burke and Randolph—to human nature,
to the ways of God toward man and civilized man toward
man, and not to the romantic or historical concepts of irrevocable "natural rights." No "right," however natural it may
seem, can exist unqualified in society. A man may have a
right to self-defense; therefore, he may have a right to a
sword; but if he is mad or wicked, and intends to do his
neighbors harm, every dictate of prudence will tell us to
disarm him. Rights have no being independent of circumstance and expediency.

Yet Bentham's materialistic view was as repugnant to
Burke and Randolph as was Rousseau's etherealism. Al-

---

[9] "Extract from a Private Letter," *Richmond Enquirer,* February 10,
1834.

though Randolph fought Jefferson's doctrines, his contemporaries spoke of him as a Republican and a liberal—a democrat, even. J. G. Baldwin settled this seeming paradox in a shrewd remark linking Burke and Randolph: "They were Whigs, in the ancient sense, because their strong love of personal freedom—alone as deep and unconquerable as their pride; and because of their strong caste feelings; in other words, devotion to their own rights and to those of their order."[10]

Randolph was what Horace Gregory calls an "aristocratic libertarian."[11] His theory of the basis of authority was not one of those metaphysical abstractions he so despised, but a deliberate defense of the old society he thought best and of the old state of which he was so fitting a representative. The unreasoning egalitarianism and idealism of Marryat's elder Mr. Easy would not do for him, and he fought with all the powers of his impatient logic the tide of the popular principles of equality and fraternity—and fought, too, that corruption of the principle of liberty which he considered libertinism.

None of the great Virginians were social radicals; as the Revolution in America was essentially a struggle for the preservation of old American ways, so were Jefferson's reforms aimed at the preservation of an agrarian society of freeholders—those freeholders who Randolph, also, considered the strength of the commonwealth. The real innovators were not Henry and Jefferson and Taylor and Randolph but the westerners of Clay's American System

---

[10] Joseph G. Baldwin, *Party Leaders,* pp. 144–45.

[11] Horace Gregory, "Our Writers and the Democratic Myth," *Bookman,* LXXV, 377–82.

and the Federalist manufacturers "north of the Patapsco."
John Taylor assailed the capitalists not with the arguments
of a modern Marxist, seeking to have the expropriated become the expropriators, but with the denunciations of an
agriculturist who saw the doom of his society in the Bank
of the United States and the tariff. But if the Virginians
were not radicals, neither were they aristocrats, in the strict
sense; their opposition to an established nobility—that is, to
a small and special class maintained by law in the possession of exclusive economic and political privileges—was
unrelenting. Nathaniel Macon, Randolph's colleague, once
wrote to Van Buren: "Banks are the nobility of the country,
they have exclusive privileges; and like all nobility, must be
supported by the people and they are the worst kind, because they oppress secretly."[12]

Yet though Randolph denounced Toryism and privilege
—unless one considers entail and primogeniture, the passing
of which Randolph regretted, forms of privilege—he was
willing to term himself an aristocrat, in the personal sense;
one of the best of his epigrams is this: "I am an aristocrat; I
love liberty, I hate equality."[13] No phrase more clearly re-
veals the gulf between the thought of Jefferson and the
thought of Randolph.

Here, with respect to the question of authority, is the
strongest proof of the power of Randolph's mind and of the
influence of his oratory. Upon the question of slavery, the
South went beyond Randolph and repudiated his opposition
to the institution; in regard to his hatred of change, Virginia

---

[12] Macon to Van Buren, May 24, 1836 (Macon Papers, North Carolina
State Department of Archives and History).

[13] Anonymous notes on Randolph (Nathan Loughborough MSS, copy
in Randolph Papers, Virginia State Library).

and the South and the nation were altered politically and economically, as decades passed, almost beyond recognition, for all his warnings; his ideal of inviolate state powers was doomed; and the agrarian society he loved has withered. Yet his theory of authority was accepted by the South of Calhoun and the South of Davis and is accepted—with little mention of Randolph—by many political thinkers today. His scorn for the Rights of Man and the Declaration of Independence, or rather, for the literal and popular interpretation of those documents, has triumphed among the scholars over the idealism—an attractive enthusiasm, to be sure—of the days of American infancy. It was the devout Randolph who helped strike down the concept of egalitarian liberty as a divine gift; it was Randolph, the lover of old ways, who helped demolish the theory of an historical compact of freedom. Perhaps the man of Roanoke, were he able to look upon this success, would find small pleasure in it, for the society in the cause of which he denounced the principles of the Declaration was long since engulfed by our world; still, although in Pyrrhic fashion, Randolph has triumphed.

Little need be said of Randolph's opinions upon the question of sovereignty, since John Austin had not yet impressed that vexed question in all its ramifications upon political consciousness. Randolph was in substantial agreement with Burke, with John Taylor, and with Calhoun. Sovereignty rested in the people of a state; it was indivisible and not transferable; the true state was Virginia or Massachusetts, not the government at Washington; and, moreover, it was vested neither in a state government nor in a federal establishment, but in the people themselves. Such was Randolph's premise when he found it necessary to discuss the matter. But his impatience with abstractions did not often allow him to consider the point in his speeches; for, like Taylor and many a man since, he considered the question idle. With Randolph, it was not so much of import where the abstraction "sovereignty" had been placed by process of law as of where it *should* rest—and where real power, which alone can maintain sovereignty, should rest. Randolph always aimed for the heart of things.

This chapter deals with the question of the origin of power in the state; with the question of who, and how many, should exercise the governance; and with the question of abstract rights against political expediency. Not until late in life did Randolph find it necessary to elucidate publicly his views on these topics; other matters were more pressing, and his disgust with government had not become so thorough. As an old man, disappointed in men and measures, he challenged the divinity of Demos—denied popular wisdom with that sort of boldness which had cost John Adams his popularity.

2

Whether in his early youth Randolph was a thorough disciple of the *philosophes,* it is not easy to say. He was a friend to France; he was an enemy to the "monocrats" and "aristocrats" of the Federalist party; and he was an adherent of Jefferson, although, as Adams is quick to point out, Randolph was no worshiper even then of the Monticello sage. But opposition to Washington and John Adams and Hamilton could be based more upon fear for the liberties of states and citizens, and distrust of the financial and commercial policies of the Federalist administration, than upon devotion to the abstractions of the Age of Reason; and, similarly, enthusiasm for the cause of France might be that sympathy with peoples struggling for independence which was Randolph's all his life, rather than a love of Jacobinism. In his speech on Gregg's Resolution in 1806, less than a decade after he had been an advocate of the French cause, Randolph referred to those days:

> Then every heart beat high with sympathy for France, for Republican France. I am not prepared to say with my friend from Pennsylvania that we were all ready to draw our swords in her cause, but I affirm that we were prepared to have gone great lengths. I am not ashamed to pay this compliment to the hearts of the American people even at the expense of their understandings. It was a noble and generous sentiment, which nations, like individuals, are never the worse for having felt. They were, I repeat it, ready to make great sacrifices for France. And why ready? Because she was fighting the battles of the human race against the combined enemies of their liberty; because she was performing the part which Great Britain now in fact sustains; forming the only bulwark against universal dominion.[14]

This lefthanded tribute to the Gallomaniacs of the 1790s hardly has the ring of a man who ever held French principles; yet in 1797, Randolph, dating his letter "Floreal 10, 5 yr.," had written to Henry Middleton Rutledge a message sanguinary enough in tone to have satisfied Marat:

> The friends of freedom and mankind are alarmed at the length to which the administration of this country has gone, but let not the emissaries and dependents of Pitt believe that any man or set of men can induce the free American people to embrue their hands in the blood of their brethren. Before that period arrives I hope to see the advisers of such measures brought to the block: this is the only atonement which can be made by them for their political sins.[15]

---

[14] *Annals of Congress* (9th Cong., 1st sess.), p. 562.
[15] Randolph to Rutledge, April 29, 1797 (copy in Randolph Papers, Virginia State Library).

Probably such expressions were only the words of a fiery youth who saw a free nation in its agony; for it is difficult to perceive any social radicalism in a letter to Nicholson, written three years later, in which Randolph stated, "I have a respect for all that is antique (with a few important exceptions)."[16] A few months afterward, he made some defense of Burr, then intriguing for the presidency, and found it necessary to add, "I am not a monarchist in any sense:"[17] The Virginian planter could not long keep company with Gallic excesses; and, clearer of vision than many an English liberal, he saw Napoleon as a far greater threat to liberty than ever the Bourbons had been.

An early instance of his principle of basing governmental action rather upon "expediency tempered by prescription and tradition," than upon assertions of inviolable right, may be seen in a letter to Creed Taylor in 1802, in which Randolph opposed the creation of a separate state in western Virginia and regretted that the area west of Blue Ridge was almost unrepresented in the Virginian legislature:

> I am sorry that so large a portion as I have been told (23,-000) was left unrepresented west of the ridge. I have not seen your new bill, but it would have been policy to have given them more than their proportion. . . . It will forever fix the aversion of those oppressed people—for such they *now* are. Was it generous to crush an insect with the club of Hercules?[18]

In short, representation should be determined by the need for harmony of interests in the state, not by counting noses.

---

[16] Randolph to Nicholson, August 12, 1800 (copy in Randolph Papers, Virginia State Library).

[17] Randolph to Nicholson, December 17, 1800 (copy in Randolph Papers, Virginia State Library).

[18] Randolph to Taylor, January 31, 1802 (copy in Randolph Papers, Virginia State Library).

As for direct representation, he had taken a similar stand in its favor earlier that year, when he had praised the character of the House of Representatives:

> In this branch alone you will find the Republican character; in the other it is not to be seen. There, is that principle virtually acknowledged which gives to Old Sarum and Newton a representation equal to that of London; a principle which is believed by some essential to the existence of that well-ordered government, or perhaps that of any other that they are willing to bestow upon man: the principle that the governors are not to be under the complete control of the governed; in other words, that the majority ought not to govern. In the appointment of the executive the same spirit prevails, although somewhat modified.[19]

These statements prove that we have no reason to doubt —that during the greater part of Jefferson's first administration Randolph retained a measure of faith in the Jeffersonian democracy. But the break came soon; not on a question of political theory, however, but on one of political morality—the Florida question. Disgust with the policies of the Republican administration doubtless had its part in strengthening the conservative tendencies already to be seen in Randolph's course. By the latter part of 1805, he was sneering at Jefferson as the "political messiah"; scorning the reliance his fellow-congressmen placed upon authority as blundering "amongst a load of quotations from Grotius, and Puffendorf, and Lord knows who"; and exhorting them to be "not dreamers and soothsayers, but men of flesh."[20] They sought to base their actions upon "natural" principles; already Randolph found a different basis of authority. Soon Sloan, of New Jersey, who disliked Randolph for his ref-

---

[19] *Annals of Congress* (7th Cong., 1st sess.), pp. 367–68.
[20] *Ibid.* (9th Cong., 1st sess.), pp. 592–605.

erence to his proposals as "Sloan's Vegetable Specific," was comparing Randolph with Burke—invidiously, Sloan thought.[21] Randolph wrote to his ally Nicholson: "Are you too denounced as a Jacobin republican? It seems there are two sorts coming into vogue, and I hear (but do not see) that I am put down in that class."[22]

The "Jacobin Republicans," whose principles are discussed in another chapter, were anything but literal Jacobins; soon they were to become the "Tertium Quids," and Randolph never was to reenter the Jeffersonian fold. His separation did not mean he would adopt Federalistic principles, as Jefferson expected;[23] in a letter of September 6, 1806, to his nephew, then in England, he praised the absence of established classes in America:

> Here is no distinction of ranks; and here, most fortunately for you, the honest means, to which your want of fortune will require you to resort, to obtain an honest livelihood, will not cast you beneath any class of your countrymen . . . much rather would I see you fixed to a workbench, or following the plough, than leading a life of unprofitable and discreditable idleness. Active employment is essential to the happiness of man.[24]

But equality of opportunity did not mean equality of political privilege; he was at war with the growing demand for popular electoral suffrage. To Francis Scott Key, he wrote, in 1813: "Electioneering is upon no very pleasant footing any where; but with you, where the 'base proletarian rout' are admitted to vote, it must be peculiarly irksome and

---

[21] *Ibid.,* pp. 1107–15.

[22] Randolph to Nicholson, October 12, 1805 (copy in Randolph Papers, Virginia State Library).

[23] See Jefferson to Monroe, May 4, 1806 (*Works of Jefferson,* XI, 106).

[24] Randolph to St. George Randolph (Randolph MSS, Duke University).

repugnant to the feelings of a gentleman."[25] As in Fenimore
Cooper, the characteristics of aristocrat and democrat min-
gled in Randolph. This was no inconsistency. For us, democracy has come to mean universal suffrage; but the people
(a term susceptible of various definitions) may rule without "one man, one vote." For Randolph, the real people of
a country were its substantial citizenry, its men of some
property, its farmers and merchants and men of skill and
learning; upon their shoulders rested a country's duties, and
in their hands should repose its government.

There is no need to trace in detail Randolph's expressions
concerning the basis of authority during the succeeding
fifteen years, for it was not until 1822 that Randolph commenced a detailed exposition of his views. One finds, however, in his speeches and letters frequent condemnation of
Jacobinism and unreality in politics, as when he wrote to
Key in 1815: "England, I sometimes think, stands on the
verge of some mighty convulsion. . . . Jacobinism has, I believe, a stronger hold in that country than in any other in
Europe. But the foolishness of human wisdom, nothing
daunted by the repeated overthrow of its plans, yet aspires
to grasp and control the designs of the Almighty."[26] In a
public letter addressed to a constituent that same year, he
assailed the "air-built theories" of the national administration: "Anarchy is the chrysalis state of despotism; and to
that state have the measures of this government long tended,
amidst the professions, such as we have heard in France
and seen the effects of, of Liberty, Equality, Fraternity."[27]

---

[25] Randolph to Key, September 12, 1813 (Hugh Garland, *Randolph of Roanoke,* II, 20).

[26] *Ibid.,* p. 71.

[27] *Richmond Enquirer,* April 1, 1815.

And egalitarianism, produced in part by Jefferson's radical alteration of the laws of descent, aroused his wrath; he wrote to Gilmer in 1821: "When our patriotic wiseacres succeeding in breaking down the distinction between the gentleman and the blackguard, it was obvious that it would at length be effected by the extinction of the former class."[28]

A strong admiration for British institutions combined with events in America—the War of 1812, the elections of Madison and Monroe, the rise of the National Republicans, the decisions of Marshall's Court, the Bank, the debt, the tariff, and many another dose that was gall to Randolph— to prejudice him even more strongly against Jeffersonian theories. It was during the debate on the apportionment bill, in 1822, that the Virginian orator commenced his prolonged assault upon Jeffersonian natural-rights thought, Jeffersonian democratic polity, and Jeffersonian optimism.

3

A blow at the power of his Virginia launched Randolph against egalitarianism. The census of 1820 had shown the necessity of increasing the number of members in the House or of increasing, as an alternative, the size of the unit of representation; Virginia's population had not grown in proportion to that of the nation at large, and, were the unit of representation to be increased, Virginia would lose at least one representative. The indignant Randolph, foreseeing the eclipse of the Old Dominion by an industrialized North and a barbarous West, made a fierce stand for

---

[28] Randolph to Gilmer, December 27, 1821 (Richard B. Davis, *Francis Walker Gilmer,* p. 117).

the honor and the rights of his state. There was no need for a fixed number of members in Congress, he insisted; it was far better to have a large House than to have congressional districts with a population so large as to sever the bond between people and representative. Here Randolph emphasized a principle he steadily maintained—that the legislator should be close to his constituents, from whom came his right to legislate. Randolph never yielded to the theory of virtual representation—that doctrine, best expressed by Mansfield during the pre-Revolutionary controversy, that lawmakers represent not a particular body of constituents but act for the people as a whole. In Randolph remained too much of the Revolutionary and Jeffersonian spirit for such an abandonment of local rights, even though the theory sometimes was gravely propounded on the floor of the House. During the debate on apportionment in January 1822 he said:

> Government, to be safe and to be free, must consist of representatives having a common interest and a common feeling with the represented. . . . When I hear, said Mr. R., of settlements at the Council Bluffs, and of bills for taking possession of the mouth of the Columbia river, I turn not a deaf ear, but an ear of a different sort, to the sad vaticinations of what is to happen in the length of time—believing, as I do, that no government extending from the Atlantic to the Pacific can be fit to govern me or those whom I represent. There is death in the pot, compound it how you will. No such government can exist, because it must want the common feeling and the common interest with the governed, which is indispensable to its existence.[29]

Randolph was right, after his fashion, for the representative federal government of his day was not the national,

---

[29] *Annals of Congress* (17th Cong., 1st sess.), p. 820.

almost imperial, government that is ours. He would not have thought this government of ours "fit to govern" him. But though he held that a legislature must be truly representative, he added that a constitution-framing body, like the federal convention of 1787, need not represent particular constituents. "They were to present a wise and free constitution to our acceptance or rejection; to act not as an ordinary legislature, but as the Lycurgus, the Solon, the Alfred of the country. . . . It would be as competent for a single individual to produce such a constitution, as for any assembly of individuals—Mr. Locke's fatal and total failure to the contrary notwithstanding."[30] Franker, perhaps, than Burke, who to the last preserved an outward show of respect for Locke's concepts while undermining them, Randolph here defied the authority of the master of Rousseau and Jefferson, and presently carried that dissent to greater lengths.

In Randolph's system small place existed for the social contract or for faith in collective popular political wisdom. And Randolph scoffed at the enthusiasts who, like Lamartine, demanded "absolute liberty":

> But, the honorable gentleman has said, we are for lighting the candle of liberty at both ends. It is true, said Mr. R., that some of us do sometimes, for the entertainment of the House and the public, endeavor to serve up a roast secretary, and get a sound basting for our pains. It is true, that the fat is sometimes thrown into the fire, and our own dinners gain nothing thereby. I hope, however, we shall not light the candle of liberty at both ends, or at either end; for, if we do, it must sooner or later burn out.[31]

---

[30] *Ibid.,* p. 933.
[31] *Ibid.,* p. 936.

Having thus disposed in his merciless way of an incautious adversary, Randolph proceeded to expose the follies of seeking abstract harmony in government, of expecting the great venerable Gothic edifice of society to conform to ideal classical proportions; with Burke, he believed that a state is better governed by the irregular patterns formed by common sense and tradition than by the laws of mathematics and the Procrustean methods of omnipotent majorities. The Constitution had not been designed with mathematical regularity, or upon abstract models, but was what later men were to call "a bundle of compromises." The very fact that small states count for as much as great states in the Senate; the equally obvious fact that the slave states possessed "black representatives"—men elected from districts in which, perhaps, slaves outnumbered freemen—these provisions revealed that the Constitution had been produced by practical statesmen, not by idealistic calculators:

> It strikes me, said Mr. R., that we are pursuing theoretical principles, which ought never to have been permitted to find their way into this Government, to lengths from which eventually the most abstract and metaphysical must recoil; for, if they do not, in the madness of their projects and of their strength, they will pull down the House over their heads. We are pursuing them to a length subversive even of the principle of union. If any man raises against me the hue and cry of being an enemy to republicanism, I cannot help that; for, if my life will not speak for me, my tongue cannot. . . . How comes it that the state of Delaware has two members in the other House? . . . What does that right depend upon? Abstract theories? No, sir. Upon what, then, does it depend? Upon common sense—although no science, fairly worth the seven, and worth all the politics of any men who study politics in the closet instead of the busy haunts of men—of professors in a university turned statesmen.[32]

---

[32] *Ibid.*, p. 944.

Gentlemen would reply, said Randolph, that such provisions in the Constitution were the consequence of compromise; they would be right; and compromise was what he recommended once more in this matter of congressional reapportionment—compromise, not a vain appeal to a misty "natural harmony."

In vain the Roanoke planter struggled against these forces of change; and, disgusted with the course of Congress, he sailed for Europe. Jacob Harvey, who accompanied him, was a Federalist and considered Randolph a representative of the democratic spirit, yet his anecdotes of the English tour show how Randolph's mind was inclining more and more toward a complete refutation of Jeffersonianism. Of Virginia, Randolph declared that "the days of her glory are past"—for with the repeal of the "good old English laws of primogeniture," the native Virginian aristocracy was supplanted by blackguards; and, in consequence, Virginia was losing her ascendancy in the national councils.[33] At a dinner in London

> Randolph was questioned closely on American affairs, and amused them very much by his replies. He exposed what he termed the sad degeneracy of Old Virginia, and became quite pathetic, in mourning over the abolition of the laws of primogeniture. Some of the company thought this a strange complaint from a republican; and, before we separated, they really had nearly mistaken Randolph for an aristocrat! . . . I could not help telling Randolph that *I* was the best republican of the two, and I laughed at him for having played the aristocrat so well.[34]

Although Randolph possessed the talents of an actor to a remarkable degree, he needed no pretense to appear aristo-

---

[33] "Randolphiana," *Richmond Enquirer,* June 18, 1833.
[34] *Ibid.,* June 21, 1833.

cratic in character, if not in politics. All the same, he was no Tory, and criticized English institutions freely. "England is Elysium for the rich; Tartarus for the poor," he observed.[35] And of the ruinous English administration of Ireland, he told Harvey: "Alluding to the oppressions of both the government and the church, he said, 'The lion and the jackal have divided the spoils between them, sir; but if I had my way, I would "unmuzzle the ox which treadeth out the corn." ' "[36]

John Randolph would have scorned to set his course by any system of unalterable universals; like Burke, he saw no need for rigid adherence to a harmonious closet philosophy. Back in the United States, he told the House: "Whatever trespass . . . I may be guilty of upon the attention of the Committee, one thing I will promise them, and will faithfully perform my promise—I will dole out to them no political metaphysics. Sir, I unlearned metaphysics almost as early as Fontenelle, and he tells us, I think, it was at nine years old."[37] In the same debate he reexpressed his doctrine of the need for direct representation of constituents, which the concept of Congress as a kind of omniscient national organ threatened:

> But, sir, how shall a man from Mackinaw, or the Yellow Stone river, respond to the sentiments of the people who live in New Hampshire? It is as great a mockery—a greater mockery than it was to talk to those colonies about their virtual representation in the British Parliament. I have no hesitation in saying that the liberties of the colonies were safer in the custody of the

---

[35] Notes on Randolph (Loughborough MSS, copy in Randolph Papers, Virginia State Library).

[36] "Randolphiana," *Richmond Enquirer,* June 25, 1833.

[37] *Annals of Congress* (18th Cong., 1st sess.), p. 1302.

British Parliament than they will be in any portion of this country, if all the powers of the states as well as those of the general government, are devolved upon this House.[38]

Thus Randolph, again like Burke, combined a love of local liberties with a denial that they were a "natural" condition; they were bestowed by the wisdom of society.

Strict constructionist though Randolph was, he saw in a written constitution only an instrument and not the final source of authority or the final appeal from injustice. Men should obey a constitution strictly so long as it was endurable; but should the interpretation of it fall into partisan hands, or should a problem transcending the constitution arise, men must defend their liberties by other means—not their "natural liberties," perhaps, but that freedom which needs no historical or juristic sanction. The basis of authority, in short, rested upon the acquiescence of the citizen in the justice of the constitution, not upon the constitution itself. Jefferson would not have dissented from this doctrine; it was the question of inherent right to participate in the control of government, regardless of station, that was the crux of difference, although even on this point Jefferson altered his stand from time to time. Randolph first appealed to a right beyond constitutional guarantees in his speech on the tariff of 1824. It was many years later before most southerners lost faith in the safeguards of the Constitution, but Randolph despaired even then. He agreed with the Federalist Fisher Ames that "constitutions are but paper; society is the substratum of government." On April 15, 1824, Randolph said:

---

[38] *Ibid.,* p. 1304.

All policy is very suspicious, says an eminent statesman, that sacrifices the interest of any part of a community to the ideal good of the whole; and those governments only are tolerable, where, by the necessary contraction of the political machine, the interests of all the parts are obliged to be protected by it. . . . With all the fanatical and preposterous theories about the rights of man (the *theories,* not the rights themselves, I speak of), there is nothing but power that can restrain power. . . . I do not stop here, sir, to argue about the constitutionality of this bill; I consider the constitution a dead letter; I consider it to consist, at this time, of the power of the states; that is the constitution. You may entrench yourself in parchment to the teeth, says Lord Chatham, the sword will find its way to the vitals of the constitution. I have no faith in parchment, sir, I have no faith in the abracadabra of the constitution; I have no faith in it. . . . If, under a power to regulate trade, you draw the last drop of blood from our veins; if *secundum artem,* you draw the last shilling from our pockets, what are the checks of the constitution to us? A fig for the constitution! When the scorpion's sting is probing us to the quick, shall we pause to chop logic? Shall we get some learned and cunning clerk to say whether the power to do this is to be found in the constitution, and then, if he, from whatever motive, shall maintain the affirmative, like the animal whose fleece forms so material a part of this bill, quietly lie down and be sheared?[39]

Randolph's "eminent statesman" here is Edmund Burke, of course; and the position of these two imaginative conservatives upon the "rights of man" is often misunderstood, as is their view of the origin of civil society. Proper constitutions, they both hold, are the product of social experience; they are rooted in custom and prescription, which have a deeper validity than mere positive law. An abstract devotion to a written "constitution," Randolph is saying above, may

---

[39] *Richmond Enquirer,* June 4, 1824.

be subversion of the actual constitution of a people, which depends upon traditional justice. Social compacts, whether alleged to have been made in the mists of antiquity or owing their creation to recent popular enactment, do not take precedence of the *real* rights of humanity which they profess to defend. Randolph joined Burke in denying the social compact as described by Rousseau and Paine. Like his preceptor, Randolph believed not that society is a contract in the ordinary sense of that word—no deliberate agreement of free individuals outside society, a historical and moral impossibility—but rather that society is a "contract" in the sense of a divinely ordained link between the dead, the living, and those yet unborn. As F. J. C. Hearnshaw observes, when "contract" is used in this sense, "language has obviously lost its ordinary meaning"; Rousseau and Paine are repudiated, and so is Locke's individualism.[40]

Similarly, Burke and Randolph denied the validity of the rights of man as erected into abstract absolutes by Paine and his fellows; they affirmed natural rights of a very different sort—natural rights in the Christian tradition, the moral view of politics which we may trace back to Hooker and Aquinas and the Stoics. Burke defines the *real* rights of men upon the classical predicate of justice, "to each his own." Men have a right to the benefits of civil society—to do justice, to the fruits of their industry, to inheritance, to the welfare of their offspring, to "instruction in life, and to consolation in death." But no rights to equality at the expense of others, no rights to political power regardless of ability and integrity, or to overthrow the traditions of so-

---

[40] F. J. C. Hearnshaw, ed., *Social and Political Ideas of Some Representative Thinkers of the Revolutionary Era,* p. 93.

ciety, can exist. These latter are parodies of rights, veiled vices.[41] Men's rights, in short, are not mysterious gifts deduced from *a priori* postulates; they are opportunities or advantages which the stability of a just society bestows upon its members. Paine and the French radicals and the American doctrinaires confused strong inclinations with abstract rights. *Wanting* prerogatives is not the same thing as possessing a right to them. These concepts are expressed repeatedly by John Randolph, sometimes by quotation from Burke, sometimes with the ardor of his own rhetoric.

Randolph's dissent from the principles of Jefferson, from *liberté, égalité, fraternité,* reached its climax two years later in his speech upon negro slavery in South America. He mauled once more the enthusiasts for absolute liberty and then took an uncompromising stand against the doctrine of abstract natural rights, independent of circumstance and expediency. Randolph must be allowed to speak for himself at some length:

> If, said Mr. R., I were, what I am not—an acute philologer—I should sometimes amuse myself with the manner in which words slip from their original meanings, and come to purport something very different from what any body ever attached to them when they first came into use; the word *sophist* (a wise man) got so much into disrepute, that *philosopher* (a lover of wisdom) had to supply its place; the word *libertine* meant what a liberal means now; that is, a man attached to enlarged and free principles—a votary of liberty; but the libertines have made so ill an use of their principles, that the word has come (even since the time of Shakespeare) to be taken in a bad sense; and *liberal* will share the same fate, I fear, if it contracts this black alliance. There are some other words, also, such as *principle, conscience,* which are also in great danger. . . .

---

[41] Burke, "Reflections on the Revolution in France," *Works,* II, 331–32.

But, sir, perhaps I may be told, that in case I do not accede
to the proposition of the gentleman from South Carolina, the
answer is very plain and triumphant to my resolution. That
the principles of these South American states are the principles
that were of high authority on another great question—the Missouri question—are the principles of the Declaration of Independence. What more will you have, what more can you ask?
What resource have you now left? Sir, my only objection is, that
these principles, pushed to their extreme consequences—that
all men are born free and equal—I can never assent to, for the
best of all reasons, because it is not true; and as I cannot agree
to the intrinsic meaning of the word Congress, though sanctioned by the Constitution of the United States, so neither can
I agree to a falsehood, and a most pernicious falsehood, even
though I find it in the Declaration of Independence, which has
been set up, on the Missouri and other questions, as paramount
to the Constitution. I say pernicious falsehood—it must be, if
true, self-evident; for it is incapable of demonstration; and there
are thousands and thousands of them that mislead the great
vulgar as well as the small. . . . There is another, which, taken
from a different source, I shall speak of as I trust I shall always
feel, with reverence—I mean faith without works, as the means
of salvation. All these great positions, that men are born equally
free, and faith without works, are in a certain sense, in which
they are hardly ever received by the multitude, true; but in
another sense, in which they are almost invariably received by
nineteen out of twenty, they are false and pernicious. . . . In
regard to this principle, that all are born free and equal, if there
is an animal on earth to which it does not apply—that is not
born free, it is man—he is born in a state of the most abject
want, and a state of perfect helplessness and ignorance, which is
the foundation of the connubial tie. . . . As to ignorance, Locke
says that we bring no innate ideas with us into the world; it is
true, but man is born with certain capacities—which assume the
impression, that may be given by education and circumstances;
but the mathematicians and the astronomers, who of all men
on earth are the most unsafe, in affairs of government and life—
who should say that all the soil in the world is equally rich, the
first rate land in Kentucky and the Highlands of Scotland, because the superficial content of the acre is the same, would be

just as right, as he who should maintain the absolute equality of man in virtue of his birth. The rickety and scrofulous little wretch who first sees the light in a workhouse, or in a brothel, and who feels the effects of alcohol before the effects of vital air, is not equal in any respect to the ruddy offspring of the honest yeoman; nay, I will go further, and say that a prince, provided he is no better born than royal blood will make him, is not equal to the healthy son of a peasant.[42]

Thus Senator Randolph, enjoying at the time a popularity to which he had long been a stranger and engaged in demolishing the policies of Henry Clay, disavowed *a priori* political deductions. Men are *not* born free and equal, in any sense commonly thought by the mass of Americans; theories of "natural right" are in fact contrary to nature; the Declaration of Independence is in part, at least, demagoguery. The immediate occasion of his invective was a threat to the southern institution of slavery; the ideas he enunciated had a broader application. Having ridiculed the concept of natural equality, in the same speech Randolph proceeded to attack infatuation with abstract harmony in government and the striving after impossible ideals of absolute liberty. These will-o'-the-wisp notions, he cried out, had led the United States to fantastic projects of interference in the affairs of South America and even Greece; these abstractions unrelated to political realities menaced the security of the South and the tranquillity of the nation. He quoted Burke upon abstraction as distinguished from principle—a distinction of considerable importance for the student of conservative ideas. "I never govern myself," Burke had said, "no rational man ever did govern himself, by abstractions and universals. I do not put abstract ideas wholly out of any

---

[42] *Register of Debates* (19th Cong., 2d sess.), II, 125–26.

question, because I well know that, under that name, I should dismiss principles; and that, without the guide of sound, well-understood principles, all reasoning in politics, as in everything else, would be only a confused jumble of particular details, without the means of drawing out any sort of theoretical or practical conclusion."

Randolph expatiates upon this theme. "If you want to know the effect of metaphysical madness, look to the history of the French Revolution, and to the undoing of the country." That intellectual tendency which Burke and Randolph decry is best described by this epithet "metaphysical madness." Both conservatives regularly employed abstract concepts themselves, for both were eminently Christians, men of letters, and political moralists: religion, literary art, and disinterested politics cannot long subsist without the nourishment of general principles in some degree. Both believed in Providence, a divine origin of society, and a spiritual bond between the generations of humanity—ideas which require as great a power of abstraction, if they are to be properly comprehended, as any man possesses. But Burke and Randolph detested presumptuous and pompous speculation upon those mysteries of human nature, society, and the cosmos which must end (because of the fallibility of human reason) either in a silly, delusory certitude or in nihilism. Still more did they contemn application of such "metaphysical madness" to practical concerns. We have remarked that Randolph and his master derided *a priori* political deductions; well, they also attacked certain *a posteriori* endeavors, the product of that speculative school which thought society could be reduced to inflexible operations determined by collection of evidence. Burke calls these latter doctrinaires "sophisters and calculators," and they were very nearly the counterparts of twentieth-century "social planners." They were the savants who Napoleon and Destutt de Tracy (the first in contempt, the latter in commendation) called "ideologues," and they had their British and American disciples. When Burke and Randolph profess their disgust with "abstractions," then, they are speaking against two separate groups of innovators: the *a priori* thinkers, best exemplified by Rousseau and Hegel, and the *a posteriori* thinkers, like the Encyclopedists and Cabanis. Both schools assumed that society and human character could be reformed deliberately and universally through the enactment of their programs.

Against such presumption the common sense of Burke and Randolph, both of whom had a good deal of experience of the world in its practical aspects and both of whom adhered to the Stoic and Christian view of errant human nature, rose up indignantly. Like Canning, Randolph was deeply impressed by Burke's emphasis upon the virtue of prudence. Prudence is the foundation of all true statesmanship; in its political application, prudence is the application of principles to *particular circumstances*. Prudence dictates that men must not be treated as undifferentiated units, nor societies as mere aggregations of humanity subject to uniform causes and effects, nor the perplexities of politics as soluble by a few neat decrees. A professor may deal in general views unmodified by circumstances, but a statesman must consider the infinite combination of social facts—differences, for instance, between man and man, between society and society, in historical development, natural resources, religious tradition, intellectual attainments, local institutions, peculiarities of character. General moral principles do indeed apply throughout the world and to all men;

but abstract political concepts, whether the product of *a priori* or *a posteriori* minds, cannot be applied abruptly and indiscriminately to that delicate growth called "society" and that sensitive moral being called "man." The political abstractions of both innovating schools were deficient in veneration, that characteristic so prominent in Burke and Randolph; they left out of account the fact that society is not a machine but a moral essence. Often the view of social nature which Burke bequeathed to modern thought is described, with questionable accuracy, as "organic." Burke and his heritors did indeed think of society as possessing a continuity like that of a living body; but their actual description of social continuity indicates that they had in mind more an immortality of spirit, much like that of the church, than a renewal of tissue. At any rate, the "sophisters and calculators" quite ignored the necessity for continuity, and for this Burke and Randolph drubbed them unmercifully.

Tocqueville repeatedly observes that democratic peoples insist upon simple ideas, capable of universal application; they are as intolerant of intellectual subtlety and qualification as they are of hierarchy. Randolph perceived with bitter clarity this marked characteristic of American opinion. It was wholly inconsonant with his own complex and mysterious nature, and he cut and slashed at it almost from instinct. Henry Clay, in so much a mirror of the American public, a kind of magnified popular opinion incarnate in a single politician, was the most conspicuous advocate of applying simple and unmodified American political concepts to enormous problems: the American System of industrial and territorial expansion and unification, the Panama Mission intended to express sympathy with simple democratic tendencies in Latin America and throughout the world—

these measures of Clay's provoked from Randolph a flow of contemptuous, despairing invective reminiscent of Swift. Clay stood for the principle of simple uniformity; Randolph, for the principle of proliferating variety. Diversity, private or social, great genius or mere eccentricity, is favored in an aristocratic milieu, Tocqueville writes; democratic ages demand conformity. Thus the future lay with Clay, but Randolph's warning against the perils of abstraction applied to reality and unitary concepts applied to complex questions has a significance enhanced by the agonies of the twentieth century.

Clay's Missouri Compromise had been the product of such democratic methods, an endeavor to gloss over a terrible problem by the application of a coat of generalities and a superficial reconciliation of interests; now, said Randolph, Clay and the body of opinion he represented were trying to extend visionary sympathies and solutions beyond the bounds of the United States by sending a minister to the congress at Panama. These vague schemes of social amelioration forwarded by President Adams and Secretary Clay would end in social destruction, after the French fashion:

> What was the consequence of this not stopping to parley with the imprescriptible rights of man, in the abstract? It is that they have now full leisure to meditate on the imprescriptible rights of their king in the concrete: that is the result of devotedness to abstract policies—of their management—look at it in Haiti and everywhere—I would say, if I was not afraid of being considered as treating that subject too lightly, which lies heavy on my heart—look at the famous academy of Lagado, and you will have a pretty fair specimen of a country governed by mathematicians and star-gazers, from lighthouses in the sky. It is mournful while ludicrous. I have seen men who could not write a book, or even spell this famous word Congress (they spelled it with a K) who had more practical sense and were more trust-

worthy, as statesmen or generals, than any mathematician, any naturalist, or any literati, under sun. . . .

I must be permitted to say, that there exists, in the nature of man, *ab ove, ab origine,* of degraded and fallen man—for the firstborn was a murderer—a disposition to escape from our own proper duties, to undertake the duties of somebody or anybody else.[43]

In the history of American political thought, only old John Adams equals Randolph in the virulence and penetration of his denunciation of "French liberty," grandiose notions that are consummated in general misery; and, like Adams, Randolph perceived the fetters which must forever bind property to power. In this very speech on South American slavery, Randolph declared that the control of property and the possession of power are eternally wedded: "You cannot divorce property from power. You can only make them change hands." Fenimore Cooper was to say the same thing a dozen years later.[44]

After this manner Randolph of Roanoke, the friend of France in 1797, ended his congressional career as the relentless foe of the theories behind the French Revolution. He had been consistent. Randolph had proved himself a champion of liberty to the point of excess, although not of equality and fraternity; but his liberty, for all its occasional eccentric passion, was the liberty prescribed by tradition and delimited by expediency, not the absolute freedom of the *philosophes.*

John Randolph retired from Congress in 1828. His final, and perhaps most important, ideas upon the question of the basis of authority in government came the following year,

---

[43] *Ibid.,* p. 128.

[44] See Fenimore Cooper, *Sketches of Switzerland,* II, 18.

when he was a delegate to the constitutional convention of Virginia. He went to Richmond to defend old ways against the egalitarianism of a melioristic age.

4

"I have lived and hope to die a *freeholder,* and when I lose that distinction I shall no longer have any reason to be proud of being your faithful servant."[45] With these frank sentiments, Randolph stalked into the Virgina Convention. Never was there another state constitutional convention like that of Virginia in 1829. Among the delegates were former Presidents, distinguished jurists, powerful legislators, and famous orators; and nowhere, except at the federal constitutional convention, perhaps, were the fundamentals of government more thoroughly discussed—the problems of right and power, of suffrage and office, of property and poverty, of permanence and change. The East stood against the West in Virginia; the old order defied the new; egalitarianism fought conservatism. The most frequent spokesmen of lower Virginia were men like Benjamin Watkins Leigh, Littleton Waller Tazewell, and Philip P. Barbour; Randolph was silent all during the first period of the convention's sessions; but men waited to hear the orator of Roanoke, and at last he satisfied them. He defended everything old against everything new and completed his denial of the philosophy of Jefferson and of Paine. King Numbers, the fetish of equality, the passion for change, and the danger of abstract speculation all encountered the lash of his temper. "I go for blood," he had declared years before;

---

[45] *Richmond Enquirer,* May 25, 1824.

and here he was savage in his detestation of tinkering in politics.

Thompson, of Amherst, one of the ablest delegates from western Virginia, listened to the speeches of Randolph and John Marshall and their allies with the alarm most Jeffersonians must have felt. Randolph and his party were declaring that "government has no principles," Thompson protested; they held that "the rights of man are a mere chimera, of distempered imaginations." No one, in the whole progress of the debate, had so much as mentioned Jefferson and Paine; once the name of Fox had been venerated and that of Burke execrated, "but now, Burke, Filmer, and Hobbes, judging from their arguments, have become the text books of our statesmen."[46]

Within bounds, this is a shrewd criticism of the ideas expounded by Randolph at the convention. Randolph did not disavow principle, of course, nor did he approve the old Tories; but he reiterated his horror at "abstractions" in politics and cited the great authority of Burke. True natural rights, said Randolph, are imperiled always by the interposition of abstract rights of men; and so they were here at this very convention. It was proposed to set an age qualification of thirty years for election to the House of Delegates. Randolph espoused the cause of youthful politicians and ridiculed the insertion of such rigid provisions into a constitution. Expediency might hint, and public opinion ensure, that very few young men should acquire much political influence; yet it was unwise and unjust to exclude absolutely the whole class of young men, regardless of merit. "But, all this, I suppose, is in obedience to the all-prevailing principle,

---

[46] *Proceedings and Debates of the Virginia State Convention,* p. 411.

that *vox populi vox dei;* aye, sir, the all prevailing principle, that numbers, and numbers alone, are to regulate all things in political society, in the very teeth of those abstract rights of man, which constitute the only shadow of claim to exercise this monstrous tyranny."[47]

An assault on King Numbers, the monarch of the West, occupies the greater part of this speech of Randolph's—that question of the arbitrary power possessed by a majority over property and liberty which was later to attract the brooding intellect of Calhoun. Randolph continued:

> Are we men? Met to consult about the affairs of men? Or are we, in truth, a Robinhood society? Discussing rights in the abstract? . . . Do we forget, that we are living under a Constitution, which has shielded us for more than half a century . . . To their monstrous claims of power, we plead this prescription; but then we are told that *nullum tempus occurrit Regi*—King who? King Numbers. And they will not listen to a prescription of fifty-four years—a period greater, by four years, than would secure a title to the best estate in the Commonwealth, unsupported by any other shadow of right. Nay, sir, in this case, prescription operates *against* possession. They tell us, it is only a case of long-continued and, therefore, of aggravated injustice. They say to us, in words the most courteous and soft (but I am not so soft as to swallow them), "we shall be—we will be— we must be your masters, and you shall submit." To whom do they hold this language? To dependents? weak, unprotected, and incapable of defense? Or is it to the great tobacco-growing and slave-holding interest, and to every other interest on this side of the Ridge? "We are numbers, you have property." I am not so obtuse, as to require any further explanation on this head. . . . Mr. Chairman, since the days of the French Revolution, when the Duke of Orleans, who was the richest subject, not only in France, but in all Europe, lent himself to the *mountain* party in the Convention . . . so great a degree of infatuation, has not been shown by any individual, as the tobacco-grower, and

---

[47] *Ibid.,* p. 313.

slave-holder of Virginia, who shall lend his aid to rivet this yoke
on the necks of his brethren, and on his own.[48]

Extortionate national tariffs had been imposed by a bare
majority in Congress, Randolph reminded the convention;
King Numbers will do the same, reckless of justice, whenever
he is given his chance. Under the pretext of democracy, a
bare majority of men, told by the head, will plunder the
minority at pleasure; but it will be to their interest to keep
the minority at "the highest point consistent with their subjugation" for the sake of the greater spoils.

> Shall we, in Virginia, introduce this deadly principle into our
> own government? and give power to a bare majority to tax us
> *ad libitum,* and that when the strongest temptation is at the same
> time held out to them, to do it? It is now a great while since I
> learned from the philosopher of Malmesbury, that a state of na-
> ture is a state of war; but if we sanction this principle, we shall
> prove that a state, not of nature, but of society, and of constitu-
> tional government, is a state of interminable war.

Then Randolph returned to his old assault upon "abstractions" as distinguished from principles; and even unmodified
principles, applied indiscriminately, can do terrible harm.
He subscribed wholly to the Bill of Rights, but the ideas it
contained were intended for guides, not inflexible rules of
procedure:

> The Bill of Rights contains unmodified principles. The decla-
> rations it contains are our lights and guides, but when we come
> to apply these great principles, we must modify them for use;
> we must set limitations to their operation, and the enquiry is,
> *quousque?* How far? It is a question not of principle, but of de-
> gree. The very moment this immaculate principle of theirs is

---

[48] *Ibid.,* p. 316.

touched, it becomes what all principles are, materials in the hands of men of sense, to be applied in the welfare of the Commonwealth. It is not an incantation. It is no talisman. It is not witchcraft. It is not a torpedo to benumb us. If the naked principle of numbers only is to be followed, the requisites for the statesman fall far below what the gentleman from Spottsylvania rated them at. He needs not the four rules of arithmetic. No, sir, a negro boy with a knife and a tally stick, is a statesman complete in this school.[49]

Subjection to King Numbers produces taxation without representation; for property inevitably will be exposed to the desires of the unpropertied. The theory that taxation is a voluntary grant for common welfare, which is expressed repeatedly by Burke, thus will be undone; taxation will become once more what it was under despotisms, an arbitrary assessment for the benefit of particular persons and classes. "I will put it in the power of no man or set of men who ever lived," cried Randolph in his piercing tones, "to tax me without my consent." Remember, he exhorted the convention, that property and power cannot be truly separated; if power be transferred to the propertyless, they will not remain long without property of some sort. Chief Justice Marshall, who sat there in the convention, had remarked that the power to tax is the power to destroy. The whole old order of society, the old commonwealth of Virginia, might be obliterated by this innovation. Just as man always had been in society, so man has always had an appetite for property, operating sometimes *per fas,* sometimes *per nefas.*

It is the first time in my life, that I ever heard of a government, which was to divorce property from power. Yet, this is seriously and soberly proposed to us. Sir, I know it is practic-

---

[49] *Ibid.,* p. 317.

able, but it can be done only by a violent divulsion, as in France —but the moment you have separated the two, that very moment property will go in search of power, and power in search of property. "Male and female created He them"; and the two sexes do not more certainly, nor by a more unerring law, gravitate to each other, than property and power. You can only cause them to change hands.

Levelers would say, he knew, that he was no "friend to the poor." But weakening the structure of society is no kindness to the poor. Look at the drunkard staggering from the whiskey shop, look at the slattern seeking him, and ask where are their children. You will be told the government has undertaken to educate them, and so provided for the idleness and the whiskey of the parents. "Among the strange notions which have been broached since I have been in the political theatre, there is one which has lately seized the minds of men, that all things must be done for them by the government, and that they are to do nothing for themselves: the government is not only to attend to the great concerns which are its province, but it must step in and ease individuals of their natural and moral obligations."[50] An admirer of Adam Smith and the classical school of political economy, Randolph feared the democratic power of positive legislation as a means for converting the economic system from one of private concern to one of public spoliation.

Rambling in this long and acid speech as was his fashion, toward the end of it Randolph returned to his original charge, the despotism of Numbers; and he pursued the topic throughout the remaining sessions of the convention. It is unnecessary to trace the whole course of his remarks. He was the sternest foe of the "white basis men," who would

[50] *Ibid.*, p. 319.

give no representation to property; he appealed to the sons of freeholders, not yet freeholders themselves, to stand by the old constitution. Only the owners of land, said Randolph, were fit to decide the policies of the commonwealth. He denounced all "tinkering" with government. He scoffed at the theories of Jefferson, never meant for practical men: "Sir, if there be any point in which the authority of Mr. Jefferson might be considered as valid, it is in the mechanism of a plow." For Mr. Jefferson had designed and sent to the savants, at Paris, a model plow, exhibited in the Jardin des Plantes. It was mightily admired by the savants; but when applied to the red Virginia clay, in competition with the ill-looking Carey plow, it was beaten as thoroughly "as common sense will always beat theory and reveries. . . . So much for authority!"[51]

The innovators did not realize half the mischief they were doing, he exclaimed; they were establishing a monstrous government, with two branches of the legislature representing the very same voters, pitted against each other until one should submit—the whole profound idea of representative government as a harmonizing of separate interests thus forgotten. "A government of numbers in opposition to property was Jacobinism, rank Jacobinism."[52] Society thus roughly handled ceases to be a concord and is transformed into malignant factions—all this in the name of reform. Randolph's view is succinctly put by a passing observation of George Santayana's: "A reformer hewing so near to the tree's root never knows how much he may be felling."[53]

---

[51] *Ibid.,* p. 533.

[52] *Ibid.,* p. 556.

[53] George Santayana, *Reason in Society,* p. 47.

Legislators must be the representatives of small con-
stituencies, of distinct local interests, or they fail to reach
their proper function, Randolph continued; but, once
chosen, a representative must be permitted to exercise his
own virtue and knowledge: "He thought the people were
trustworthy—just so far as this—they were very capable of
choosing their own agents. They had sagacity and virtue
enough to decide between worth and wisdom and intelligence on the one side, and their opposites on the other; and
they having established their agents with power to act for
them, he was for leaving more to those agents than some
gentlemen seemed willing to do."[54] On the last day of the
convention, once more he praised true representative government and denounced fulsome flattery of the people, who
can act safely only through agents. Once he had been
thought an overviolent Republican, he knew, but now the
innovators had left him far behind, "thought an aristocrat
by those whom I think ultra-Jacobins." Like the uninformed
owner of a plantation, the people can be secure only if they
obtain the services of honest overseers rather than undertaking the conduct of affairs themselves: "Yet they may be
lured to their destruction by elections in November, and
elections in April . . . when they are called to pass upon an
act of Assembly, containing thirty or forty sections—of
which one-tenth—no, sir, not one-tenth—even of the Assembly that passed it—know the true meaning."[55]

The legislative initiative, the recall, direct primaries, and
those other instruments of popular power which have grown
up since Randolph's time would have met no warmer wel-

---

[54] *Proceedings and Debates of the Virginia State Convention*, p. 815.
[55] *Ibid.*, p. 870.

come from him than did this variety of the referendum; and no doubt he would have loathed the political consequences of these devices, though he might have been surprised that government still can function at all, despite such excrescences.

Marshall, Randolph, and the other leaders from the eastern counties succeeded in modifying the proposals of the western delegates, but they could not prevent the adoption of the new constitution, for which lower Virginia voted in the fear that, if it should be rejected, a worse might be framed. Even Randolph was forced to yield after this fashion; and a year later he wrote to President Jackson (rather a curious confidant on such a topic) in terms quite as bitter as those of Sir Walter Scott after the reform bill which Parliament passed in 1833. Abolishing the freehold franchise had thrown the government into the hands of the scum of the country; referring to the route from Roanoke to Charlotte Court House, he declared: "On the whole road there is not one person who can read or write and hardly one that is not a sot or notorious receiver of stolen goods, from slaves instigated to steal by the wretched 'House Keepers' who by the votes of Fenton Mercer and Madison and Monroe! were made voters at our elections by our new Constitution."[56] Randolph's "people," the farmers and men of substance, had given way to poor white trash.

J. R. Cooke, of Frederick, one of the "white basis men" who had thus succeeded in forcing the adoption of a general suffrage, expressed his astonishment, now the convention was done, that Randolph and his Tidewater colleagues had

---

[56] Randolph to Jackson, March 1, 1832 (*Correspondence of Jackson,* IV, 413–14).

repudiated the doctrines of Locke and, infatuated with their own brilliance, had contended that there are no original principles of government; that natural freedom and equality are mere abstractions; that the doctrine of majority rule is "a vulgar fallacy"; that a government of numbers is legalized rapine; that the distribution of political power must be decided by "an enlarged expediency," without reference to natural rights.[57] Though Cooke somewhat misstated Randolph's position upon two of these points, it certainly was perfectly true that by 1830 Randolph had severed completely any ties to Locke, Paine, and Jefferson. In the last year of his life he wrote: "I cannot live in this miserable, undone country, where, as the Turks follow their sacred standard, which is a pair of Mahomet's green breeches, we are governed by the old red breeches of that Prince of Projectors, St. Thomas of Can*ting*bury; and surely Becket himself never had more pilgrims at his shrine than the saint of Monticello."[58] The old families of Virginia, he predicted, would sink into the mass of overseers' progeny, extinguishing the aristocracy of blood which Randolph prized as highly as any peer: "And this is the legitimate, nay, inevitable conclusion to which Mr. Jefferson and his leveling system have brought us."[59]

5

"I was not born to endure a master," Randolph wrote.[60] He might have added that he was not born to endure many

---

[57] *Richmond Enquirer,* February 13, 1830.

[58] Garland, *op. cit.,* II, 346.

[59] *Ibid.,* I, 19.

[60] *Ibid.,* II, 360.

equals; his impatient genius could not bear the failings of other men, nor could it descend to demagoguery. Had the basis of the franchise been earlier what it became in 1830, probably Randolph could not have gained office, for the distinction of "freeholder" upon which he prided himself also provided the only kind of constituency which would have tolerated Randolph's course as a political free lance. Tocqueville remarks the dislike of democratic peoples for eccentricity, and only Southside Virginia, perhaps, retained sufficient of the ancient aristocratic temper to elect so startling a man to high responsibility as late as 1828. Natural liberty, equality, and fraternity were ideas congenitally foreign to such a character as Randolph's, especially when a mind of his temper was joined to the possession of great estates and hundreds of slaves. Jefferson remained constant to these egalitarian principles, but Jefferson had little of Randolph's intolerant hauteur.

Far more than temperament, all the same, lay behind Randolph's dissent from Revolutionary principles. He saw clearly to what conclusions such ideas led and to what limbo they would consign the old life he loved. Whether his society or ours be the better, he was a true prophet, for the America of his time has been obliterated; perhaps he was wiser than Jefferson, since a change of this description was more than Jefferson bargained for.

Randolph found the source of authority not in a mystic Nature but fundamentally in force—force tempered by the experience of man and softened by the wise conventions of society. With Aristotle, he believed that man out of society must be either a beast or a god; there never had been a condition of truly human existence which was not a state of society. The real and ineradicable sources of political power are vigor of mind and body, possession of property. Equality and fraternity, far from being natural rights, are artificial conventions, to be extended or contracted as the requirements of a particular society dictate. As for liberty, individual and national freedom, although it was not an abstract right of man, it was a natural objective, a longing inherent in the character of men; and the Roanoke statesman never -denied its blessings, although the exigencies of society might require that in particular cases liberty be restrained. "Art is man's nature," Burke had said; and Randolph, never forgetting this precept, declared that the art of politics consists in a prudent conformity of practice to principle, not in a fanatic devotion to abstraction.

Nothing of the leveler endured in Randolph, but he, like John Taylor, held that government should not deliberately produce inequality through legislation.[61] An aristocracy of this sort he roundly condemned: "Must we, too, have these Corinthian ornaments of society because those countries have given in to them?"[62] But men should not vainly endeavor to use the power of the state for equalizing natural distinctions, either; that, Randolph said, would be bleeding a healthy animal to aid a sick creature. Randolph dreaded the power of positive law, controlled by democracies, to sweep away the variety and liberty of life.

Real freedom and proper station in society must be determined by a noble expediency, guided by traditional moral principle. Fundamental principles of government can be discerned; individual liberty is one of them; but such principles admit exceptions—they are not legislative enactments. Or-

---

[61] See John Taylor, *Definition of Parties,* p. 9.

[62] *Richmond Enquirer,* June 4, 1824.

dinarily Randolph assailed the theories expressed in the Declaration of Independence "in the sense in which they are commonly understood by the multitude"; he did not wish to be thought an enemy to equality of civil rights, the sensible meaning to be got from the assertion that "all men are created free and equal." Equality before the law had no more determined advocate than Randolph, but there was no stronger opponent of political and economic leveling. Justice and democracy are not synonymous; courage and vigilance are required to keep them even compatible. It is no paradox that a government professedly egalitarian, like that of Cleon or that of the Soviets, can be as arbitrary as a government professedly autocratic, like that of Critias or that of Spain. Randolph's warning that enfranchisement does not bring tranquillity needs recalling.

If, then, men cannot enjoy equal political and economic status, the degree of popular participation in government should be decided by enlightened expediency. Power and property cannot be separated permanently, said Randolph; and, if they change hands, usually it is with a disastrous interlude. Power, therefore, should be in the trust of men of property, landed property—freeholders, the strength of the commonwealth, qualified by interest and ability to comprehend the nature of government. They need not be the Federalists' "rich and well-born"; they need only be sturdy farmers and planters. It is to their interest that government be just; they, the pride of any state, are deserving of this prerogative; and they are numerous enough to maintain government. Perhaps Randolph's system never could have endured, whatever the course of national events, for the egalitarian spirit was immensely strong, and in industrial America (which would have been anathema to Randolph) freeholders are not more than a small proportion of the population. At any rate, the tariff, the rise of capitalism on a vast scale, and the decay of Virginian agriculture quashed the society of Jefferson and Randolph.

As Randolph declared during his famous denunciation of the "corrupt bargain" of J. Q. Adams and Clay, the "Blifil and Black George" speech, he was, in his day, "beaten down, horse, foot, and dragoons!" But his political ideas were to attain a fleeting triumph in the South. Fifteen years after Randolph's death, Calhoun was to write concerning natural-rights doctrine, specifically acknowledging the influence of Randolph:

> We now begin to experience danger of admitting so great an error to have a place in the declaration of our independence. For a long time it lay dormant; but in the process of time it began to germinate, and produce its poisonous fruits. . . . Instead, then, of all men having the same right to liberty and equality, as is claimed by those who hold that they are all born free and equal, liberty is the noble and highest reward bestowed on mental and moral development, combined with favorable circumstances.[63]

In Calhoun, who he distrusted, Randolph found his disciple; and in the minds of the political metaphysicians, who he despised, he found his victory.

---

[63] John C. Calhoun, *Discourse on the Constitution, Works,* I, 511–12.

Chapter Four

The Division
of Power

1

In 1813 John Randolph, the bitter opponent of a war that had been popular in its inception, told a hostile Congress and a hostile people who were accustomed to his acerbity:

> I have said, on a former occasion, and if I were Philip, I would employ a man to say it every day, that the people of this country, if ever they lose their liberties, will do it by sacrificing some great principle of free government to temporary passion. There are certain great principles, which if they be not held inviolate, at all seasons, our liberty is gone. If we give them up, it is perfectly immaterial what is the character of our Sovereign; whether he be King or President, elective or hereditary—it is perfectly immaterial what is his character—we shall be slaves—it is not an elective government which will preserve us.[1]

This was Randolph's exhortation to the nation—commonly an unheeding nation—throughout his fiery career: a demand for government of law and precedent, not of men and enthusiasm; for a known and unbending delimitation

---

[1] *Annals of Congress* (12th Cong., 2d sess.), pp. 184–85.

and balancing of the governing power, not the constitutional construction of opportunism; for a maintenance of the principles of freedom, whatever their passing inconvenience, and not a grasping at temporary benefits, whatever their ultimate consequence. Randolph was a strict constructionist, a state-powers man, a jailer of that necessary evil, government; he fought the Federalists, the imperialists, the latitudinarians, the centralists, the "energymen," and, if they often forced him to give ground, still he held them back from the keep of his Old Republican castle and maintained the fight until a later generation took up the battle.

The state-powers, strict-construction views Randolph held were in no sense peculiar to him, of course; they were the tenets of all the Virginians of his school and of many men throughout the Union, particularly in the seaboard states of the South; but his constituents of Charlotte County called him, with truth, in a resolution passed after his death, "the most intelligent, the most consistent, and the most intrepid, advocate of the rights and sovereignty of the states."[2] John Taylor of Caroline held the pen of the Old Republican faction—a rather unwieldy pen, perhaps, although Taylor's style has been too harshly criticized, in part because of Randolph's complaint that Taylor needed a translator for his books—but Randolph was the orator of the cause, and his tongue was as dextrous as Taylor's pen was ponderous. Other men maintained these doctrines; but none defended them more ably, clung to them more inveterately, or impressed them more thoroughly upon the minds of the younger generation of political leaders. More than a century

---

[2] See William Cabell Bruce, *Randolph,* II, 228.

and three quarters since Randolph commenced his career, these issues of state prerogative and constitutional construction are debated with scarcely less heat than in his day. Let us look at some of his more important declarations on these questions—still acid, still lucid.

The great object of Randolph and the Old Republicans, in a political sense, was the restriction of the power of government to that sphere specifically assigned by constitution and precedent. They admitted that at times such a jealous interpretation might lead to a passing difficulty; they conceded that temporary benefits might sometimes be got by exceeding the letter and spirit of the law. But, they declared, these annoyances or restrictions must be endured if free government and constitutional rights are to be maintained. The Old Republicans, respecters of precedent, perceived how dangerous and how irresistible a force is faulty precedent; the exception becomes the rule, war powers become peace powers, and, if a stand ever is to be made, it must be at the outset. Once the dike of constitutional guarantees is out, innovation pours through without interruption. The stern reluctance of the Old Republicans to allow government one jot more power than was specifically granted seemed a splitting of hairs to many of their contemporaries, and certainly seems so to most men today; but often the question with the Old Republicans was not the problem immediately at stake but the far vaster principle of the rule of law. It was upon this point of rigid construction of the federal compact, this insistence that principles are not to be abandoned no matter how tempting the prospect opened by making exceptions, that Randolph must have separated from the party of Jefferson even had there been no Yazoo debate, no Florida affair, no embargo; for those issues passed away, and Randolph was not reconciled to the Jeffersonian body; the difference was more fundamental. Whether or not Randolph was correct, historically and philosophically, it still is noteworthy that the three Presidents whose straying from the principles of republicanism he so condemned did not deny his premises; they, too, agreed that the Constitution must be construed strictly; but they, once in office, began to sacrifice construction to the demands of the hour, rightly or wrongly. Power corrupts, said Randolph. The time was to come when all three—Jefferson, Madison, and Monroe—were to lament the pass to which loose construction had brought the nation and were to return to the faith which Randolph never had abandoned.

A discussion of Randolph's thought on the subject of the division of power must embrace a number of subjects: the construction of the Constitution; the powers of states and the nature of the Union; limitations upon authority, by whomever exercised; and the struggle between sections. As Randolph's life neared its end, that question of the division of power became the problem of the hour in the form of the ominous nullification controversy.

It may seem strange that one aspect of the question is not discussed, except incidentally, in this chapter—the problem of sovereignty. It is omitted because Randolph omitted it, with his impatience of abstractions. He understood the problem, and, like John Taylor, considered it vain; while Taylor undertook the trouble of proving that sovereignty was indivisible and irremovable from the people of the separate states, Randolph only made this explanation implicit in his speeches. "Asking one of the states to surrender part of her sovereignty is like asking a lady to surrender part of her chastity," said Randolph.[3] For him, there was no half-mystic body of sovereignty, divisible or indivisible; there was only the question of how men best could govern themselves, as experience and their circumstances permitted. He was willing to allow the metaphysicians to place sovereignty where they willed, so long as power itself remained properly allotted.

2

Whatever charges hostile critics of Randolph may bring against him, they cannot deny his early and enduring devotion to the principle of strict construction of the Constitution, although they may attempt to prove his defense of the constitutionality of the Louisiana Purchase a momentary wandering from that narrow path. Randolph's whole congressional career is a record of protest against measures on the ground of their unconstitutionality, whether or not he favored their ends. Equally constant was his advocacy of the powers of the states. In 1802 he insisted that representatives were the delegates of the states in their respective individual capacities, not of the people of the United States at large, or as a nation: this was a deliberate distortion of the plain intent of the men who made the Constitution, Randolph pointed out, for, if such had been the intent of the Convention, representation in the House would have been allotted by federal districts, without regard for state lines. Make such assumptions, and you destroy the federal character of government.

---

[3] Notes on Randolph (Nathan Loughborough MSS, copy in Randolph Papers, Virginia State Library).

Another of his early speeches on the question of federal power against state sovereignty was delivered in 1805; it concerned the proposed exemption of colleges from the duties imposed in the tariff schedule. Randolph spoke against this bill and, at some length, dealt with the limited powers of the federal government and with the need for uniformity of legislation and the danger of special concessions and discriminations; he told of the importance of strict constitutional construction and of previous false construction, the work of his great fellow-Virginian, friend, and political adversary, John Marshall.[4] Not long afterward, during the debate on "preservation of the peace," he asserted the power of a state to serve processes in federal territory and the concurrent jurisdiction of the state with the national authority over coastal waters—a question still perplexed.[5] The doctrines of strict construction and of state powers even then were inseparably joined in his mind, and their union became more important as the years passed. These were the doctrines of the Republican party—or had been the doctrines of that party before it had attained power; yet, even in Jefferson's first term of office, Randolph found Republicans who opposed him, by word or implication, and the time was not long before he discovered himself, with his adherence to old principles, in the minority. For President Jefferson, too, was leaning—or was being forced to lean, by circumstances—toward interpretation of power more federalistic and latitudinarian than Republican. Some biographers defend Jefferson's vacillations on the ground that they only show how the man of Monticello was not slavishly devoted

[4] *Annals of Congress* (8th Cong., 2d sess.), pp. 705–6.
[5] *Ibid.,* pp. 768–70.

to abstract principles; but Jefferson was to regret the consequences of cutting the dikes of strict construction, precisely as Randolph, much sooner, came to regret the Louisiana Purchase. Many of the Republicans of the North were only superficially strict-construction men and champions of state powers, and, as Henry Adams points out repeatedly in his history of Jefferson's administration, it was upon them that Jefferson came to depend for his most constant support—upon devoted followers like Smilie of Pennsylvania and Sloan of New Jersey, legislators of a type far different from Randolph. The satirist Hugh Brackenridge sneered at the northern democrats in Congress and called election to that body "a stain worse than stealing sheep";[6] at all events, they were more egalitarian democrats and personal followers of Jefferson than they were adherents to the famous Virginian school of thought, and it is not surprising that Randolph soon parted company with them. As early as 1801, he was writing of these doubtful allies:

> Parties here consist of the old Federalists courting popularity—these are a small minority; the same kind of characters, Republicanized, and lukewarm Republicans, who added to the former, will perhaps constitute a bare majority of the House, and Republicans who hold the same principles now that they professed under adverse fortune, and who, *if they were all here,* might amount to about fifty members. These are determined to pay the debt off, to repeal the internal taxes, to retrench every unnecessary expense, military, naval, and civil, to enforce economy as well upon men calling themselves Republicans as upon Federalists, and to punish delinquents without respect to their political professions.[7]

---

[6] Hugh Henry Brackenridge, *Modern Chivalry*, p. 17.

[7] Randolph to St. George Tucker, January 15, 1801 (copy in Virginia State Library).

Four years later, Randolph was to find his band of what
he considered true republicans reduced to half the fifty he
had numbered in 1801; and, after Jefferson had left office,
he was to say of that President's administration:

> It had my hearty approbation for one-half of its career. As
> to my opinion of the remainder of it, it has been no secret. The
> lean kine of Pharaoh devoured the fat kine. The last four years,
> with the embargo in their train, ate up the rich harvest of the
> first four, and, if we had not some Joseph to step in, and change
> the state of things, what would have been now the condition
> of the country? I repeat it; never has there been any admin-
> istration which went out of office and left the country in a state
> so deplorable and calamitous as the last.[8]

Randolph of Roanoke often was to refer in nostalgic
fashion, in later years, to the first administration of
Thomas Jefferson, with all its reforms. Indeed, there was not
one administration after that time to which Randolph gave
his continued support, although, had he lived until the
succession of Tyler, he might have approved of the policies
of that Virginian President; but by Tyler's time it was too
late to turn back the course of events to Old Republican
ways, and if the South Carolina school, and many leaders in
other states of the South, later adopted the principles of the
Old Republicans, still they remained a national minority
and finally were crushed by force. The triumph of Randolph's republicanism—of antifederalism—was brief indeed; but enough of that spirit survived after 1804 to feed
a flame which is not yet wholly out.

> I confess that I have (and I am not at all ashamed to own
> it) an hereditary attachment to the state which gave me birth.
> I shall act upon it as long as I act on this floor, or anywhere else.

---

[8] *Annals of Congress* (10th Cong., 1st sess.), p. 68.

I shall feel it when I am no longer capable of action anywhere. . . . I recollect an old motto, that always occurs to me at the approach of every thing in the shape of an attack upon my country—it is, *Nemo me impune lacesset*.[9]

This passion for personal and local liberties meant a distrust not only of national authority and congressional tinkering but of the executive branch, the judiciary, and, within the states, of the state governments themselves. Randolph sometimes repeated, "This is a government of suspicion, not of confidence"; and his suspicion, certainly, never slumbered. He was ever alert to denounce executive usurpation of authority, to deny the power of the Supreme Court to define the Constitution, and to check the inclination of Congress for legislating. Even concerning government in his own Virginia, he spoke of "the puzzle of state politics," of pettiness and corruption. Closely linked with the problems of the division of power is the problem of constitutional construction. A great part of Randolph's life was spent in demonstrating that American state and private liberties are dependent upon a rigorous interpretation of the Constitution.

It often has been asserted that the strict-construction men interpreted the Constitution strictly only when their interests were threatened by a loose interpretation; and it also has been held that state powers were asserted only when a state found involved some immediate interest. These contentions cannot be maintained in the case of John Randolph. Many a southerner of a later day, many a defender of slavery, held that Congress had no exclusive right of government over the territories; but Randolph, southerner

---

[9] *Ibid.*, (17th Cong., 1st sess.), p. 903.

and defender of slaveholding against northern assaults, still maintained that Congress governed the territories—and the District of Columbia, too—absolutely, as an empire. This was, undeniably, a proof of the penetration of his thought; for if he had said, as many did, that Congress was compelled to govern the territories in the "spirit" of the Constitution, he would have admitted that there was a "spirit," presumably to be defined by loose-construction men, outside the letter of the Constitution, and then where would have been strict construction? But Randolph, although he stated that congressional power over the territories was unrestrained, still was not an advocate of making that power a tyranny, and it was he who, in Jefferson's administration, condemned the territorial government of Louisiana and introduced a petition from that region requesting more liberal institutions.

Many a southerner held the protective tariff unconstitutional; but Randolph, the foremost opponent of the tariff, admitted it to be probably within the letter of the law, although he said the true test of constitutionality was not the effect of the act but the intention of the act; a tariff designed primarily to raise revenue, but incidentally protective, although folly, would be within the aim of the Constitution; one designed expressly to exclude foreign products would be contrary to the intention of the founders. To Neale Alexander, he wrote:

> The man who supports the Bank and denounces the tariff as unconstitutional, may take his choice between knave and fool, unless he admits that he is both.
>
> In one case, the power to lay duties, excises, etc., is granted; in the other, no such power is given. The true key is, that the *abuse, under pretense of exercise of any* power (midnight judiciary, etc.) is unconstitutional. This unlocks every difficulty.

Killing a man may be justifiable homicide, chance-medley, man-slaughter or murder, according to the motives and circumstances of the case. An unwise, but honest exercise of a power, may be blamed, but it is not unconstitutional. But every usurped power (as the Bank) is so.[10]

There could hardly be better proof than this that Randolph was fully sincere in his strict interpretation of the Constitution. To detail his whole course would be to write a political history; but we may see, at any rate, how able a teacher Randolph was for that later great exponent of the same doctrine, Calhoun.

3

Perhaps Randolph's greatest contribution to the cause of a just distribution of governmental powers was his untiring opposition to the centralizing tendencies of the federal government during the period between 1805 and 1820. With the aid only of a few admirers, he waged the fight against internal improvements, the tariff, foreign wars and entanglements, the Bank, and every other measure which threatened the principles of state powers and the planter economy. By the second decade of the century, the South had begun to come round to his stand; during the first years of the 1820s he was more popular than he was at any other period of his life except during the first administration of Jefferson; but before that, he was braving the storm. In addition to Randolph's native audacity, the sternest of convictions must have been required to withstand popular apathy and con-

---

[10] Randolph to Alexander, June 26, 1832 (Hugh Garland, *Randolph of Roanoke,* II, 353).

gressional hatred. Doubtless Randolph's clear perception that the cause of strict construction and state powers was united with that of the planter economy—that the sundering of the two issues meant death for either—had a sustaining influence.

To state that Randolph and his Old Republicans—sometimes reduced, in the House, to a half-dozen members—carried on the controversy unaided would be an exaggeration, however; they had strange allies, for a time, in the Federalists of New England. New England, indeed, maintained even more resolutely the doctrines of strict construction and state powers during the era of the embargo and the war with England. For it appeared to the New Englanders that their region faced ruin in consequence of the measures of the government at Washington; Randolph, however, perceiving more clearly long-run consequences, declared that the Old Dominion, for all its devotion to the Virginia dynasty, would pay "so dearly for the war whistle." He found Quincy, Otis, and Pickering closer to him then than such Virginians as Thomas Mann Randolph and John Eppes, to mention no greater names. Among his valuable correspondence with Josiah Quincy of Massachusetts appears this revealing letter of January 29, 1814:

> What a game of round-about has been played since I was initiated into the mysteries of politics! I recollect the time when to your Mr. Otis, *state rights* were as nothing in comparison with the proud prerogative of the federal government. *Then* Virginia was building an armory to enable her to resist *federal usurpation.* . . . It was always my opinion that Union was the means of securing the safety, liberty, and welfare of the confederacy, and not in itself an end to which these should be sacrificed. But the question of resistance to any established government is always a question of expediency; and the resort ought

never to be had to this last appeal, except in cases where the grievance does not admit of palliative or temporizing remedies. The one is a case to be decided by argument, the other by feeling.[11]

To the "good old thirteen states" and their common ties, Randolph felt a real attachment. He did not gloss over the perils and disasters of possible disunion. Resistance to injustice, however justifiable in the abstract, must be only the last resort of men denied an appeal. Still, this is the ancestor of the fire-eaters, repeatedly crying out to centralizers and northern industrial interests and western empire-builders that they were provoking no mere human cattle but rather the enormous might of the planting and slaveholding and free-trading interest. Sometimes his hints of resistance in the South by armed force against the injustice of the general government probably should be considered chiefly a threat calculated to obtain the "temporizing remedies" of which he wrote. He held the states to be sovereign, nevertheless, and free to sever their ties to the Union if tyranny were put upon them. As for Calhoun, armed resistance was for Randolph the last justifiable resort of a community intolerably oppressed.[12] Randolph, in theory, might have been the more ready of these two to evoke force, for he lacked the faith in constitutional guarantees which the Carolinian professed; but when the test of 1832 came, it was Calhoun who dared the issue of war or peace, although Randolph called for Virginian assistance to South Carolina if the Force Act were put into effect. Henry Adams writes of this facet of Randolph's politics in a sentence which displays the

---

[11] Edmund Quincy, *Life of Josiah Quincy*, p. 339.
[12] John C. Calhoun, *Discourses on the Constitution, Works*, I, 300.

acuity which was Adams' so often: "Patrick Henry and Mr. Madison shrank from this last appeal to arms, which John Randolph boldly accepted; and, in his defense, it is but fair to say that a right which has nowhere any ultimate sanction of force is, in law, no right at all."[13]

Yet to the Hartford Convention, Randolph wrote in terms remonstrating though sympathetic, admitting their grievances while entreating them to endure, as Virginia was enduring. He prophesied the ruin secession would bring—an opinion he very probably still held at the time of South Carolinian nullification, nearly two decades later. He remarked, in part:

> When I exhort to further patience—to resort to constitutional means of redress only, I know that there is such a thing as tyranny as well as oppression; and that there is no government, however restricted in its power, that may not, by abuse, under pretext of exercise of its unconstitutional authority, drive its unhappy subjects to desperation. . . . Our Constitution is an affair of compromise between the states, and this is the master-key which unlocks all its difficulties. If any of the parties to the compact are dissatisfied with their share of influence, it is an affair of amicable discussion, in the mode pointed out by the constitution itself, but no cause for dissolving the confederacy.[14]

Here is a suggestion of the doctrines of concurrent powers and special constitutional checks which Calhoun was later to develop. But nullification is not implied.

All during these years, the Southside orator declared, his stand was consistent: the defense of the states against federal encroachment, the liberty of the citizen against all encroachment. He would vote for no new tax, for no new

---

[13] Henry Adams, *John Randolph*, p. 37.
[14] Garland, *op. cit.*, II, 51–62.

accession of power to any division of government.[15] By a curious destiny he found his most formidable adversary in the debates upon these questions of war powers and national expansion to be an intense young South Carolinian, the rising Calhoun, then a War Hawk, filled with nationalistic enthusiasm, a proponent of liberal construction of the Constitution, internal improvements at national expense, defiance of Britain, and the democratic creed of progress. From the beginning of their acquaintance Randolph treated Calhoun with a respect he very rarely accorded to his enemies—and a suspicion nearly as profound. The high authority of Henry Adams insists that, with the passage of the years, Randolph converted Calhoun. Certainly those concepts of southern unity and peculiar character, of the danger of consolidatory tendencies to the existence of slavery, of the necessary union between strict construction and states' rights, of even concurrent powers and an appeal beyond Congress and the Supreme Court—those theories, after 1824 so relentlessly expounded by Calhoun, had been expressed by Randolph ever since he broke with Jefferson. With what seems to have been a touch of the gift for prophecy that was Randolph's, the Virginian singled out this young representative from upcountry South Carolina, in a speech which (for a change) was more an appeal or lecture than a denunciation, as the special object of his plea for the powers of the states. In January, 1816 the dominant party in Congress proposed a revenue program by the terms of which the direct taxation levied during the late war would be retained as a principle and many of the wartime duties

---

[15] Letter to Edward Booker, 1816 (copy in Randolph Papers, Virginia State Library); see Bruce, *op. cit.,* II, 240.

continued also. Randolph, the unacknowledged leader of
the motley opposition, rose in fury to denounce this proposal, for he detested wars and tariffs with an equal vehemence. Calhoun, in turn, answered Randolph by declaring
that federally financed roads and canals were a part of the
effort toward an enduring defense of the country, and so was
the subsidy to manufactures which the tariff provided. The
nation must prepare for war in time of peace. Randolph retorted at his usual length, but in a tone of solemn warning,
almost entreaty, which he seldom deigned to employ. Did
Randolph, for the moment, spy out his successor in Calhoun? The Roanoke planter's slaves, and many of his constituents, credited wild Jack Randolph—a man who could
see devils on the stairs and fancy dead men writing in the
next room—with powers more than human. At any rate, in
one of those flashes of intuition which startled all his contemporaries, he turned his burning dark eyes upon Calhoun, pointed at him his bony finger, and in his high and
piercing voice called upon the young politician to penetrate
deeper into the mysteries of politics. Randolph's cadaver-
ous form, his grand gentleman's manner, his strange and
wrinkled face, his imagination heightened by the brandy
with which he choked the pain from his perpetual sickness
—this nervous and sometimes terrible being, with all these
attributes of genius and madness intertwined, cried out to
the sober backcountry Calvinist Calhoun that one must
judge of political measures by their distant but immense
effect:

> I have long believed there was a tendency in the administra-
> tion of this government, in the system itself indeed, to consoli-
> dation, and the remarks made by the honorable gentleman from
> South Carolina have not tended to allay any fears I have enter-

tained from that quarter. Make this a simple integral government, said Mr. R., and I subscribe to the doctrines of the honorable gentleman; because they are drawn from the same fountain
from which I have drawn my own principles. Mr. R. said he
was glad to see that the gentleman had not raked in the kennels
(he would say) of democracy, for the principles of which he
formed his political creed. But, said Mr. R., ours is not an
integral government, but a government of states confederated
together. He put it to the committee, to the gentleman himself,
whether the honorable gentleman's principles (which he had
demonstrated with an ability honorable to the state he represented, to the House, and to himself) did not go to the destruction of the state governments. It was not, Mr. R. said, from the
preference of present good to a little self-denial, that he opposed
the system of the gentleman and his political friends. I say, Mr.
R. repeated, that these doctrines go to prostrate the state governments at the feet of the general government. If the warning
voice of Patrick Henry had not apprised me long ago, the events
of this day would have taught me that this Constitution does
not comprise one people, but that there are two distinct characters in them. Mr. R. said, he had been led heretofore to question
whether the fact was so; he now believed it as much as any
article of his political creed. When speaking of the value of our
form of government, the gentleman might have added to his
remarks, Mr. R. said, that while in its federative character it
was good, as a consolidated government it would be hateful;
that there were features in the Constitution of the United States,
beautiful in themselves, when looked at with reference to the
federal character of the Constitution, were deformed and monstrous when looked at with reference to consolidation. The gentleman was too deeply read in Aristotle, too well versed in
political lore, to deny the fact.[16]

Here, in five minutes' impromptu utterance, was the essence of Calhoun's later creed. "Randolph's answer was one
which Calhoun passed over at the time," writes the chief
biographer of the Cast-Iron Man, "but to which he paid

---

[16] *Annals of Congress* (14th Cong., 1st sess.), p. 840.

tribute many years later."[17] The direct tax was adopted, as Randolph, inured to defeat, had quite expected. But Calhoun had begun to listen to him. "John Randolph stands in history as the legitimate and natural precursor of Calhoun," declares Henry Adams with the characteristic bluntness of that family which Randolph called "the American house of Stuart." "Randolph sketched out and partly filled in the outlines of that political scheme over which Calhoun labored so long, and against which Clay strove successfully while he lived—the identification of slavery with states' rights. All that was ablest and most masterly, all except what was mere metaphysical rubbish, in Calhoun's statesmanship had been suggested by Randolph years before Calhoun began his states' rights career."[18] This speech of Randolph's against the revenue measures of 1816 was the inception of a long and curious relationship between two brilliant and almost fanatic southerners, marked on Calhoun's part by a pondering courtesy, on Randolph's by a suspicion that sometimes descended to flaming public abuse, even while Calhoun, become Vice-President, brooded over the Senate and refused to suppress the invective of Senator Randolph. Two other paragraphs from Randolph's reply to Calhoun are worth examination. In a tenor of that pathos which is a strong characteristic of all his better speeches. Randolph flung at Calhoun a query that in the long run, as the South Carolinian mulled it over, may have converted the Cast-Iron Man to the views of his adversary:

> The question is, whether or not we are willing to become one great consolidated nation, under one form of law; whether

[17] Charles W. Wiltse, *John C. Calhoun, Nationalist*, p. 108.

[18] Adams, *op. cit.*, p. 272.

the state governments are to be swept away; or whether we have still respect enough for those old respectable institutions to regard their integrity and preservation as part of our policy? I, for one, said Mr. R., cling to them, because I love my country as I do my immediate connections; for the love of country is nothing more than the love of every man for his wife, child, or friend. I am not for a policy which must end in the destruction, and speedy destruction, too, of the whole of the state governments.

And Randolph proceeded to show how Calhoun's recommendations for preparing for future war—building of roads and encouragement of manufactures by the federal power—would establish precedents ruinous to the sovereignty of the states. "It was his policy, Mr. R. said, to stick to the states in contests arising between them and the general government—to the people in all collisions between them and the government, and between the popular branches and the unpopular branches of the government—he was wrong, however, he said, to call it unpopular; for, unfortunately, its popularity was that which gave it an irresistible weight in this House and in the nation."[19]

During the same month, Randolph delivered a speech on the treaty-making power of the President and the Senate, in which he denied that a treaty could override an act of Congress and pointed out the dangers of such a power, were it to be conceded. It destroyed all balancing of authority, within the national government and between the general government and the states, he declared.[20]

But to prolong this survey of Randolph's opinions during those years of lonely struggle, however interesting, is impracticable here. This period of his career ends with the

---

[19] *Annals of Congress* (14th Cong., 1st sess.), p. 844.
[20] *Ibid.,* pp. 533–38.

second Missouri debate, in which Randolph took so active a part, denying the right of Congress to refuse to accept the electoral vote of any state in the Union, as he had denied the right of Congress to insist upon the insertion of certain provisions in the constitution of Missouri. By 1821 the South and the adherents of Jefferson, alarmed at the projects of the National Republicans, and convinced, in part, by the warnings of Randolph and his colleagues, had begun to rally to the cause of strict construction and the states. Upon the publication of John Taylor's *Construction Construed and Constitutions Vindicated,* the aged Jefferson, who had been aroused by the Missouri "firebell in the night," wrote: "I acknowledge it has corrected some erring opinion into which I had slidden without sufficient examination."[21] William Leigh, referring to some letters he had read, later wrote of Jefferson to Randolph: "The old gentleman seems from this correspondence, to be more alarmed at the rapid and increasing encroachments of the federal government than I could have imagined."[22] And Jefferson himself wrote to Nathaniel Macon:

> You probably have seen in the newspapers a letter of mine recommending Col. Taylor's book to the notice of our fellow citizens. . . . There are two measures which if not taken, we are undone. 1st, how to check these unconstitutional invasions of states rights by the federal judiciary. How? Not by impeachment in the first instance, but by a strong protestation of both houses of Congress that such and such doctrines, advanced by the supreme court, are contrary to the constitution: and if they afterward relapse into the same heresies, impeach and set the whole

---

[21] *Richmond Enquirer,* January 24, 1822.

[22] Leigh to Randolph, April 3, 1826 (Randolph Letters, University of North Carolina).

adrift. For what was the government divided into three branches, but that each should watch over the others, and oppose their usurpations. 2. to cease borrowing money to pay off the national debt, if this cannot be done without dismissing the army and putting the ships out of commission, have them up high and dry, and reduce the army to the lowest point at which it was ever established.[23]

Randolph—who, like the Adamses, thought most men humbugs—must have experienced a grim pleasure on beholding these symptoms of fright at the tendencies which Randolph had been fighting since 1805. The man of Roanoke enjoyed a degree of triumph and popularity again; no longer was he almost alone in his demand for a nice division of power, and his best speeches upon the subject were made during this period.

On January 31, 1824, Randolph delivered his long speech on the proposed surveys for roads and canals. There has been no better exposition of the argument for strict constitutional construction. First he assailed the passion for attempting to exercise to the utmost every power conceivably granted by the Constitution, and then he launched into a condemnation of the latitudinarians of constitutional interpretation, who took the authority to *establish* post roads as signifying authority to *build* post roads. By words—"the counters of wise men, the money of fools"—the lovers of political manipulation and governmental spending intend to cajole Americans out of their rights and liberties. The makers of the Constitution had intended to grant Congress only a minimum power over the economy; indeed, if the Constitution when submitted for ratification had included

---

[23] Jefferson to Macon, August 19, 1821 (Macon Papers, North Carolina Department of Archives and History).

a specific provision for laying a duty of ten percent *ad valorem* on imports, the Constitution never would have been adopted.

Nor had the power to "regulate" commerce ever been intended at the convention as a power to hamper, restrict, or prohibit. "It is rather unfortunate for this argument, that, if it applies to the extent to which the power to regulate foreign commerce has been carried on by Congress, they may prohibit altogether this domestic commerce, as they have heretofore, under the other power, prohibited foreign commerce."[24] Years before, Randolph had pronounced Jefferson's embargo unconstitutional because it constituted a destruction of commerce, no mere regulation. Are these unconstitutional augmentations of power now to be extended over interstate commerce? What might not this usurpation do to the peculiar institution of the southern states?

Quite as dangerous would be a loose interpretation of the "general welfare" clause, Randolph continued. Commenced by Hamilton, this device was now carried to new extremes by "a new sect" determined to "so far transcend Alexander Hamilton and his disciples, as they outwent Thomas Jefferson, James Madison, and John Taylor of Caroline."[25] Under the pretext of general welfare, anything might be done; there might better be no constitution at all. In a passage glowing with that curious, random wit and learning which Randolph always sandwiched into his most solemn appeals, he proceeded to show that, the principle of "liberal" constitutional construction once conceded, security under law exists nowhere:

---

[24] *Annals of Congress* (18th Cong., 1st sess.), I, 1300.
[25] *Ibid.*, p. 1303.

But, sir, it is said . . . we have a right to regulate commerce between the several states, and it is argued that "to regulate" commerce is to prescribe the way in which it shall be carried on—which gives, by a *liberal* construction, the power to *construct* the way, that is, the roads and canals on which it is to be carried: Sir, since the days of that unfortunate man, of the German coast, whose name was originally Fyerstein, Anglicized to Firestone, but got, by translation, from that to Flint, from Flint to Pierre-a-Fusil, and from Pierre-a-Fusil to Peter Gun— never was greater violence done to English language, than by the constitution, that, under the power to prescribe the way in which commerce shall be carried on, we have the right to construct the way on which it is to be carried. Are gentlemen aware of the colossal power they are giving to the general government? Sir, I am afraid, that that ingenious gentleman, Mr. Macadam, will have to give up his title to the distinction of the *Colossus of Roads,* and surrender it to some gentlemen of this committee, if they succeed in their efforts on this occasion. . . .

Nay, we may go further. We may take it into our heads— Have we not the power to provide and maintain a navy? What is more necessary to a navy than seamen? And the great nursery of our seamen is (besides fisheries) the coasting trade—we may take it into our heads, that those monstrous lumbering wagons that now traverse the country between Philadelphia and Pittsburgh, stand in the way of the raising of seamen, and may declare that no communication shall be held between these points but coastwise; we may specify some particular article in which alone trade shall be carried on. And, sir, if, contrary to all expectation, the ascendancy of Virginia, in the general government, should again be established, it may be declared that coal shall be carried in no other way than coastwise, etc. Sir, there is no end to the purposes that may be affected under such constructions of power.[26]

Once the principle of "liberal" construction should prevail, in short, the party in power at Washington might manipulate government to its special advantage; continuity of

---

[26] *Ibid.,* pp. 1306–7.

policy in the common interest would give way to the particular and selfish interests of section and class. The Constitution, strictly adhered to, is the shield of minorities; it
is therefore of general benefit; for any interest, state, or
section, no matter how mighty, is liable some day to find
itself a minority. The temptation to use positive law as an
instrument of special advantage, once all barriers to its operation should be overthrown, is too great for man to resist;
security can be had only if the people agree to restrain the
operation of legislatures to provinces clearly defined and if
the state and general governments keep themselves rigidly
to their prescribed areas of action. Sometimes states had endeavored to encroach on the powers of the federal government, Randolph admitted; this is as dangerous a course as
federal encroachment upon the states; the great balance of
authority must be preserved. The advocates of omnicompetent legislatures and amorphous constitutions will in the
end destroy their own interests as well. But for the present
these centralizers are insensate. Having allowed the general
government to assume the powers of the purse and the
sword, the states discover that everything else they possess
is at the mercy of Washington. "We did believe there were
some parchment barriers—no! What is worth all the parchment barriers in the world—that there was, in the power of
the states, some counterpoise to the power of this body;
but, if this bill passes, we can believe so no longer."[27]

A general government restricted to the powers precisely
described in the Constitution must necessarily have been a
simple and comparatively weak government, unable to plan
the national economy or to direct social change in appre-

[27] *Ibid.,* p. 1305.

ciable degree: and this is precisely the sort of government Randolph wanted. Such a government could not have built deliberately a great industrial system in America. Be it so, said Randolph and his associates; they feared and detested the new industrial order. They looked upon society as a spiritual essence which grows healthily only when it grows slowly. If its development is forced, society may become monstrous, spiritually enormous. Leave economic change, like private life, to the management of Providence and individuals. They abhorred what a recent writer calls "the cult of the colossal."[28] Strict constitutional construction of the commerce power and the general-welfare clause would keep federal authority from molding the national character as the men who run the general government please; in short, the molding of national character would be left to tradition and Providence, which is precisely what Randolph desired. He railed at "planners" of every description. His assertions of the lengths to which construction of the commerce clause may be carried have been entirely sustained by the subsequent course of American history, and the Virginia, the South, and the America he loved have been swept away by the industrial society thus stimulated.

Prescient as Cassandra, Randolph beheld in his imagination this immense standardizing force which glowered from behind "liberal construction"; and to redress the balance, he summoned up southern sectionalism. Previously contemptuous of many politicians and policies to the south of Virginia, from 1824 onward he relied increasingly upon a self-conscious southern regional interest to furnish a counterpoise for the vast northern industrial interest which had

---

[28] Wilhelm Röpke, *The Social Crisis of Our Time.*

proved too ruthless to be restrained by the Constitution alone. Probably Randolph had been the first statesman to define the South as the quasi-nation bounded by "Mason and Dixon's line" (for which expression he sometimes substituted "south of the Patapsco"); and now he incessantly reminded that region of its distinct and common character:

> Should this bill pass, one more measure only requires to be consummated; and then we, who belong to that unfortunate portion of this Confederacy which is south of Mason and Dixon's line . . . have to make up our own minds to perish like so many mice in a receiver of mephitic gas, under the experiments of a set of new political chemists; or we must resort to the measures which we first opposed to British aggressions and usurpations—to maintain that independence which the valor of our fathers acquired, but which is every day sliding from under our feet. I beseech all those gentlemen who come from that portion of the Union to take into serious consideration, whether they are not, by the passage of this bill, precipitately, at least without urgent occasion, now arming the general government with powers hitherto unknown—under which we shall become, what the miserable proprietors of Jamaica and Barbados are to their English mortgagees, mere stewards—sentinels—managers of slave labor—we ourselves retaining, on a footing with the slave of the West Indies, just enough of the product of our estates to support life, while all the profits go with the course of the Gulf stream. Sir, this is a state of things that cannot last. If it shall continue with accumulated pressure, we must oppose to it associations, and every other means short of actual insurrection. We must begin to construe the Constitution like those who treat it as a bill of indictments, in which they are anxious to pick a flaw—we shall keep on the windward side of treason—but we must combine to resist, and that effectually, these encroachments, or the little upon which we now barely subsist will be taken from us.[29]

"The windward side of treason"—how might this uneasy check upon consolidation and the new economic order be

---

[29] *Annals of Congress* (18th Cong., 1st sess.), I, 1310–11.

ascertained and persevered in? Randolph referred to two courses of action still open to the states in extremity:

> This government is the breath of the nostrils of the states. Gentlemen may say what they please of the preamble to the Constitution; but this Constitution is not the work of the amalgamated population of the then existing confederacy, but the offspring of the states; and however high we may carry our heads, and strut and fret our hour, "dressed in a little brief authority," it is in the power of the states to extinguish this government at a blow.[30]

In short, the states might dissolve the general government by refusing to send senators to Washington, so that the lack of a quorum in the upper chamber would make the passing of legislation impossible; or they might refuse to appoint presidential electors and thus obliterate the executive power. Indeed, Randolph is said to have recommended the former course to Clay at the time of the Missouri Compromise.[31] For all the violence of his language on occasion, Randolph was no disunionist, and he would have resorted to these measures only under intolerable provocation; and then, supposing a government to be carried on in defiance of the lack of constitutional authority, forceful resistance would be justified as the final appeal to equity.

Even as he spoke, an opinion on these recourses more extreme than his was beginning to rise in South Carolina. Only three months later, Calhoun's uneasiness at the growing arrogance of industrialism and the North came to a head as a result of the debate over the tariff of 1824. From that time on, Calhoun turned toward strict construction, states' rights, southern sectionalism, and conservative mea-

---

[30] *Ibid.*, p. 1300.
[31] See *Reminiscences of Benj: Perley Poore,* I, 210.

sures.[32] South Carolina began to assume that leadership in the struggle against consolidation which Virginia formerly had maintained. The tariff of 1824, frankly protective and brutally indifferent to the southern agricultural interest, was provocation sufficient to rouse to anger men far less irascible than Randolph. Being put in a substantial majority by the congressional reapportionment three years earlier, the congressional party which represented the northern and western protectionists proposed an increase in duties averaging thirty-seven percent, doubling the previous rate. Agriculture in the southeastern states, already in great difficulties and reduced to a return of only two percent on investment as compared with the swelling profits of northern industrialism,[33] was awakened to its perilous situation as all the previous exhortations of Randolph and the Old Republicans had never been able to excite that sluggish interest. Once more, after many years of unpopularity as the erratic spokesman of a "lean and proscribed minority," Randolph became the orator of a great and determined part of Congress:

> I speak with the knowledge of what I say, when I declare, that this bill is an attempt to reduce the country south of Mason and Dixon's line, and east of the Allegheny Mountains, to a state of worse than colonial bondage; a state to which the domination of Great Britain was, in my judgment, far preferable . . . for the British Parliament never would have dared to lay such duties on our imports, or their exports to us . . . as is now proposed to be laid upon the imports from abroad. . . . It marks us out as the

---

[32] See Gerald M. Capers, "Reconsideration of John C. Calhoun's Transition from Nationalism to Nullification," *Journal of Southern History,* XIV, 34–48; and Wiltse, *op. cit.,* p. 289.

[33] Wiltse, *op. cit.,* p. 286.

victims of a worse than Egyptian bondage. It is a barter of so much of our rights, of so much of the fruits of our labor, for political power to be transferred to other hands. It ought to be met, and I trust it will be met, in the southern country, as was the Stamp Act, and by all those measures, which I will not detain the House by recapitulating, which succeeded the Stamp Act, and produced the final breach with the mother country, which it took about ten years to bring about; as I trust in my conscience, it will not take as long to bring about similar results from this measure, should it become a law.[34]

Quoting Burke, Randolph declared all policy suspicious that sacrifices the interest of a part to the alleged good of the whole. This bill was precisely a measure of that description; it was candidly designed for the benefit of special interests at the expense of a minority already hard pressed. The Constitution having been torn up by this majority of protectionists and consolidators who valued immediate gain above the rule of law, the South must be prepared to meet insolent power, if need be, with righteous power. "With all the fantastic and preposterous theories about the rights of man (the *theories,* not the rights themselves, I speak of), there is nothing but power that can restrain power. . . . We are proscribed, and put to the ban; and if we do not feel, and feeling do not act, we are bastards to those fathers who achieved the Revolution; then shall we deserve to make our bricks without straw."[35] Forcible resistance to injustice was implicit here; but separation was the remedy only of desperation, and Randolph declared his attachment to the Union—"But there is no magic in this word *union.* . . . The marriage of Sinbad the sailor, with the corse of his deceased wife, was an union,

---

[34] *Annals of Congress* (18th Cong., 1st sess.), II, 2359–60.
[35] *Ibid.,* p. 2360.

and just such an union as will this be, if, by a bare majority in both Houses, this bill becomes a law."[36]

He trusted that the President would veto the bill, should it be passed; and if he did not—why, the "Union" is really a confederation which "contains within itself the seeds of preservation, if not of this Union, at least of the individual commonwealths of which it is composed."[37] Secession was a right undeniable, Randolph maintained, although a desperate remedy.

> Self-defense is the first law of nature. You drive us into it. You create heats and animosities amongst this great family, who ought to live like brothers; and, after you have got this temper of mind roused among the southern people, do you expect to come among us to trade, and expect us to buy your wares? Sir, not only shall we not buy them, but we shall take such measures (I will not enter into the detail of them now) as shall render it impossible for you to sell them.[38]

He would boycott the "wooden nutmegs" of the North; he would repel northern avarice after the fashion of the Tea Party. This still is resistance "to windward of treason." And then he came to the peroration of this brilliant speech:

> We are the eel that is being flayed, while the cook-maid pats us on the head, and cries, with the clown in King Lear, "Down, wantons, down!" There is but one portion of the country that can profit by this bill, and from that portion of the country comes this bare majority in favor of it. I bless God that Massachusetts and Old Virginia are once again rallying under the same banner, against oppressive and unconstitutional taxation; for, if all the blood be drawn from out the body, I care not

---

[36] *Ibid.,* p. 2368.

[37] *Ibid.,* p. 2369.

[38] *Ibid.,* p. 2376.

whether it be drawn by the British Parliament or the American Congress—by an emperor or a king abroad, or by a President at home.[39]

The tariff was passed, of course; and the President did not veto it; and once the new tariff had crushed the valetudinarian maritime interest of Massachusetts, Webster and his state went over to the protectionists, leaving the South solitary in its plea for strict construction and low duties. Four years more Randolph carried on the struggle for states' rights and the old Constitution and then relinquished his place in Congress to others; but he was not to be silent during his last years in Southside Virginia.

4

Federal appetite for power made a sectionalist of John Randolph. For years he had sneered at the "cotton barons" of the lower South; he had been enraged by the acquiescence of Georgia and South Carolina in previous measures of consolidation, loose construction, and internal improvements at federal expense; he had disliked the rough and covetous ways of flush times in Alabama and Mississippi; he had liked Massachusetts men of Josiah Quincy's sort far better than the southern War Hawks. But strict construction of the constitution having given way before the innovating and capitalistic majority, he turned now to southern unity as a means of salvation. In 1829 he wrote to Dr. Brockenbrough:

> The operation of this present government, like a debt at usurious interest, must destroy the whole South. It eats like a canker

[39] *Ibid.*, p. 2379.

into our very core. South Carolina must become bankrupt and depopulated. She is now shut out of the English market for her rice, with all the premium of dearth in Europe. I am too old to move, or the end of this year should not find me a resident of Virginia, against whose misgovernment I have full as great cause of complaint as against that of the U.S. It has been one mass of *job* and abuse—schools, literary funds, Charlottesville conventions, and their spawn.[40]

Virginia, too, was changing, and even the ardent champion of the Old Dominion's rights could not endure her failings. But it was Virginia, he said in the Virginia Convention later that year, that long had maintained, almost alone, the cause of the states; and to alter the constitution of Virginia would be to endanger the continuance of that opposition to federal usurpation:

> What provision is there, Mr. Chairman, either in the Constitution of Virginia or the Constitution of the United States, which establishes it as a principle, that the Commonwealth of Virginia should be the sole restraining and regulating power on the mad and unconstitutional usurpations of the Federal Government? There is no such provision in either;—yet, in practice, and in fact, too, the Commonwealth of Virginia has been, to my certain knowledge, for more than thirty years, the sole counterpoise and check on the usurpations of the Federal Government—so far as they have been checked at all; I wish they had been checked more effectually.
>
> For a long time, our brethren of the South, because we were the frontier state of the great southern division of the Union, were dead to considerations to which we have, I fear, awaked too late. Virginia was left alone and unsupported, unless by the feeble aid of her distant offspring, Kentucky. It is because I am unwilling to give up this check, or to diminish its force, that I am unwilling to pull down the edifice of our state government from

---

[40] Randolph to Brockenbrough, January 12, 1829 (Garland, *op. cit.,* II, 318).

the garret to the cellar; aye, to the foundation stone. I will not put in hazard this single good, for all the benefits the warmest advocate of reform can hope to derive from the results of this body.[41]

If to Virginia, as a state, went the credit of this struggle, to Randolph, as a man, the recognition as the prime mover of that course was due; and Randolph was not to abandon the cause in that controversy of which the first mutters were then to be heard; for nullification was in the air.

John Randolph of Roanoke, who rarely forgave a political foe, always distrusted John C. Calhoun, who was to fill, in the years to come, the place that Randolph had occupied in national politics. Perhaps the memory of his debates with Calhoun the War Hawk on the floor of the House made Randolph suspect the permanency of Calhoun's conversion to the ideals for which the man of Roanoke had waged the battle relentlessly; and, like many another southerner, Randolph believed Calhoun to be personally ambitious, ruthlessly ambitious. The South Carolinian made an effort to obtain Randolph's valuable support, and, for a time, in 1827, almost succeeded. Randolph wrote to Brockenbrough, "I saw the V. P. yesterday. He is in good spirits; he is sustained by a powerful passion."[42] But later letters show how this slight confidence waned, and Benjamin Perley Poore relates an incident which, accurately told or not, illustrates Randolph's attitude toward the Carolinian. Randolph, who had been accustomed to addressing the Speaker of the House, rose, and exclaimed, "Mr. Speaker! I mean

---

[41] *Proceedings and Debates of the Virginia State Convention*, p. 315.

[42] Randolph to Brockenbrough, February 11, 1827 (Garland, *op. cit.,* II, 284).

Mr. President of the Senate and would-be President of the United States, which God in his infinite mercy avert."[43] But whatever Randolph thought of him, Calhoun must have felt the influence of the Virginian's mind and tongue, both in the House and in the Senate. Henry Adams says that "Randolph converted Calhoun."[44] Circumstances converted him, too, naturally; but Randolph's statement of the great political issues in America charted the course for Calhoun and his school.

Nullification, however, was not the policy of Randolph; he assailed it as one of those theories of abstract metaphysics he had denounced so often, and, while he upheld vigorously the right of secession, he proclaimed that a state could not remain in the Union and still refuse to obey the Union's laws. He was enraged at Calhoun, moreover, for dividing the South and attacking the leadership of Jackson, upon whom Randolph relied to defend southern interests. After South Carolina's proclamation of nullification, but before Jackson's force bill, Randolph wrote to the President: "The infamous conduct of Calhoun and his wretched creatures has damned him and them everlastingly in Virginia, Pennsylvania and New York, and in the West also. Clay has 'trained off.' He has cut his throat with his own tongue."[45] And a little later he informed Jackson: "I told my noble friend Hamilton in my letter to him (which you shall see) that the throwing over board Mr. Jonah Calhoun was a condition precedent to any aid from *our* quarter, especially

---

[43] *Reminiscences of Benj: Perley Poore*, I, 65.

[44] Adams, *op. cit.*, p. 291.

[45] Randolph to Jackson, March 28, 1832 (*Correspondence of Jackson*, IV, 420).

from me."[46] Randolph sent Beverley Tucker to remonstrate, in vain, with Calhoun.[47]

Jackson's proclamation against the nullifiers changed Randolph's sympathies utterly; "nullification was nonsense," but the federal government could not coerce a sovereign state, and Virginia should prepare to come to the aid of threatened South Carolina. Randolph declared himself ready to have his dying body strapped to his horse "Radical" and enter the field against the federal troops;[48] to a friend he spoke of "the ferocious and bloodthirsty proclamation of our Djezzar Pacha," and added:

> The apathy of our people is most alarming. If they do not rouse themselves to a sense of our condition and put down this wretched old man, the whole country is irretrievably ruined. The mercenary troops who have embarked for Charleston have not disappointed me; they are working in their vocation, poor devils! I trust that no quarter will be given to them.[49]

The dying man made a final great effort; he addressed the freeholders at Charlotte Court House, where he had made many a speech for thirty years, and forced down the throats of Jackson men and old Federalists a set of resolutions denouncing the conduct of the President. "Here I remark I am no nullifier," he said. "The doctrine of nullification is sheer nonsense."[50] But he could not endure Jackson's measures, and the dying orator, with his ruined body and flickering

---

[46] Randolph to Jackson, March 28, 1832 (*ibid.*, p. 429).

[47] Beverley Tucker to James Henry Hammond, March 26, 1850 (Hammond Papers, Library of Congress).

[48] Garland, *op. cit.*, II, 358.

[49] *Ibid.*, p. 359.

[50] Powhatan Bouldin, *Home Reminiscences of John Randolph*, p. 180.

mind, charmed the people of his district into signing the
resolutions which declared Virginia to be a sovereign state
that had but delegated the exercise of certain powers to
federal government; that she retained the right to secede
"whenever she shall find the benefits of union exceeded by its
evils"; that Jackson had been won over to the cause of every
evil influence; that, while the doctrine of nullification was
"weak and mischievous," the doctrines of Jackson were
equally unfounded and more dangerous; and that the signers approved of the mission of Benjamin Watkins Leigh to
South Carolina. The ninth resolution stated that "although
we believe that we shall be in a lean and proscribed minority,
we are prepared to take up our cross, confident of success
under that banner, so long as we keep faith and can have
access to the public ear."[51]

Thus John Randolph of Roanoke made his final stand for
the powers of the states and against federal encroachment.
Even in the passion of these last resolutions, his desire to resort first to consultation and conciliation is conspicuous; for,
although secession was a right, it was not a good. For more
than a third of a century Randolph had endeavored to maintain what he considered the just distribution of power between federal and state governments; he had given his
allegiance to what he thought the only honest construction of
the Constitution; and he had attempted, even while rallying
the South to resistance against the measures of the national-
ists and the North, to remain true to the principles upon
which the federal system had been established. Henry Adams writes: "The doctrine of states' rights was in itself a
sound and true doctrine; as a starting point of American

---

[51] *Ibid.,* p. 181.

history and constitutional law, there is no other which will bear a moment's examination."[52] That parchment guarantees could be a permanent barrier against usurpation, Randolph knew to be impossible; but if men could be persuaded that solely by strict fidelity to parchment could tranquillity and union be perpetuated, the ruin he foresaw might be averted. A consolidated government he thought the worst of all evils; and, surely, a consolidated government in this nation—or a government approaching what Randolph would have called consolidation—has proved incompatible with the society he represented. To the cause of local liberties and the guarantees of the federal Constitution he gave all the chivalric valor that was his.

While the nullification quarrel was at its height, the lugubrious man of Roanoke wrote to Harvey: "I could not have believed that the people would so soon have shown themselves unfit for free government. I leave to General Jackson, and the Hartford men, and the ultra-Federalists and Tories, and the office-holders and office-seekers, their triumph over the liberties of the country. They will stand damned to everlasting flame."[53]

The fate of all Randolph's adversaries has not been so bitter as that; and one of them, John Quincy Adams, shares with Randolph the honor of being the most candid and honest public men of their generation. But with respect to political constancy and purity, John Randolph's struggle for a proper division of the powers of government entitles him to a position almost unique among American statesmen.

---

[52] Adams, *op. cit.*, p. 273.
[53] Garland, *op. cit.*, II, 359.

Chapter Five

The Planter-Statesman

1

John Taylor of Caroline declared that land is the basis of all wealth and that therefore land deserves power in government.[1] Whether Randolph of Roanoke, the admirer of Smith, Ricardo, and Say, admitted the truth of the first part of this physiocratic contention is doubtful; something more modern is implied in Randolph's political economy; and, indeed, old John Taylor belonged to the generation which preceded Randolph's. But whatever opinion the man of Roanoke held concerning the economic preeminence of land, no ambiguity shrouded his conviction that the agricultural life is the best state of society man can ask. Randolph was one of the greatest of the planter-statesmen who filled so large a role in the history of the southern states, from the time of Washington to the time of Davis; and among all those memorable names, the agrarian society had no more consistent, shrewd, and fierce defender than John Randolph.

"Defender" is a word chosen deliberately here; for the agricultural interest almost always was reeling before the assault of other interests, and, too often, agriculture lost

---

[1] John Taylor, *Definition of Parties,* p. 8.

ground, for all the illustrious muster-roll of its partisans. Probably the successive defeats of the farm and the plantation in national political contests were a result neither of any innate weakness of rural people nor yet of timidity on the part of their leaders; the cause lay in the conservative nature of the agricultural interests, which had little to gain from change, while the commercial, financial, and industrial interests were full of youthful vigor and rapacity; agriculture could hardly encroach upon them, but they could extort tribute from agriculture. The agrarian party was generous enough at times, moreover—upon the plea of national security—to sacrifice its own advantage to embargo and tariff, while the other economic interests rarely made such concessions.[2] In the West, it is true, the agricultural interest was so linked with expanding industrial forces, and so heartily in accord with that speculative spirit which has always been a danger to American farming and agricultural life— Tocqueville remarks that an American clears a farm only with the intention of selling it for a profit—that for years the western states remained the political allies of the industrial and financial North. Before 1824 the rural party was self-conscious and articulate only in the southeastern states, notably Virginia.

Between 1800 and 1828, between Jefferson and Jackson, the planters and farmers pressingly required a champion in Congress; for although the Virginia dynasty, theoretically fond of the rural ideal, and the Republican party, professedly representative of the agricultural interest, maintained control of national politics during the greater portion of this era, still the agricultural economy was exposed to a

---

[2] See Henry Adams, *History of the United States,* IV, 281.

series of distressing blows all during these years. The farmer always tends to be weaker politically than his numbers seem to indicate. "It is the choicest bounty to the ox," said Randolph, "that he cannot play the fox or the tiger; so it is to one of the body of agriculturalists that he cannot skip into a coffeehouse and shave a note with one hand, while with the other he signs a petition to Congress portraying the wrongs and grievances and sufferings he endures, and begging them to relieve him."[3] Lacking the collective cunning and proximity to administration which commercial and industrial forces possessed, the country population was badly prepared to make a stand in Congress. Who was to be their spokesman at Washington? Old John Taylor, that indefatigable writer of treatises, entered Congress with reluctance and departed with alacrity, for he was no popular orator; Jefferson and his successors, however much they praised the life of the farmer, found themselves compelled to pursue policies which left that farmer in a state nearly as disastrous as that in which Jefferson was to find his own lands; Nathaniel Macon and other planter-legislators, great and small, had the requisite devotion but not the requisite genius. The duty fell to John Randolph.

Acerbity of temper and indifference to popularity were flaws which kept Randolph from being a really successful leader of the opposition; but in some other ways he was admirably qualified to maintain the responsibility. He could command public attention—like a necromancer fascinating a snake—in a way no other man of his time could. He could join to the agricultural party other factions which, for a time, had the same objectives: the slavery interest, the states' rights

---

[3] *Annals of Congress* (14th Cong., 1st sess.), p. 688.

thinkers, and on occasion even the commercial classes of New England. He was himself a successful planter, supervising the cultivation of his thousands of acres; he lived like a pre-Revolutionary Virginia gentleman, bumping over the wretched roads in his old-fashioned English coach, and his slaves rode blooded horses; but he inhabited a two-room cabin and spent the greater part of each year in the oppressive routines of growing tobacco and grains. More, he was devoted by inheritance and principle to the society of the country gentleman and the Virginia landlord. The agricultural ideal occupied as important a place in his system as in Jefferson's, though Randolph's ideal was the old Tidewater life and Jefferson's a yeoman population destined never really to develop as the President hoped.

In some ways a very practical man, Randolph was a severe critic of the rural life he defended, just as he criticized all that he loved. To Josiah Quincy he wrote of "the sordid cares of a planter," to which he was condemned every long and dreary winter: "They remind me of Cromwell, when he turned farmer at St. Ives; for without vanity I may compare myself to what Oliver was *then,* and may with truth declare, that my 'mind, superior to the low occupations to which I am condemned, preys upon itself.' "[4] Randolph's solitary and half-mysterious existence as a Roanoke planter must have had its effect upon his delicate temperament; even while he was still living at Bizarre, away from the shadows of Roanoke, his half-brother, Henry St. George Tucker, wrote to James M. Garnett of Randolph's brooding bitterness: "It is manifest that his solitude has great influence

---

[4] Randolph to Quincy, August 30, 1813 (Edmund Quincy, *Life of Josiah Quincy,* p. 336).

upon his feelings."[5] Yet probably Randolph could have endured no other life; certainly his detestation of towns, his
revolt against social mediocrity, and his devotion to field
sports would have made Tucker's life as a successful Winchester lawyer anathema to him. In the view of Randolph,
Macon, Stanford, and William Leigh, of southern Virginia
and northern North Carolina, only in the country, on his
own land and free from debt, did a man experience real
liberty; and only such men, as a class, were competent to
determine the policies of the state.

What did Randolph believe to be the model agricultural
economy? We have remarked that he found his model in
the image of pre-Revolutionary Virginia; Jefferson sought
for his in the visions of an egalitarian future. Jefferson's
successful campaign for the abolition of entail and primogeniture was intended to equalize landholding, to establish
upon a broad base a state—perhaps a nation—of freeholders, small farmers, each nearly self-sufficient economically, producing their foodstuffs and the bulk of their other
necessities. Labor on these holdings was to be chiefly that of
freemen, the possessors. Such an economy never did come
to prevail in Virginia; and, while the radical revision of the
laws of descent did indeed greatly diminish the prosperity
and influence of the old families that had led the Old Dominion, still it failed signally to produce a general equaliza-
tion of landowning. Tocqueville attributes to the American
abolition of entail and primogeniture a very great share
in the restlessness, cupidity, and wistful materialism of the
American people; it destroyed one of those artifices which,

---

[5] Tucker to Garnett, July 5, 1811 (Henry St. George Tucker Papers,
Duke University).

in Burke's phrase, enable "generation to link with generation" and distinguish men from "the flies of a summer."

John Randolph, for his part, roundly damned this alteration of the laws of descent; that act of innovation had ener-
vated the great families which contributed, in previous
generations, so much to Virginia's glory. Frequently he referred to this topic and once wrote, while in Europe, to
Brockenbrough, that he had no hope for a restoration of the
ancient Virginian spirit, "the state of society and manners
which existed in Virginia half a century ago; I should as
soon expect to see the Nelsons, and Pages, and Byrds, and
Fairfaxes, living in their palaces, and driving their coaches
and sixes; or the good old Virginia gentlemen in the assembly, drinking their twenty and forty bowls of rack punches,
and madeira, and claret, in lieu of a knot of deputy sheriffs
and hack attorneys, each with his cruet of whiskey before
him, and puddle of tobacco-spittle between his legs."[6] Yet
he fought for the old ways toward which he was already
looking back with a nostalgia so many Virginians later
were to share.

The old Virginian life Randolph praised had not been
simply a society dominated by great slaveholding landlords.
He spoke contemptuously of Wade Hampton and his fellows as "cotton barons" and declared the real substance of
society to be the independent planters and farmers of
small freeholds, which class he eulogized in the Virginia
Convention of 1829, speaking of "the good old Virginia
planter—the man who lived by hard work, and who paid
his debts."[7] That which Randolph desired was a society

---

[6] Randolph to Brockenbrough, July 24, 1824 (Hugh Garland, *Randolph
of Roanoke*, II, 225).

[7] *Proceedings and Debates of the Virginia State Convention*, p. 790.

with a great number of small freeholders to furnish the bulk of the governing class and a scattering of wealthier and better-educated great planters to furnish suitable leadership for the commonwealth. Indeed, his own congressional district was made up of such a society, with a few great landholders like Randolph, the Carringtons, and the Leighs, and a numerous class of less wealthy landowners who, like the Bouldins, sometimes achieved important political office. Randolph, like Jefferson, believed in an aristocracy of nature, not of station; but he thought that aristocracy of nature largely determined by the gifts of good family and of possession of property.

Jefferson apparently held that his agricultural class should devote its energies principally to the raising of foodstuffs for their own consumption rather than to a money crop like tobacco. While Randolph raised the greater part of the food for his slaves on his own lands, still tobacco was his chief crop, and he was the foremost advocate of the old trade with England, exchanging Virginian agricultural staples for British manufactures.[8] Although Jefferson wrote his famous phrase comparing cities to the sores of the body and recommended an economy strictly agricultural, trading with the "workshops of Europe," this stand of his was altered after the embargo days, and he came to recommend the encouragement of American factories. This, Randolph could not tolerate; he would not buy from the North, out of resentment at protective tariffs, and he even sent his books to England to be bound. As in Jefferson's literary taste, a certain old-fashioned element lingered in Jefferson's economic thought; the President spoke of the advantage in interna-

---

[8] See Randolph to Quincy, July 1, 1824 (Edmund Quincy, *op. cit.*, p. 353).

tional trade as lying in the disposal of "national surpluses," in his letters to Du Pont de Nemours and others.[9] Randolph, much read in Smith and Ricardo, perceived more distinctly the nature of specialization and the economic advantages of unrestricted international commerce, and contended that America was as unsuited for really profitable manufacturing as England was for really profitable agriculture.[10]

Such, then, was Randolph's specific for a satisfactory agricultural society—concepts shared by the Old Republicans. Randolph failed to gain the restoration or perpetuation of his system; but so did Jefferson fail to achieve his agrarian ideal. The Old Republicans failed because they were in an irremediable political minority; because they could not rid themselves of the burden of negro slavery; and because, very possibly, Malthus' geometrical increase of population was against them—overpopulation, the problem of problems. Their system of landholding was suited to a static population but hardly to a swelling one; and even the rapid advance of the agricultural frontier could not preserve their nation from the necessity of adopting a complicated economy of large-scale manufactures, intricate finance, rapid transportation, and urban life. The Republicans might have retorted that the swelling of population, through immigration and commerce, was deliberately encouraged by the classes and regions which stood to gain by change; but it was too much to expect mankind not to fill a void as rapidly as air fills a vacuum. Desperately the successors of the Old Republicans endeavored to maintain their

[9] Jefferson to Du Pont, June 28, 1809 (*Correspondence Between Jefferson and Du Pont de Nemours,* pp. 124–27).

[10] *Annals of Congress* (18th Cong., 1st sess.), 1, 2362.

position by the acquisition of western territories to be amal-
gamated with the southern agricultural system; and the very
endeavor brought closer the war which was to strike down
their society. Time and space were against the planter-statesmen. But in many ways the life they sought to perpetuate
was good; not a few men would think it a better state of
society than that our age must accept; and they are hardly
to be censured for standing like men for the old ways. For
Cato to stand against Caesar and the forces that Caesar
represented was hopeless; but it was not ridiculous. No fatal
weakness existed in the Old Republicans' economy *per se;*
but for them the time was out of joint. Their principles of
public and private conduct are not invalidated by time's
annihilation of the economic system in which their ideas
developed. On the management of government, the conduct
of foreign relations, and the commercial policy of the state,
Randolph and his fellows spoke out boldly to defend the
plantation. Although the plantation is gone, there remains a
need for honest politics, intelligent statecraft, and sound
public economics. In Randolph's career is exhibited the
doomed course of the plantation-politicians, and in his principles are elements still worth attention in this very different
epoch.

2

Their most consistent spokesman, Randolph, permanently defined the platform of the planter-statesmen when
he told the House of Representatives, early in 1813:

> Is it necessary for men at this time of day to make a declara-
> tion of the principles of the Republican party? Is it possible
> that such a declaration could be deemed orthodox when pro-

ceeding from lips so unholy as those of an excommunicant from that church? It is not necessary. These principles are on record; they are engraved upon it indelibly by the press and will live as long as the art of printing is suffered to exist. It is not for any man at this day to undertake to change them; it is not for any men, who then professed them, by any guise or circumlocution to conceal apostasy from them, for they are there—there in the book. . . . What are they? Love of peace, hatred of offensive war, jealousy of the state governments toward the general government; a dread of standing armies; a loathing of public debt, taxes, and excises; tenderness for the liberty of the citizen; jealousy, Argus-eyed jealousy, of the patronage of the President.[11]

From the advocacy of these principles, Randolph and his faction did not retreat. They had been the principles of Jefferson and his devotees in 1800, Randolph declared; they remained the principles of true Republicans. A simple, economical, limited, peaceful government was the only government consistent with the society they represented—a government fit for a stable, rural nation. But there remains a great deal of room for increase of these virtues in the state in our own more complex society.

Always prominent in the Old Republican creed was a demand for purity and simplicity in public affairs, retrenchment and reform. The sincerity of Randolph's long campaign against profligacy, corruption, and time-serving in governmental affairs never has been successfully impeached, even by his most hostile critics. From his fiery Yazoo speeches to his duel with Clay, Randolph was the dread of every self-seeker in Congress; and although some writers have believed Randolph's ideals of purity impossible of attainment and his stand as a political St. Michael too top-

---

[11] *Richmond Enquirer,* April 1, 1813.

lofty, few have condemned his general course of action. Randolph and the other Old Republicans were men of private honesty, of economical and self-sufficient habits; they saw no reason why private morals should not be public morals or why the government should plunder, or be plundered, when the citizen should not. Out of their very nature they were opposed to regular party organization, to all intricacies of party machinery, to caucus and convention. Their dislike for practical politics, then, was another obstacle between them and success.

Although they were resolute supporters of the rights of private property, they did not hold that private property dishonestly obtained had a clear title against government; as John Taylor wrote, "If Jugurtha had been rich enough to buy Rome, ought the nation to have submitted to the sale, because the bargain was made with the government?"[12] Thus it was that Randolph denounced the Yazoo land companies and prevented, until 1818, any compensation of those associations. That Jefferson did not take a firm stand against the Yazoo speculators helped provoke John Randolph's initial opposition to his administration, and the Roanoke orator detested Madison in the belief that he was a "Yazoo man." Yazoo left a rift between Jefferson and his congressional leader which never could be bridged. Speculative land companies had obtained immense grants of territory from a Georgia legislature they had corrupted by shameless bribery; a well-purged legislature indignantly repealed the land grants; and those companies of speculators in lands along the Yazoo River appealed to Congress to

---

[12] John Taylor, *Inquiry into the Principles and Policy of the United States,* p. 61.

compensate them for their losses. The same measures
toward persuasion which had been exercised in Georgia now
appeared in Washington, the notorious Gideon Granger,
postmaster general, presuming to lobby for the bill on the
floor of the House—until Randolph denounced him as one
accustomed to "buy and sell corruption in the gross." Jefferson and the northern Republicans winked at the affair, out
of expediency (indeed, in later years Jefferson actually
would have liked to appoint Granger to the Supreme
Court); but Randolph and the Old Republicans now began
to take shape as a faction, outraged at this violation of the
purity of the Republican party. They never would compromise with great selfish interests; they had a terror of what
has since come to be known as the "pressure group."

This was barefaced corruption; but the Old Republicans
dreaded scarcely less that double-dealing, secrecy, and pretense in public affairs which come with governmental meddling in economic concerns. "I was not born into this order
of things, and I will never consent, voluntarily, to become
the vassal of a privileged order of military and monied men,
by whom, as by a swarm of locusts, the produce of my land
is to be devoured, and its possessor consigned to indigence
and scorn. He who will not assert his place in society deserves to be trampled under foot."[13]

Faithful to Randolph's declaration, the Old Republicans
asserted their place with great wrath and did their best to
prevent the devouring of the produce of their lands; even
when the government was in their own hands, they did not
trust it. In 1803, when he exerted high influence upon the

---

[13] See Randolph's letter, signed "Decius," *Richmond Enquirer*, August 15,
1806.

course of the federal administration, Randolph wrote to Nicholson: "To me the tendency of the power of appointment to office (no matter to what individual it may be trusted) to debauch the nation and to create a low, dirty, time-serving spirit is a . . . serious evil."[14]

Going beyond their assault on the abuse of public funds, the Old Republicans demanded strict economy in lawful and necessary expenditures. Randolph's opposition to the proposal of a sword for the adventurer Eaton and to a mausoleum for Washington, while in these days they may seem petty wrangling, were matters of principle; for Randolph believed that if governmental appropriations for baubles were not checked at the outset, they never would be halted. One of his chief objections to the program of internal improvements was that it would require funds which should be used instead to pay the federal debt, which he considered a drain upon the public for the benefit of special interests: "Let us leave the profits of labor in the pockets of the people, to rid them of that private embarrassment under which they so extensively suffer, and apply every shilling of the revenue, not indispensable to the exigencies of the government, to the faithful discharge of the public debt, before we engage in any new schemes of lavish expenditure."[15] From an early period, the Old Republicans foresaw that progressive inflation of credit and currency which has been a prominent characteristic of the American economy since the foundation of the Republic. Financial inflation means instability and the ruin of old ways; the innate conservatism of the

---

[14] Randolph to Nicholson, October 15, 1803 (copy in Randolph Papers, Virginia State Library).

[15] *Annals of Congress* (18th Cong., 1st sess.), I, 1310.

Old Republicans, agrarian reformers though they were, revolted at the prospect of a society forever in flux and
change.

Debt, Randolph maintained, was slavery; and once he
startled the House by crying out, "Mr. Speaker, I have discovered the philosopher's stone. It is this, sir—Pay as you
go! Pay as you go!"[16] In 1828 Macon, who was lodging with
Randolph in Washington, wrote to a friend an expression of
his and Randolph's view of the course of Congress:

> Almost every bill reported is to take money out of the
> Treasury or taxes from the U.S. It must be thought by some, I
> wish not by too many, that a public debt is a public blessing and
> all who live on the public, no doubt think, the more taxes the
> better, and that every tax adds to industry, and the harder people
> are put to it, the more easy they will be to govern; from such I
> wish to be delivered and hope the country may be free from
> them.[17]

Something of a late-twentieth-century flavor is in this paragraph. Randolph might have expressed such an opinion
more elegantly than did his old friend from North Carolina,
but he would have put it no less energetically.

Yet he was not so fanatically devoted to economy that
he neglected stability in government; for when it was suggested at the Virginia Convention that the number of state
representatives be reduced in order to cut legislative expenses, he opposed this false saving: "These savings made
by paring down the legislature, and lopping off the council,
may not prove to be true economy. Remember the fable—

---

[16] Edmund Quincy, *op. cit.,* p. 343.

[17] Macon to N. W. Edwards, February 17, 1828 (Macon Papers, North
Carolina State Department of Archives and History).

if the sheep will not spare enough of their fleece to feed the dogs, they may have to spare the whole of it, and the carcass to boot, to the wolf."[18]

And at this same constitutional convention of 1829, Randolph aptly expressed his whole distrust of government, with its passion for positive law, innovation, and regulation, with its powers of corruption and exploitation, with its demand for haste and uniformity:

> I am much opposed, said Mr. R., except in a great emergency—and then the legislative machine is always sure to work with sufficient rapidity—the steam is then up—I am much opposed to this "dispatch of business." The principles of free government in this country (and if they fail—if they should be cast away—here—they are lost forever, I fear, to the world) have more to fear from armies of legislators, and armies of judges, than from any other, or from all other causes. Besides the great manufactory at Washington, we have twenty-four laboratories more at work, all making laws. In Virginia we have now two in operation, one engaged in making ordinary legislation, and another *hammering* at the fundamental law. Among all these lawyers, judges, and legislators, there is a great oppression on the people, who are neither lawyers, judges, nor legislators, nor ever expect to be—an oppression barely more tolerable than any which is felt under the European governments. Sir, I never can forget, that in the great and good book to which I look for all truth and all wisdom, the Book of Kings succeeds the Book of Judges.[19]

This attitude it is which, in large degree, clears the Old Republicans from any imputation of seeking advantage for themselves or their class in their stand against power in the state. They fought for the planter life, for the life they

---

[18] *Proceedings and Debates of the Virginia State Convention*, p. 493.
[19] *Ibid.*, p. 802.

thought best; but they did not ask special advantage for that agricultural society, unlike the farm bloc of a later day. They asked only to be left unmolested, allowed to buy and sell in a free market, not to be taxed for the benefit of other interests, not to be forced into another mode of life. All government, said Randolph, was menacing; the only safety for every interest and class and section lay in limitation of the power of governments, in jealous supervision of governmental operation. Let government leave men to their own concerns and be economical, equitable, and honest. Randolph's principles of political purity and social organization gave way to a different order of things chiefly because other great interests, reckless of such concepts, found it advantageous to conduct government along very different lines; and although the Old Republicans experienced temporary victories in their struggle for honesty and simplicity, their campaign was a stubborn retreat. From 1805 onward, Randolph's school of the agricultural interest and the earlier Republican idealism was hopelessly outnumbered.

3

In order to flourish, or even to exist, the society of the planters was dependent upon the guarantees of a strictly construed Constitution, upon a reasonably free trade with the world, upon simple and austere government, and upon lasting peace. From all these motives, and also because men of the sturdy conservative convictions held by the Old Republicans were naturally lovers of tranquillity and foes of aggression, Randolph's faction stood opposed to war and foreign alliances. They resisted as best they could the approach of the War of 1812; and, when apparently the struggle had become inevitable, John Randolph, Stanford, and a few other congressmen struggled almost unaided against the tide. Randolph experienced his sole defeat for a seat in the House in consequence of his opposition; but events seemed to vindicate his conduct, and he was returned by his constituents, in the following election, to continue for the remainder of his career the advocacy of diplomatic isolation and economic internationalism for America.

From his Jacobin days in 1797, when Randolph opposed war with France, until the days of the Panama Congress in 1826, Randolph was the foe of all proposals for hostilities or foreign entanglements—if one excepts some remarks of his recommending retaliation against England, after the "Chesapeake" affair. From the inception of the embargo until the last echoes of the second war with England had died, the danger of war, together with denunciations of the American restrictive commercial policy, was the great theme of his speeches. His remarks—some of them nearly as pertinent now as then—are worth sampling with a view toward their relation to his planter society.

In John Adams' administration Randolph called the federal troops "ragamuffins," and in Jackson's administration he sneered at them as "mercenaries." He declared them a threat to the powers of the states, for he placed his reliance for state sovereignty chiefly in the physical superiority of the states to the federal government and not in parchment guarantees; moreover, they were a drain upon the public purse. His own plan for efficiently arming the militia, and substituting flying trains of artillery for permanent harbor fortifications and Jefferson's gunboats, never was adopted; but it had merit, John Taylor writing of it: "Mr. Randolph's proposal . . . is the most effectual, principled, and grand measure, which has been introduced since the government has been in operation. He ought to nurse his popularity in Congress, if for no other end, but to carry the one point."[20]

Nursing popularity was a talent in which Randolph was totally deficient; instead, sarcasm and terror were his weapons. He opposed the increase of the national army with great bitterness; his speeches from 1807 until the close of hostilities with Britain expound his views with a thoroughness that cannot be imitated here.[21] On November 21, 1812, he delivered one of his most significant speeches on the question of military establishments and preparations for war, holding that he derived his principles from the old and true doctrines of the Republican party and that he would not yield them for the sake of popularity.[22] He declared that Britain was our shield against Napoleonic tyranny; he exposed the "agrarian cupidity" of the West, which sought war in order to provide markets for its hemp and foodstuffs; and he proclaimed that the Republicans were following the path disastrously trodden by the Federalists:

> There is a fatality, sir, attending plenitude of power. Soon or late, some mania seizes upon its possessors; they fall from the dizzy height, through the giddiness of their own heads. Like a vast estate, heaped up by the labor and industry of one man, which seldom survives the third generation, power gained by patient assiduity, by a faithful and regular discharge of its attendant duties, soon gets above its own origin. Intoxicated by their own greatness, the Federal party fell. Will not the same causes produce the same effects now as then? Sir, you may raise

---

[20] Taylor to J. M. Garnett, December 17, 1807 (Garnett MSS, Duke University).

[21] See especially *Annals of Congress* (10th Cong., 1st sess.), pp. 1904–12.

[22] *Richmond Enquirer,* December 5, 1812.

this army, you may build up this vast structure of patronage, this mighty apparatus of favoritism; but—"lay not the flattering unction to your souls"—you will never live to enjoy the succession. You sign your political death warrant. . . .

He was not surprised at the war spirit which is manifesting itself in gentlemen from the South. In the year 1805–06, in a struggle for the carrying-trade of belligerent colonial produce, this country was most unwisely brought into collision with the great powers of Europe. By a series of most impolitic and ruinous measures, utterly incomprehensible to every rational sober-minded man, the Southern planters, by their own votes, succeeded in knocking down the price of cotton to seven cents, and of tobacco (a few crops excepted) to nothing, and in raising the price of blankets (of which a few would not be amiss in a Canadian campaign), coarse woollens, and every article of first necessity, three or four hundred percent. And, now that by our own acts we have brought ourselves into this unprecedented condition, we must get out of it in any way but by an acknowledgement of our own want of wisdom and forecast. But is that the true remedy? Who will profit by it? Speculators; a few lucky merchants who draw prizes in the lottery; commissaries and contractors. Who must suffer by it? The people. It is their blood, their taxes, that must flow to support it. . . .[23]

In speech after speech, Randolph demonstrated how ruinous the war was for his own Virginia—more ruinous even than the nonimportation and embargo acts. And the young men of Virginia, he added, their prospects of employment and independence ruined, drift away to Washington, there "dancing attendance for a commission." War and an omnipotent administration breed similar servility in politicians of all parties, who begin to sink into "very good courtiers"; thus effective opposition withers, and free government with it.[24]

There is evident here Randolph's dread of the corrupting

[23] *Annals of Congress* (12th Cong., 1st sess.), pp. 442–48.
[24] *Richmond Enquirer,* April 1, 1815.

power of government in general and the federal government
in particular. The greatest danger did not come from abroad,
maintained Randolph; it was domestic and a real threat to
liberty. As he replied to Calhoun in 1816:

> The gentleman had represented this country as contending
> with Great Britain for existence. Could the honorable gentle-
> man, or any other man, Mr. R. asked, believe that we would
> ever have a contest with any nation for existence? No, said Mr.
> R., we hold our existence by charter from the great God who
> made this world; we hold it in contempt of Great Britain—I
> speak of civil freedom—I am addressing myself to one who
> understands these distinctions. We do not hold our right to
> physical being or political freedom by any tenure from Europe;
> yet we hold our tenure of civil liberty by a precarious tie, which
> must be broken; for, from the disposition to follow the phantom
> of honor, or from another cause, this country is fairly embarked
> on a course of policy like that which is pursued by other govern-
> ments in Europe.[25]

Randolph's unyielding opposition to war and expansion
and his advocacy of the most unpopular of courses at that
time brought general condemnation upon him; the town of
Randolph, in Georgia, named in his honor, was renamed
Jasper, in wrath;[26] and even the poets assailed him. Referring to his habit of sucking stick candy in the House chamber, one wrote of Randolph:

> When *bitter* Randolph *candy* ate,
> We wondered, one and all!
> But, see the strange decree of fate
> Turn *Candy* into *Gall!*[27]

---

[25] *Annals of Congress* (14th Cong., 1st sess.), p. 845.

[26] *Richmond Enquirer,* January 14, 1813.

[27] *Ibid.,* January 27, 1816.

Randolph endured the storm, and the disasters of the war with England proved him a true prophet and restored him to a measure of favor; thereafter he pursued relentlessly his attacks on intervention in foreign quarrels. Such intervention would disrupt the finances of the country, he knew; it would divert attention from disturbed and pressing domestic affairs; it would endanger, by the possible exercise of the treaty power, the guarantees of the Constitution and the authority of the House. In the debate on the Greek question and in that on the Panama Congress, he delivered particularly important speeches, and, since it is not possible to review his whole course of defense of American political isolation, we may obtain a fair picture of his stand by glancing at a part of one of his speeches on the former subject. The passion for intervening in the concerns of Europe and Latin America led, he maintained, to unconstitutional projects and policies, to ends and means never contemplated by the framers of the Constitution; he, who before 1812 had declared, "We will come out of this war without a Constitution," believed this would be the result of foreign meddling short of war, as well.

It has once been said, of the dominions of the king of Spain—thank God! it can no longer be said—that the sun never set upon them. Sir, the sun never sets on ambition like this; they who have once felt its scorpion sting are never satisfied with a limit less than the circle of our planet. I have heard, sir, the late coruscation in the heavens attempted to be accounted for by the return of the lunar cycle, the moon having got back into the same relative position in which she was nineteen years ago. However this may be, I am afraid, sir, that she exerts too potent an influence over our legislation. . . .

Let us, said Mr. R., adhere to the policy laid down by the second, as well as the first founder of our Republic—by the Camillus, as well as Romulus, of the infant state—to the policy

of peace, commerce, and honest friendship with all nations, entangling alliances with none; for to entangling alliances you must
go, if you once embark in such projects as this. And with all
his British predilections, Mr. R. said, he suspected he should,
whenever that question should present itself, resist as strongly
an alliance with Great Britain as with any other power. We are
sent here, said he, to attend to the preservation of the peace of
this country, and not to be ready, on all occasions, to go to war
whenever anything like what in common parlance is termed *a
turn up* takes place in Europe.

I can, however, assure the committee, for one, that the public
burdens on those whom I represent here (though they are certainly better off than those to the North and the West of them:
that is till you come to the favored states, where the interest of
the public debt is paid and where almost all the public moneys
are disbursed)—their burdens, sir, are as great as they can bear,
because their private engagements are greater than they can
discharge—and if this is not a self-evident proposition, I am at a
loss to know what can be such. And this universal distress in the
country has been the effect of freaks of legislation in the past.
I do not deny but there may be some who have drawn great
prizes in the lottery, but that is not the case with the great mass
of the nation. And what *is this* scheme but a lottery? If it should
end in war, there will be more great prizes to be drawn, but it
will be for me, for those whom I represent, to pay them. . . .

For my part, I would sooner put the shirt of Nessus on my
back than sanction these doctrines—such as I never heard from
my boyhood until now. They go the whole length. If they prevail, there are no longer any Pyrenees—every bulwark and
barrier of the Constitution is broken down; it is become a *tabula
rasa,* a *carte blanche,* for every one to scribble on it what he
pleases.[28]

Randolph always could sum up his own views more con-
cisely and more eloquently than another could hope to do;
and this speech expressed the dislike of the Old Republicans
for governmental measures which went beyond the bound-

---

[28] *Ibid.,* January 31, 1824.

aries of the United States, containing within the space of a few thousand words probably the most able refutation of imperialism that has been heard in Congress. War and imperialism meant the undermining of the society and the constitution for which Randolph and his friends stood; they meant the economic ruin of their institutions; and they meant that spirit of managing other men's affairs which was so repugnant to these lovers of freedom. It was the War of 1812 which struck an awful blow at their cause, and it was a later war which crushed them to earth.

4

In 1808 John Brockenbrough wrote to Randolph: "Patriotism is a mighty precious thing when it costs nothing, but the mass of mankind consider it a very foolish thing when it curtails their self-indulgence."[29] This was during the days of Jefferson's embargo. The Old Republicans, in whom there was little of self-indulgence and a great deal of true patriotism, opposed with all their strength what they considered the ruinous stifling of their economy; and not long after Brockenbrough wrote, the mass of the people, long faithful to the Jeffersonian program, began to turn toward repeal of the prohibition of commerce. For once the Old Republican school triumphed, and they were to win other victories of this sort—in the South, at least. Essential in the Old Republican program was opposition to all regulation of commerce and finance by the federal government —opposition of the embargo and its kindred measures, to

---

[29] Brockenbrough to Randolph, (?) 1808 (?) (copy in Randolph Letters, University of North Carolina).

the tariff, to the Bank of the United States. Gradually the
Old Republicans and their political inheritors brought the
majority of the electorate in the southern states to adopt
this hostility toward federal control of trade and industry.

The fear and hatred of restrictive measures and special
legislative privilege to economic interests, which had been
perhaps the chief characteristics of the Republican party in
the first Congress, were kept alive from the second administration of Jefferson to the first administration of Jackson
principally by the Old Republicans. The Virginia dynasty
and the National Republicans came to look with a most
favorable eye upon the protective tariff, the neomercantile
system, and even the federally chartered Bank. The Old
Republicans saw the doom of their institutions in such establishments, for they knew that wealth, and power with it,
would flow to other classes and other regions than their
own were those policies to continue; and they thought such
a society far inferior to theirs. Not only would there be these
economic consequences, but the constitutional precedents
set by such a loose interpretation of federal authority would
demolish utterly strict construction; and strict construction
was an end in itself with these lovers of liberty. John Taylor
expressed their viewpoint at great length and with admirable strength in his books; but it is worth our time to see
what Randolph's more eloquent tongue had to say.

John Randolph's great speech, in 1806, against Gregg's
Resolution commenced his onslaught upon those restrictions on exports and taxes on imports which would ruin his
Old Virginia. Randolph's economics were the doctrines of
the classical school, and their consistency was unassailable.
Calhoun opposed them, in his earlier years, because he
considered domestic manufacturing necessary for national

strength in war; but he did not deny that Randolph's premises were economically sound, laying aside questions of political expediency. No one could successfully deny the fact; and certainly no one could successfully meet Randolph in a debate on the question. The argument on Gregg's Resolution, however, was not so much a question of economic principle as it was of the constitutionality of restraint of trade and of its possible effect upon the matter of war or peace. Said Randolph:

> As in 1798 I was opposed to this species of warfare, because I believed it would raze the constitution to its very foundation— so, in 1806, I am opposed to it, and on the same grounds. No sooner do you put the constitution to this use—to a test which it is by no means calculated to endure—than its incompetency becomes manifest, and apparent to all. I fear, if you go into a foreign war for a circuitous, unfair carrying-trade, you will come out without your constitution. Have you not contractors enough yet in this House? Or do you want to be overrun and devoured by commissaries and all the vermin of contract? I fear, sir, that what are called the "energy men" will rise up again; men who will burn the parchment. We shall be told that our government is too free; or, as they would say, weak and inefficient. Much virtue, Sir, in terms! That we must give the President power to call forth the resources of the nations. That is to filch the last shilling from our pockets—to drain the last drop of blood from our veins.[30]

Yet Gregg's Resolution to forbid importation from Great Britain and her possessions was as nothing in comparison with Jefferson's embargo, soon to follow. Randolph supported the embargo when it first was introduced in the House, but, after realizing its purpose, voted against it; he had thought it designed only as a temporary measure, which he previously had recommended, for securing American

---

[30] *Annals of Congress* (9th Cong., 1st sess.), p. 560.

shipping in American harbors before undertaking retaliation against Britain or France. But an indefinite suspension of commerce was wholly another matter; Randolph thought the first form of embargo to be a simple regulation of commerce and therefore constitutional; the second, however, amounted to a prohibition or destruction of commerce and did not accord with the spirit of the commerce clause in the Constitution. For its duration, Randolph assailed the embargo; in its comparatively short span of existence, it did incalculable harm to the agrarian cause, since it ruined half of Virginia and stimulated the manufacturers of New England and the Middle Atlantic States, which demanded tariff protection once the embargo vanished.

Randolph's assaults on the embargo and that greater evil, the war which followed it, are matters of political history; both events hastened the decline of his Virginia and led to the establishment of that national mercantile policy he so deplored—the protective tariff. He proclaimed that "the embargo, like Achilles' wrath, was the source of our Iliad of woes!"[31] To Brockenbrough he wrote of "the exploded mercantile system, revived and fastened, like the Old Man of the Sea, around our necks." In 1816 he delivered one of the most searching criticisms of that policy, during the discussion of the tariff bill. It was nothing more than a system of bounties to manufacturers, he said with passion, "to encourage them to do that which, if it be advantageous to do at all, they will do, of course, for their own sakes." The productive labor of the country would be distorted and molded into a thousand fantastic shapes to suit the intent and the profit of these special interests. It was simply a question of whether

---

[31] Garland, *op. cit.*, I, 213.

a planter would consent to be taxed to enable another man to set up a spinning jenny. Randolph would sell in the best market and buy in the cheapest and never would agree to this intricate neomercantilism of bounties, even though the proponents of protection should agree to establish bounties for the raising of tobacco, too. The agriculturalist bore the brunt of the war and taxation. The agriculturalist, that great stable element of society, was to be pillaged for the benefit of a class of speculators and note-shavers:

> The agriculturalist has his property, his lands, his all, his household goods to defend; and like that meek drudge, the ox, who does the labor and plows the ground, and then, for his reward, takes the refuse of the farmyard, the blighted blades and the mouldy straw, and the mildewed shocks of corn for his support—while the commercial speculators live in opulence, whirling in coaches and indulging in palaces; to use the words of Dr. Johnson, coaches which fly like meteors and palaces which rise like exhalations. Even without your aid, the agriculturalists are no match for them. Alert, vigilant, enterprising and active, the manufacturing interest are collected in masses and ready to associate at a moment's warning for any purpose of general interest to their body. . . . The cultivators, the patient drudges of other orders of society, are now waiting for your resolution; for on you it depends whether they shall be left further unhurt or be, like those in Europe, reduced, *gradatim,* and subjected to another squeeze from the hard grasp of power.[32]

Despite all its passion, this defense of the agrarian society was as unavailing as most such pleas since Randolph's time. His remarks upon the tariff of 1824, already quoted partially in a previous chapter, were similar in vein: England, he said, possessed a natural advantage in manufacturing; she was welcome to it, for that condition of society meant only

---

[32] *Annals of Congress* (14th Cong., 1st sess.), pp. 683–88.

misery for the bulk of her inhabitants.[33] He fought the tariff throughout the last year of his congressional career, at the time his colleague Macon wrote to Edwards: "I have heard that the tariff would be taken up today or tomorrow in the H. of R. We must wear old clothes, and put patch on patch, and not be ashamed, provided we owe nothing, though we may not be dressed in the fashion, there is no better fashion, than to be out of debt."[34] Such was the simplicity of these Old Republicans, whom northerners sometimes described as luxurious proprietors supported by the labor of slaves.

Linked with their opposition to restrictions upon commerce was the hatred of the Old Republicans for the federally chartered Bank of the United States. Their opposition (or, at least, that of many of them) was not limited to that great institution; they disliked the state banks, as well. There was nothing fundamentally ridiculous in their position. They were opposed to borrowing and debt; they were advocates of a simple agricultural economy; they were "hard-money men"; and the states, or the colonies, had prospered earlier without banks. Had they been able to perpetuate the society they loved, banks might not have been a necessity, though they might have been a convenience. But many of the Old Republicans thought such convenience outweighed by the evils of concentration of economic power, complication of the economy, and encouragement to extravagance the banks brought with them. The federal Bank was unconstitutional, moreover, they contended; and, in time, the people were to accept the latter contention of the Old Republicans.

---

[33] *Ibid.* (18th Cong., 1st sess.), II, 2360.

[34] Macon to N. W. Edwards, March 3, 1828 (Macon Papers, North Carolina State Department of Archives and History).

Randolph wrote to Brockenbrough, president of the Bank of Virginia, that a banking house was a house of ill fame.[35] He saw the Bank of the United States as an unconstitutional monster, created for the benefit of an avaricious class and serving as a tool of the centralizers. His chief assault on the Bank came in 1816, during the debate over rechartering the institution. Randolph agreed that the circulating currency of the day was in a deplorable state of fluctuation, but he saw no remedy in the Bank—and, most certainly, no remedy worthy of the price that would have to be paid. True payments never can be made solely by credit and paper; precious metals, or paper bottomed on them, are indispensable. He foresaw a consequent management of the national economy by the federal executive to suit the will and discretion of politicians. The banks had become so powerful, such an influence upon almost all men of consequence, that "we are tied hand and foot to this great Mammon, which is set up to worship in this Christian land"; and the government, while denouncing religious hierarchy, establishes a new economic hierarchy:

> The stuff uttered on all hands, and absolutely got by rote by the haberdashers' boys behind the counters in the shops, [is] that paper now in circulation would buy anything you want as well as gold and silver. . . .
>
> He despaired, he said, almost of remedying the evil when he saw so many men of respectability directors, stockholders, debtors of the banks. To pass this bill, he said, would be like getting rid of the rats by setting fire to the house; whether any other remedy could be devised, he did not now undertake to pronounce. The banks, he said, had lost all shame, and exemplified a beautiful and very just observation of one of the finest writers,

---

[35] W. C. Bruce, *Randolph,* I, 430.

that men banded together in a common cause, will collectively do that at which every individual of the combination would spurn.[36]

And Randolph declared, several days later, that he was

the holder of no stock whatever, except live stock, and had determined never to own any; but if this bill passed, he would not only be a stockholder to the utmost of his power, but would advise every man, over whom he had any influence, to do the same, because it was the creation of a great privileged order of the most hateful kind to his feelings, and because he would rather be the master than the slave. If he must have a master, let him be one with epaulettes, something that he could fear and respect, something that he could look up to—but not a master with a quill behind his ear.[37]

The Bank was chartered; but Randolph was to triumph in death, for Jackson, whom he first supported and then cursed, carried on, in this respect at least, the Old Republican tradition. Nevertheless, time has brought the complicated credit economy Randolph dreaded, with finance the master of man. "Who can bind posterity?" Randolph exclaimed despairingly.

5

As early as 1811 John Randolph said of the Republicans of true principles:

He feared, if a writ were to issue against that old party—as had been facetiously said of another body, of our valiant army —it would be found impossible for a constable with a search warrant to find it. There must be a return *non est inventus.*

---

[36] *Annals of Congress* (14th Cong., 1st sess.), 1110–13.
[37] *Ibid.,* p. 1339.

Death, resignation, and desertion had thinned their ranks. They had disappeared. New men and new doctrines had succeeded.[38]

The Republican principles of 1800 were indeed deserted by most of their champions, out of necessity or inclination; but Randolph and his allies were constant. Right or wrong, they were faithful, and such fidelity in politics merits a high reward which the Old Republicans never did receive. True, their principles coincided with the measures which would best protect their class, and in that they may be said to have yielded to self-interest; but Randolph, with his abhorrence of natural-rights doctrine, would have admitted freely the impeachment. He sought to safeguard himself and his society; that, and not abstract theory, he would have maintained, was the whole basis of politics. Randolph and his friends fought for the agricultural life. They were vanquished.

Yet those doctrines of 1800 did not perish; they were guarded, battered but obdurate, by the Old Jacobins and were passed on to a later generation of southern thought (and, in a measure, of northern thought) which gave them a more hearty welcome than they had long experienced. Those principles of a society of freeholders have in them an attraction for some natures which does not perish with the times. Those political standards, in part the product and in part the corollary of this school of thought, have been sorely trampled, but they have not been refuted. Purity and economy in government, peace and prudence in foreign relations, and freedom from economic oppression by special interests are ideals which, if remote of achievement, still are worth striving toward.

---

[38] *Ibid.* (12th Cong., 1st sess.), p. 525.

Chapter Six

The Cancer

1

George Mason, one of the three Virginians most admired by John Randolph, declared: "Every master of slaves is born a petty tyrant. They bring the judgment of heaven on a country."[1] Jefferson, Randolph's kinsman, attacked slavery as a deprivation of the divine gift of liberty, and added, "Indeed I tremble for my country when I reflect that God is just; that his justice cannot sleep forever."[2] And St. George Tucker, stepfather of Randolph, wrote his admirable *Dissertation on Slavery*, prefaced by the words of Montesquieu: "Slavery not only violates the laws of nature, and of civil society, but also wounds the best Forms of Government: in a Democracy, where all Men are equal, Slavery is contrary to the spirit of the Constitution."[3]

A half-century later, Calhoun, who considered himself the heir of Jefferson—and so he was, in many respects—said of slavery:

---

[1] See K. M. Rowland, *The Life of George Mason*, II, 161.

[2] Thomas Jefferson, *Notes on the State of Virginia*, p. 237.

[3] St. George Tucker, *A Dissertation on Slavery*, p. 1.

Be it good or bad, it has grown up with our society and institutions, and is so interwoven with them that to destroy it would
be to destroy us as a people. But let me not be understood as admitting, even by implication, that the existing relation between
the two races in the slaveholding States is an evil—far otherwise.
I hold it to be a good, as it has thus far proved itself to be, to
both, and will continue to prove so if not disturbed by the fell
spirit of abolition.[4]

The bridge between these two schools of thought was
John Randolph, the slaveholding *ami des noirs,* and possibly
he faced reality more clearly than did his predecessors or
his inheritors. On the question of slavery, more than any
other single issue, the development of Randolph's thought
is an index to the alteration of the southern mind during
those years.

In his youth Randolph was a sturdy opponent of negro
slavery; he never ceased to deplore the institution; his consistency cannot be impeached; and yet, by the end of his
life, his stand had become only a step removed from Calhoun's praise of servitude. In Randolph, too, the development of that dread of the negro, emphasized by U. B. Phillips in his studies of the Old South, may be discerned clearly.

The problem of slavery, in its larger aspect, is closely
bound to that of natural rights. As Randolph's degree of
faith in natural rights is obscure during his early years, so
is the precise extent of his earlier opposition to slavery.
Henry Adams implies that Randolph was an ardent eman-
cipator, literally the American *ami des noirs* he called himself, and quotes with some malice the Virginian's account
of his boyhood: "brought up among Quakers, an ardent

---

[4] *Register of Debates* (24th Cong., 2d sess.), p. 2186.

ami des noirs, to scuffle with negroes and overseers for something like a pittance of rent and profit upon my land and stock."[5] But to paint a Virginian of that day as an admirer of L'Ouverture, Dessalines, and Christophe, a fellow of Condorcet, Mirabeau, Pétion, and Gregoire, is a strain upon credulity; Randolph's use of the expression must be considered an example of his half-whimsical adoption of current political labels, just as he termed his Old Republicans "the old Jacobins *enragés*," though they were anything but literal Jacobins. The French program of racial fraternization could hardly have attracted Randolph. One might be an advocate of gradual abolition and yet not an egalitarian, and Randolph, in 1826, spoke of his youthful disgust with the institution:

> From my early childhood, all my feelings and instincts were in opposition to slavery in every shape; to the subjugation of one man's will to that of another; and from the time that I read Clarkson's celebrated pamphlet, I was, I am afraid, as mad—as Clarkson himself. I read myself into this madness, as I have read myself into some agricultural improvements; but, as with these last, I worked myself out of them, so also I worked myself out of it.[6]

Although Randolph thus purged himself of what he considered the folly of governmental interference with slavery, he never altered his own humane treatment of his hundreds of slaves. As a master, Randolph did indeed prove himself a friend of the blacks. The childless man of Roanoke, embittered against his era, treated his slaves with paternal pity

[5] Henry Adams, *Randolph,* p. 21; Hugh Garland, *Randolph of Roanoke,* II, 224.

[6] *Register of Debates* (19th Cong., 1st sess.), p. 118.

and kindness, tempered by the necessity of keeping them in a proper awe. Powhatan Bouldin tells us that Randolph, with his glittering eye, was held in awe by every negro of the neighborhood;[7] but he was loved by them, also. The younger Josiah Quincy, an earnest advocate of emancipation, related this incident of Randolph's return to Roanoke, where he was met by his slaves: "Men and women rushed toward him, seized him by the hand with perfect familiarity, and burst into tears of delight at his presence among them. His conduct to these humble dependents was like that of a most affectionate father among his children."[8]

In his letters he frequently refers to his slaves as if they were friends or kinsmen. From London, in 1830, he wrote to William Leigh, referring to his two favorite household servants, "Before this Juba is at home. . . . Johnny was delighted to hear from home and sends his kind How D'ye? to all."[9] Johnny, who was with Randolph at the time of the Virginian's death in Philadelphia, had accompanied Randolph on his tours of Britain, and Randolph told Jacob Harvey, "Much as I was prepared to see misery in the South of Ireland, I was utterly shocked at the condition of the poor peasantry between Limerick and Dublin. Why, sir, John never felt so proud of being a *Virginia slave.* He looked with horror upon the mud hovels and miserable food of the *white slaves,* and I had no fear of *his* running away."[10] On the same trip, Randolph informed some Irish gentlemen that "if any of you should visit old Virginia, I shall promise

---

[7] Powhatan Bouldin, *Home Reminiscences of John Randolph,* p. 32.

[8] Josiah Quincy, *Figures of the Past,* p. 228.

[9] Randolph to Leigh, December 15, 1830 (Randolph Letters, University of North Carolina).

[10] Garland, *op. cit.,* II, 222; also "Randolphiana," *Richmond Enquirer,* June 25, 1833.

you a fair hearing, at all events; and you may compare *our* system of slavery with yours—aye, and be the judges yourselves!"[11]

A conscientious master of fields and slaves in declining Virginia after the embargo and 1812 might very well be hard pressed to keep his slaves properly fed and clothed; and a patriarchal proprietor like Randolph, who looked upon his slaves more as wards than as a source of income, had reason to inveigh against the original introduction of slavery, no matter how difficult it might be to remedy the evil now. After the devastating flood of the Roanoke in 1814, Randolph wrote to Brockenbrough: "With a family of more than two hundred mouths looking up to me for food, I feel an awful charge on my hands. It is easy to rid myself of the burden if I could shut my heart to the cry of humanity and the voice of duty. But in these poor slaves I have found my best and most faithful friends; and I feel that it would be more difficult to abandon them to the cruel fate to which our laws would consign them, than to suffer with them."[12] Even the rogues among his blacks seemed like children to him; writing to an overseer of Benjamin Watkins Leigh's plantation, he remarked: "I send you a hand in lieu of Bull's (Moses') wife who had parted from him because he has deserted her and taken up with other women. His name is Davy. He is a sheep stealer and a hog stealer. Have an eye upon him. He is weak breasted, predisposed to consumption. You must therefore not put him to any *hard* work or expose him to wet or cold."[13]

---

[11] Garland, *op. cit.*, II, 223.

[12] *Ibid.*, p. 44.

[13] Randolph to Leigh, September 17, 1832 (Randolph MSS, Duke University).

Such was the master who was the South's foremost opponent of federal interference with slavery. More like a baron
among his peasants than a slaveowning entrepreneur of the
Deep South, he never wavered in his hatred of the slave
trade and never bought or sold slaves, no matter how great
his immediate need for money might be. If he had ever
wished to emancipate his slaves during his lifetime, he could
not have done so, for they were included in the mortgage
upon the Randolph estates which his father had given British creditors.[14] But the failure of the settlement at Israel Hill,
where his brother Richard had established his own emanci-
pated slaves, probably would have deterred Randolph from
hoping to set up his blacks as freedmen in the South; what
provision he made in his will, we shall say a trifle about
presently. At any rate, he was the terror of slave traders,
and the abolitionist Whittier was accurate when, in "Randolph of Roanoke," he praised the dead Virginian:

> He held his slaves, yet kept the while
>   His reverence for the Human;
> In the dark vassals of his will
>   He saw but Man and Woman.
> No hunter of God's outraged poor
>   His Roanoke valley entered;
> No trader in the souls of men
>   Across his threshold ventured.[15]

Though Randolph was no literal *ami des noirs,* he certainly was a southern friend to the blacks in his own con-

---

[14] Garland, *op. cit.,* II, 150.

[15] Written in 1846. See Mary H. Coleman, "Whittier on Randolph," *New England Quarterly,* VIII, 551–54.

duct. What his attitude became in public life is a more important question.

2

John Randolph had been a member of the House of Representatives only a year when a number of free blacks presented a petition requesting revision of the slave-trade laws and the fugitive-slave regulations, as well as the inception of a program of general emancipation. His stand on the matter was the beginning of his uncompromising defense of the right of the South to be free from external interference with her peculiar institution. He hoped that the House would act so decidedly in the negative as to deter petitioners from ever presenting a similar appeal. "The Constitution had put it out of the power of the House to do anything in it, and therefore he hoped the motion for a reference would be lost by a decided majority, and this would be the last time the business of the House would be entered upon, and the interest and feelings of the southern states be put in jeopardy, by similar applications."[16] At this time Randolph ruled the House literally booted and spurred, the master of the new Republican Congress as much from terror as from love, and congressmen hastened to obey his edict: the House passed, eighty-five to one, a resolution declaring the parts of the petition referring to emancipation "have a tendency to create disquiet and jealousy, and ought therefore to receive no encouragement."[17] Randolph, with his accustomed prescience, had foreseen the probable consequence of such

[16] *Annals of Congress* (6th Cong., 1st sess.), pp. 233–34.
[17] *Ibid.,* p. 244.

agitation, and for a long time he had squelched it. But four
decades later, similar petitions were to split the House into
vituperative northern and southern camps.

During Randolph's second year in Congress occurred
Gabriel's insurrection, the first of those servile rebellions
which were to influence southern emotions so profoundly
and, in the long run, to reinforce Randolph's plea for state
rights and strict construction. At Bizarre, Randolph wrote
to Nicholson, in Maryland, concerning the rising: "The
accused have exhibited a spirit, which, if it becomes general,
must deluge the southern country with blood. They manifested a sense of their rights, and a thirst for revenge, which
portend the most unhappy consequences."[18] Whether the
phrase "a sense of their rights" indicated a recognition of
natural rights possessed by slaves, it is hard to say. Less than
two years later, Randolph's opposition to slavery appears to
have been still virulently strong. As the chairman of a committee of the House to consider a petition of the people of
Ohio (among them William Henry Harrison the chief
mover) for a temporary suspension of the prohibition of
slavery under the Ordinance of 1787, Randolph wrote a report denying their request and condemning the institution.
It is noteworthy that Randolph never disputed the power of
Congress to prohibit slavery in the territories, or, for that
matter, in the District of Columbia; Congress, he said, governed the territories as an empire, before they became states.
His report follows:

> That the rapid population of the State of Ohio sufficiently
> evinces, in the opinion of your committee, that the labor of slaves

---

[18] Randolph to Nicholson, September 26, 1800 (copy in Randolph Papers,
Virginia State Library).

is not necessary to promote the growth and settlement of colonies in that region. That this labor, demonstrably the dearest of any, can only be employed to advantage in the cultivation of products more valuable than any known to that quarter of the United States: that the committee deem it highly dangerous and inexpedient to impair a provision wisely calculated to promote the happiness and prosperity of the northwestern country, and to give strength and security to that extensive frontier. In the salutary operation of this sagacious and benevolent restraint, it is believed that the inhabitants of Indiana will, at no very distant day, find ample remuneration for a temporary privation of labor and emigration.[19]

And Randolph was opposed to slavery in the South, as well. He condemned South Carolina's reopening of the slave trade; to Littleton Waller Tazewell he wrote in 1804:

To her [South Carolina's] indelible disgrace she has legalized this abomination and all her rice and indigo and cotton is to be converted into slaves. The labor of the miserable negro is to procure fresh companions of his wretchedness. I tremble for the dreadful retribution which this horrid thirst for African blood, which the legislators of that state are base enough to feel and yet more base to avow, may bring upon us. But a few years past, and the opulent nabobs of St. Domingo looked down with disdain on the feeble splendor of the beggarly noble class of Europe. In less than five years, the cause of the wretches will be recruited by 200,000 native Africans. It behooves Virginia, in my opinion, to look to the consequences.[20]

The question of slavery was not raised again in Randolph's congressional career until 1806, during the debate on a proposal to prohibit the importation of slaves after

---

[19] *American State Papers,* Class VIII: *Public Lands,* I, No. 76, 160 (7th Cong., 2d sess.), "Indian Territory."

[20] Randolph to Tazewell, January 8, 1804 (copy in Randolph Papers, Virginia State Library).

1807—a dispute excited principally by the Carolinian re-opening of the foreign slave trade, which we have seen Randolph denounce above. Yet he was among the most vigorous opponents of the particular bill introduced, a surprising fact in view of his detestation of the traffic; but his opposition was based upon jealousy for state and individual rights and upon fear of the precedent that would be established. He objected to that provision in the bill which implied that, under the constitutional proviso for halting the foreign slave trade, a master might be forbidden by the federal government from taking his own slaves out of one state into another. This, Randolph declared, was interference not with the foreign slave traffic but with the relation between master and slave—a power the federal government never should possess. Representative Early, of Georgia, made a declaration which Randolph neither endorsed nor contested and which reflected the growing resentment south of Mason and Dixon's line at northern criticism: "A large majority of the people in the southern states do not consider slavery as a crime. They do not believe it immoral to hold human flesh in bondage. Many deprecate slavery as an evil; as a political evil; but not as a crime."[21]

On February 19 Randolph spoke on the topic. The Senate had rejected a House amendment to the effect that the right of a slaveowner to transport his property from one state to another be specifically guaranteed; and Randolph declared that the House ought to stand firm on the amendment.

> If the bill passed without the amendment, the Southern people would set the law at defiance. He would begin the example. He

---

[21] *Annals of Congress* (9th Cong., 2d sess.), p. 238.

would go with his own slaves, and be at the expense of asserting the rights of slaveholders. The next step would be to prohibit the slaveholder himself going from one state to another. This bill, without the amendment, was worse than the exaction of ship money. The proprietor of sacred and chartered rights is prevented the constitutional use of his property.[22]

Already the determination of southerners to "set at defiance" what it considered unconstitutional interference with its peculiar institution was manifest here. On February 26 Randolph spoke again, remarking that the bill, if passed, might provide precedent for some future scheme of universal emancipation. "It went to blow up the Constitution in ruins. Mr. R. said, if ever the time of disunion between the states should arrive, the line of severance would be between the slaveholding and the nonslaveholding states."[23] Representative Goldsborough defended the bill, and Randolph replied: "He considered it no imputation to be a slaveholder, more than to be born in a particular country. It was a thing with which they had no more to do than with their own procreation."[24]

Finally the bill passed in a form more satisfactory to Randolph, but the great issue had been opened to public view. Henceforth Randolph often was to refer defiantly to his fellow congressmen from the South as "my fellow slaveholders," in reply to New England's reproaches. His prediction as to the "line of severance" was to prove fatally penetrating, although in 1806, with separatist movements in the West and in Massachusetts apparently more ominous,

[22] *Ibid.*, p. 528.
[23] *Ibid.*, p. 626.
[24] *Ibid.*, p. 627.

the nature of future disunion was hardly so obvious as it later became. And here we see the first instance of Randolph's deliberate utilization of southern fear for slavery to gain support for his states' rights principles—the aspect of Randolph's career which Henry Adams considers most important.[25] Randolph, the purist in politics, the St. Michael disappointed in men and measures, came to appeal most successfully to men's economic motives and vague dreads in order to raise bulwarks for the society he loved. He might himself oppose slavery, but he would not refuse the support of those who inclined toward the institution. From this date forward, Randolph appealed to the slaveowners of the South to stand by strict constitutional construction and states' rights, or else their slave property must be at the mercy of the North—indeed, the whole security of white people in the South would be imperiled. This appeal carried weight which no other argument could have furnished; it sufficed to convert southern members of the National Republican faction, former Federalists in the South, and others given to centralizing and loose-construction tendencies.

Randolph's fear of the consequences arising from federal interference with slavery was quite genuine, and strongly influenced his support of the doctrines of strict construction and state powers; but it was not the only motive, nor the most important motive with him, for he had been a champion of those causes before the question of congressional intervention in slavery assumed any prominence. He used it, however, as a rallying cry for the Old Republicans; and he utilized the issue of slavery to advance his views upon questions other than constitution construction and local liberties.

---

[25] Adams, *op. cit.*, chap. xi.

He appealed to the southern fear of black insurrection—a fear which he shared—to further his program of isolation from European quarrels. His next expression of opinion upon slavery and the South is found in his speech on foreign relations, December 9, 1811. The War Hawks, bitterly opposed by Randolph, had rendered almost inevitable a conflict with England, and Randolph made a last passionate appeal against the coming war. The recent and then continuing horrors in Haiti must have chilled many a southerner— Gabriel's insurrection was thought to have been inspired by the successful example of Santo Domingo—and the Southsider's skillful tongue dealt mercilessly with this delicate problem.

> Mr. R. dwelt on the danger arising from the black population. He said he would touch this subject as tenderly as possible—it was with reluctance that he touched it at all—but in cases of great emergency, the State physician must not be deterred. . . . What was the situation of the slaveholding States? During the war of the Revolution, so fixed were their habits of subordination, that when the whole Southern country was overrun by the enemy, who invited them to desert, no fear was ever entertained of an insurrection of the slaves. . . . But should we therefore be unobservant spectators of the progress of society within the last twenty years—of the silent but powerful change wrought by time and chance, upon its composition and temper? When the fountains of the great deep of abomination were broken up, even the poor slaves had not escaped the general deluge. The French Revolution had polluted even them. Nay, there had not been wanting men in that House, witness their legislative *Legendre,* the butcher who once held a seat there, to preach upon that floor these imprescriptible rights to a crowded audience of blacks in the galleries—teaching them that they are equal to their masters—in other words, advising them to cut their throats. Similar doctrines were disseminated by peddlers from New England and elsewhere, throughout the Southern country— and masters had been found so infatuated, as by their lives and

conversation, by a general contempt of order, unthinkingly to cherish these seeds of self-destruction to them and their families. What was the consequence? Within the last ten years, repeated alarms of insurrection among the slaves—some of them awful indeed. From the spreading of this infernal doctrine, the whole Southern country had been thrown into a state of insecurity. Men dead to the operation of moral causes, had taken away from the poor slave his habits of loyalty and obedience to his master, which lightened his servitude by a double operation; beguiling his own cares and disarming his master's suspicions and severity; and now, like true empirics in politics, you are called upon to trust to the mere physical strength of the fetter which holds him in bondage. You have deprived him of all moral restraint, you have tempted him to eat of the fruit of knowledge, just enough to perfect him in wickedness; you have opened his eyes to his nakedness; you have armed his nature against the hand that has fed, that has clothed him, that has cherished him in sickness; that hand, which before he became a pupil of your school, he had been accustomed to press with respectful attention. You have done all this—and then show him the gibbet and the wheel, as incentives to a sullen, repugnant obedience. God forbid, sir, that the southern states should ever see an enemy on their shores, with these infernal principles of French liberty in the van! While talking of Canada, some of us were shuddering for our own safety at home. He spoke from facts, when he said that the night-bell never tolled for fire in Richmond that the mother did not hug her infant more closely to her bosom.[26]

Such was not the speech of a literal *ami des noirs*. But it should not be thought that these eloquent injunctions against racial equality meant that Randolph was reconciled to slavery. Four years later he delivered a denunciation of the domestic slave trade that Garrison would not have hesitated to publish, recommending its abolition in the District of Columbia. Nowhere in the world, not even in

---

[26] *Annals of Congress* (12th Cong., 1st sess.), I, 450–51.

Africa, he said, was there "so great and so infamous a slave market as in the metropolis, in the very Seat of Government of this nation, which prided itself on freedom." Randolph disavowed any intention of interfering with the delicate relation between slave and owner; but he would not endure a slave market, where were sold persons "bought either from cruel masters or kidnapped; and of those who were kidnapped . . . there were two kinds—slaves stolen from their masters, and free persons stolen, as he might say, from themselves." He pointed out that recent economic developments in southern cultivation of cotton, tobacco, and especially sugar had increased the price of slaves, which provided temptation to "their base, hard-hearted masters" to sell "out of their families the negroes who had been raised among them." Washington ought to afford no countenance to inhumanity of this sort—"an assemblage of prisons where the unfortunate beings, reluctant, no doubt, to be torn from their connexions, and the affections of their lives, were incarcerated and chained down, and thence driven in fetters like beasts, to be paid for like cattle." Randolph moved that the Committee for the District of Columbia should be "instructed to inquire into the inhuman and illegal traffic in slaves carried on in the District, and to devise some speedy means to put a stop to it."[27]

But in a later Congress, Randolph criticized Cuthbert's proposal for establishing a registry of slaves on the ground that it might lead to unjustified federal interference in state and private affairs; he insisted that federal regulation of the slave traffic remain within constitutional bounds. "In exterminating the slave trade, Mr. R. said, he would join heart

---

[27] *Ibid.* (14th Cong., 1st sess.), pp. 1115–16.

and hand with the gentleman from Georgia, if he chose, in carrying the war into the enemy's country, even into Africa, and endeavor to put it down there, so they did not go beyond the definite landmarks of the Constitution."[28]

Perhaps these speeches, delivered with Randolph's accustomed indifference to popularity, had some part in creating the doubt expressed by many as to the course Randolph would take when, in 1820, the Missouri question confronted Congress. Indeed, such southern misgivings as to Randolph's stand on federal interference with slavery are hardly explicable otherwise. The Old Republican, so detested during the war with Britain, by 1820 was becoming more popular than ever he had been since his break with Jefferson; events had begun to convince Virginia and the South of Randolph's foresight; Jefferson was bestirring himself against loose construction of the Constitution; and letters were beginning to appear in the *Richmond Enquirer* commending the master of Roanoke. Only Randolph's confirmed dislike for slavery and his apparent consent to allow Congress power to interfere with the institution in the territories could have induced anyone to think that Randolph might not stand for the freedom of Missouri to determine her own laws. A friend informed Randolph of these popular misgivings and wrote to Ritchie of the *Enquirer* that Randolph "expressed his astonishment, that a doubt could arise in the mind of anyone who has observed his course. He disclaimed all intention of abandoning state rights, much less the right of the people to *self-government*."[29]

---

[28] *Ibid.* (16th Cong., 1st sess.), pp. 925–26.
[29] *Richmond Enquirer,* January 18, 1820.

Of what Randolph said during the first Missouri debate, we know little, although references to his remarks by other congressmen show that he must have made one of his greatest speeches; he had quarreled, not long before, with the editors of the *National Intelligencer* and had demanded their expulsion from the House, so their omission of his address may have been intentional. He appears to have said little concerning slavery itself but to have discussed the constitutional powers of states—with him, the real question at issue. On February 26, 1820, he spoke four hours on the matter; we know the substance of his remarks only by hearsay. On March 1 he made a second oration, dealing with constitutional aspects of the Compromise. After the debate was done, Randolph wrote to Rutledge: "The slaveholding interest has been sacrificed by southern and western men from slaveholding states, who have wanted to curry favor for very obvious purposes. . . . Your Mr. Lowndes, Mr. Speaker, Barbour of the Senate (a mere bladder of wind) and some other would-be leaders who want also to curry favor for the same reasons (these I need not specify) are the true fathers of the compromise."[30]

Calhoun had voted for the Compromise then; but eighteen years later he paid this tribute to John Randolph:

He now believed that it was a dangerous measure, and that had it been met with such uncompromising zeal as a then distinguished and sagacious member from Virginia, now no more, opposed to it, abolition might have been crushed forever in its birth. He then thought of Mr. Randolph, as, he doubts not, many think of him now, who have not looked into this subject, that

---

[30] Randolph to Rutledge, March 20, 1820 (Randolph MSS, Duke University).

he was too unyielding, too uncompromising, too impracticable; but he had been taught his error, and took pleasure in acknowledging it.[31]

In the second Missouri debate, Randolph's stand against federal interference with the institutions of particular states was unaltered, but we have only one sentence in which he referred to the blacks: "I do now appeal to the nation, said he, whether this pretended sympathy for the rights of free negroes and mulattoes is to supersede the rights of the free white citizens, of ten times their whole number."[32] Such comparative silence on the slavery question could not endure long, however; the threat to slavery within the South was becoming too distinct for equivocation, and the centralizing tendencies of the general government again provoked Randolph's appeal to the fears of his fellow slaveholders. In the debate of January 1824 on internal improvements, he delivered what Henry Adams considers his greatest speech. After remarking the danger of loose construction with reference to the project for internal improvements, he added:

> If Congress possesses the power to do what is proposed in this bill, they may not only enact a sedition law—for there is precedent—but they may emancipate every slave in the United States, and with stronger color of reason than they can exercise the power now contended for. And where will they find the power? They may follow the example of the gentleman who preceded me, and hook the power on to the first loop they find in the Constitution. They might take the preamble, perhaps the war-making power; or they might take a greater sweep, and say, with some gentlemen, that it is not to be found in this or that of

---

[31] *Congressional Globe* (25th Cong., 2d sess.), Appendix, p. 70.
[32] *Annals of Congress* (16th Cong., 2d sess.), p. 1161.

the granted powers, but results from all of them, which is not only a dangerous but *the most* dangerous doctrine. Was it not demonstrable, Mr. R. asked, that slave labor is the dearest in the world, and that the existence of a large body of slaves is a source of danger? Suppose we are at war with a foreign power, and freedom should be offered them by Congress as an inducement to them to take a part in it; or suppose the country not at war, at every turn of this federal machine, at every successive census, that interest will find itself governed by another and increasing power, which is bound to it neither by the common tie of interest or feeling. And if ever the time shall arrive, as assuredly it has arrived elsewhere, and in all probability may arrive here, that a coalition of knavery and fanaticism shall, for any purpose, be got up on this floor, I ask gentlemen, who stand in the same predicament as I do, to look well to what they are now doing—to the colossal power with which they are now arming this government. The power to do what I allude to is, I aver, more honestly inferable from the war-making power than the power we are now about to exercise. Let them look forward to the time when such a question shall arise.[33]

Many thought Randolph's assertions exaggerated, but none of his prophecies was to prove more accurate than this. In the next decade John Quincy Adams was to threaten the South that the war power was the power of emancipation; and four decades later the prophecy would become the Emancipation Proclamation. This question would not down, nor would Randolph allow his fellow legislators to forget it; he was carrying the war into Africa, as Calhoun later was to do; in part, he raised the slavery controversy because of his own fears on the subject and in some degree as a tool to gain southern support for his general political ideas. During the same month he forced the subject into a debate on the Greek

---

[33] *Ibid.* (18th Cong., 1st sess.), p. 1308.

problem. Webster had announced that one reason for intimidating Turkey was that Moslems held slaves. But what did our Constitution say about slavery? Randolph inquired.

> Sir, I am not going to discuss the abstract question of liberty, or slavery, or any other abstract question. I go for matters of fact. But I would ask gentlemen in this House, who have the misfortune to reside on the wrong side of a certain mysterious parallel of latitude, to take this question seriously into consideration—whether the government of the United States is prepared to say, that the act of holding human beings as property, is sufficient to place the party so offending under the ban of its high and mighty displeasure?[34]

Three months later the issue appeared in his speech on the tariff; for the tariff would impose dreadful privations upon the slaves, he said, depriving them of their annual blankets and their woolen suits. "It was notorious that the profits of slave labor had been, for a long time, on the decrease, and that, on a fair average, it scarcely reimbursed the expense of the slave, including the helpless ones, whether from infancy or age." The new tariff seemed calculated to produce emancipation by the curious method that "in case the slave shall not elope from his master, his master will run away from him." Such deliberate impoverishment of the South would be pushed further, Randolph predicted, as reapportionment of the House gave the North a dependable majority. Slave labor, he added in a note appended to this speech, was ruinously expensive, and Virginia would have been far more prosperous, and free from the humiliation of being dominated by the North, if she had sent all her blacks northward

---

[34] *Richmond Enquirer,* January 31, 1824.

across the Ohio, in 1785, instead of ceding her northwest territory to Congress.[35]

Randolph's vehemence was redoubled in his speech of March, 1826, denouncing the proposed Panama Mission. Never did he turn the problem of slavery more deftly to general political purposes. That he fully felt the fears which he expressed is proved by his letters to friends, but he had also the purpose of dissuading Congress from embarking upon a program of intervention in Latin America. "You can no more make liberty out of Spanish matter than you can make a seventy-four out of a bundle of pine saplings," he had said. The Spanish-Americans had liberated their blacks. Could the United States join in friendship and alliance with such revolutionaries? He introduced a resolution requiring the President to lay before the Senate information concerning the emancipation program in Spanish America, and he followed this proposal with one of his most impassioned speeches. As with so many of his orations, it is real pain to chop it into excerpts, but it is too long for inclusion here. He discussed slavery at length. The revolutionists threatened Cuba, he said; once in Cuba, they would menace the United States with servile insurrection.

> Sir, I know there are gentlemen, not only from the Northern, but from the Southern states, who think that this unhappy question—for such it is—of negro slavery—which the Constitution has vainly attempted to blink, by not using the term—should never be brought into public notice, more especially into that of Congress, and most especially, here. Sir, with every due respect for the gentlemen who think so, I differ from them *toto*

---

[35] *Annals of Congress* (18th Cong., 1st sess.), II, 2381.

coelo. Sir, it is a thing which cannot be hid—it is not a dry rot that you can cover with your carpet, until the house tumbles about your ears—you might as well try to hide in a volcano in full operation—it cannot be hid—it is a cancer in your face, and must be treated *secundum artem;* it must not be tampered with by quacks, who never saw the disease or the patient, and pre-scribe across the Atlantic; it must be, if you will, let alone; but on this very principle of letting it alone, it is that I have brought in my resolution. . . . I know that on it depends the life's blood of the little ones, which are lying in their cradles, in happy ig-norance of what is passing around them; and not the white ones only; for shall not we too kill?[36]

He traced the development of the English movement against the slave trade; he showed how gradually that society, of which he had been a member, became a society for abolition of slavery itself; he blamed Wilberforce, Stephen, and Zachary Macaulay for the alteration. Their benevolence had become madness. "Fanaticism, political or religious, has no stopping place short of Heaven—or Hell." These insensate idealists had come to love the blacks of Jamaica, Haiti, and Sierra Leone more than their own countrymen. These fanatics were devoted to the universal extirpation of slavery; they were not content to let a dying institution sink naturally into oblivion. Randolph foresaw that the English abolitionist movement would spread to America—as, of course, it did by the time of Van Buren's administration. The states must be awakened to the danger and must begin to meet it at once. "But, no, sir, the politico-religious quack, like the quack in medicine, and in every-thing else, will hear of nothing but his nostrum—all is to be forced—nothing can be trusted to time, or to nature." In the

---

[36] *Register of Debates* (19th Cong., 1st sess.), pp. 117–18.

North, slavery already had run its course; it was senescent in Maryland, sick in Virginia's meadow and grain country (where no staple crop made slavery necessary or profitable). and doomed to decay with the lapse of time, elsewhere. Just as freeborn Englishmen's ancestors once were serfs, just as the serfs of Russia and Poland were even now going through the transition to liberty, so would the operation of natural economic causes bring about the emancipation of American negroes.

> And shall we be made to suffer shipwreck, we of the South, in steering our bark through this *Euripus,* by the madness of our pilot and our own folly—steering between this Scylla and the Charybdis (not of the Bahama passage) but of the imprescriptible rights of kings (*jure divino*) on the one hand, and the imprescriptible rights of negro slaves on the other? Is there no medium? . . . I am contented to act the part of Cassandra, to lift up my voice, whether it will be heeded, or heard only to be disregarded, until too late.[37]

This was Randolph's last important congressional speech on the question of slavery—and his greatest. Langdon Cheves was to quote from it at the Nashville Convention in 1850.

That Randolph was genuinely alarmed at the danger of servile uprisings as a result of Latin American influence is shown by a letter to William Leigh, in which he wrote of the Panama Mission scheme, "If the states and people of the Union can 'go' this, I predict the most awful consequences to the happiness of the country, and the security especially of the southern and southwestern states."[38] It seems equally

---

[37] *Ibid.,* pp. 130–31.
[38] Randolph to Leigh, April 3, 1826 (copy in Randolph Letters, University of North Carolina).

true, however, that he used the Panama question as an anvil on which to forge his weapons for use in the debates over constitutional construction and political isolation.

The Panama Mission proposal came to nothing, however; two years later Randolph left Congress forever, his hopes at least partially satisfied by the election of Jackson, and, after attending the Virginia Constitutional Convention, went to Russia as American minister. Augustus Foster, the British diplomat, thought Randolph "would have made an excellent Russian nobleman," and asserted that Randolph told him "slaves were necessary to form a gentleman."[39] Whatever the measure of accuracy in Foster's statements, the master of Roanoke, in defending the right of the South to settle her own problems, had not lost his old antipathy toward human bondage. In the year of the Panama debate, *Niles' Register* reported that Randolph declared: "I have no hesitation in saying slavery is a curse to the master. I have been held up, as any man will be, who speaks his mind fairly and boldly, as a blackish sort of a white and a whitish sort of a black—as an advocate for slavery in the abstract."[40] He told Josiah Quincy the younger that the greatest orator he had ever heard was a woman. "She was a slave. She was a mother, and her rostrum was the auction block." But, he added to Quincy, "we must concern ourselves with what is, and slavery exists. We must preserve the rights of the states, as guaranteed by the Constitution, or the negroes are at our throats. The question of slavery, as it is called, is to us a question of life and death. . . . You will find no instance in history

---

[39] Foster to Josiah Quincy, July 18, 1839 (Edmund Quincy, *Life of Josiah Quincy,* pp. 462–63).

[40] *Niles' Register,* VI (3d ser.), 453.

where two distinct races have occupied the soil except in the relation of master and slave."[41]

These latter remarks are as good a summary of Randolph's views as can be found. To slavery he was opposed on principle all his life; but he saw it as a problem almost insoluble in the South, and he prepared, with increasing sternness, to wall it away from external interference. As he told the Virginia Convention, in 1829: "I have nothing to do with the consciences of men. The abolitionist is as free to hold his opinions as I am to hold mine—I do not find fault with him. I impute no demerit to him for them. But I will never suffer him to put a torch to my property, that he may slake it in the blood of all that are dear to me. I will arrest his hand if I can—by reason if I can—but if not, by force."[42]

In his last years this defensive policy led Randolph into expressions of intolerance on the subject foreign to his nature, and which would well serve those who seek to find in slavery the cause of the decline of liberalism in the South. This attitude of the last months of his life came, indeed, at a time when he was insane, according to the judgment of a court after his death; yet it is difficult to see in Randolph's insanity, here, anything but an exaggeration, provoked by tormenting disease and disappointment, of the conclusions toward which the southern mind was moving. Even in his madness, Randolph was prophetic of changing times and ways. One fearful slave rising had occurred during the inception of his career—Gabriel's revolt; another marked his last decline—Nat Turner's insurrection. To the debates in the Virginia legislature upon the question of gradual emanci-

[41] Josiah Quincy, *op. cit.*, pp. 212–13.
[42] *Proceedings and Debates of the Virginia State Convention*, p. 838.

pation of the slaves, which followed the suppression of the
Southampton rising, Randolph gave no encouragement;
indeed, if we consider him to have been sane at the time, he
would have taken drastic action to prevent any discussion of
such a subject. Bolling told the legislature, in December
1831: "Every intelligent individual admits that slavery is
the most pernicious of all the evils with which the body politic can be afflicted. By none is this position denied, if we except the erratic John Randolph, who goes about like a
troubled spirit, malignantly assaulting every individual
against whom his spleen is excited." Only a few months before his death, Randolph, very much indeed like a troubled
spirit, made his last speech to his constituents, at Charlotte
Court House; he advocated the cause of South Carolina; he
denounced the North, and grew angry at the fact that not
long before a black preacher had spoken in a meetinghouse
in Charlotte, and warned of the dangers such racial equality
brought with it; he then referred to the late insurrection and
the debates in the legislature:

> I am no prophet, but I then predicted the insurrection. The
> insurrection came; was ever such a panic? Dismay was spread
> throughout the country. I despised it when it was here. Look
> at the conduct of our last General Assembly. The speeches that
> were made there were little dreamed of. What kind of doctrine
> was preached on the floor of the House of Burgesses? If I had
> been there I should have moved that the first orator who took
> the liberty to advance that doctrine, should be arrested and
> prosecuted by the state's attorney.[43]

One might doubt the accuracy of the report of this speech,
recorded only fragmentarily, were it not for a letter, scrawled

---

[43] Bouldin, *op. cit.*, pp. 189–90.

in a feeble hand, which was written by Randolph nearly a year before he made this last address. It was the product of a dying man, provoked to an expression of passion by the course of the North and the centralizers; but it cannot be considered the letter of a man politically insane, for it recommended what was to be the sober policy of later southerners. There must be drudges in every state of society, Randolph wrote: "Take your choice of slaves or *nominal* free men. . . . There is no equality that a liberal spirit will brook that is not composed of men equal to each other because elevated on the pedestal of slavery, or as rich capitalists, peers." Before the War of Independence, Virginia flourished, though her proportion of negroes was much larger than at present. Virginia had *gentlemen*, then; now she would lack the spirit to oppose Great Britain in similar circumstances.

> I look for civil war. You may live to see Winchester and Richmond in two different states. All south of the river will join S. Carolina and if the Rope of Sand miscalled the fedl. govt. does not take Cuba somebody else will do it. We have no choice. If England gets Havana we are ruined. We *must and will* have it and then is vent for all our now unprofitable slaves. It will be a noble empire from Rappahannock to St. Jago de Cuba. Having Havana and the Bay of Tampa, we can throttle the Mississippi and give law to the West.[44]

Here is the dream of William Walker forecast. The next day Randolph wrote to President Jackson in similar vein; to the very President of the United States he recommended immediate secession:

> Let the fools and knaves in the two Houses of Congress disband and then strike at Cuba. It will give vent and profit-

---

[44] Randolph to William Wallace, March 17, 1832 (Randolph MSS, Duke University).

able employment for all our now burdensome slaves. It will strengthen the *great slaveholding interest*. We shall have at least every thing south of James River with the naval depot at Norfolk. I say therefore, with Earl Grey, if the struggle does begin as I happen to know it will unless you avert it by a prompt redress of our intolerable wrongs, "I shall stand by my order." It is slavery versus antislavery; and if the fanatics and fools in England drive matters over hard with Jamaica, she will be glad to throw herself under our protection. With the Havana and the Bay of Tampa, the only port in the Gulf capable of receiving a first rate line of Battle Ship, we have a slip-knot around the throat of the Mississippi and we can strangle the commerce of the *"free* states" northwest of the river Ohio, if those states give us any annoyance. . . .

Nations, like men, can be governed only by *Interest;* and the slave interest has the knife at its throat in the hands of fanatics and rogues and fools and we *must* and *shall* and *will* defend ourselves. . . . Everything south of Ohio, except perhaps Kentucky and the Western District of Virginia, must be with us. With this noble country and Cuba, where we can make a hogshead of sugar as easily as a pound can be grown on the Mississippi or in Florida, we shall have a vast empire capable of indefinite improvement and of supporting easily forty millions of people.[45]

The opinions of the *ami des noirs* in his last days, these. They might not have been his expressions had he been fully rational during those final months, but they indicate the way his thought was turning. Beverley Tucker, his half-brother and disciple, was to become one of the most ardent advocates of slavery; Calhoun, who listened to Randolph's Panama Mission speech, soon was to declare himself a supporter of the peculiar institution; and in Polk's administration a be-

---

[45] Randolph to Jackson, March 27, 1832 (*Correspondence of Jackson,* IV, 421–22).

ginning was to be made in the contemplated program of expanding southward and westward the domain of slavery. The growing wrath of the debate on slavery had driven even the consistent Randolph into the position of advocating what he abhorred.

3

One might expect of a statesman like Randolph, who was personally opposed to slavery but politically committed to the defense of the institution from external meddling, that he would seek an internal remedy. True, Jefferson and Mason, though they disapproved of bondage, did little enough to alter matters; and Randolph was too deeply involved in the attack on the centralizers and his own concerns to take much part in Virginian politics, but he was a member of the English society for suppression of the slave trade and for a time gave encouragement to the Colonization Society, as did John Taylor.[46] But he, like Taylor, seems to have hoped only for amelioration of the evil, not for its extirpation; and, with the increase of abolitionist activity in the North, he despaired of much improvement, condemning the foreign and domestic abolitionists for their ignorance. The course of his opinions is a gauge of southern reaction against northern radicalism. He was willing to confess to northerners his hatred of slavery, and wrote to Josiah Quincy: "Like you, I feel a veneration for the place of my residence. . . . The curse of slavery, however—an evil daily magnifying, great as it already is—embitters many a moment of the Vir-

---

[46] See John Taylor, *Arator*, p. 55; *Construction Construed*, p. 301.

ginian landholder who is not duller than the clod beneath
his feet."[47]

Before the American abolitionist movement became vigorous, Randolph's letters and remarks in Congress evince an
admiration for Wilberforce and the other English opponents
of the slave trade. "When I think on Wilberforce and his
worthy compeers, I cannot despair. Ten such would have
saved Sodom."[48] In 1816 Randolph addressed a public meeting of the African Colonization Society in Washington, at
which Henry Clay presided, and gave the organization his
mild endorsement; thousands of slaveholders, he said, would
manumit their slaves and, in consequence, of their cares, if a
satisfactory place of refuge for the freedom were provided.[49]
This was the year of Randolph's speech against the District
slave trade, cited previously. Two years later he again condemned that traffic and, indeed, all the abuses of slavery in
a letter to Brockenbrough: "Avarice alone could have produced the slave trade; avarice alone can drive, as it does
drive, this infernal traffic, and the wretched victims of it,
like so many post horses, whipped to death in a mail coach.
Ambition has its reward in the pride, pomp, and circumstance of glorious war; but where are the trophies of avarice?
the handcuff, the manacle, and the bloodstained cowhide?
What man is worse received in society for being a hard
master?"[50]

But Randolph grew cool toward projects for improving
the lot of the black as the North grew warm in the black's

---

[47] Randolph to Quincy, March 22, 1814 (Edmund Quincy, *op. cit.*,
p. 351).
[48] Garland, *op. cit.*, II, 59–60.
[49] *Ibid.*, p. 71.
[50] *Ibid.*, pp. 100–101.

cause and as the Missouri question loomed up. On February 24, 1820, during the time of the first Missouri debate, he wrote to Brockenbrough, "These Yankees have almost reconciled me to negro slavery. They have produced a revulsion even on my mind, what then must the effect be on those who had no scruples on the subject?"[51] All the same, Randolph was not reconciled to slavery, as one learns from the will he had written in 1819 and which he rewrote in 1821 with substantially the same provisions. "I give my slaves," his first paragraph commences, "their freedom, to which my conscience tells me they are justly entitled. It has a long time been a matter of the deepest regret to me, that the circumstances under which I inherited them, and the obstacles thrown in the way by the laws of the land, have prevented my emancipating them in my lifetime, which it is my full intention to do, in case I can accomplish it."[52] Other paragraphs provided for the purchase of land outside Virginia on which to settle the freed slaves and for defraying their initial outlay. To have released his negroes immediately and left them destitute in hostile Virginia—even had not law forbidden such action—would hardly have been kindness.

And as Randolph's general conservatism grew in intensity, so his suspicion of slavery-reform projects increased. As late as 1822 he was recognized abroad as a firm opponent of slavery, and upon his tour of England he spoke at the London meeting of the African Institution, accompanied to the hall by Wilberforce, Lord Calthorpe, Lord Lansdowne, Lord Nugent, and Henry Brougham—strange company for a slaveholder. Brougham praised Randolph's opposition to

---

[51] *Ibid.*, p. 133.
[52] *Ibid.*, pp. 149–50.

the slave trade, and Randolph himself declared, "He was impelled . . . to assure them that all that was exalted in station, in talent and in moral character among his country-men, was, as in England, firmly united for the suppression of this infamous traffic."[53] He continued to maintain an interest in the English movement after his return to America; but, as the course of affairs in the United States began to alter, Randolph broke with his British colleagues and attacked the African Colonization Society. "I am more and more set against all new things," he wrote to Brockenbrough, on January 30, 1826. "I am against all colonization, etc., soci-eties—am for the good old plan of making the negroes *work,* and thereby enabling the master to feed and clothe them well, and take care of them in sickness and old age."[54]

During the next month Randolph delivered the Panama Mission speech, in which he referred to the English reform-ers and the Colonization Society. They had first commenced as men professing to have no object but the abolition of the slave trade; by degrees, however, they had revealed another object, the doctrinaire abolition of slavery itself, regardless of circumstances and consequences. "I could name illustrious names that are laboring under delusion as strong as that which led away the French Convention, when they thought they were establishing liberty, equality, and fraternity, on a foundation slippery and red with human blood and judicial murder."[55] They should not be permitted to make the south-ern states another Haiti. Freedom could not be granted

---

[53] See the *Richmond Enquirer,* July 2 and July 5, 1822; also *Niles' Register,* I (2d ser.), 327.

[54] Garland, *op. cit.,* II, 193.

[55] *Register of Debates* (19th Cong., 1st sess.), p. 117.

immediately and unconditionally to the negroes without terrible social consequences, equally injurious to either race; an ignorant, debased, and impoverished mass of people, deprived of the authority to which they had always looked for guidance, would ruin themselves and their former masters. Randolph may somewhat have exaggerated the violence of the probable consequences of general emancipation, as did almost all southerners; but the lamentable economic and social condition of most of the South ever since 1865 and the unhappy status of the negro throughout America for the last century are considerable vindication of Randolph's warnings against a hasty and indiscriminate application of positive law to a great social evil which could not be cured by mere legislation. Randolph and most later southern leaders —Rhett, for instance—seemed to have expected a deadly social or servile war in consequence of compulsory emancipation; and this, of course, never took place between southern whites and blacks; but certainly the arbitrary forcing of a "solution" upon the South, after 1865, has produced violence, evasion, and economic vexations that do incalculable harm to southern society and character.

"Without meaning to say a word, at this time, against the society, as an experiment, I must say it has failed; and, so far as it has done any thing, it has done mischief instead of good." With these words, Randolph of Roanoke severed his connection with the humanitarian societies. Their visionary solution could not be his. He had analyzed the problem of slavery and had offered what, perhaps, was the only satisfactory answer—to let time have its way. He anticipated Calhoun in arguing that two races cannot live together on equal terms; and our age has yet to solve that conundrum. He saw that foreign colonization of freed blacks could not be even a palliative and perceived the only immediate hope for improving the condition of negroes in amicable relations and joint endeavor by master and slave. Northern agitation made Randolph hate the abolitionist, but it never made him hate the black. Ultimately, Randolph declared, only the erasing force of time could moderate the evil; economic change would render slavery unprofitable anywhere in the South and, consequently, impossible to continue. Few men in the decades before the Civil War admitted the truth of that analysis, but its accuracy would be upheld by a great many modern students of history and political economy. Whether Randolph could ever have brought himself to approve of that inevitable solution is hard to determine; he hated bondage, but the old Virginian society he loved had many of its roots in servitude. He compared the gradual process of emancipation that would come to the gradual rise from serfdom to liberty in England; but he hardly would have approved of the racial intermingling which should accompany the parallel, although Randolph did not emphasize the racial inferiority of the African as Calhoun and his contemporaries were to do. This appeared to Randolph to be time's untying of the knot of slavery—unless fanaticism should sever it in Gordian fashion, the threat against which he warned the South.

Staving off that threat of interference from the North was too much even for the genius of Randolph. Dying, he stood by his libertarian principles, and with almost his last words confirmed his grant of freedom and land to his "poor slaves." It must have given him grim satisfaction that he, the fierce defender of the slave states, should thus accomplish what the egalitarian Jefferson could not. "I always have believed that St. Thomas of Cantingbury's jewels were Bristol stones

—in other words, that he was insolvent," he had written to Brockenbrough, years before. "What else could be expected from his gimcracks and crackbrained notions and 'improvements'?"

He died, and his freed blacks were sent to their lands in Ohio; there the people of an abolitionist state met them with violence and drove them from the farms the southern champion had purchased for them. The bitter humor of John Randolph would have been required to deal properly with this irony; and perhaps even his wit would have proved inadequate before the terrible solemnity that was the question of human bondage.

Chapter Seven

Change Is Not Reform

1

A gloomy statesman generally has been an anomaly in these United States. Similarly, truly conservative statesmen—leaders whose chief desire is the preservation of the ancient values of society—have been rare here; often men called conservatives have been eager for alteration of a nature calculated to encourage a very different kind of society—Hamilton most conspicuous among them. Professed devotion to the cause of undefined progress and innovation has been virtually a prerequisite for political advancement in this land of territorial and economic expansion. Clay, with his American system; Webster, with his sonorous nationalism—such names have lived. Calhoun, true enough, was both conservative and somber, but most men of a brooding character who obtained a temporary success in their day are almost forgotten now—witness Fisher Ames. John Randolph is one of the few conservative leaders this age has remembered, but he survives in the popular mind more for his eccentricities than for his statesmanship.

The idea of progress has so permeated modern American thought that one sometimes has difficulty convincing professors of history and politics that Randolph was a statesman at all. They ask, perhaps, that you give them an instance of some great constitutional change or social innovation which Randolph promoted; for, in their consciousness, "statesmanship" has come to imply political surgery, cutting at the organic structure of society. But Edmund Burke describes the statesman as possessing "a disposition to preserve and an ability to reform": the former talent takes precedence of the latter. This disposition to preserve was the ruling passion of Randolph's character. And his attempted reforms, his attacks upon political corruption, legislation for special interests, and the new industrial power, were all calculated to defend old ways against an ugly new order. Many a speech and phrase of Randolph's have a modern ring—not only by reason of the acuteness of his thought but for the clarity of his language, since he despised the floridity which even then was engulfing American oratory. But nothing of his has greater meaning for us than his remarks upon permanence and innovation, old against new. The concept of progress was absent from Randolph's political thought; he stood fast against change in federal and state constitutions, dreaded the West, and lamented the decay of the times and the men.

Randolph said at the Virginia Convention, "This is a cardinal principle, that should govern all statesmen—never, without the strongest necessity, to disturb that which is at rest."[1] Probably no man ever has expressed more succinctly the conservative instinct. He spoke thus at the end of his life, but since the inception of his political career, almost his every action had found its motive in that thought. His most thorough and eloquent exposition of this idea came in 1829.

The origins of Randolph's conservatism can no more be

---

[1] *Proceedings and Debates of the Virginia State Convention,* p. 802.

determined precisely than can the prejudices of most men. His congenital antipathy toward cant had a part; the accident of birth which made him a great landholder had a part; but most important, probably, was Randolph's love for the life of old Virginia—the Virginia which had begun to fade away in Randolph's youth. That life must be protected and preserved, he declared; it was the best state of society he could see possible for Virginia and the nation, and he scoffed at striving for impossible perfection. His poetic imagination, whch overleaped the obstacles ordinary politicians encountered, saw clearly the relation between political cause and social consequence: he knew that the life for which he struggled could not endure in an industrial civilization or in an egalitarian political system.

Yet Jefferson, too, was one of the planter-statesmen; and the liberalism of his mind contrasts most remarkably with the conservatism of Randolph's, the optimism of Monticello with the gloom of Roanoke. To Jefferson, John Adams wrote: "Your taste is judicious in liking better the dreams of the future than the history of the past."[2] For Randolph, future was gray and the past resplendent. What accounts for this divergence of opinion? The difference between their ideals of the agricultural life had its share; Randolph's admiration of Burke contrasted with Jefferson's allegiance to the tradition of Locke; and, besides, perhaps Randolph, defeated, had not Jefferson's illusions. That persistent hopefulness of Jefferson's, that reluctance to adhere to any rigid standard, that very liberalism—willingness to experiment— of the author of the Declaration, made it difficult for him to accept the logic which Randolph expounded. Acceptance

---

[2] *Works of John Adams*, X, 226.

would have meant a partial sacrifice of the democratic principle, and that Jefferson could not have endured. Jefferson
may have been the wiser in that he changed with times and
saved at least a part of his American dream; but Randolph
saw the issue bitterly clear, and he, who had expressed his
wish to die like a gamecock in the pit, would yield to no man
and no force.

2

Randolph the conservative statesman has three aspects:
as a critic of men and manners; as an opponent of expansion; and as a foe of constitutional change. Randolph's
significant observation as early as 1800, "I have a respect
for all that is antique (with a few important exceptions),"
hinted that what was for most Americans the age of public
infancy was for Randolph the age of public decay; the "few
exceptions" soon vanished from his system. America had
no harsher critic of her failings.

Some may ascribe Randolph's despair to the irritations of
his mental and physical constitution; but the matter seems
to go far deeper than that, for he was joined in many of his
complaints by men whose health was uninjured and whose
minds always were lucid—Nathaniel Macon for one, John
Brockenbrough for another. Randolph spoke of the decline
of morality in public affairs; and there was such decadence,
perhaps inevitable as the enthusiasms of the Revolutionary
era faded and as an expanding economy offered prizes to
the unscrupulous. He described the decay of old Virginia—
his *country,* he said—and he was accurate, for socially and
economically Virginia did decay from the inception of the
Jeffersonian embargo onward, and the Revolution had

seriously weakened the planter of the old sort. Perhaps it is with Randolph that we discern the beginning of the tendency, later so general in the South even before the Civil War, to look back to a happier past.

The tongue of the Southside orator was terrible to malefactors, particularly to the Yazoo men; it could prevent, for a space, the rewarding of guilt; but it could not change the time. Randolph might be called St. Michael, but though he possessed the archangel's wrath, he lacked his sword.

One observes in Randolph's reflections a deep discontent with the nation even during the first administration of Jefferson; and after he had broken with Jefferson's party upon the decency of the Yazoo affair, the morality of the abortive purchase of Florida, and the costly embargo—all, in part, questions of political conservatism against the spirit of the age— his disgust became despair. To George Hay he wrote, early in 1806: "The old Republican party is already ruined, past redemption. New men and new passions are the order of the day—except such of the first as have sunk into time servers, usurers, and money changers."[3]

And the country, too, was declining, said Randolph; his pathetic observations upon the decline of his Virginia commenced with the adoption of the embargo and were intensified by the ruinous effects of the War of 1812. To Josiah Quincy he wrote in March, 1814, that Tidewater Virginia was one desolate expanse of dismantled houses, ruinous churches, abandoned fields, mournful evergreens replacing the prosperous old countryside. The old families were gone, too, and their place taken by "the rich vulgar," sprung up

---

[3] Randolph to Hay, January 6, 1806 (Randolph Letters, University of North Carolina).

from commerce and war profits. "These fellows will 'never
get rid of Blackfriars'; and they make up in ostentation for
their other deficiencies, of which they are always uncon-
scious and sometimes ashamed."[4]

Here was the old Virginia planter with a vengeance, in
high disdain for trade. An even more melancholy letter was
sent to Quincy on July 1. Whatever prosperity remained in
Virginia, Randolph observed, had retreated west of Petersburg, Richmond, and Alexandria, and east of the mountains;
the West was a wilderness, the Tidewater nearly deserted,
though so well situated for commerce. Deer and wild turkeys
had become more plentiful near Williamsburg than in Kentucky; bears and panthers had reappeared in the neighborhood of the Dragon and Dismal swamps. He looked back
with regret to the Old Dominion:

> Before the Revolution the lower country of Virginia, pierced
> for more than a hundred miles from the seaboard by numerous
> bold and navigable rivers, was inhabited by a race of planters,
> of England descent, who dwelt on their principal estates on the
> borders of those noble streams. The proprietors were generally
> well educated, some of them at the best schools of the mother
> country, the rest at William and Mary, then a seminary of *learn-
> ing,* under able classical masters. Their habitations and establish-
> ments, for the most part spacious and costly, in some instances
> displayed taste and elegance. They were the seats of hospitality.
> The possessors were gentlemen—better-bred men were not to
> be found in the British dominions. As yet party spirit was not.
> This fruitful source of mischief had not then poisoned society.
> Every door was open to those who maintained the appearance of
> gentlemen. Each planter might be said, almost without exagger-
> ation, to have a harbor at his door. . . .
> Free living, the war, docking entails (by one sweeping act of

---

[4] Randolph to Quincy, March 22, 1814 (Edmund Quincy, *Life of Josiah
Quincy,* p. 351).

Assembly), but chiefly the statute of distributions, undermined these old establishments. Bad agriculture, too, contributed its share. The soil of the country in question, except on the margin of the rivers, where it *was* excellent, is (originally) a light, generous loam upon a sand; once exhausted, it is *dead*. . . . The tide swamps—a mine of wealth in South Carolina—here produce only miasma. You will find some good thoughts on this head, and on the decay of our agriculture generally, in our friend J. T.'s whimsical but sensible work *Arator*.

Unlike you, we had a *church* to pull down, and its destruction contributed to swell the general ruin. The temples of the living God were abandoned, the *glebe* sold, the University pillaged. The old mansions, where they have been spared by fire (the consequence of the poverty and carelessness of their present tenants), are fast falling to decay; the families, with a few exceptions, dispersed from St. Mary's to St. Louis; such as remain here sunk into obscurity. They whose fathers rode in coaches and drank the choicest wines now ride on saddlebags, and drink grog, when they can get it. What enterprise or capital there was in the country retired westward. . . .[5]

For Randolph, the forces behind this decay were in part the irresistible strength of time and nature, in part the failure of the men of his day, and in part the result of restrictive commercial policies enacted by Congress. He fought hard against all three. The next year, Randolph admitted gloomily of Virginia: "We are not only centuries behind our northern neighbors, but at least forty years behind ourselves."[6]

The nation was censured even more severely by Randolph. Of his frequent railings against the degeneracy of the time, perhaps the best is contained in his speech against the Bank bill, in 1816. "We deceive ourselves; we are almost in the day of Sulla and Marius; yes, we have almost got

[5] *Ibid.*, pp. 353–55.

[6] Randolph to James M. Garnett, February 10, 1815 (copy in Randolph Papers, Virginia State Library).

down to the times of Jugurtha." The spirit of avarice was
corrupting the whole American people, so that "a man
might as well go to Constantinople to preach against Christianity, as to get up here and preach against the Banks." He
lamented that restless covetousness which Tocqueville
found so strong a decade and a half later:

> The evil of the times is a spirit engendered in this republic,
> fatal to the republican principles—fatal to republican virtue: a
> spirit to live by any means but those of honest industry; a spirit
> of profusion: in other words, the spirit of Catiline himself—*alieni
> avidus sui profusus*—a spirit of expediency, not only in public
> but in private life; the system of Didler in the farce—living any
> way and well; wearing an expensive coat, and drinking the finest
> wines, at any body's expense. . . . If we mean to transmit our
> institutions unimpaired to posterity; if some, now living, wish
> to continue to live under the same institutions by which they
> are now ruled—and with all its evils, real or imaginary, I pre-
> sume no man will question that we live under the easiest govern-
> ment on the globe—we must put bounds to the spirit which
> seeks wealth by every path but the plain and regular path of
> honest industry and honest fame.[7]

In this vein Randolph steadily denounced the deterioration of American character, especially in congressmen. Both
the House and the Senate, he wrote to Gilmer, in 1821,
"abound in men not merely without cultivation (that was to
be looked for), but in men of mean understandings, and
meaner principles and manners."[8] These were not merely the
complaints of a dreamer of ideal political purity, for even in
his hopeful youth Randolph had recognized the limitations
of men and governments. Party and faction, for instance,

---

[7] Hugh Garland, *Randolph of Roanoke,* II, 80–81.
[8] Richard B. Davis, *Francis Walker Gilmer,* p. 176.

cannot be eliminated in any society, as he wrote to Monroe in 1803: "We rail at faction without reflecting that the remedy which, alone, can remove her, is worse than the disease. I speak of forms; for madmen alone can expect to see a whole nation deterred from intrigue and calumny by mere moral considerations. Let us not, then, be so childish as to expect from government effects utterly inconsistent with it."[9] And the next year he told Tazewell that "cabal is the necessary effect of freedom. Where men are left free to act, we must calculate on their being governed by their interests and passions."[10] This is very like Burke. Character, said Randolph, was giving way because the simple society which had produced the grand old Virginian and American character was undermined by economic alteration and governmental tinkering. "But I am becoming censorious—and how can I help it, in this canting and speaking age, where the very children are made to cry or laugh as a well-drilled recruit shoulders or grounds his firelock."[11]

The white population of Virginia, the old amusements and holidays, the very inns, were sinking into a listless decrepitude, Randolph wrote to Brokenbrough, near the end of his life:

> On my road to Buckingham, I passed a night in Farmville, in an apartment which in England they would not have thought fit for my servant; nor on the Continent did he ever occupy so mean a one. Wherever I stop, it is the same—walls black and filthy—bed and furniture sordid—furniture scanty and mean,

---

[9] Randolph to Monroe, June 15, 1803 (copy in Randolph Papers, Virginia State Library).

[10] Randolph to Tazewell, April 21, 1804 (copy in Randolph Papers, Virginia State Library).

[11] Garland, *op. cit.*, II, 274.

generally broken—no mirror—no fire-irons—in short, dirt and discomfort universally prevail, and in most private houses the matter is not mended. . . . The old gentry are gone and the *nouveaux riche,* where they have the inclination, do not know how to live. . . . Poverty stalking through the land, while we are engaged in political metaphysics, and, amidst our filth and vermin, like the Spaniard and Portuguese, look down with contempt on other nations, England and France especially. We hug our lousy cloaks around us, take another *chaw of tub-backer,* float the room with nastiness, or ruin the grate and fire-irons, where they happen to be rusty, and try conclusions upon constitutional points.[12]

Neglecting the pleasures of simplicity and the satisfactions which honest work brings, the Americans were corrupted by a passion for tinkering with politics and the taxing power, Randolph often repeated. "It won't do for a man, who wishes to indulge in dreams of human dignity and worth, to pass thirty years in public life. . . . The country is ruined past redemption; it is ruined in the spirit and character of the people."[13] He told Jackson that he much preferred the permanence of English institutions to those of America, "where all is ceaseless and senseless change."[14] "In truth, we are a fussical and fudgical people. We do stand in need of 'internal improvement'—beginning in our own bosoms, extending to our families and plantations, or whatever our occupation may be; and the man that stays at home and minds his own business, is the one that is doing all that can be done *(rebus existentibus)* to mitigate the evils of the times."[15]

---

[12] Randolph to Brockenbrough, November 15, 1831 (*ibid.,* p. 345).

[13] Randolph to Brockenbrough, January 12, 1829 (*ibid.,* p. 317).

[14] *Correspondence of Jackson,* IV, 428.

[15] Randolph to Brockenbrough, August 10, 1826 (Garland, *op. cit.,* II, 309).

So much for Randolph's verdict upon American instability. He was one of the few statesmen who have been hostile critics of their whole society and yet have managed to
retain a considerable political influence. Very probably John
Randolph of Roanoke would have been a critic of any
society in which he found himself; but the bedraggled egalitarianism of early nineteenth-century America drove him
close to fury. He perceived in his day that corruption and
perversion of republican institutions to private advantage
which ever since have been so lamentably conspicuous a
feature in our governmental system. He saw, clearly, the
doom of his Virginia, and the causes of that doom. Perhaps
he was wiser than Jefferson in his view of the laws of descent;
for if Jefferson expected the abolition of entail to bring
about the predominance of prosperous yeoman farmers in
Virginia, he was disappointed; and Randolph discerned in
that act, with truth, the ruin of many an old Virginian
family. Randolph's analysis of the consequences of the
American laws of inheritance is strikingly similar to that
made by the political sagacity of Tocqueville. Of men and
morals in his age, Randolph held an opinion thoroughly
contemptuous; probably the sight of humanity in industrialized and standardized America, a century and a half
later, would have left even Randolph speechless. Toward
the end, he felt sure that what Tocqueville was to call
"democratic despotism," the triumph of dull and intolerant
mediocrity, could hardly be averted; one could not bind
future generations, and he told Brockenbrough:

> Of all the follies that man is prone to, that of thinking he can
> regulate the conduct of others, is the most inveterate and pre-
> posterous. . . . What has become of all the countless genera-
> tions that have preceded us? Just what will become of us, and
> of our successors. Each will follow the devices and desires of its

own heart, and very reasonably expect that its descendants will
not, but will do, like good boys and girls, as they are bid. . . .
If ever I undertake to educate, or regulate any matter, it shall
be a thing that cannot talk. I have been a Quixote in this matter,
and well have I been rewarded—as well as the woeful Knight
among the galley slaves in the Brown mountain.[16]

3

Westward expansion always has been too popular a subject in America for many congressmen to offer opposition
to the program. The Federalists and their inheritors, indeed,
sometimes stood against western enthusiasm, avowedly
or covertly; but a Republican planter, John Randolph, declared unequivocally that the West was a curse to the Union,
not a blessing, and opposed the admission of any new
states. This is the second principal distinction of Randolph
as the champion of permanence against change.

It may seem strange that an advocate of the agricultural
interest, like Randolph, should be foremost in opposition to
the pioneer communities beyond the mountains; but his motives were numerous and weighty. Although the West was at
first agricultural, it had no desire to remain in that condition
and was hardly second to the manufacturing interests of the
Middle Atlantic States in the demand for stimulation of domestic industries. Then, too, the West was the home of belligerent nationalism; thence came most of the War Hawks,
"the Grundys, Clays, and Seavers," that Randolph hated.[17]
Moreover, the West was the seat of radical egalitarianism,
and the western state constitutions were anathema to Ran-

---

[16] Randolph to Brockenbrough, December 15, 1827 (*ibid.*, p. 295).
[17] See J. W. Pratt, *Expansionists of 1812*, p. 147.

dolph. But most important was the fact that Randolph knew old constitutions and old ways could not survive in a vast federated—or centralized—empire stretching from Atlantic to Pacific; aside from the physical obstacles to true federal union, the Western states, with their arbitrarily determined boundaries, had not the tradition of local rights and local distinctiveness—the spirit of particularism—which made the old Union in truth the confederacy Randolph called it. Expansion meant nationalism or centralism and destruction of the confederate spirit. The interests of the West were opposed to those of the East, said Randolph, and their provinces would come to govern them. Randolph was a sectionalist or regionalist only out of political necessity and had little more love for sectional unity than for national unity; but the rise of the West was a blow at "the good old thirteen United States" of Randolph's phrase; and Randolph set his face against it.

Yet it was the western question which led Randolph into the only act of his political career which his hostile critics may with some justice term inconsistency: he was the champion, in the House, of Jefferson's Louisiana Purchase, and he defended both the expediency and the constitutionality of that measure. This was less an inconsistency than that on the tariff question charged against Calhoun, or that on the Bank question charged against Clay. Randolph had not then broken with the Jeffersonian party; the danger of western domination of national policies was not then apparent; the possibility of general loose constitutional construction by the Republicans had not then appeared, and Randolph seems to have stood for the purchase more on the ground that it would remove a dangerous foreign neighbor—a part of his program of American aloofness from foreign quarrels—than as a matter of aggrandizement and manifest destiny.[18] Randolph never specifically recanted his declaration of the constitutionality of the purchase, but he freely admitted his error in recommending congressional approval of Jefferson's action, for, as he said later, that purchase had been a severe blow at constitutional precedent and at the older states of the Union. As early as 1805 Randolph proclaimed that, because of the precedent it had established, "the Louisiana purchase was the greatest curse that ever befell us."[19] His war against the West had commenced. Seventeen years later he said of the purchase:

> He remembered well the predictions, the sad vaticinations, on the acquisition of Louisiana. . . . We were then called on, Mr. Randolph continued, by some of the very men who had a hand in framing the Constitution, and whose wisdom has been so loudly, and not unjustly, applauded, to pause before we signed that treaty, admitting vast regions of country into the Confederation. We were forewarned, but not forearmed, said he, as we are now experiencing—what we are now beginning to experience, I repeat—for we are yet in the green tree; and, when the time comes when the whole country is filled up, if these things are now done in the green tree, what will be done in the dry? I, for one, although forewarned, was not forearmed. If I had been, I have no hesitation in declaring, that I would have said to the imperial Dejanira of modern times—take back your fatal present! I would have staked the free navigation of the Mississippi on the sword, and we must have gained it.[20]

In short, Randolph would have had the nation acquire the commercial advantages of the Mississippi by intimidation or by force, and not have incorporated, in the process, those

---

[18] *Annals of Congress* (8th Cong., 1st sess.), p. 434.

[19] *Ibid.* (9th Cong., 1st sess.), p. 928.

[20] *Ibid.* (17th Cong., 1st sess.), p. 943.

vast areas which were to change the whole character of the United States. Only three years after the purchase, he was speaking contemptuously of the "newfangled country over the Mississippi" and beginning to call Kentucky "the Australia of Virginia." One of his most vigorous statements of his stand is to be found in a letter to that other—and Federalist—champion of the East, Josiah Quincy:

> We are the first people that ever acquired provinces, either by conquest or purchase (Mr. Blackstone says they are the same), not for us to govern but that they might *govern us*—that we might be ruled to our ruin by people bound to us by no common tie of interest or sentiment. But such, whatever may be the incredulity of posterity, is the fact. Match it, if you can, in the savage laws of Lycurgus, or the brutal castes of Hindustan.[21]

The following year, Randolph wrote to Brockenbrough, "Louisiana is not my country. I respect as much the opinions of the people of London as of the western states."[22] And yet Randolph, with his prophet's vision, sensed that the struggle against the West was in vain and said as much to the northerners who, at the time of the Missouri debate, would have sought to exclude that state from the Union:

> I do look with a sentiment I cannot express, said Mr. R.—I look with a sentiment of pity—and that has been said to be nearly allied to love, as I know it to be allied to a very different emotion—I look with pity on those who believe, that, by their feeble efforts in this House, governed by forms and technicalities . . . they can stop the growth of the rising empire in the West. Let gentlemen lay a resolution on the table, let it be engrossed by a fair hand, and do you, Mr. Speaker, sign it, that the waves of the Mississippi shall not seek the ocean, and then send your

---

[21] Randolph to Quincy, October 18, 1813 (Quincy, *op. cit.*, p. 337).
[22] Randolph to Brockenbrough, March 2, 1814 (Garland, *op. cit.*, II, 33).

John Randolph of Roanoke

sergeant-at-arms to carry it into execution, and see whether you can enforce it with all the force, physical and moral, under your control.[23]

All the same, Randolph himself did not vote in favor of the admission of Missouri; although he vehemently opposed the terms proposed for Missouri by the antislavery faction, doubtless he was sorry to see any great new western state enter the Union. "No government, extending from the Atlantic to the Pacific, can be fit to govern me or those whom I represent."[24] So he proclaimed in 1822; and in that same year he pointed out what a danger the West was to the preservation of the Union: the Missouri debate had been only the signpost indicating a series of such perils. He said of Virginia's generous early cession of her lands north of the Ohio to the nation, "By that act, the great river Ohio, in itself a natural limit—that natural limit is made (I speak in the spirit of foresight) the permanent and unfading line of future division, if not in the Government, in the councils, of the Country."[25]

And in his last major congressional speech, that on retrenchment and reform, in 1828, Randolph defended unflinchingly the course of opposition to the West he had long pursued. The new states had been vast deserts, rightfully belonging to the Indians. Although very dense populations, the rabble of great cities, are a terrible danger to good political institutions, barbaric lands scarcely settled are no less dangerous to social tranquillity. Most important of all, this giving inchoate and almost uninhabited regions a voice in

---

[23] *Annals of Congress* (16th Cong., 1st sess.), p. 942.

[24] *Ibid.* (17th Cong., 1st sess.), pp. 819–22.

[25] *Ibid.*, p. 942.

the Senate equal to that of ancient and populous communities, possessed of traditions and property, was political stupidity and injustice:

> I have always said, and shall forever hold it to be the height of injustice (and of folly, too, on the part of the old states) that thirty or forty thousand persons, who so long as they remained in Pennsylvania or Virginia, were represented in the Senate, only as the rest of the Pennsylvanians and Virginians, should, by emigrating to one of the geographical diagrams beyond the Ohio or the Mississippi, acquire, *ipso facto,* an equipollent vote in the other House of Congress with the millions that they left behind at home. In case of the old states, necessity gave this privilege to Rhode Island, etc. . . .
>
> Sir, do not understand me as wishing to establish injurious or degrading distinctions between the old and the new states, to the disadvantage of these last. . . . No, sir, my objection was to the admission of such states (whether south or north of the Ohio, east or west of the Mississippi) into the Union, and by consequence, to a full participation of power in the Senate with the oldest and largest members of the confederacy, before they had acquired a sufficient population that might entitle them to it, and before that population had settled down into that degree of consistency and assimilation which is necessary to the formation of a body politic. . . . If I had been an emigrant myself to one of these new states—and I have near and dear connexions in some of them—I could not have murmured against the denial to forty or fifty thousand new settlers . . . of a voice in the Senate, potential as New York's, with a million and a half of people.[26]

In this defense by a man who boasted of never having voted for the admission of a new state we discern one of Randolph's primary political theories: that governmental questions should be determined not by abstract claims of

---

[26] Powhatan Bouldin, *Home Reminiscences of John Randolph,* pp. 276–78.

natural equality but by enlightened expediency founded upon considerations of practicality and traditional experience. The western regions should not be admitted simply upon their claim to be independent and equal bodies of freemen; they must first show some physical equality, some equality of power, with the older states.

Such was the view Randolph's conservative mind took of the West. Randolph seems not to have hoped to have overcome the West forever but only to have delayed the admission of new states until they could become states in truth. He was not wrong in his analysis of the nature of the West, whether or not one agrees with his conservative opposition. From the West came the radical constitutional ideas which swept back over the eastern region of Virginia in 1829; from the West came nationalism, jingoism, and egalitarianism. Randolph knew what he fought, and, although he failed, he did not relent. He was buried with face to the setting sun, tradition says, so that he might keep his sharp eyes on Henry Clay and the West.[27]

4

In Randolph's short sentence "Change is not reform," spoken at the Virginia Convention of 1829, was epitomized the thought of the great Virginian free lance. Many a man of his day must have thought such a stand inexplicable, even more would think so today; for in the minds of most Americans, "change" has become synonymous with "progress," and progress has become the object of a sort of new deism; whole schools of philosophy and of educational

---

[27] See "Randolph's Grave," *Littell's Living Age*, XI, 195.

thought have accepted mystic "progress" as their only goal, without attempt at definition of terms. But John Randolph of Roanoke had his ideal—the ideal of individual freedom, the freedom he thought best exemplified by the life of old Virginia—too clearly delineated in his imagination for him to be tempted into theories of "progress" and "cooperation for a higher freedom." His contention that change and progress are not one but sometimes mutually exclusive received scant consideration in an American vision of grandeur. He fought all major alterations in federal and state constitutions, not because he thought those constitutions perfect, but because he knew they would be replaced by worse; and no conservative thinker has more cogently expressed his creed than, late in life, did Randolph.

Only once was Randolph the proponent of constitutional change; and that was during the period of the impeachment and trial of Justice Chase in 1805. He recommended, before that unsuccessful prosecution, a constitutional amendment providing for removal of federal judges by vote of Congress, but it never was passed by House or Senate. Randolph spoke contemptuously of the "go-cart of precedent" and held that constitutions faced "amendment or deterioration"[28] then. Unchecked judicial interpretation of the Constitution always was a sore spot with Randolph, for the decisions of his friend John Marshall did more injury to Randolph's Constitution than did Federalist or Republican congresses. But his recommendation of reconsideration of constitutional questions was not to become a permanent part of his thought, since the Old Republicans soon found they had more to lose than to gain by constitutional alteration. Still,

---

[28] *Annals of Congress* (9th Cong., 1st sess.), pp. 500–502.

Randolph did not possess the reverence for the federal Constitution that was John C. Calhoun's; the man who had seen the "poison under the wings" of the federal butterfly thought the Constitution hardly perfect. The preceding disorders, he said, had induced the framers of the Constitution "to have a King Stork substituted for King Log." The American Constitution, he wrote to Quincy, possessed the faults inherent in political systems which are "made" rather than slowly developed; it lacked at once the elasticity and the prescriptive veneration of governmental institutions that grow out of centuries of experience. "I see nothing of this in our system. I perceive only a bundle of theories (bottomed on a utopian ideal of human excellence) and in practice a corruption the most sordid and revolting."[29] This statement of principles is significant of Randolph's affection for English political institutions; but since no other federal constitution was to be had, Randolph became the most able and constant advocate of strict construction of this Constitution.

The American passion for enacting positive law to cover every possible exigency—which, in essence, is a question of constitutional nature—roused Randolph's contempt and despair. He declared himself, like Jefferson, averse to making the extreme medicine of the Constitution our daily food. "We see, about November," he told the House in 1816, "about the time the fog sets in, men enough assembled in the various legislatures, general and state, to make a regiment; then the legislative maggot begins to bite; then exists the rage to make new and repeal old laws. I should not think we would find ourselves at all worse off if no law of a general

---

[29] Randolph to Quincy, October 18, 1813 (Quincy, *op. cit.*, pp. 337–38).

nature had been passed by either general or state governments for ten or twelve years last past."[30] Eight years later
he expressed his futile wish that Congress had done nothing
but talk—or, still better, had slept—for many years previous. "If I could once see a Congress meet and adjourn
without passing any law whatever, I should hail it as one of
the most acceptable of omens."[31]

Of all Randolph's expressions, in Congress, of opposition
to governmental haste and tinkering and innovation, the
best came in a speech of May, 1824:

> In all beneficial changes in the natural world, and the senti-
> ment is illustrated by one of the most beautiful effusions of imagi-
> nation and genius that I ever read—in all those changes, which
> are the work of an all-wise, all-seeing and superintending provi-
> dence, as in the insensible gradation by which the infant but
> expands into manhood, and from manhood to senility; or if you
> will, to caducity itself, you will find imperceptible changes; you
> cannot see the object move, but take your eyes from it for a
> while, and like the index of that clock, you can see that it has
> moved. The old proverb says, God works good, and always by
> degrees. The devil, on the other hand, is bent on mischief, and
> always in a hurry. *He* cannot stay; his object is mischief, which
> can best be effected suddenly, and he must be gone to work
> elsewhere. . . .[32]

It was at the Virginia Convention, in 1829, that the dying
Randolph made his most eloquent defiance of the forces of
innovation and experiment. He filled the role which Chancellor Kent played at the similar reforming constitutional
convention in New York. Virginia, by 1829, remained one

---

[30] *Annals of Congress* (14th Cong., 1st sess.), p. 1132.
[31] *Ibid.* (17th Cong., 1st sess.), pp. 820–21.
[32] *Richmond Enquirer,* June 8, 1824.

of the few states which possessed an old-style constitution—
a constitution, that is, with special safeguards for property,
with a limited franchise, with some remnant of the institutions that had been hers in colonial times. Representation in
the legislature was weighted heavily in favor of the old Tidewater counties. Randolph fought hard for the preservation
of the old constitution; he struggled especially for retention
of the county courts, of jury trial, and of freehold suffrage—
all of them old institutions in the English tradition; he endeavored to prevent the insertion of a clause providing for
future amendments, for the old constitution of Virginia, like
North Carolina's, had not flaunted that "grin of death," as
Randolph called it.

In Randolph's first speech at the convention, he defined
the conditions under which he would consider reform ad-
visable; and, analyzing the situation of Virginia, he found
the state constitution in no need of alteration.

> As long as I have had any fixed opinions, I have been in the
> habit of considering the Constitution of Virginia, under which
> I have lived for more than half a century, with all its faults and
> failings, and with all the objections which practical men—not
> theorists and visionary speculators, have urged or can urge
> against it, as the very best constitution; not for Japan; not for
> China; not for New England; or for Old England; but for this,
> our ancient Commonwealth of Virginia.
>
> But, I am not such a bigot as to be unwilling, under any cir-
> cumstances, however imperious, to change the constitution un-
> der which I was born, I may say, certainly under which I was
> brought up, and under which, I had hoped to be carried to my
> grave. My principles on that subject are these: the grievance
> must first be clearly specified, and fully proved; it must be vital,
> or rather, deadly in its effect; its magnitude must be such as will
> justify prudent and reasonable men in taking the always deli-
> cate, often dangerous step, of making innovations in their fun-

damental law; and the remedy proposed must be reasonable and adequate to the end in view. When the grievance shall have been made out, I hold him to be not a loyal subject, but a political bigot, who would refuse to apply the suitable remedy.

But, I will not submit my case to a political physician; come his diploma from whence it may; who would at once prescribe all the medicines in the Pharmacopoeia, not only for the disease I now have, but for all the diseases of every possible kind I might ever have in future. These are my principles, and I am willing to carry them out; for, I will not hold any principles which I may not fairly carry out in practice.

Judge, then, with what surprise and pain, I found that not one department of this government—no, not one—was left untouched by the spirit of innovation (for I cannot call it reform). . . . Many innovations are proposed to be made, without any one practical grievance having been even suggested, much less shown.

I have by experience learned that changes, even in the ordinary law of the land, do not always operate as the drawer of the bill, or the legislative body may have anticipated; and of all things in the world, a government, whether ready made, to suit casual customers, or made to order, is the very last that operates as its framers intended. Governments are like revolutions: you may put them in motion, but I defy you to control them after they are *in* motion. . . .

Mr. Chairman, the wisest thing this body could do, would be to return to the people from whom they came, *re infecta*. I am very willing to lend my aid to any very small and moderate reforms, which I can be made to believe that this our ancient government requires. But, far better would it be that they were never made, and that our constitution remained unchangeable like that of Lycurgus, than that we should break in upon the main pillars of the edifice.[33]

In this speech, of which only a fragment is given here, Randolph's principle of determining particular cases by par-

---

[33] *Proceedings and Debates of the Virginia State Convention,* pp. 313–21.

ticular circumstances, not by abstract laws, is most notice-
able. He spoke in similar vein some time later:

> It has been better said, than I am capable of saying it, that
> the lust of innovation—for it is a lust—that is the proper term
> for an unlawful desire—this lust of innovation—this *rerum no-
> varum lubido*—has been the death of all republics. All men of
> sense, ought to guard and warn their neighbors against it. Sir,
> I have felt deep affliction—mortification—and humiliation, at
> seeing this venerable fabric of our government treated with as
> little ceremony as a mouse in the receiver of a natural philoso-
> pher and experimenter. . . .
>
> Recollect that change is not always amendment. Remember
> that you have to reconcile to new institutions the whole mass of
> those who are contented with what they have, and seek no
> change—and besides these, all the disappointed of the other
> class; and what possible chance is there that your new consti-
> tution can be accepted?[34]

Randolph's grand speech against any provision for future
amendment of the constitution they were framing came on
December 30, 1829. He said, in part:

> I have remarked since the commencement of our deliberations
> —and with no small surprise—a very great anxiety to provide
> for *futurity*. Gentlemen, for example, are not content with any
> present discussion of the constitution, unless we will consent
> to prescribe for all time hereafter. I had always thought him the
> most skillful physician who, when called to a patient, relieved
> him of the existing malady, without undertaking to prescribe
> for such as he might by possibility endure thereafter. . . .
>
> Dr. Franklin, who, in shrewdness, especially in all that related
> to domestic life, was never excelled, used to say, that two mov-
> ings were equal to one fire. So to any people, two constitutions
> are worse than a fire. And gentlemen, as if they were afraid that
> this besetting sin of republican governments, this *rerum no-*

---

[34] *Ibid.*, p. 492.

varum lubido (to use a very homely phrase but one that comes pat to the purpose), this *maggot* of innovation, would cease to bite, are here gravely making provision, that this constitution, which we should consider as a remedy for all the ills of the body politic, may itself be amended or modified at any future time. Sir, I am against any such provision. I should as soon think of introducing into a marriage contract a provision for divorce; and thus poisoning the greatest blessing of mankind and its very source—at its fountain head. He has seen little and has reflected less, who does not know that "necessity" is the great, powerful governing principle of affairs here. Sir, I am not going into that question which puzzled Pandemonium, the question of liberty and necessity: "Free will, fix'd fate, foreknowledge absolute"; but, I do contend, that necessity is one of the principal instruments of all the good that man enjoys.

The happiness of the connubial union itself depends greatly on necessity; and when you touch this, you touch the arch, the key-stone of the arch, on which the happiness and well-being of society is founded. . . .

Sir, what are we about? Have we not been undoing what the wiser heads—I must be permitted to say so—yes, sir, what the wiser heads of our ancestors did more than half a century ago? Can any one believe that we, by any amendments of ours—by any of our scribbling on that parchment—by any amulet—any legerdemain—charm—abracadabra—of ours, can prevent our sons from doing the same thing? that is, from doing as they please, just as we are doing what we please? It is impossible. Who can bind posterity? When I hear gentlemen talk of making a constitution "for all time"—and introducing provisions into it, "for all time"—and yet see men here, that are older than the constitution we are about to destroy . . . it reminds me of the truces and peaces in Europe. They always begin, "In the name of the most holy and undivided Trinity," and go on to declare, "there shall be perfect and perpetual peace and unity between the subject of such and such potentates, for all time to come"— and, in less than seven years, they are at war again. . . .

It would seem as if we were endeavoring (God forbid that I should insinuate that such was the intention of any here) as if we were endeavoring to corrupt the people at the fountainhead. Sir, the great opprobrium of popular government, is its *instability*. It was this which made the people of Anglo-Saxon stock cling with such pertinacity to an independent judiciary, as the only means they could find to resist this vice of popular governments. By such a provision as this, we are now inviting, and in a manner prompting, the people, to be dissatisfied with their government. Sir, there is no need of this. Dissatisfaction will come, soon enough. . . .

Sir, I see no wisdom in making this provision for future changes. You must give governments time to operate on the people, and give the people time to become gradually assimilated to their institutions. Almost any thing is better than this state of perpetual uncertainty. A people may have the best form of government that the wit of man ever devised; and yet, from its uncertainty alone, may, in effect, live under the worse government in the world. Sir, how often must I repeat, that *change* is not *reform*. I am willing that this new constitution shall stand as long as it is possible for it to stand, and that, believe me, is a very short time. Sir, it is vain to deny it. They may say what they please about the old constitution—the defect is not there. It is not in the form of the old edifice, neither in the design nor the execution: it is in the *material;* it is in the people of Virginia. To my knowledge that people are changed from what they have been. The four hundred men who went out to David were *in debt*. The fellow laborers of Catiline were *in debt*. And I defy you to show me a desperately indebted people anywhere, who can bear a regular sober government. I throw the challenge to all who hear me. I say that the character of the good old Virginia planter—the man who owned from five to twenty slaves, or less, who lived by hard work, and who paid his debts, is passed away. A new order of things is come. The period has arrived of living by one's wits—of living by contracting debts that one cannot pay—and above all, of living by office hunting. . . . I say, that in such a state of things, the old constitution was too good for them, they could not bear it. No, sir, they could not bear a freehold suffrage and a property representation. I have always endeavored to do the people justice—but I will not flatter them—I will not pander to their appetite for change. I will not agree to any rule of future apportionment, or to any provision for changes called amendments to the constitution. They who love change—who delight in public confusion—who wish to feed the caldron and make it bubble—may vote if they please for future changes. But by what spell—by what formula are you going to bind all the people to all future time? *Quis custodiet custodes?* The days of Lycurgus are gone by, when he could swear the people not to alter the constitution until he should return—*animo non revertendi.* You may make what entries upon parchment you please. Give me a constitution that will last for half a century—that is all I wish for. No constitution that you can make will last for the one-half of half a century. Sir, I will stake anything short of my salvation, that those who are malcontent now will be more malcontent three years hence than they are at this day. I have no favor for this constitution. I shall vote against its adoption, and I shall advise the people of my district to set their faces—aye—and their shoulders against it. But if we are set to have it—let us not have it with its death warrant in its very face; with the *facies hypocratica*—the Sardonic grin of death upon its countenance.[35]

Randolph's prediction was accurate enough: the new constitution of Virginia endured only from 1830 to 1850, and by 1831 those who had agitated for the new constitution were assailing the document of 1830. Jefferson had argued that each generation must form its own institutions; Randolph recognized that men cannot be prevented from altering what they will in their time, but he deplored this risky power.

A few days later Randolph uttered that remark which is his best expression of the conservative spirit.

Mr. Randolph said, that he should vote against the amendment, and that on a principle which he had learned before he came into public life; and by which he had been governed during the whole course of his life, that it was always unwise—yes—highly unwise, to disturb a thing that was at rest. This was a great cardinal principle that should govern all wise statesmen

---

[35] *Ibid.,* pp. 789–91.

—never without the strongest necessity to disturb that which was at rest.[36]

With this maxim, and with that phrase he so often re-peated at the convention, "Change is not reform," we may leave Randolph. By 1832 he was writing: "The country is ruined past redemption by political and religious factions bidding at the auction of popularity where every thing is *'knocked down'* to the *lowest bidder."*[37] He had fought the good fight for the old ways, but the sands were fast running out, and, as he was dying, so was the old life he loved.

5

A recent writer lists three principal tenets of our demo-cratic creed: belief in a fundamental law (natural-rights theory of the Enlightenment); belief in the freedom of the individual; and belief in the "mission of America."[38] If we are to accept this analysis, we find John Randolph of Roa-noke in agreement with only one of the chief doctrines in the body of American political sentiment—the champion-ship of the rights of the individual. Surely no man could be more jealous of his liberty, more resentful of governmental intrusion upon his privileges, than was the great Southside Virginian: he accepted with all his heart the principle of de-votion to liberty. But he rejected "Rights of Man" theories utterly and took his stand with Burke; he sneered at the "American mission," advocated in his day by his enemies,

---

[36] *Ibid.,* p. 802.

[37] Randolph to William Wallace, March 17, 1832 (Randolph MSS, Duke University).

[38] R. H. Gabriel, *The Course of American Democratic Thought,* p. 12.

Clay, Webster, and John Quincy Adams; he placed his faith in old ways and old Virginia. Randolph was in scant accord with the political tendencies of his time, and those of our age would find still less favor with him. Yet to disagree with *demos* need not be to err; the consequences of such dissent may be unpleasant, but the dissenter can have the truth with him. Certainly Randolph's opinions upon "fundamental law" and "America's mission" have prevailed in the sense that they are widely accepted now by students of politics, who, indeed, sometimes go farther than did Randolph, and declare that the desire for individual liberty, too, is vain— futile in this time of troubles, at least. Randolph, knowing what a world with the characteristics of ours would be like, fought doggedly to stave off its coming.

This, then, was the political thought of John Randolph, greatest of the Old Republicans. He found the basis of authority not in "natural right," not in Nature and Nature's God, but in the Christian concept of ordination and subordination, power balanced by tradition; and he thought that authority best wielded by freeholders. He stood for the liberty of individuals, localities, and states, and strove to maintain the division of power so as to guarantee such liberty; as a part of that endeavor and in accord with his belief that his position was historically sound, he maintained a strict interpretation of the federal Constitution. He, the planter-statesman, saw contentment for man in an agricultural life and fought all policies—the tariff, foreign wars and alliances, special privileges—which endangered that society. He perceived slavery, the greatest problem of his state and section and nation, to be a cancer; but he thought that radical remedies would be worse than the disease. He looked upon innovation as decadence, not progress. Such was his credo; he upheld it with the sternest consistency and devoted his tortured life to a vain battle in its defense.

Whatever the eccentricities of his private character, they did not affect his political beliefs; as Beverley Tucker wrote, "Many of his constituents seemed to think of him as the Muhammadans do of madmen—that in regard to politics he was inspired."[39] Perhaps nothing else in American political philosophy is more brilliant than are Randolph's greatest speeches. "His political teaching never, of course, approached the dizzy mystic heights along which Burke alone could walk in safety," writes Keith Feiling of a great contemporary of Randolph, Canning;[40] and the remark may be applied nearly as well to John Randolph. But Randolph was one of the very few American thinkers to realize that society is more than a contract for mutual convenience and to declare that political constitutions cannot be adjusted like clockwork.

Statecraft is no uniform system; it is, instead, a patchwork concept. There are statesmen whose talent it is to manage, like Walpole; and statesmen whose talent it is to rebuild, like Sully; and statesmen whose talent it is to forge, like Cavour; and statesmen whose talent it is to criticize, like Burke. Randolph of Roanoke stands with the last category, of course; and acute self-criticism not being a virtue conspicuous in America, a man of Randolph's daring and penetration was required for the task of exposing American complacency after 1800. He was the sort of statesman who points out the natural boundaries of the state rather than the sort of states-

---

[39] Nathaniel Beverley Tucker, "An Account of John Randolph," *Historical Magazine*, III, 187—88.

[40] Keith Feiling, *Sketches in Nineteenth Century Biography*, p. 39.

man who is determined to enlarge those frontiers. After 1800 it seemed as if America were wholly convinced of her own omniscience—convinced that change was reform, that majorities were always just, that expansion was necessarily progress, that America could safely disregard the precepts of history and the formulas previously supposed to regulate society. America still believes in these generalizations, for the most part; but that these ideas never have been carried wholly to extremes, that our American complacency is leavened with a tiny, chastening grain of doubt—such limitations upon the reckless self-confidence of the United States are in part the contribution of Randolph and his colleagues.

Randolph's ideas spread throughout the South after 1820. The Missouri question, the tariff of 1824, congressional reapportionment, and presently nullification were the material causes of this alteration of the southern temper, of course, and it is hardly likely that Randolph could have revived the principles of the Old Republicans otherwise. But popular impulses cannot take coherent form without some system of ideas to arrange themselves upon, any more than ideas can achieve political consequences without the matter of popular impulse to sustain them; and Randolph's speeches provided that intellectual frame for southern alarm at the tariff, the slavery question, and consolidation. To Jefferson or John Taylor, with their eighteenth-century egalitarianism, the southerners of this new generation hardly could turn for guidance: the doctrine of majorities and the doctrine of natural equality both worked against the conservation of southern society. John Randolph, on the other hand, had outlined a political theory radically different, based upon the values of continuity and prescription, denying that rights exist in the abstract and that profound problems can be

settled by the application of positive law. As the South became a conscious minority in the nation, southern leaders
began to listen to Randolph with renewed interest, to re-
read his old speeches, and to imitate his uncompromising
defiance.

When one leafs through yellow-old newspapers of the
1820s in the South, or blackens his fingers with the dust that
lies upon the heavy volumes of *The Annals of Congress* and
The Register of Debates, he becomes conscious of this
southern revival of Randolph's influence, particularly after
1824. Resolutions are passed in southern towns and counties commending Randolph as the champion of state rights;
he is quoted increasingly in Congress, as the years pass, and
it is old John Randolph whose words Hayne utters against
Webster in 1830; his ideas and his methods are echoed in
Washington and Richmond and Charleston. Oratory then
retained an influence over American public opinion which,
for the most part, it has since relinquished; and Randolph
became the inspiration of that later school of southern orators whose efforts, all too often, were hardly better than
burlesques of the nervous genius that Randolph possessed.

One indefatigable disseminator of Randolph's principles
was Judge Nathaniel Beverley Tucker, of Missouri and Virginia, professor and novelist and southern sectionalist, Randolph's own half-brother. You see his grave close by the
door of Bruton Parish Church, in Williamsburg; in his day
Tucker was aflame with resentment against the North, a fire
which produced that curious novel *The Partisan Leader*. He
did not let the South forget Randolph.

Other disciples of Randolph had begun as his adversaries
—in particular, Langdon Cheves and John C. Calhoun. The
aged Cheves invoked the shade of John Randolph at the

Nashville Convention of 1850 and in aid of his plea for immediate secession; thus the National Republican of 1811 had become the secessionist of four decades later. Calhoun's case is at once more important and more intricate. In earlier chapters, Calhoun's gradual conversion to Randolph's views has been touched upon. Although Calhoun to the end remained friendly toward American expansion, in almost all other respects he came to share the great Virginian orator's ideas. The tariff of 1824 revealed to Calhoun that nationalism was not synonymous with common interest; but the arguments furnished by Randolph lay ready to his hand, and Randolph's scintillating and discursive eloquence, which Calhoun could not imitate, made clear to the South Carolinian the real nature of that enormous controversy which until then he had discerned only vaguely.

"The man, the force that drove Calhoun into his realizations was none other than John Randolph," writes Calhoun's recent biographer, Margaret Coit. "For with all his vagaries, the Virginian was a realist. As early as 1816, he had seen through the 'tariff humbug,' long before bitter experience had brought a similar comprehension to Calhoun. All the throbbing, storm-tossed issues which were to torment the South and the nation for the next thirty years were passing before Randolph's tortured vision. . . . Calhoun listened."[41] Presently John C. Calhoun commenced that series of tributes to Randolph which runs through his later speeches and papers. In 1826, after Randolph's taunts in the Senate had provoked Clay to call him out—and had produced in consequence one of the most famous duels in American history—Vice-President Calhoun found it ad-

---

[41] Margaret Coit, *John C. Calhoun*, p. 171.

visable to defend in the newspaper his own conduct as
presiding officer of the Senate. "And who is Mr. Randolph?"
he wrote. "Is he or his manners a stranger in our national
councils? For more than a quarter of a century he has been
a member of Congress, and during the whole time his character has remained unchanged. Highly talented, eloquent,
severe, and eccentric; not unfrequently wandering from the
question, but often uttering wisdom worthy of a Bacon, and
wit that would not discredit a Sheridan, every Speaker had
freely indulged him in his peculiar manner, and that without
responsibility or censure."[42] This admiration presently became emulation. And, through Randolph's ideas, the spirit
of Burke entered into Calhoun. So far as we can tell, Calhoun had read little of Burke; his references to the Whig
genius are infrequent; but certainly a considerable part of
that devotion to prudence and expedience, that contempt
for abstract political ideals, and that suspicion of omnipotent majorities which we find in *A Disquisition on Government* seem to echo Burke. That Burke was not much more
widely read, South and North, came to be a great pity.

In April, 1865, John S. Wise, a boy officer who was a
courier from the wreck of the Army of Northern Virginia
to President Jefferson Davis, galloped by the desolate
plantation of Roanoke, " 'Oh, John Randolph, John, John!'
thought I, as I rode by, 'you have gotten some other Johns,
in fact the whole breed of Johnnies, into a peck of trouble
by the governmental notions which you left to them as a
legacy.' "[43] No other man did so much, perhaps, to steel the
resolution of the South. In 1837, replying to Webster, Cal-

---

[42] John C. Calhoun, *Works,* VI, 347.
[43] John S. Wise, *The End of an Era,* p. 441.

houn had observed, "I regard it as one of the wisest maxims in human affairs, that when we see an inevitable evil, . . . not to be resisted, approaching—to make concessions in time, when we can do it with dignity; and not to wait until necessity compels us to act, and when concession, instead of gratitude, will excite contempt. The maxim is not new. I have derived it from the greatest of modern statesmen, Edmund Burke."[44] Calhoun was speaking of the cession of the public lands to the several states, but of course his words apply with remarkable precision to those great issues which provoked the Civil War. That Randolph and Calhoun emulated the fiery determination of Burke more than they emulated his cautious "sounding the lead" is in some degree true; but, in the perspective of history, northern abstract humanitarianism and northern industrial appetites are more guilty than these southerners of contempt for compromise and concession. With all the enduring evils it produced, the Civil War demonstrated at least one truth: that the power of government is not omnicompetent; that the alteration of social institutions is no mere automatic consequence of legislation; and that, when the government transcends certain bounds and threatens great interests and classes, it must be prepared to employ military force. Legislatures have no right to tamper with the delicate social arrangements which only time can properly mend, Randolph and Calhoun declared. When government does usurp such powers, men will resist. The North never quite believed Randolph and Calhoun. The terror of the Civil War, the shameful years that followed—North and South—and much of the present sullen tone of American society are consequences.

---

44 Calhoun, *op. cit.*, II, 649.

The thirty-five years of Randolph's public career were spent in marking out the road which the South was to follow from the time of Jefferson to the time of Lincoln. From the Declaration of Independence to *A Discourse on the Constitution;* from the national democracy of 1800 to the southern nationalism of Yancey and Rhett; from *A Dissertation on Slavery* to Walker's filibusters and bloody Kansas; from the first tariff debate to Edmund Ruffin at his gun—this was to be the path. Had Randolph wholly foreseen the culmination, he might have been appalled, but he would not have flinched. For what else, he would have asked, could his Virginia and the South do? What else could men of honor do? They could not yield, and they could not triumph.

In the southerners of the two generations that followed his, the Virginian patriot found his disciples, and their name was legion. And although Randolph's sovereign states have been beaten down at one time and bribed into submission at another; although every economic measure he denounced has been made a permanent policy of our national government; although the plantation is desolate and the city triumphant—still, Randolph's system of thought has its adherents. He has helped to insure us against reckless consolidation and arbitrary power. His love of personal and local liberties, his hatred of privilege, his perception of realities behind political metaphysics, his voice lifted against the god Whirl—these things endure.

Randolph of Roanoke died in a Philadelphia inn, strange and wonderful to the last. There is no statue in his memory. The fierce lover of permanence was buried in the woods of Roanoke. But in 1879 his body was exhumed and taken to Hollywood Cemetery in Richmond. The roots of a great tree, penetrating through his coffin, had twined through the dead man's long black hair and filled his skull. So, doubtless, he would have wished to lie forever. Yet modern America, ill at ease in the presence of things immutable, will not permit even the bones of genius to rest secure.

Against the lust for change Randolph had fought with all his talents. And though he lost, he fell with a brilliancy that was almost consolation for disaster.

Appendix I

Selected Letters

Although a great many of Randolph's letters have been
lost, several hundred remain—some in holograph,
others in copies made by biographers, a considerable number printed in the several lives of Randolph or in periodicals. Among American political leaders, very few have been
his equals in this branch of literature.

Space permits only a brief selection here; a complete collection of the correspondence is much to be desired. The
specimens which follow are intended to illustrate some of
Randolph's social opinions, facets of his character, and his
style. Those addressed to Harmanus Bleeker have not been
published previously.

To St. George Tucker, Williamsburg,
Virginia*

New York, Dec. 25, 1788.
I received my dear Papa's affectionate Epistle, and was
sorry to find that he thought himself neglected. I assure you,

---

* Written to his stepfather, from Columbia College, when Randolph was
fifteen years old. The blanks occur in the source from which this letter is
reprinted: Bouldin, *Home Reminiscences of John Randolph*, pp. 219–20.

my dear sir, that there was scarcely a fortnight elapsed since Uncle's absence without my writing to you, and [I] would have paid dearly for you to have received them. I sent them by the Post, and indeed no other opportunity except by Capt. Crozier, and I did not neglect that. Be well assured, my ever dear sir, that our Expenses since our arrival here, have been enormous and by far greater than our Estate, especially loaded as it is with Debt, can bear; however, I flatter myself, my dear Papa, that upon looking over the Accounts you will find that my share is, by comparison, trifling, and hope that, by the wise admonitions of so affectionate a Parent, one who has our welfare and interest so much at Heart, we may be able to shun the rock of Prodigality, upon which so many people continually split, and by which the unhappy Victim is reduced, not only to Poverty, but also to Despair and all the Horrors attending it.

Brother R. writes you, that I am lazy. I assure you, my dear Papa, he has been egregiously mistaken. I attend every lecture that the class does. Not *one* of the Professors have ever found me dull or ever said that I was irregular. All my leisure Time, I devote to the study of _____, and then read the Poets from five o'clock in the morning till twelve. I am constantly reading in my Room. The rest of my time is allotted to College Duty. If Brother Richard had written you, that I did nothing all the Vacation, he would have been much in the dark—neither was it possible for me. We lived in this large building without a soul in it, but ourselves, and it was so desolate and dreary that I could not bear to be in it. I always was afraid that some Robber, of which we have a plenty (as you will see by the enclosed paper) was coming to kill me, after they made a draught on the house.

Be so good, my dear sir, when it is convenient, to send me

the debate of the Convention of our State. My love to the families of Butler, ⸻, and Cawsons. My love to Mr. Tucker, Jr., Miss Maria, and the children. Tell them I wish them a Merry Christmas. That you, my ever dear Papa, may enjoy many happy and merry ones, is the sincere Wish of your ever affectionate Son,

John Randolph, Jun'r.

P.S.: My best love to Aunt Betty Carlos. Capt. Henry of Bermuda says that Cousin F. Tucker of the Hermitage is to be married to young Jack Tucker.

To Theodore Dudley*

Georgetown, Jan. 31, 1806

My dear Theodore,

I send you by the New Orleans mail, "letters written by the great Mr. Pitt, afterwards Earl of Chatham, to his nephew, when at college." You know my opinion of Lord Chatham: that he was at once the greatest *practical* statesman that ever lived, and the most transcendent orator. With all this, he was a truly *good man,* (indeed, he *must have been,* since *virtue* is *essential* to *great excellence* in *laudable pursuits,*) and the most elegant and polished gentleman of his time.

When I speak of a practical statesman, I wish you to understand me. A man may possess great theoretic knowledge on any subject, and yet be a poor practitioner. To take an example from the profession which you seem to have chosen, in preference to any other,—a man might have all

---

* Randolph had taken under his wing, in addition to his two nephews, his young kinsman Theodore Dudley, who became a physician. This letter is printed in Dudley's *Letters of John Randolph to a Young Relative,* pp. 9–11.

the best medical authors by heart, know the treatment which is best considered to be most judicious for every disease, and the properties of every medicine, so as, in *conversation,* to vie with any, and to outshine the greater part of his profession, and yet be so deficient in *practice,* as, when brought to a patient, to be unable to tell what his disease was, and, of course, how it was to have been treated,—whether the pulse indicated depletion or stimulants. Such is the difference between theory and practice; one is disease on paper, where all goes smoothly, and the *patient infallibly recovers:* the other is disease in the subject of malady, in man himself, where symptoms are complicated, and the various considerations of age, sex, and condition, in the patient, baffle the most skilful, and dismay the most experienced—*where the patient dies.*

I fear, from the shortness of your letter, from the incorrectness of its *orthography* and *syntax,* and from the omission of some material words, that want of paper was not your only cause for omitting to write the week before last. Enclosed you have something to obviate that objection.—

"There *is* only 20 more to carry down."
    Note.—A verb DOES NOT agree with its nominative in *number* and person.
"Plowing"—which in the preceding line you have spelt correctly.
"No accidents *has* befallen." A verb does *not,* &c.
"The reason that I did not (the word write omitted) last week, was, &c." No attention to points, at all.
Number of lines in your letter, nine,

——————— —— errors ————— ———, four;*

---

* Besides omitting the year 1806. [Randolph's note]

Surely you cannot have read over once what you wrote. Moreover, the hand is a very bad one; many words blotted, and every part of it betrays negligence and a *carelessness* of *excelling*—a most deplorable symptom in a young man.

Is Dr. Robinson in Farmville, and is he likely to remain there? Would you prefer being at Hamp. Sid. Coll. to staying at Bizarre? I am very uneasy about you, my dear boy. In your letters I see no trace of your studies—no mention made of Ovid or Homer—nothing as to your manner of disposing of your time. As soon as I am well enough, I shall set off for Bizarre. God bless you.

Your affectionate friend
and relation,
John Randolph

What has become of the journal that I directed you to keep?

Have you ever received the two bank notes that I sent you?

Do not imitate your father's handwriting—it is a running hand, unfit for you at present. You must learn to write *distinctly* first, as children learn to read, letter by letter, syllable by syllable, word by word. The first page of this letter is a very good copy for you—particularly the date.

To Theodore Dudley*

Georgetown, Saturday, Feb. 15, 1806

My dear boy,

After I had gone to bed last night, and lay tumbling and tossing about, uneasy and unable to rest, my thoughts running upon many an anxious subject, among which you

---

* Printed in Dudley, *Letters of John Randolph to a Young Relative,* pp. 13–16.

were not forgotten, I was relieved by the entrance of a servant, who handed me your letter of the 9th, with some others. But that relief was only temporary. My mind fixed itself on your situation for the remainder of the night, and I have determined to settle you at school at Winchester, unless (of which I have no expectation) I shall find Hampden-Sydney *very greatly* altered for the better. At your time of life, my son, I was even more ineligibly placed than you are, and would have given worlds for quiet seclusion and books. I never had either. You will smile when I tell you that the first map that I almost ever *saw* was one of Virginia, when I was nearly fifteen; and that I never (until the age of manhood) possessed any treatise on geography, other than an obsolete Gazetteer of Salmon, and my sole atlas were the five maps, if you will honour them with that name, contained in the Gazetteer, each not quite so big as this page, of the three great eastern divisions, and two western ones, of the earth. The best and only Latin dictionary that I ever owned, you now have. I had a small Greek lexicon, bought with my own pocket money, and many other books, acquired in the same way, (from 16 to 20 years of age;) but these were merely books of amusement. I never was with any preceptor, one only excepted, (and he left the school after I had been there about two months,) who would deserve to be called a Latin or Greek scholar; and I never had any master of modern languages, but an old Frenchman, (some gentleman valet, I suppose), who could neither write nor spell.

I mention these things, my child, that you may not be disheartened. 'Tis true, that I am a very ignorant man, for one who is thought to have received a learned education. You (I hope) will acquire more information, and digest it better.

There is an old proverb, "You cannot teach an old dog new tricks." Yours is the time of life to acquire knowledge. Hereafter you must *use* it; like the young, sturdy labourer, who lays up, whilst he is fresh and vigorous, provision for his declining age.

When I asked you whether you had received the bank notes I sent you, I did not mean to *inquire how you had laid them out*. Don't you see the difference? From your not mentioning that they had come to hand, (a careless omission; you should break yourself of this habit,) and your cousin informing me that she had not received two packets sent by the same mail, I concluded that the notes were probably lost or embezzled. Hence my inquiry after them. No, my son; whatever cash I send you (unless for some special purpose) is yours: you will spend it as you please, and I have nothing to say to it. That you will not employ it in a manner that you ought to be ashamed of, I have the fullest confidence. To pry into such affairs would not only betray a want of that confidence, and even a suspicion discreditable to us both, but infringe upon your rights and independence. For, although you are not of an age to be your own master, and independent in all your actions, yet you are possessed of rights which it would be tyranny and injustice to withhold, or invade. Indeed, this independence, which is so much vaunted, and which young people think consists in doing what they please, when they grow up to man's estate, (with as much justice as the poor negro thinks liberty consists in being supported in idleness, by other people's labour,)—this independence is but a name. Place us where you will,—along with our rights there must coexist correlative duties,—and the more exalted the station, the more arduous are these last. Indeed, as the duty is precisely correspondent to the power, it follows that the richer, the wiser, the more powerful a man is, the greater is the obligation upon him to employ his gifts in lessening the sum of human misery; and this employment constitutes happiness, which the weak and wicked vainly imagine to consist in wealth, finery, or sensual gratification. Who so miserable as the bad Emperor of Rome? Who more happy than Trajan and Antoninus? Look at the fretful, peevish, rich man, whose senses are as much jaded by attempting to embrace too much gratification, as the limbs of the poor post horse are by incessant labour. (See the Gentlemen and Basket-makers, and, indeed, the whole of Sandford and Merton.)

Do not, however, undervalue, on that account, the character of the *real* gentleman, which is the most respectable amongst men. It consists not of plate, and equipage, and rich living, any more than in the disease which that mode of life engenders; but in *truth,* courtesy, bravery, generosity, and learning, which last, although not *essential* to it, yet does very much to adorn and illustrate the character of the true gentleman. Tommy Merton's gentlemen were no gentlemen, except in the acceptation of innkeepers, (and the *great* vulgar, as well as the small,) with whom he who rides in a coach and six, is three times as great a gentleman as he who drives a post-chaise and pair. Lay down this as a principle, that *truth* is to the other virtues, what vital air is to the human system. They cannot exist *at all* without it; and as the body may live under many diseases, if supplied with pure air for its consumption, so may the character survive many defects, where there is a rigid attachment to *truth*. All *equivocation* and subterfuge belong to falsehood, which consists, not in using *false* words only, but in conveying false impressions, no matter how; and if a person deceive himself, and I, by my silence, suffer him to remain in that error, I am implicated in the deception, unless he be one who has no right to rely upon me for information, and, in that case, 'tis plain, I could not be instrumental in deceiving him.

I send you two letters, addressed to myself, whilst at school—of which I now *sorely repent me* I did not then avail myself, (so far, at least, as my very ineligible situation would admit.) Will you accept a little of my experience, instead of buying some of your own at a very dear rate?— and so, God bless you, my son.

Your affectionate uncle,

John Randolph

P.S.: In consideration of my being surrounded with company, and having, at the same time, a horrible headache, excuse this *scratch*.

I shall send you Walker's Dictionary, for pronouncing the English language. Among other vulgarisms, I hope it will break you and Buona of saying horrubble, sensubble, indolunce, &c. You will soon get over this, by accustoming yourself to say horri, sensi, (as if spelled horry, &c.,) dividing the word, and then adding the final syllable (ble.) You know I've long been contending against this barbarism, which deforms the pronunciation of Virginia.

"Mah," instead of my, pronounced sometimes mie, and, at others, me, the e short, as bring me my hat.

Famully—family.

Possubul—possible, &c., &c.

Vigilunt—vigilant, &c., &c.

Another omission:—

You say nothing of Duchess, or the other mares and the foals. Are they with foal? (or as the sportsmen say, *"in foal?"*)

When you write, have my letter before you, and (after telling me every thing that suggests itself to your mind) examine and reply to the points it contains.

Copy the enclosed letters, and take special care of the originals. I am glad that you have read Lord Chatham's letters, and yet more, that you are pleased with them. They will *bear,* and, I hope, *receive,* repeated readings.

Enclosed are ten dollars, United States Bank, payable at Washington, No. 7045, E.

To the Freeholders of Charlotte, Prince Edward, Buckingham, and Cumberland*

May 30, 1812

Fellow Citizens,

I dedicate to you the following fragment. That it appears in its present mutilated shape, is to be ascribed to the successful usurpation which has reduced the freedom of speech in one branch of the American Congress to an empty name. It is now established, *for the first time, and in the person of your representative,* that the House may and will refuse to hear a member in his place, or even to receive a motion from him, upon the most momentous subject that can be presented for legislative decision. A similar motion was brought forward by the republican minority in the year 1798, before these modern inventions for stifling the freedom of debate were discovered. It was discussed as a matter of *right,* until

---

* This public letter to his constituents, published in Virginian newspapers, is a concise version of a speech opposing war with Britain, which he was prevented from delivering on the floor of the House of Representatives. The text is taken from Garland's *Life of John Randolph,* I, 299–303.

it was abandoned by the mover, in consequence of additional information (the correspondence of our envoy at Paris) laid before Congress by the President. In the "reign of terror," the father of the sedition law had not the hardihood to proscribe liberty of speech, much less the right of free debate on the floor of Congress. This invasion of the public liberties was reserved for self-styled republicans, who hold your understandings in such contempt, as to flatter themselves that you will overlook their every outrage upon the great first principles of free government, in consideration of their professions of tender regard for the privileges of the people. It is for you to decide whether they have undervalued your intelligence and spirit, or whether they have formed a just estimate of your character. You do not require to be told that the violation of the rights of him whom you have deputed to represent you is an invasion of the rights of every man of you, of every individual in society. If this abuse be suffered to pass unredressed—and the people alone are competent to apply the remedy—we must bid adieu to a free form of government for ever.

Having learned from various sources that a declaration of war would be attempted on Monday next, *with closed doors,* I deemed it my duty to endeavor, by an exercise of my constitutional functions, to arrest this heaviest of all calamities, and avert it from our happy country. I accordingly made the effort of which I now give you the result, and of the success of which you will have already been informed before these pages can reach you. I pretend only to give you the substance of my unfinished argument. The glowing words, the language of the heart, have passed away with the occasion that called them forth. They are no longer under my control. My design is simply to submit to you the views which have induced me to consider a war with England, under existing circumstances, as comporting neither with the *interest* nor the *honor* of the American people; but as an idolatrous sacrifice of both, on the altar of *French rapacity, perfidy and ambition.*

France has for years past offered us terms of undefined commercial arrangement, as the price of a war with England, which hitherto we have not wanted firmness and virtue to reject. That price is now to be paid. We are tired of holding out; and, following the example of continental Europe, entangled in the artifices, or awed by the power of the destroyer of mankind, we are prepared to become instrumental to his projects of universal dominion. *Before these pages meet your eye, the last republic of the earth will have enlisted under the banners of the tyrant and become a party to his cause.* The blood of the American freemen must flow to cement his power, to aid in stifling the last struggles of afflicted and persecuted man, to deliver up into his hands the patriots of Spain and Portugal, to establish his empire over the ocean and over the land that gave our fathers birth —to forge our own chains! And yet, my friends, we are told, as we were told in the days of Mr. Adams, *"the finger of heaven points to war."* Yes, the finger of heaven *does* point to war! It points to war, as it points to the mansions of eternal misery and torture—as a flaming beacon warning us of that vortex which we may not approach but with certain destruction. It points to desolated Europe, and warns us of the chastisement of those nations who have offended against the justice, and almost beyond the mercy, of heaven. It announces the wrath to come upon those who, ungrateful for the bounty of Providence, not satisfied with the peace, liberty, security, and plenty at home, fly, as it were, into the face of the Most High, and tempt His forbearance.

To you, *in this place,* I can speak with freedom; and it becomes me to do so; nor shall I be deterred by the cavils and the sneers of those who hold as "foolishness" all that savors not of worldly wisdom, from expressing fully and freely those sentiments which it has pleased God, in His mercy, to engrave on my heart.

These are no ordinary times; the state of the world is unexampled; the war of the present day is not like that of our revolution, or any which preceded it, at least in modern times. It is a war against the liberties and the happiness of mankind; it is a war in which the whole human race are the victims, to gratify the pride and lust of power of a single individual. I beseech you, put it to your own bosoms, how far it becomes you as freemen, as Christians, to give your aid and sanction to this impious and bloody war against your brethren of the human family. To such among you, if any such there be, who are insensible to motives not more dignified and manly than they are intrinsically wise, I would make a different appeal. I adjure you by the regard you have for your own safety and property, for the liberty and inheritance of your children—by all that you hold dear and sacred—to interpose your constitutional powers to save your country and yourselves from the calamity, the issue of which it is not given to human foresight to divine.

Ask yourselves if you are willing to become the virtual allies of Bonaparte? Are you willing, for the sake of annexing Canada to the Northern States, to submit to that overgrowing system of taxation which sends the European laborer supperless to bed, to maintain, by the sweat of your

brow, armies at whose hands you are to receive a future
master? Suppose Canada ours; is there any one among you
who would ever be, in any respect, the better for it?—the
richer, the freer, the happier, the more secure? And is it for a
boon like this that you would join in the warfare against the
liberties of man in the other hemisphere, and put your own
in jeopardy? Or is it for the *nominal* privilege of a licensed
trade with France that you would abandon your lucrative
commerce with Great Britain, Spain, and Portugal, and
their Asiatic, African, and American dependencies; in a
word, with every region of those vast continents?—that
commerce which gives vent to your tobacco, grain, flour,
cotton; in short, to all your native products, which are
denied a market in France? There are not wanting men so
weak as to suppose that their approbation of warlike measures is a proof of personal gallantry, and that opposition to
them indicates a want of that spirit which becomes a friend
of his country; as if it required more courage and patriotism
to join in the acclamation of the day, than steadily to oppose
one's self to the mad infatuation to which every people and
all governments have, at some time or other, given way. Let
the history of Phocion, of Agis, and of the De Witts, answer
this question.

My friends, do you expect to find those who are now
loudest in the clamor for war, foremost in the ranks of
battle? Or, is the honor of this nation indissolubly connected
with the political reputation of a few individuals, who tell
you *they* have gone too far to recede, and that you must pay,
with *your ruin,* the price of their *consistency.*

My friends, I have discharged my duty towards you,
lamely and inadequately, I know, but to the best of my poor
ability. The destiny of the American people is in their own

hands. The net is spread for their destruction. You are enveloped in the toils of French duplicity, and if—which may Heaven in its mercy forbid—you and your posterity are to become hewers of wood and drawers of water to the modern Pharaoh, it shall not be for the want of my best exertions to rescue you from the cruel and abject bondage. This sin, at least, shall not rest upon my soul.

John Randolph of Roanoke

To Francis Scott Key*

Roanoke, May 10, 1813.

Dear Frank—

For so, without ceremony, permit me to call you. Among the few causes that I find for regret at my dismissal from public life, there is none in comparison with the reflection that it has separated me—perhaps for ever—from some who have a strong hold on my esteem and on my affections. It would indeed have been gratifying to me to see once more yourself, Mr. Meade, Ridgely, and some few others; and the thought that this may never be, is the only one that infuses any thing of bitterness into what may be termed by disappointment, if a man can be said to be disappointed when things happen according to his expectations; on every other account, I have cause of self-congratulation at being disenthralled from a servitude at once irksome and degrading. The grapes are *not* sour—you know the manner in which you always combated my wish to retire. Although I have

---

* This letter to the author of "The Star-Spangled Banner" was written after Randolph's loss of his congressional seat, in consequence of his having led the antiwar faction. It is printed in Garland, *Life of John Randolph,* II, pp. 11–12; the original is lost.

not, like you, the spirit of a martyr, yet I could not allow but great force to your representations. To say the truth, a mere sense of duty alone might have been insufficient to restrain me from indulging the very strong inclination which I have felt for many years to return to private life. It is now gratified in a way that takes from me every shadow of blame. No man can reproach me with the desertion of my friends, or the abandonment of my post in a time of danger and of trial. "I have fought the good fight, I have kept the faith." I owe the public nothing; my friends, indeed, are entitled to every thing at my hands; but I have received my discharge, not indeed *honestam dimissionem,* but passably enough, as times go, when delicacy is not over fastidious. I am again free, as it respects the public at least, and have but one more victory to achieve, to be so in the true sense of the word. Like yourself and Mr. Meade, I cannot be contented with endeavoring to do good for goodness' sake, or rather for the sake of the Author of all goodness. In spite of me, I cannot help feeling something very like contempt for my poor foolish fellow-mortals, and would often consign them to Bonaparte in this world, and the devil, his master, in the next; but these are but temporary fits of misanthropy, which soon give way to better and juster feelings.

When I came away I left at Crawford's a number of books, letters, papers, &c., in (and out of) an open trunk; also a gun, flash, shot-belt, &c. Pray take them in charge for me, for although one-half of them are of no consequence, the *rest* are; and you may justly ask why I have been so careless respecting them?—because I am the most lazy and careless man on earth (LaBruyère's absent man is nothing to me), and because I am in love. Pray give the letters special protection.

To Harmanus Bleeker, Albany, New York*

Roanoke, Tuesday, July 26, 1814.

Your kind letter of the 13th was received last night—& altho' a week must elapse before this can commence its snail-paced journey of six days & a half to Richmond—(a distance of 110 miles—you see we still retain some vestiges of the terrapin system) I cannot refrain from thanking you for it—altho' you have not said one syllable about Mrs. G. —for in such employment alone do I find refuge from myself. My poor nephew remains a sad spectacle of a human being *without a soul.* Alas, this is not a pious fraud, such as was practised by M. upon his pupil. It is melancholy reality daily before my eyes, operating upon my mind as a pestiferous atmosphere or unwholesome diet does upon the body; gradually destroying, by sure and deadly process, all the springs of health. For some time, I have had scarcely any other companion—if he can be called—except this unfortunate youth. Dudley has been incessantly engaged with his patients, amongst whom the greater part are persons in extreme indigence. They know very little of this country, who do not know that it is excessively poor. It could not be otherwise even if the lands were generally fertile which is far from being the case. *There is no market for the produce of the soil.* The greater part of the inhabitants possess nothing beyond the bare necessities of life—few enjoy the

---

* A letter written by Randolph during his retirement at Roanoke, after losing his congressional seat to Eppes, in 1813. He refers to his two nephews, sons of his dead brother Richard, of whom one, John St. George Randolph—born deaf and dumb—had gone mad, and the other, Theodorick Tudor Randolph, was dying. Holograph in Bleeker letterbook, Alderman Library, University of Virginia.

comforts & none (estimated by the standard of Baltimore, Philada. or New York) the luxuries; which you meet with no where in Virginia except in Richmond. 'Tis true we have some rich men—but as each man has been the architect of his own fortune, they are more distinguished for their parsimony than their wealth. They never leave home except on business & their whole time is absorbed in the most minute attention to their affairs. They will seldom call in a physician unless the case be very urgent—never to their slaves, altho the most highly valued property, upon a principle, 'tis said *(I speak impersonally)* of *calculation*. When I told you that there was no market for the produce of the land, I might have stopped there—the inference which a political economist could not fail to draw is that society must necessarily be in its rudest state, consistent with a life of agriculture. I should do great injustice, however, to the middle and lower ranks of our people, were I to represent them otherwise than as, for the most part, kind, well disposed & beyond comparison more social & hospitable than the rich. Have you ever remarked a solitary tree in a field starving the plants for a great distance around & absorbing to itself all the nourishment of the earth. Such have been & are *our* rich folks, all of whom commenced by "keeping store". These stores (we have no villages) are generally ten or twelve miles apart; it requiring from fifty to a hundred square miles to maintain one. By offering credit the people are first tempted & afterwards compelled to buy the few West Indian & English commodities they consume, at four or five times the price you pay in Albany. A hawk's eye is kept upon the property of the debtor & the transaction ends by a sale under "deed of trust" & the removal of the family to the "western country". I have been credibly informed that three men, all of whom began the world with nothing, had it in their power to turn out of house & home, five hundred families in a single county; near a fourth of the whole population, and yet a senseless clamour is raised to the North & South, that "in Virginia Lands are not liable for debt". Less is lost in Virg. by bad debts than in any other state in the Union.

I have not answered your numerous questions, because they are beyond my scope, but I have given you a more just picture of the state of things, here, than has ever, I believe, been yet drawn. A word as to Society. I have actually none. Day after day, week after week, aye! month after month, do I rise up & go to bed without any change of scene except what the weather affords. My best friends are a few faithful slaves, who attend to my domestic concerns & minister to my few wants without troubling me for orders. They are a loyal & for their opportunity good people. Not very scrupulous perhaps in distinguishing betweed meum & tuum, but this ought not to surprise us. The resource of fraud & over-reaching is shut to them—they have none other than the breach of the 8th Commandment—but they are eminently Liberal in sharing what they have one with another. I sleep with windows open to the floor, my doors are never fastened, seldom shut. In a separate house, also open is the chief of my household goods—my smoke house, hardly in sight, about one hundred yards off; for I live in the midst of some thousands of acres of woodland. I might be robbed or knocked on the head any night of the week—frequently I am entirely alone, not even a servant within call: but I lie down without apprehension & awake in safety.

I have little doubt of peace, because the war can no longer be prosecuted. The cow has gone dry. I have not seen *"patronage"*. I wrote to Richmond for it as soon as Field

Marshal Coleman's Herald announced it. But alas! in matters of literature Richmond is as far behind Geo. Town,— you know George Town—as *it* is behind New York. The same as to manufactures generally. I have read however the Edinb: & Quart: Reviews of the work & preferred the latter, as I think Miss Edgeworth also will. My relish for reading is greatly impaired. Except Burke and Lord Byron's poems I have read nothing for a long time past. Of the former I have reperused with additional delight his first posthumous volume—"the reflections"—"the appeal"—"the matchless diatribe on the D. of B's attack" & the "Regicide Peace". The thoughts on scarcity & the third Regicide letter shew a minute acquaintance with matters of detail that is surprising. Burke was not one of those "who talked of *things in general,* because he knew nothing of *things in particular"*. Who but he would have hunted thro' Doctors commons to shew that there had not been in England one fifth of the number of divorces in a century, that had taken place in Paris alone, during three months? Apropos of Paris. I expect that the government will be effectively that of Talleyrand & Co: The restored king seems made not of stern stuff. The Bourbons will dread another revolution & resign themselves to favourite senators and marshals. I should like to know the state of the French military force. Adieu! I envy you Mr & Mrs Lloyd. You have no cause to thank me for this letter. In writing it I have escaped, for a few moments at least, from the misery which benumbs all my faculties. Believe me in truth yours

J.R. of. Roanoke.

Poor old Eutas! I was mortified to see him reduced to the ranks—but the remark on "that last cut," I recognise as his. The anniversary of our independence was marked here by inundation that destroyed three fourths of the largest & finest crop I ever had. An intense drought since has burnt up the remainder, or as *we* say "the balance".

West is not a correspondent of mine. I some times hear from Frank Key & could I acquire his piety might be at peace: but I cannot. I strive but it is in vain. It must come from above. A quick arrival from Europe will solve all your doubts before this letter can reach you. It will lie several days at an intermediate Post Office whence a private hand (my servant's) brought yours. As soon as the legislature abandoned the restrictive system the Gen¹. Post Office took it up.

July 28. 1814

Since writing the above—, I learn that my nephew at Cambridge, is proceeding by slow journies towards Virginia, which perhaps he may never reach, & whence there is no probability of his return. He is in (I fear a confirmed) pulmonary consumption. I must announce to his mother the decay of this last prop of her widowhood! The Cup is full. I have no more to do with this world.

To a New England Senator*

Philadelphia, Dec. 15, 1814.

DEAR SIR,—You will doubtless be surprised, but (I trust) not offended at the receipt of this letter. Of the motives

---

* Although Randolph bitterly opposed war with England, he addressed this formal letter of remonstrance against New England's proposed secession to a Hartford Convention man. Garland (from whose *Life*, II, 51–62, this text is taken) does not give the name of the New England senator in question. It was, however, James Lloyd, senator from Massachusetts.

which dictate it I shall forbear to speak: let them be gathered from its context. But should you ascribe my selection of you as the object of its address to any other cause than respect for your character and confidence in your love of country, you will have done much injustice to me; but more to yourself.

At Washington, I learned the result of the dispatches brought by the John Adams (a name of evil omen), and there rumours were afloat, which have since gathered strength, of a disposition in Massachusetts, and indeed throughout New England, to follow the example of Nantucket, and declare for a neutrality in the present contest with Great Britain. I will not believe it. What! Boston, the cradle of American independence, to whose aid Virginia stept forth unsolicited, when the whole vengeance of the British ministry was wreaked on that devoted town. Boston! now to desert us, in our utmost need, to give up her old ally to ravage, at the price of her own impunity from the common enemy—I cannot, will not believe it. The men, if any such there be among you, who venture to insinuate such an intent by the darkest innuendo, do they claim to be the disciples of Washington? They are of the school of Arnold. I am not insensible to the vexations and oppressions, with which you have been harassed, with little intermission, since the memorable embargo of 1807. These I am disposed, as you well know, neither to excuse, nor to extenuate. Perhaps I may be reminded of an authority, to which I always delight to refer, *Segnius irritant animum,* &c., but let me tell such gentlemen, that our sufferings under political quacks of our own calling in, are not matter of *hearsay.* It is true they are considered by the unhappy, misguided patient, as evidence of the potency and consequently (according to his system of logic) of the efficacy of the medicine, as well as the inveteracy of the disease. It is not less true that this last has become, from preposterous treatment, in the highest degree alarming. The patient himself begins to suspect something of the sort, and the doctors trembling, each for his own character, are quarrelling and calling hard names among themselves. But they have reduced us to such a condition, that nothing short of the knife will now do. "We must *fight,* Mr. Speaker!" said Patrick Henry in 1775, when his sagacious mind saw there was nothing else left for us but manly resistance or slavish submission; and his tongue dared to utter what his heart suggested. How much greater the necessity now, when our country is regarded not as a property to be recovered, and therefore spared, so far as is compatible with the end in view; but as an object of vengeance, of desolation.

You know my sentiments of the men at the head of our affairs, and of the general course of administration during the last eight years. You know also that the relation, in which I stand towards them, is one of my own deliberate choice; sanctioned not more by my judgment than by my feelings. You, who have seen men (in the ranks, when I commanded in chief in the House of Representatives, and others, at that time too green to be on the political muster roll—whose names had never been pronounced out of their own parish) raised to the highest offices; you who are thoroughly acquainted with the whole progress of my separation from the party with which I was once connected in conduct, do not require to be told, that "there was a time in which I stood in such favor in the closet, that there must have been something extravagantly unreasonable in my wishes, if they might not ALL have been gratified." But I must acknowledge that you have seen instances of apostasy among your quondam political associates, as well as my own, that might almost justify a suspicion, that I too, tired of holding out, may wish to make my peace with the administration, by adding one more item "to the long catalogue of venality from Esau to the present day." Should such a shade of suspicion pass across your mind, I can readily excuse it, in consideration of the common frailty of our nature, from which I claim no peculiar exemption, and the transcendent wickedness of the times we live in; but you will have given me credit for a talent which I do not possess. I am master of no such ambidexterity; and were I to attempt this game, which it is only for adepts (not novices) to play! I am thoroughly conscious, that like other bungling rogues, I should at once expose my knavery and miss my object—not that our political church refuses to open her arms to the vilest of heretics and sinners who can seal their abjuration of their old faith by the prosecution of the brethren with whom they held and professed it: but I know that my nerves are of too weak a fibre to hear the question ordinary and extra-ordinary from our political inquisitors. I can sustain with composure and even with indifference the rancorous hatred of the numerous enemies whom it has been my lot to make in the course of my unprosperous life—but I have not yet steeled myself to endure the contemptuous pity of those noble and high-minded men, whom I glory to call my friends, and I am on too bad terms with the world, to en-counter my own self-disrepect.

You may however very naturally ask, why I have chosen you for the object of this address? Why I have not rather selected some one of those political friends, whom I have yet found "faithful among the faithless," as the vehicle of my opinions? It is because the avenue to the public ear is shut against me in Viriginia, and I have been flattered to believe that the sound of my voice may reach New England. Nay, that it would be heard there, not without attention and respect. With us the press is under a virtual *imprimatur,* and it would be more easy, at this time, to force into circulation the treasury notes, than opinions militating against the administration, through the press in Virginia. We were indeed beginning to open our eyes in spite of the opiate with which we were drugged by the newspapers, and the busy hum of the insects that bask in the sunshine of court patronage, when certain events occurred, the most favorable that could have happened for our rulers; whose "luck," verifying the proverb, is in the inverse ratio of their wisdom; or, perhaps I ought to say, who have the cunning to take advantage of glaring acts of indiscretion, in their adversaries at home and abroad, as these may affect the public mind; and such have never failed to come to their relief, when otherwise their case would have been hopeless. I give you the most serious assurance, that nothing less than the shameful conduct of the enemy and the complexion of certain occurrences to the eastward could have sustained Mr. Madison after the disgraceful affair at Washington. The public indignation would have overwhelmed, in one common ruin, himself and his hireling newspapers. The artillery of the press, so long the instrument of our subjugation, would, as at Paris, have been turned against the destroyer of his country: when we are told that old England says he "shall," and New England that he "must," retire from office, as the price of peace with the one, and of union with the other, we have too much English blood in our veins to submit to this dictation, or to any thing in the form of a threat. Neither of these people know any thing of us. The ignorance of her

foreign agents, not only of the country to which they are
sent, but even of their own, has exposed England to general
derision. She will learn, when it is too late, that we are a
high-minded people, attached to our liberty and our country, because it is free, in a degree inferior to no people under
the sun. She will discover that "our trade would have been
worth more than our spoil," and that she has made deadly
enemies of a whole people, who, in spite of her and of the
world, of the sneers of her sophists, or of the force of her
arms, are destined to become, within the present session, a
mighty nation. It belongs to New England to say, whether
she will constitute a portion, an important and highly respectable portion of this nation, or whether she will dwindle
into that state of insignificant, nominal independence, which
is the precarious curse of the minor kingdoms of Europe.
A separation made in the fulness of time, the effect of
amicable arrangements, may prove mutually beneficial to
both parties: and such would have been the effect of American independence, if the British ministry could have listened to any suggestion but that of their own impotent rage:
but a settled hostility embittered by the keenest recollections, must be the result of a disunion between you and us,
under the present circumstances. I have sometimes wished
that Mr. Madison (who endeavored to thwart the wise and
benevolent policy of General Washington "to regard the
English like other nations, as enemies in war, in peace
friends,") had succeeded in embroiling us with the Court of
St. James, twenty years sooner. We should in that case, have
had the father of his country to conduct the war and to
make the peace; and that peace would have endured beyond
the lifetime of the authors of their country's calamity and

disgrace. But I must leave past recollections. The present and the immediate future claim our attention.

It may be said, that in time of peace, the people of every portion of our confederacy find themselves too happy to think of division; that the sufferings of a war, like this, are requisite, to rouse them to the necessary exertion: war is incident to all governments; and wars I very much fear will be wickedly declared, and weakly waged, even by the New England confederacy, as they have been by every government (not even excepting the Roman republic), of which we have any knowledge; and it does appear to me no slight presumption that the evil has not yet reached the point of amputation, when peace alone will render us the happiest (as we are the freest) people under the sun; at least too happy to think of dissolving the Union, which, as it carried us through the war of our revolution, will, I trust, bear us triumphant through that in which we have been plunged, by the incapacity and corruption of men, neither willing to maintain the relations of peace, nor able to conduct the operations of war. Should I, unhappily, be mistaken in this expectation, let us see what are to be the consequences of the separation, not to us, but to yourselves. An exclusion of your tonnage and manufactures from our ports and harbors. It will be our policy to encourage our own, or even those of Europe in preference to yours; a policy more obvious than that which induced us of the South, to consent to discriminating duties in favor of American tonnage, in the infancy of this government. It is unnecessary to say, to you, that I embrace the duties on imports, as well as the tonnage duty, when I allude to the encouragement of American shipping. It will always be our policy to prevent your ob-

taining a naval superiority, and consequently to cut you off
entirely from our carrying trade. The same plain interest will
cause us to prefer any manufactures to your own. The intercourse with the rest of the world, that exchanges our
surplus for theirs, will be the nursery of our seamen. In the
middle States you will find rivals, not very heartily indisposed to shut out the competition of your shipping. In the
same section of country and in the boundless West, you
will find jealous competitors of your mechanics—you will
be left to settle, as you can, with England, the question of
boundary on the side of New Brunswick, and unless you can
bring New York to a state of utter blindness, as to her own
interests, that great, thriving, and most populous member
of the southern confederacy will present a hostile frontier
to the only States of the union of Hartford, that can be estimated as of any efficiency. Should that respectable city be
chosen as the seat of the Eastern Congress, that body will
sit within two days' march of the most populous county of
New York (Dutchess), of itself almost equal to some of the
New England States. I speak not in derision, but in sober-
ness and sadness of heart. Rather let me say, that like a
thorough-bred diplomatist, I try to suppress every thing like
feeling, and treat this question as a dry matter of calculation;
well knowing, at the same time, that in this, as in every
question of vital interest, "our passions instruct our reason."
The same high authority has told us that jacobinism is of no
country, that it is a sect found in all. Now, as our jacobins
in Virginia would be very glad to hear of the bombardment
of Boston, so, I very much fear, your jacobins would not be
very sorry to hear of a servile insurrection in Virginia. But
such I trust is the general feeling in neither country, otherwise, I should at once agree that union, like the marriages

of Mezentius, was the worst that could befall us. For, with every other man of common sense, I have always regarded union as the means of liberty and safety; in other words of happiness, and not as an end, to which these are to be sacrificed. Neither, at the same time, are means so precious, so efficient (in proper hands) of these desirable objects, to be thrown rashly aside, because, in the hands of bad men, they have been made the instrument almost of our undoing.

You in New England (it is unnecessary I hope to specify when I *do not* address myself personally to yourself) are very wide of the mark, if you suppose we to the south do not suffer at least as much as yourselves, from the incapacity of our rulers to conduct the defence of the country. Do you ask why we do not change those rulers? I reply, because we are a people, like your own Connecticut, of steady habits. Our confidence once given is not hastily withdrawn. Let those who will, abuse the fickleness of the people; I shall say such is not the character of the people of Virginia. They may be deceived, but they are honest. Taking advantage of their honest prejudices, the growth of our revolution, fostered not more by Mr. Jefferson than by the injuries and (what is harder to be borne) the insults of the British ministry since the peace of 1783, a combination of artful men, has, with the aid of the press, and the possession of the machinery of government (a powerful engine in any hands) led them to the brink of ruin. I can never bring myself to believe, that the whole mass of the landed proprietors in any country, but especially such a country as Virginia, can seriously plot its ruin. Our government is in the hands of the landed proprietors only. The very men of whom you complain, have left nothing undone that *they* dared to do, in order to destroy it. Foreign influence is unknown among us. What we feel of it is through the medium of the General Government, which acted on, itself, by foreign renegadoes, serves as a conductor, between them and us, of this pernicious influence. I know of no foreigner who has been, or is, in any respectable office in the gift of the people, or in the government of Virginia. No member of either House of Congress, no leading member of our Assembly, no judge of our Supreme Courts: of the newspapers printed in the State, as far as my knowledge extends, without discrimination of party, they are conducted by native Virginians. Like yourselves, we are an unmixed people. I know the prejudice that exists against us, nor do I wonder at it, considering the gross ignorance on the subject that prevails north of Maryland, and even in many parts of that neighboring State.

What member of the confederacy has sacrificed more on the altar of public good than Virginia? Whence did the General Government derive its lands beyond the Ohio, then and now almost the only source of revenue? From our grant, —a grant so curiously worded, and by our present Palinurus too, as to except ourselves, by its limitations, from the common benefit.

By its conditions it was forbidden ground to us, and thereby the foundation was laid of incurable animosity and division between the States on each side of that great natural boundary, the river Ohio. Not only their masters, but the very slaves themselves, for whose benefit this regulation was made, were sacrificed by it. Dispersion is to them a bettering of their present condition, and of their chance for emancipation. It is only when this can be done without danger and without ruinous individual loss that it will be done at all. But what is common sense to a political Quixote?

That country was ours by a double title, by charter and

by conquest. George Rogers Clark, the American Hannibal, at the head of the State troops, by the reduction of Post Vincennes, obtained the lakes for our northern boundary at the peace of Paris. The march of that great man and his brave companions in arms across the drowned lands of the Wabash, does not shrink from a comparison with the passage of the Thrasimene marsh. Without meaning any thing like an invidious distinction, I have not heard of any cession from Massachusetts of her vast wilds; and Connecticut has had the address, out of our grant to the *firm,* to obtain, on her own private account, some millions of acres: whilst we, yes we, I blush to say it, have descended to beg for a pittance, out of the property once our own, for the brave men by whose valor it had been won, and whom heedless profusion had disabled us to recompense. We met the just fate of the prodigal. We were spurned from the door, where once we were master, with derision and scorn; and yet we hear of undue Virginian influence. This fund yielded the Government, when I had connection with it, from half a million to eight hundred thousand dollars annually. It would have preserved us from the imposition of State taxes, founded schools, built bridges and made roads and canals throughout Virginia. It was squandered away in a single donative at the instance of Mr. Madison. For the sake of concord with our neighbors, by the same generous but misguided policy, we ceded to Pennsylvania Fort Pitt, a most important commercial and military position, and a vast domain around it, as much Virginia as the city of Richmond and the country of Henrico. To Kentucky, the eldest daughter of the Union, the Virginia of the west, we have yielded on a question of boundary, from a similar consideration. Actuated by the same magnanimous spirit at the instance of other states (with the exception of New York, North Carolina, and Rhode Island), we accepted, in 1783, the present Constitution. It was repugnant to our judgment, and fraught, as we feared, with danger to our liberties. The awful voice of our ablest and soundest statesmen, of Patrick Henry, and of George Mason, never before or since disregarded, warned us of the consequences. Neither was their counsel entirely unheeded, for it led to important subsequent amendments of that instrument. I have always believed this disinterested spirit, so often manifested by us, to be one of the chief causes of the influence which we have exercised over the other States. Eight States having made that Constitution their own, we submitted to the yoke for the sake of union. Our attachment to the Union is not an empty profession. It is demonstrated by our practice at home. No sooner was the Convention of 1788 dissolved, than the feuds of federalism and anti-federalism disappeared. I speak of their effects on our councils. For the sake of union, we submitted to the lowest state of degradation: the administration of John Adams. The name of this man calls up contempt and derision, wheresoever it is pronounced. To the fantastic vanity of this political Malvolio may be distinctly traced our present unhappy condition. I will not be so ungenerous as to remind you that this personage (of whom and his addresses, and his answers, I defy you think without a bitter smile) was not a Virginian, but I must in justice to ourselves, insist in making him a set-off against Mr. Madison. They are of such equal weight, that the trembling balance reminds us of that passage of Pope, where Jove "weighs the beau's wits against the lady's hair."

> The doubtful beam long nods from side to side,
> At length the wits mount up, the hairs subside.

Intoxicated not more by the fulsome adulation with which he was plied, than by the fumes of his own vanity, this poor old gentleman saw a visionary coronet suspended over his brow, and an air-drawn sceptre "the handle towards his hand," which attempting to clutch, he lost his balance, and disappeared never to rise again. He it was, who "enacting" Nat. Lee's Alexander, raved about the people of Virginia as "a faction to be humbled in dust and ashes," when the sack-cloth already was prepared for his own back.

But I am spinning out this letter to too great a length. What is your object—PEACE? Can this be attained on any terms, whilst England sees a prospect of disuniting that confederacy, which has already given so deep a blow to her maritime pride, and threatens at no very distant day to dispute with her the empire of the ocean? The wound which our gallant tars have inflicted on her tenderest point, has maddened her to rage. Cursed as we are with a weak and wicked administration, she can no longer despise us. Already she begins to hate us; and she seeks to glut a revenge as impotent as it is rancorous, by inroads that would have disgraced the buccaneers, and bulletins that would only not disgrace the sovereign of Elba. She already is compelled to confess in her heart, what her lips deny, that if English bull-dogs and game-cocks degenerate on our soil, English MEN do not:—and should (which God forbid) our brethren of the East desert us in this contest for all that is precious to man, we will maintain it, so long as our proud and insulting foe shall refuse to accede to equitable terms of peace. The Government will then pass into proper hands—the talents of the country will be called forth, and the schemes of moon-struck philosophers and their disciples pass away and "leave not a track behind."

You know how steady and persevering I endeavored, for eight years, to counteract the artful and insidious plans of our rulers to embroil us with the country of our ancestors, and the odium which I have thereby drawn upon myself. Believing it to be my duty to soften, as much as possible, the asperities which subsisted between the two countries, and which were leading to a ruinous war, I put to hazard, nay, exposed to almost certain destruction, an influence such as no man, perhaps, in this country, at the same age, had ever before attained. (The popularity that dreads exposure is too delicate for public service. It is a bastard species: the true sort will stand the hardest frosts. Is it my fault [as Mr. Burke complained of the crowned heads of Europe] that England will no longer suffer me to find palliatives for her conduct?) No man admired more than I did her magnanimous stand against the tyrant, before whom all the rest of Christendom at one time bowed: No man, not even her own Wilberforce and Perceval, put up more sincere prayers for her deliverance. In the remotest isle of Australasia, my sympathy would have been enlisted, in such a contest, for the descendants of Alfred and Bacon, and Shakespeare, and Milton, and Locke, on whom I love to look back as my illustrious countrymen—in any contest I should have taken side with liberty; but on this depended (as I believed and do still believe) all that made my own country in my sight. It is past—and unmindful of the mercy of that protecting Providence which has carried her through the valley of the shadow of death, England "feels power and forgets right." I am not one of the whining set of people who cry out against mine adversary for the force of his blow. England has, unquestionably, as good a right to conquer us, as we have to conquer Canada; the same right that we have to conquer

England, and with about as good prospect of success. But let not her orators declaim against the enormity of French principles, when she permits herself to arm and discipline our slaves, and to lead them into the field against their masters, in the hope of exciting by the example a general insurrection, and thus render Virginia another St. Domingo. And does she talk of jacobinism! What is this but jacobinism? and of the vilest stamp? Is this the country that has abolished the slave trade? that has made the infamous, inhuman traffic a felony? that feeds with the bread of life all who hunger after it, and even those who, but for her, would never have known their perishing condition? Drunk with the cup of the abominations of Moloch, they have been roused from the sleep of death, like some benighted traveller perishing in the snows, and warmed into life by the beams of the only true religion. Is this the country of Wilberforce and Howard? It is;—but, like my own, my native land, it has fallen into the hands of evil men, who pour out its treasure and its blood at the shrine of their own guilty ambition. And this impious sacrifice they celebrate amidst the applauses of the deluded people, and even of the victims themselves.

There is a proneness in mankind to throw the blame of their sufferings on any one but themselves. In this manner, Virginia is regarded by some of her sister States; not adverting to the fact, that all (Connecticut and Delaware excepted) are responsible for the measures that have involved us in our present difficulties. Did we partition your State into those unequal and monstrous districts which have given birth to a new word in your language, of uncouth sound, calling up the most odious associations? Did we elect the jacobins whom you sent to both Houses of Congress—the Bidwells, and Gannetts, and Skinners,—to spur on the more moderate men from Virginia to excesses which they reluctantly gave in to at the time, and have since been ashamed of? Who hurried the bill suspending the privilege of the writ of HABEAS CORPUS through a trembling servile Senate, in consequence, as he did not blush to state, of a *verbal* communication from the President? A Senator from Massachusetts, and professor in her venerable university. In short, have not your first statesmen (such I believe was the reputation of the gentleman in question at the time), your richest merchants, and the majority of your delegation in Congress vied in support of the men and the measures that have led to our present suffering and humiliated condition?

If you wished to separate yourselves from us, you had ample provocation in time of peace, in an embargo the most unconstitutional and oppressive; an engine of tyranny, fraud, and favoritism. Then was the time to resist (we did not desert England in a time of war), but you were then under the dominion of a faction among yourselves, yet a formidable minority, exhibiting no signs of diminution; and it is not the least of my apprehensions, from certain proceedings to the eastward, that they may be made the means of consigning you again, and for ever, to the same low, insolent domination. The reaction of your jacobins upon us (for although we have some in Virginia, they are few and insignificant) through the men at Washington, ("who must conciliate good republicans") is dreadful. Pause, I beseech you, pause! You tread on the brink of destruction. Of all the Atlantic States you have the least cause to complain. Your manufactures, and the trade which the enemy has allowed you, have drained us of our last dollar. How then can we carry on the war? With men and steel—stout hearts, and willing hands—and these from the days of Darius and

Xerxes, in defence of the household gods of freedom, have proved a match for gold. Can they not now encounter paper? We shall suffer much from this contest, it will cut deep; but dismissing its authors from our confidence and councils for ever, (I speak of a few leaders and their immediate tools, not of the deluded, as well in as out of authority), we shall pass, if it be the good pleasure of Him whose curses are tempered with mercies, through an agony and a bloody sweat, to peace and salvation; to that peace which is only to be found in a reconciliation with Him. "Atheists and mad-men *have* been our lawgivers," and when I think on our past conduct I shudder at the chastisement that may await us. How has not Europe suffered for her sins! Will England not consider, that, like the man who but yesterday bestrode the narrow world, she is but an instrument in his hands, who breaketh the weapons of his chastisement, when the measure of his people's punishment is full?

When I exhort to further patience—to resort to constitutional means of redress only, I know that there is such a thing as tyranny as well as oppression; and that there is no government, however restricted in its powers, that may not, by abuse, under pretext of exercise of its constitutional authority, drive its unhappy subjects to desperation. Our situation is indeed awful. The members of the Union in juxtaposition—held together by no common authority to which men can look up with confidence and respect. Smitten by the charms of Upper Canada, our President has abandoned the several States to shift for themselves as they can. Congress is *felo de se*. In practice there is found little difference between a government of requisitions on the States, which these disregard, a government of requisitions on the people, which the governors are afraid to make until the

public faith is irretrievably ruined. Congress seemed barred
by their own favorite act of limitations, from raising supplies; prescription runs against them. But let us not despair
of the Commonwealth. Some master-spirit may be kindled
by the collision of the times, who will breathe his own soul
into the councils and armies of the republic; and here indeed is our chiefest danger. The man who is credulous
enough to believe that a constitution, with the skeleton of an
establishment of 10,000 men, not 2,000 strong, (such was
our army three years ago), is the same as with an army of
60,000 men, may be a very amiable neighbor, but is utterly
unfit for a statesman. Already our government is in fact
changed. We are become a military people, of whom more
than of any other it might have been said *fortunatos sua si
bona norint*. If under such circumstances you ask me what
you are to do, should a conscription of the model of Bonaparte be attempted? I will refer you to its reputed projector,
Colonel Monroe. Ask him what he would have done, whilst
governor of Virginia, and preparing to resist Federal usurpation, had such an attempt been made by Mr. Adams and
his ministers; especially in 1800. He *can* give the answer.

But when you complain of the representation of three-
fifths of our slaves, I reply that it is one of the articles of
that compact, which you submitted to us for acceptance,
and to which we reluctantly acceded. Our Constitution is
an affair of compromise between the States, and this is the
master-key which unlocks all its difficulties. If any of the
parties to the compact are dissatisfied with their share of
influence, it is an affair of amicable discussion, in the mode
pointed out by the Constitution itself, but no cause for dissolving the confederacy. And when I read and hear the
vile stuff against my country printed and uttered on this

subject, by fire-brands, who ought to be quenched for ever, I would remind, not these editors of journals and declaimers at clubs, but their deluded followers, that every word of these libels on the planters of Virginia, is as applicable to the father of his country as to any one among us; that in the same sense we are "slave-holders," and "negro-drivers," and "dealers in human flesh," (I must be pardoned for culling a few of their rhetorical flowers), so was *he,* and whilst they upbraid Virginia with her Jeffersons and her Madisons, they will not always remember to forget that to Virginia they were indebted for a Washington.

I am, with the highest respect and regard, dear sir, your obedient servant,

John Randolph of Roanoke.

To Dr. John Brockenbrough*

September 25. [1818]

My good friend,—I am sorry that Quashee should intrude upon you unreasonably. The old man, I suppose, knows the pleasure I take in your letters, and therefore feels anxious to procure his master the gratification. I cannot, however, express sorrow—for I do not feel it—at the impression which you tell me my last letter made upon you. May it lead to the same happy consequences that I have experienced—which I now feel—in that sunshine of the heart, which the peace of God, that passeth all understanding, alone can bestow!

Your imputing such sentiments to a heated imagination

---

* This letter concerning Randolph's religious convictions is taken from Garland's *Life,* II, 100–103.

does not surprise me, who have been bred in the school of Hobbes and Bayle, and Shaftesbury and Bolingbroke, and Hume and Voltaire and Gibbon; who have cultivated the skeptical philosophy from my vain-glorious boyhood—I might also say childhood—and who have felt all that un-utterable disgust which hypocrisy and cant and fanaticism never fail to excite in men of education and refinement, super-added to our natural repugnance to Christianity. I am not, even now, insensible to this impression; but as the excesses of her friends (real or pretended) can never alien-ate the votary of liberty from a free form of government, and enlist him under the banners of despotism, so neither can the cant of fanaticism, or hypocrisy, or of both (for so far from being incompatible, they are generally found united in the same character—may God in his mercy preserve and defend us from both) disgust the pious with true religion.

Mine has been no sudden change of opinion. I can refer to a record, showing, on my part, a desire of more than nine years' standing, to partake of the sacrament of the Lord's Supper; although, for two-and-twenty years preced-ing, my feet had never crossed the threshold of the house of prayer. This desire I was restrained from indulging, by the fear of eating and drinking unrighteously. And although that fear hath been cast out by perfect love, I have never yet gone to the altar, neither have I been present at the per-formance of divine service, unless indeed I may so call my reading the liturgy of our church, and some chapters of the Bible to my poor negroes on Sundays. Such passages as I think require it, and which I feel competent to explain, I comment upon—enforcing as far as possible, and dwelling upon, those texts especially that enjoin the indispensable accompaniment of a good life as the touchstone of the true faith. The Sermon from the Mount, and the Evangelists generally; the Epistle of Paul to the Ephesians, chap. vi.; the General Epistle of James, and the First Epistle of John; these are my chief texts.

The consummation of my *conversion*—I use the word in its strictest sense—is owing to a variety of causes, but chiefly to the conviction, unwillingly forced upon me, that the very few friends which an unprosperous life (the fruit of an ungovernable temper) had left me were daily losing their hold upon me, in a firmer grasp of ambition, avarice, or sensuality. I am not sure that, to complete the anti-climax, avarice should not have been last; for although, in some of its effects, debauchery be more disgusting than avarice, yet, as it regards the unhappy victim, this last is more to be dreaded. Dissipation, as well as power or prosperity, hardens the heart; but avarice deadens it to every feeling but the thirst for riches. Avarice alone could have produced the slave-trade; avarice alone can drive, as it does drive, this infernal traffic, and the wretched victims of it, like so many post-horses, whipped to death in a mail-coach. Ambition has its reward in the pride, pomp, and circumstances of glorious war; but where are the trophies of avarice?—the handcuff, the manacle, and the blood-stained cowhide? What man is worse received in society for being a hard master? Every day brings to light some H_____e or H_____ns in our own boasted land of liberty! Who denies the hand of a sister or daughter to such monsters? Nay, they have even appeared in "the abused shape of the vilest of women." I say nothing of India, or Amboyna, of Cortez or Pizarro.

When I was last in your town I was inexpressibly shocked (and perhaps I am partly indebted to the circumstance for accelerating my emancipation) to hear, on the threshold of

the temple of the least erect of all the spirits that fell from
heaven, these words spoken, by a man second to none in this
nation in learning or abilities; one, too, whom I had, not
long before, seen at the table of our Lord and Saviour: "I do
not want the Holy Ghost (I shudder while I write), or any
other spirit in me. If these doctrines are true (St. Paul's),
there was no need for Wesley and Whitefield to have separated from the church. The Methodists are right, and the
church wrong. I want to see the old church," &c. &c.: that
is, such as this diocese was under Bishop *Terrick,* when
wine-bibbing and buck-parsons were sent out to preach "a
dry clatter of morality", and not the word of God, for 16,000
lbs. of tobacco. When I speak of morality it is not as condemning it; religion includes it, but much more. Day is now
breaking and I shall extinguish my candles, which are better
than no light; or if I do not, in the presence of the powerful
king of day they will be noticed only by the dirt and ill savor
that betray all human contrivances, the taint of humanity.
Morality is to the Gospel not even as a farthing rushlight to
the blessed sun.

By the way, this term Methodist in religion is of vast compass and effect, like tory in politics, or aristocrat in Paris,
"with the lamp-post for its second," some five or six-and-
twenty years ago.

Dr. Hoge? "a Methodist parson." Frank Key? "a fanatic,"
(I heard him called so not ten days ago,) "a Methodistical,
whining, &c., &c." Wilberforce? "a Methodist," Mrs. Han-
nah More? "ditto." It ought never to be forgotten, that real
converts to Christianity on opposite sides of the globe agree
at the same moment to the same facts. Thus Dr. Hoge and
Mr. Key, although strangers, understand perfectly what
each other feels and believes.

If I were to show a MS. in some unknown tongue to half a dozen persons, strangers to each other and natives of different countries, and they should all give me the same translation, could I doubt their acquaintance with the strange language? On the contrary, can I, who am but a smatterer in Greek, believe an interpreter who pretends to a knowledge of that tongue, and yet cannot tell the meaning of τυπτω?

I now read with relish and understand St. Paul's epistles, which not long since I could not comprehend, even with the help of Mr. Locke's paraphrase. Taking up, a few days ago, at an "ordinary," the life of John Bunyan, which I had never before read, I find an exact coincidence in our feelings and opinions on this head, as well as others.

Very early in life I imbibed an absurd prejudice in favor of Mahomedanism and its votaries. The crescent had a talismanic effect on my imagination, and I rejoiced in all its triumphs over the cross (which I despised) as I mourned over its defeats; and Mahomet II himself did not more exult than I did, when the crescent was planted on the dome of St. Sophia, and the cathedral of the Constantines was converted into a Turkish mosque. To this very day I feel the effects of Peter Randolph's Zanga on a temper naturally impatient of injury, but insatiably vindictive under insult.

On the night that I wrote last to you I scribbled a pack of nonsense to Rootes, which serves only to show the lightness of my heart. About the same time, in reply to a question from a friend, I made the following remarks, which, as I was weak from long vigilance, I requested him to write down, that I might, when at leisure, copy it into my diary. From it you will gather pretty accurately the state of my mind.

I have been up long before day, and write with pain, from a sense of duty to you and Mrs. B., in whose welfare I take the most earnest concern. You have my prayers: give me yours, I pray you.

Adieu!

John Randolph of Roanoke.

I was on top of the pinnacle of Otter this day fortnight: a little above the earth, but how far beneath heaven!

NOTE.—It is my business to avoid giving offence to the world, especially in all matters indifferent. I shall therefore stick to my old uniform, blue and buff, unless God sees fit to change it for black. I must be as attentive to my dress, and to household affairs, as far as cleanliness and comfort are concerned, as ever, and indeed more so. Let us take care to drive none away from God by dressing religion in the garb of fanaticism. Let us exhibit her as she is, equally removed from superstition and lukewarmness. But we must take care, that while we avoid one extreme we fall not into the other; no matter which. I was born and baptized in the Church of England. If I attend the Convention at Charlottesville, which I rather doubt, I shall oppose myself then and always to every attempt at encroachment on the part of the church, the clergy especially, on the rights of conscience. I attribute, in a very great degree, my long estrangement from God to my abhorrence of prelatical pride and puritanical preciseness; to ecclesiastical tyranny, whether Roman Catholic or Protestant; whether of Henry V or Henry VIII; of Mary or Elizabeth; of John Knox or Archbishop Laud; of the Cameronians of Scotland, the Jacobins of France, or the Protestants of Ireland. Should I fail to attend, it will arise from a repugnance to submit the religion, or church, any more than the liberty of my country, to foreign influence. When I speak of my country, I mean the Commonwealth of Virginia. I was born in allegiance to George III; the Bishop of London (*Terrick!*) was my diocesan. My ancestors threw off the oppressive yoke of the mother country, but they never made me subject to *New England* in matters spiritual or temporal; neither do I mean to become so, voluntarily.

To Harmanus Bleeker*

Salem, Virginia, Oct. 10, 1818

Dear Bleeker

Stepping accidentally into the Post-Office at Fincastle a few days ago, with our sometime fellow-labourer Breckenridge, I was most unexpectedly saluted by your well known hand on the cover of a pamphlet addressed to me, which had strayed only about 100 miles & almost as many degrees out of the course to my habitation. If you have Madison's miserable map of Virginia look for Bottetourt County— Fincastle, the county town—near which B. has a spacious & opulent establishment—Salem lies about 20 miles to the South near the Roanoke. It is on the great western road, along which the tide of emigration pours its redundant flood to the wide region that extends from the gulf of Mexico to the Missouri. Alabama is at present the lodestone of attraction—Cotton, Money, Whiskey, & the means of obtaining

---

* The "Mrs. G." mentioned in this letter is a lady (presumably Mrs. Christopher Gore) to whom Randolph had been presented by Bleeker a few years before, and with whom—this correspondence suggests—he had fallen in love. Randolph did not acquire the twenty thousand acres he mentions. Holograph, University of Virginia.

all these blessings, *Slaves*—The road is thronged with droves of these wretches & the human carcass-butchers, who drive them on the hoof to market & recalls to memory Clarkson's Prize Essay on Slavery & the Slave trade, which I read upwards of thirty years ago. One might almost fancy one's self on the road to Catibar or Bonny. The impression made on my mind by that dissertation sunk deep, as it did into that of the author, & altho it may have been obscured by pleasure, or business, it has renewed itself, as I advance in life. Just so, forty years ago, kneeling at my mother's feet, I repeated, ignorantly but reverently, the Lord's Prayer & "the belief", night and morning. The seed was trodden under foot of man, but blessed be *His* name! it was sown with a mother's care & watered with a mother's tears—& altho late the harvest, hath brought forth if not an ample, yet I humbly trust a *saving* crop. He has been most gracious to me, my good friend, & at last, in his good time & at his good plea-sure, hath shewn me the way that leadeth into eternal life. May he so guide & support my footsteps that they not stray from it, into that broad road of which it is written "Many there be that find it".

I have been passing a good deal of time lately among our mountains—making a flying trip home, where your letter of the 9th of Sept. met me, together with one from Phila. postmarked "feb. 5" & again "Richmond feb. 9." The cover of which I have enclosed to the P.M.G. who will probably send it to the Land office, as they did our military de-spatches, to lie, like Lord North's until a successor comes into office to read them. By the way, I have omitted to thank you for Mr. Clere's pamphlet. The sight of your hand was as that of an old friend in a far country. I cried out " 'tis Bleeker's hand"—but B. did not recognize it. You will be glad to hear that my poor nephew is better—much better, in every respect. I have well grounded hopes of his entire recovery.

I am much gratified to hear of our fair friend, Mrs. G. Present me to her, I pray you, not merely as an admirer of beauty, but of what is fairer & more attractive than even beauty itself—grace, modesty & a certain indefinable charm of manner that is resistless in its sway over the affections of all within its sphere. Your own words applied to another, "whom Mercer could tell me of" describe her almost too well—intelligence, delicacy & sweetness.

The Review you mention I have read & admired long ago, but have never seen the work it criticizes. Mrs. Hutchinson reminded me in the strongest manner of my own ever honoured mother, whose image is now before me & of whom I could relate to you some interesting circumstances. Harry Tucker was just a week old when she left her bed & fled with him in her arms from that Hartford-Convention-man, Arnold; who was at Petersburg, but two & a half miles off. I see her the evening that she fled again (by night) from Tarleton & his Pandours, as she flung my deceased father's most valuable papers into a pillow case & put his steel hilted dagger into her stays. I could just get my chin over the leaf of the old fashioned desk she was searching, & asked her "what that was for?". "My son, your mother shall never be insulted"—was the reply, & I now understand the look that accompanied it. She was a lone woman with five children (one at the breast—the oldest only eleven) & two adult relations, hanging with all the weight of female imbecility an incumbrance upon her—"Cleopatra's Majesty" always brought her figure up before me. She taught me to read & indeed all I know that is worth knowing—from her I learned to relish Shakespeare—to aspire to something better than a mere Country Squire. To her I am indebted for my enunciation—& my brother's was more perfect, many think, than mine—She taught us also to dance; for with all her household qualifications she was of ethereal temper—"She was a matron of Cornelia's mien"—& in her presence impudence itself stood abashed—her natural temper however was eminently cheerful & I have known her after a day of unremitting household drudgery, order her carriage & spend half the night at assembly in the neighouring market Town.

Would you like to see a sort of Virginian Rob Roy? Look for the Bent Mountain at the head of the South Fork (branch) of Roanoke on the confines of Bottetourt & Montgomery where I propose to buy 20,000 acres of rich grass land, provided the legal proprietors can give possession It has been long held by a hardy mountaineer in defiance of them & the laws, & they have been obliged to compromise by letting him hold possession, he consenting to pay 1/3 of the profits of their stock, slaves & land, all of which were once his own—& in fact are so yet. It is a caricature of highland life. The climate is delicious; a plain gently undulating some times broken elevated about 4,000 feet above the tide, irrigated by ten thousand springs & rills—rich in grass & timber—but too cold for grain, except rye.

Lord Byron's fourth Canto has been one of my travelling companions—I read however but little—"flumina amen sylvasque inglorias". In spite of my dear mother's precautions, "Gaudete equis canes basque" might be my designation. The fourth Canto is inferior to the first part of Childe Harold but yet very fine. More unequal perhaps but rising to the proudest level of this writer's other works in particular passages. I long to see the "Niobe of Nations" & the "Sea Cybell". I (too) loved her from boyhood—& for the same

cause. Madness, suicide or Piety—(perhaps both the first!)
in some of these must Lord Byron take refuge. I think I see
passages that shadow out my own story.

> "The thorns which I have reaped are of the Tree I
> planted."

[Manuscript of this letter apparently incomplete.]

TO HARMANUS BLEEKER*

Roanoke Nov. 16, 1818

My dear Sir

Your last letter of the 2d is felt almost like a reproach &
I will endeavor to make amends for my late dilatory conduct
by the promptitude of my present acknowledgement of your
goodness. Should I fall in with our good friend the Patroon,
I shall take delight in sharing in every way in my power the
respect & regard I bear him—but there are few things less
probable than this—since to use your words I am in a
manner "rivetted to home"—for some time at least, and
indeed, my dear Sir, this from being a matter of irksome
duty, has become a source of gratification to me, of which
the reflection that it is a discharge of duty constitutes not the
least part. The nature of the property that I hold obliges me
to endeavor to extort from the labouring portion of my
slaves as much profit as will support them & their families in
sickness & in health, in infancy and when past labour;
reserving to myself, if practicable, a fair rent for my land &
profit on my stock. To do this without severity to the slaves

---

* Holograph, University of Virginia. Despite the humor and sound
sense of this and the preceding letter, during 1818 Randolph was in
retirement from Congress, suffering from his first really disabling period
of dementia.

or pinching them in necessaries of life is an arduous problem. If Irish absentees be blameworthy, Virginian absentees are more so. And thus with a passion for travelling not excelled by any that I ever knew—which has been upon me since my first sea voyage thirty-four years ago when I read Sinbad the Sailor & Robinson Crusoe—I am in a manner "fixed to the freehold". The master's presence is the only check (& that insufficient) upon the malpractices of the overseers & of the negroes too, poor creatures. I have often bewailed the lot that made me "their keeper". I now bow with submission to the decree of Him who has called me to this state, & pray to be enabled to discharge the duties of it. And yet it is possible I may find some excuse to go a wandering, if my life should be spared another year, when my resources will probably be more abundant & my affairs more settled: for you must know, that after all charges are honestly defrayed the balance (as we Virginians say) often stands on the wrong side of the Ledger.

At present I am plaistering my house; another cause of detention at home. So that if you should come to see me at Christmas I can give you a snug apartment, almost in the style of Low Dutch neatness. You will see leafless trees in abundance & the earth strewed with the foliage, "Which as autumnal leaves that strew the brooks in Vallombrosa, where the Etrurian shades, High over-arch'd, imbower"— but for the human face divine, my wrinkles & the cheerful countenance of my father's old Servant Essar must suffice you. Within doors we can have Books, conversation, a temperate glass of wine & a real Spanish Cigar & may "reason high of Providence, Fore-Knowledge, will & Fate, Fix'd Fate, free will, Fore-Knowledge absolute, and find no end in wand'ring mazes lost." But this I think is to the full as well let alone.

I have read, with what sensation I leave you to guess, the Heart of Mid Lothian. Jeanie Deans is my heroine. She is the true example of Religious Principle acting upon a naturally kind & cheerful temperament. Effie I pronounced a b—— very early in the work & a b—— of the worst sort she at last becomes, a b—— of Quality. The IV Canto of Childe Harold I had marked & made a list of such stanzas & parts of them as I peculiarly admired intending to send it to you—but the shorter way is to adopt Horace Walpole's plan of confining the few people in their senses & letting the insane go at large. It is an endless source of pleasure to me—at least I have not found the end yet. I have long thought that I discerned traces, in Manfred especially, of a spirit that was too much perturbed not to find peace—even that peace that passeth all understanding, the peace of God!

Your good wishes thro my favourite Jeanie are cordially returned. I hope soon to hear from you. My correspondence is daily languishing from my own increasing averseness to writing. To say the truth, my dear Sir, old age creeps on me a pace. My hands & eyes cannot flatter if they would.

I am most sincerely & affectionately
Yours
John Randolph of Roanoke

To Dr. Theodore Dudley*

Washington, Dec. 30, 1821
Your letter of the 20th, has lain several days on my table. The difficulty of writing, produced by natural decay, is so increased by the badness of the materials furnished by our

---

* Printed in Dudley, *Letters of John Randolph to a Young Relative*, pp. 312–33.

contractors, (who make the public pay the price of the best,) that I dread the beginning of a letter. At this time, it requires my nicest management to make this pen do legible execution.

So true is your remark, that I have tried to strike root into some of the people around me—one family, in particular; but I found the soil too stony for me to penetrate, and, after some abortive attempts, I gave it up—nor shall I ever renew the attempt, unless some change in the inhabitants should take place.

The medical gentleman, whom you suppose to be actuated by no friendly spirit towards you, made the observation in question, to one whom he believed well disposed towards you; and he mentioned it to another, of the same description, who told it to me. I do not believe the remark extended beyond us three.

One of the best and wisest men I ever knew, has often said to me that a decayed family could never recover its loss of rank in the world, until the members of it left off talking and dwelling upon its former opulence. This remark, founded in a long and close observation of mankind, I have seen verified, in numerous instances, in my own connexions —who, to use the words of my oracle, "will never thrive, until they can become 'poor folks:' "—he added, "they may make some struggles, and with apparent success, to recover lost ground; they may, and sometimes do, get half way up again; but they are sure to fall back—unless, reconciling themselves to circumstances, they become in form, as well as in fact, poor folks."

The blind pursuit of wealth, for the sake of hoarding, is a species of insanity. There are spirits, and not the least worthy, who, content with an humble mediocrity, leave the field of wealth and ambition open to more active, perhaps more guilty, competitors. Nothing can be more respectable than the independence that grows out of self-denial. The man who, by abridging his wants, can find time to devote to the cultivation of his mind, or the aid of his fellow-creatures, is a being far above the plodding sons of industry and gain. His is a spirit of the noblest order. But what shall we say to the drone, whom society is eager to "shake from her encumbered lap?"—who lounges from place to place, and spends more time in "Adonizing" his person, even in a morning, than would serve to earn his breakfast?—who is curious in his living, a connoisseur in wines, fastidious in his cookery; but who never knew the luxury of earning a single meal? Such a creature, "sponging" from house to house, and always on the borrow, may yet be found in Virginia. One more generation will, I trust, put an end to them; and their posterity, if they have any, must work or steal, *directly*.

Men are like nations. One founds a family, the other an empire—both destined, sooner or later, to decay. This is the way in which ability manifests itself. They who belong to a higher order, like Newton, and Milton, and Shakespeare, leave an imperishable name. I have no quarrel with such as are content with their original obscurity, vegetate on from father to son; "whose ignoble blood has crept through *clodpoles* ever since the flood"—but I cannot respect them. He who contentedly eats the bread of idleness and dependence is beneath contempt. I know not why I have run out at this rate. Perhaps it arises from a passage in your letter. I cannot but think you are greatly deceived. I do not believe the world to be little clear-sighted.

What the "covert insinuations" against you, on your

arrival in Richmond, were, I am at a loss to divine. I never heard the slightest disparagement of your moral character; and I know nobody less obnoxious to such imputations.

When you see the C's, present my best wishes and remembrance to them all. I had hoped to hear from Richard. He is one of the young men about Richmond, with whom it is safe to associate. *Noscitur è Sorio* is older than the days of Partridge; and he who is the companion of the thriftless, is sure never to thrive: tavern haunters and loungers are no friends to intellectual, moral, or literary improvement, any more than to the accumulation of wealth.

I have seen nobody that you know but Frank K. and Gen. S. The last asked particularly after you. That you may prosper in this life, and reach eternal happiness in the life to come, is my earnest prayer.

John Randolph of Roanoke.

To Dr. John Brockenbrough*

Paris, July 24, 1824.

This date says every thing. I arrived here on Sunday afternoon, and am now writing from the Grand Hotel de Castile, rue Richelieu and Boulevard des Italiens—for, as the French say, it gives upon both, having an entrance from each.

I need not tell either of *you*, that it is in the very focus of gayety and fashion; and if the maitre d'hotel may be credited, it is always honored by the residence of "M. le Duc de Davuansaire," whenever his Grace pays a visit to his birth-

---

* Here Randolph's European travels are a foil for his reflections on Virginia. The text is from Garland's *Life*, II, 223–27.

place. The civilities which, through the good offices of my friend, Mr. Foster, were tendered to me two years ago, from "Davuansaire House," and "Chisong," would render this circumstance a recommendation, if the neatness and comfort of my apartments did not supersede all necessity for any other recommendation.

Here, then, am I, where I ought to have been thirty years ago—and where I would have been, had I not been plundered and oppressed during my nonage, and left to enter upon life overwhelmed with a load of DEBT, which the profits of a nineteen years' minority ought to have more than paid; and ignorant as I was (and even yet am) of business, to grope my way, without a clue, through the labyrinth of my father's affairs, and brought up among Quakers, an ardent *ami des noirs,* to scuffle with negroes and overseers, for something like a pittance of rent and profit upon my land and stock.

Under such circumstances, that I have not been utterly ruined, is due (under God) to the spirit I inherited from my parents, and to the admirable precepts, and yet more admirable example of my revered mother—honored and blessed be her memory. Then I had to unravel the tangled skein of my poor brother's difficulties and debts. His sudden and untimely death threw upon my care, helpless as I was, his family, whom I tenderly and passionately loved, and with whom I might be now living, at Bizarre, if the reunion of his widow with the ———— of her husband had not driven me to Roanoke; where, but for my brother's entreaty and forlorn and friendless condition, I should have remained; and where I should have obtained a release from my bondage more than twenty years ago. Then I might have enjoyed my present opportunities; but time misspent and faculties misemployed, and senses jaded by labor, or impaired by excess, cannot be recalled any more than that freshness of the heart, before it has become aware of the deceits of others, and of its own.

"But how do you like Paris? for all this egotism you might have poured out from Washington."

Not in the least. And I stay here only waiting for my letters, which are ———— to the return of this day's post from London. To you I need not say one word of the Lions of Paris, but will, in a word, tell you, that crucifixes, and paintings of crucifixions, and prints of Charlotte Corday and Marie Antoinette, &c., are the fashion of the day. That the present dynasty, infirmly seated in the saddle; and that by little and little every privilege, acquired not by the designs of its authors, but by the necessary consequences of such a revolution, will be taken from the people; nay, I am persuaded that the lands will be resumed, or (what is the same thing) an ample equivalent will be plundered from the public, to endow the losers with. At the next session of the deputies, the measure of reimbursing the emigrants—a measure the very possibility of which was scouted, only three years ago. The Marquis de La Fayette had sailed for the United States about ten days before my arrival here. I am sorry he has taken the step. It will do no good to his reputation, which at his time of life he ought to nurse. I take it for granted, that Ned Livingston, or some other equally pure patriot, will propose *another* donation to him; the last, I think, was on the motion of Beau Dawson. I hope I may be there, to give it just such another reception as M. Figaro had at my hands. Although it is certainly a species of madness (and I hear that this malady is imputed to me) to be wearing out my strength and spirits, and defending the rights (whether of things or of persons) of a people who lend their countenance to them that countenance the general plunder of the public, in the expectation either that they may share in the spoil, or that their former peculations will not be examined into.

I consider the present King of France, and his family, to be as firmly seated on the throne of the Tuilleries, as ever Louis XIV was at Versailles; all possibility of counter-revolution is a mere chimera of distempered imagination. It would be just as possible to restore the state of society and manners which existed in Virginia a half a century ago; I should as soon expect to see the Nelsons, and Pages, and Byrds, and Fairfaxes, living in their palaces, and driving their coaches and sixes; or the good old Virginia gentlemen on the assembly, drinking their twenty and forty bowls of rack punches, and madeira, and claret, in lieu of a knot of deputy sheriffs and hack attorneys, each with his cruet of wiskey before him, and puddle of tobacco-spittle between his legs.

But to return to Paris. It is wonderfully improved since you saw it; nay, since the last restoration, but it is still the filthiest hole, not excepting the worst parts of the old town of Edinboro', that I ever saw *out of Ireland.* I have dined, for your sake, *chez Beauvilliers,* and had bad fare, bad wine, and even bad bread, a high charge, and a surly *garçon.* Irving, whom you know by character (our ex-minister at Madrid), was with me. He says all the *Traiteurs* are bad, and the crack ones worst of all. I have also dined with Very, the first restaurateur of the Palaise Royal, four times; on one of which occasions I had a good dinner and a *fair* glass of champagne—next door to Very, once, at the Café de Chartres—with Pravot—Pastel; all in the Palaise

Royal; all bad, dear, and not room enough, even at *Beau-villier's* or Very's, to sit at ease. I can have a better dinner for half a guinea at the Traveller's, in a saloon fit for a prince, and where gentlemen alone can enter, and a pint of the most exquisite Madeira, than I can get here for fifteen francs. I have dined like a marketman for 5 fr. 10 sous; that is the cheapest. All the wine, except le vin ordinaire, is adulterated shockingly. The English, that made every thing dear, and spoiled the garçons and filles, whose greediness is only equalled by their impudence. Crucifixes, madonnas, and pictures and prints of that cast, with Charlotte Corday, &c., are the order of the day. Paris swarms with old priests, who have been dug up since the restoration, and they manufacture young ones (Jesuits especially) by hundreds at a single operation.

Monsieur, whom you saw at Edinburgh, is remarkable, as I hear, for consuming a hat per day, when one is each morning put upon his toilet. Hats were not so plenty then.

I made a strange mistake in my order to Leigh. I intended to have given him control over all my funds, except the tobacco sold after that period, which I wished to reserve as a fund, on which to play here—I mean in Europe. Pray, let it be so, deducting my check for the passage money.

And now, my good friend, let me tell you that the state of my eyes, and of my health, and of my avocations too—for I have a great deal of writing to do—*may* cause this to be the last letter that you shall receive from me until my return, when we shall, I hope, chat about these and other matters once more.

In case you should not have gone to Kentucky, I expect a regular bulletin from you. There is one subject very near my heart that you must keep me informed about. I know that women (with great plasticity on other subjects) never will take advice upon that. I know that they rush into ruin with open eyes, and spend the rest of their lives in cursing the happier lot of their acquaintances, who have in the most important concern of life been governed by the dictates of common sense. The man is too old; he has not *nous* enough; he is helpless. If he had ten thousand a year, he would not be a match for her. I don't know who is worthy of her. But let him be of suitable age, with *mind* and *taste* congenial with her own, and of an *erect spirit* as well as carriage of body. They shall have my blessing.

Adieu,

J.R. of R.

Except a few of the English, with which people Paris swarms, I have not seen, either in the streets or elsewhere, any thing that by possibility might be mistaken for a gentleman. The contrast in this respect with London is most striking; indeed I would as soon compare the Hottentots with the French as these last with the English. No Enquirer yet received, and I pine for news from home.

To Dr. John Brockenbrough*

Washington, January 12, 1829; Monday

My dear Doctor—

It won't do for a man, who wishes to indulge in dreams of human dignity and worth, to pass thirty years in public life. Although I do believe that we are the meanest people in the world, I speak of this "court" and its retainers and followers. I am supersaturated with the world, as it calls itself, and have now but one object, which I shall keep

---

* Here Randolph writes two months before his final retirement from Congress. Printed in Garland, *Life of John Randolph,* II, 317.

steadily in view, and perhaps some turn of the dice may enable me to obtain it: it is, to convert my property into money, which will enable me to live, or rather to die, where I please; or rather where it may please God.

As to state politics I do not wish to speak about them. The country is ruined past redemption: it is ruined in the spirit and character of the people. The standard of merit and morals has been lowered far below *"proof."* There is an abjectness of spirit that appals and disgusts me. Where now could we find leaders of a revolution? The whole South will precipitate itself upon Louisiana and the adjoining deserts. Hares will hurdle in the Capitol. "Sauve qui peut" is my maxim. Congress will liberate our slaves in less than twenty years. Adieu.

To JOHN BROCKENBROUGH*

Thursday, Feb. 12, 1829

My good friend,

Your letter of Monday came to hand yesterday, after I had written & too late to thank you for it. Tom Miller writes this morning that the Convention Bill has passed & that my friends expect me to be a candidate for a post in that Body. If any one can & will devise a plan by which abler and better men shall be necessarily brought into our councils, I will have him as my *Magnus Apollo!* But as I have no faith in any such scheme, & a thorough detestation & contempt for political metaphysicks and for an arithmetical & geometrical constitution, I shall wash my hands of all such business. The

---

* Despite his resolution, in this letter, to have no hand in the Constitutional Convention, in fact Randolph was elected a delegate. Holograph, University of Virginia.

rest of my life if not passed in peace, shall not be spent in legislative wrangling. I am determined, absolutely, not to expose myself to collision where victory could confer no honour. No, my dear friend, let political and religious fanaticks rave about their dogmas, while the country is going to ruin under the one & the others are daily becoming worse members of society—"I'll none of it." "By their *fruits* shall ye know them."

I am still very low. My nights are horrible—Last night I underwent the operating of cutting for *fistula in ano*; & the reality would hardly have been worse than the dream.

It is now bitter cold. I do not remember so villainous a winter. Where the rest (if I live to see it) is to be spent by me I cannot tell. I have had some thoughts of Williamsburg. Farewell. Pray write to me.

Yours ever

J.R. of R.

By the time you receive this you will have seen the Boston Correspondence of Mr. Adams. The reply is, I'm told, by Mr. Jackson. Meanness is the key word that deciphers every thing in Mr. Adams' character.

To Thomas A. Morton, of Prince Edward*

London, Warwick St. Charing Cross
Dec. 6, 1830. Monday

My Dear Sir:

Since the sailing of the last packet from Liverpool, I received *via* St. Petersburg your letter of the 21st of August

---

* Written to his business agent, when Randolph returned, dying, from St. Petersburg. Printed in Bouldin, *Home Reminiscences of John Randolph,* pp. 227–28.

—the only one that I have had the pleasure to get from you.

It is with no small difficulty that I summon strength to thank you for it; for I am as low as I can be to be able to write at all.

In case that you shall not have contracted for the house at Bizarre, I wish to countermand the request. I intended it for a purpose that now can never be.

My expectations from the tobacco were very small; but I had hoped it would not turn out quite so badly. Meanwhile, I have no supply from Government. Congress and the Virginia Assembly both meet this day, and I pray God to send us, the people, a safe deliverance.

It will be very unlucky in case of a general war in Europe, which some look forward to, that we shall have eaten all our wheat, for I learn that there is a total destruction of Indian corn.

I must refer you to the newspapers for European politics. Nothing will preserve peace but the dread of the "Great Powers," lest their subjects should catch the French and Belgic disease (for such they deem it). If they touch Belgium, France will strike. This country is in a deplorable condition of splendid misery. A great discovery has been made on the Continent, far surpassing any of Archimedes or Newton. The people have discovered the secret of their strength; and the military have found out that *they* are the people. The teeth and nails of despotism are from that day drawn and pared.

Commend me earnestly to all my old friends and constituents. I shall be among them (dead or alive) next Summer. I have provided for a leaden coffin, feeling as I do an inexpressible desire to lie by the side of my dear mother and honored father at old Matoax.

Remember me to the old servants—particularly Syphax, Louisa, Sam and Phil, and be assured, my dear sir, that I set the highest value on the good opinion with which you have honored me, and I fully reciprocate it.

Most sincerely and faithfully,

J. R. of *Roanoke.*

John, my servant, is quite well; he has not been otherwise since we left the U.S.; and is a perfect treasure to me. He desires his remembrance to Syphax, &c., &c.

Appendix II

Selected Speeches

Almost without exception, Randolph spoke extemporaneously, or at least with only sketchy preparation. The high eloquence and frequent wisdom of his rhetoric are the more impressive, in this light. Despite the discursive and sometimes repetitious character of many of his addresses, generally he held his audiences fascinated. Though these speeches almost always are works of humane letters, and sometimes ascend to political philosophy, they never have been collected.

Randolph often corrected reporters' notes on his remarks, but his revisions were slight. The texts in newspapers of the period sometimes are more reliable than those in *The Annals of Congress,* since Randolph occasionally endeavored to have his congressional speeches published in papers in different parts of the country, and so sent correspondents corrected versions.

From the great bulk of his oratory, I have selected thirteen speeches, at different periods throughout Randolph's career, with a view to illustrating his rhetoric, his mode of thought, and some of the principal subjects with which he was concerned.

DEBATE ON THE GEORGIA CLAIMS,
IN COMMITTEE OF THE WHOLE,
January 29, 1805

[This denunciation of the Yazoo claims marks the beginning of Randolph's break with the Jeffersonians. The "agent at the head of an executive department," excoriated by Randolph, was Gideon Granger, postmaster general. The text of this speech is that of a manuscript written by Randolph's secretary, now in the Alderman Library, the University of Virginia.]

After reading over the report of the committee of claims, which concludes with submitting the following resolution:

RESOLVED, That three commissioners be authorized to receive propositions of compromise and settlement from the several companies or persons having claims to public lands within the present limits of the Mississippi territory, and finally to adjust and settle the same in such manner as in their opinion will conduce to the interest of the United States: PROVIDED, That in such settlement the commissioners shall not exceed the limits prescribed by the convention with the State of Georgia.

Mr. Dana moved that the committee rise, and report the resolution.

Mr. Randolph wished before the committee rose, that the gentleman from Connecticut (Mr. Dana) would assign some reason for the adoption of the resolution. No two things could be more opposite than the prefatory Statement made by the committee of claims, and the resolution which terminated the report. As there were no reasons assigned, he suspected the gentleman had kept them back with a view to surprising the House by their novelty; but he hoped the committee would not agree to the motion, unless some better cause were assigned for its adoption than had been hitherto made known.

Perhaps it may be supposed, from the course which this business has taken, that the adversaries of the present measure indulged the expectation of being able to come forward at a future day—not to this House, for that hope is desperate, but to the public, with a more matured opposition than it is in their power now to make. But past experience has shewn them that this is one of those subjects which pollution has sanctified—that the hallowed mysteries of corruption are not to be profaned by the eye of public curiosity.—No, Sir, the orgies of Yazoo speculation are not to be laid open to the vulgar gaze. None but the initiated are permitted to behold the monstrous sacrifice of the best interests of the nation on the altars of corruption. When this abomination is to be practised we go into conclave. Do we apply to the press? That potent engine, the dread of tyrants, and of villains, but the shield of freedom and of worth:—No, Sir, the press is gagged. On this subject we have a virtual sedition law—not with a specious title, but irresistible in its operation, which in the language of a gentleman from Connecticut (Mr. Griswold) goes directly to its object. The demon of speculation at one sweep has wrested from the Nation their best—their only defence, and closed every avenue of information. But a day of retribution may yet come. If their rights are to be bartered away, and their property squandered, the people must not, they shall not be kept in ignorance, by whom, or for whom it is done.

We have often heard of party spirit, of caucusses as they are termed, to settle Legislative questions—but never have I seen that spirit so visible as at this time. The outdoor intrigue is too palpable to be disguised. When it was proposed to abolish a Judiciary system, reared in the last moments of an expiring administration, the detested offspring of a midnight hour, when the question of repeal was before this House it could not be taken until midnight, in the third or fourth week of the discussion.—When the great and good man who now fills, and who (whatever may be the wishes of our opponents) I hope and trust will long fill the executive chair, not less to his own honour, than to the happiness of his fellow citizens: When he, Sir, recommended the repeal of the internal taxes, delay succeeded delay, and discussion was followed by discussion, until patience itself was worn thread bare.—But now when public plunder is the order of the day, how are we treated? Driven into the committee of the whole, and out again, in a breath, by an inflexible majority, exulting and stubborn in their strength, a decision must be had, instanter. The advocates for the proposed measure feel that it will not bear a scrutiny. Hence this precipitancy. They wince from the touch of examination, and are willing to hurry through a painful and disgraceful discussion. But it may be asked why this tenacious adherence of certain gentlemen to each other on every point connected with this subject? As if animated by one spirit, they perform all their evolutions with the most exact discipline, and march in firm phalanx directly up to their object. Is it that men combined to effect some evil purpose, acting on previous pledge to each other, are ever more in unison, than those who seeking only to discover truth, obey the impulse of that conscience which God has placed in their bosoms? Such men do not stand compromitted.—They will not stifle the suggestions of their own minds, and sacrifice their private opinions to the attainment of some common, perhaps nefarious object.

Having given vent to that effusion of indignation which I feel, and which I trust I shall never fail to feel and to express on this detestable subject, permit me now to offer some crude and hasty remarks on the points in dispute. They will be directed chiefly to the claim of the New England Mississippi Land Company, whom we propose to debar (with all the other claimants under the Act of 1795) from any benefit of the five millions of acres, reserved by our compact with Georgia, to satisfy such claims not specially provided for in that compact, as we might find worthy of recompense. I shall direct my observations more particularly to this claim, because it has been more insisted upon, and more zealously defended than any other. It is alleged by the memorialists who style themselves the agents of that Company, that they and those whom they represent, were innocent purchasers:—in other words, ignorant of the corruption and fraud, by which the Act, from which their pretended title was derived, was passed. I am well aware that this fact is not material to the question of any legal or equitable title, which they may set up—but as it has been made a pretext for exciting the compassion of the Legislature, I wish to examine into the ground upon which this allegation rests. Sir, when that Act of stupendous villainy was passed in 1795, attempting under the forms and semblance of law, to rob unborn millions of their birth right and inheritance, and to convey to a band of unprincipled and flagitious men, a territory more extensive, and beyond comparison more fertile, than any State of this union, it caused a sensation scarcely less violent than that produced by the passage of the Stamp Act, or the shutting up of the port of Boston:—with this difference, that when the port bill of Boston passed, her Southern brethren did not take advantage of the forms of law, by which a corrupt Legislature attempted to defraud her of the bounty of nature:— they did not speculate on the necessities and wrongs of their abused and insulted Countrymen.——I repeat that this infamous Act, was succeeded by a general burst of indignation throughout the Continent. This is a matter of public notoriety—and those—(I speak of men of intelligence and education, purchasers too of the very Country in question) those who effect to have been ignorant of any such circumstance I shall consider as guilty of gross and willful prevarication. They offer indeed to virtue the only homage which she is ever likely to receive at their hands—the homage of their hypocrisy. They could not make an assertion within the limits of possibility less entitled to credit.

Yes, the Act of the 7th of January, 1795, excited emotions, of detestation and abhorrence, equal to those produced by the Stamp Act or port bill of Boston. But this was not all. It drew upon it, the immediate attention of the Federal Government. The authority which is about to be produced to the House is one, which I am not in the habit of prostituting to every light occasion. It is one from which those who are daily endeavouring to shelter their crimes and their follies under its venerable shade, will not dare to appeal.

Upon looking in the Journals of this House, I find the

following message from the President, dated on the 17th February 1795.

"Gentleman of the Senate, and Gentlemen of the House of Representatives.

"I have received copies of two Acts of the Legislature of Georgia, one passed on the 28th of December 1794." (This, Sir, is the Act which the wavering virtue of the Governor induced him to reject.) "The other on the 7th of January 1795" (the Act under which the different Companies, from one of which the memorialists derive their pretended title claim) "for appropriating and selling the Indian Lands, within the territorial limits claimed by that state. These copies though not officially certified, have been transmitted to me in such a manner as to leave no room to doubt their authenticity. These Acts embrace an object of such magnitude, and in their consequences may so deeply affect the peace and welfare of the United States, that I have thought it necessary now to lay them before Congress."

Here, Sir, is ample notice to the whole world. This message was referred to a select Committee; consisting of Mr. John Nicholas, Mr. Mason, Mr. Findley, Mr. Murray, Mr. Boudinot, Mr. Ames, and Mr. Sherburne; on whose report after solemn deliberations in the committee of the whole, the House on the 26th of the same month came to the following resolution.

"RESOLVED that the President of the United States be authorised to obtain a cession from the State of Georgia of their claim to the whole, or any part of the land, within the present Indian boundaries." (The very land which the Act of the 7th January had attempted to alienate, and sell:) and the bill which I now hold in my hand was accordingly brought in, pursuant to the resolution, and passed the House on the second day of March. But unfortunately the session closed of necessity on the following day, and this House is well apprised that the forms of the Senate will not permit any bill to be hurried through that body. A single negative is sufficient to prevent it. The subject however was not suffered to sleep. An Act was subsequently passed opening a negotiation with Georgia for the Territory in question, of which we have received from her a solemn transfer. Is this notice, or is it not? On a formal message from the President laying before them the Act of 1795—so totally invalid and worthless was that Act in their eyes, in such utter contempt did they hold the pretended rights of the grantees under it— that the House of Representatives immediately passed a bill empowering the President to receive a grant of the very land, which that Act had previously and fraudulently attempted to convey to the four Companies. With what face could the President recommend or Congress endeavour to obtain from Georgia a cession of the whole or any part of the Land within her Indian boundaries, if they believed that the land in question had been conveyed to others by a fair and bona fide sale? If they attached to the Act of January 1795 any idea of validity? The man who answers this objection shall have my thanks. But perhaps I shall be told that this was the Act of a single branch of the Legislature and not a law. True, Sir; but it was a solemn averment to the world, that Congress had a right to Legislate on the subject. It was, notice, on the 17th and 26th days of February, 1795, that the Act passed by the State of Georgia, in the preceding month, was void and of no effect—it was loudly proclaimed by the convention of that state, which met in the succeeding May, and was finally consummated by the rescinding Act of the 13th of February, 1796, which was subsequently engrafted on the Constitution of Georgia. And yet the New England Mississippi Land Company, under a deed of contemporaneous date (as they say) with this last Act, a deed containing not merely a special warranty, but a special covenant that no recourse shall be had against the sellers for any defect of title in them; a covenant which clearly indicates notice on the part of the buyers of such defect; claiming under a deed by which they purchased such title only as the grantees of 1795 had to sell, in whose stead and place they agreed to stand; this Company affects to have no notice of any defect of title in those of whom they bought. Sanction the claim of this Company or any other derived from the Act of 1795, and what in effect do you declare? You record a solemn acknowledgement that Congress have unfairly and dishonestly obtained from Georgia a grant of land, to which that state no longer possessed a title, having previously sold it to others for a valuable consideration, of which transaction Congress was at that time fully apprised. Are you prepared to make this humiliating concession? To identify yourselves with the swindlers of 1795? To acknowledge that you have unfairly obtained from another that to which you knew he had no title? I trust, Sir, we have not yet reached this point of moral and political depravity.

The agents of the New England Land Company are unfortunate in two points. They set out with a formal endeavour to prove that they are entitled to their proportion of fifty millions of acres of land, under the law of 1795, and this they make their plea to be admitted to a proportional share of five. If they believe what they say, would they be willing to commute a good legal or equitable claim for one

tenth of its value? Their memorial contains moreover a suggestion of falsehood. They aver that the reservation of five
millions, for satisfying claims not otherwise provided for in
our compact with Georgia was specially intended for the
benefit of the Claimants under the Act of 1795, and that we
are pledged to satisfy them out of that reservation. Now, Sir,
turn to the 6th Volume of your laws, and what is the fact?
In the first place so much of the reserved five millions, as
may be necessary, is appropriated specifically for satisfying
claims derived from British grants, not regranted by Spain,
and as much of the residue as may be necessary is appropriated for compensating other claims, not recognized in our
compact with Georgia. An appropriation for certain British
grants specially, and for other claims generally, is falsely
suggested to have been made for the especial benefit of the
claimants of 1795—and the reservation of a power in the
United States to quiet such claims, as they should deem
worthy of compensation, is perverted into an obligation to
compensate a particular class of claims; into an acknowledgement that such claims are worthy of compensation. Can
this House be inveigled by such bare-faced effrontery? Sir,
the Act containing this appropriation clause was not brought
to a third reading till the first of March. Our powers expired
on the 4th: It was at the second session of the 7th Congress.
It was in the power of those opposed to the corrupt claims
of 1795 to have defeated the bill by a discussion. But, Sir,
they abstained on this ground. If the appropriation of the
five millions had not been made at that session, the year,
within which by our agreement with Georgia it was to be
made, if at all, would have expired before the meeting of
the next Congress: and it was urged by the friends of the bill
that there were several descriptions of claims to which no

imputation of fraud could attach; that by making a general appropriation we secured to ourselves the power of recompensing such claims, as on examination, might be found worthy of it, whilst we pledged ourselves to no class of claimants whatever. But that if we should suffer the term specified, in our compact with Georgia to elapse without making any appropriation, we should preclude ourselves from the ability to compensate any claims not specially provided for, however just and reasonable we might find them, on investigation to be. Under these circumstances, and I appeal to my excellent friend from Maryland who brought it in for the correctness of my Statement, the opponents of the bill gave it no other opposition than a silent vote. And now, Sir, we are told that we stand pledged, and that an appropriation for British grants, not regranted by Spain, specially, and for such other claims against the State of Georgia, generally as Congress should find quite worthy, was made for the especial benefit of a particular description of claimants, branded to be the deepest odium; who dare to talk to us of public faith, and appeal to the national honour.

The conclusion of the memorial is amusing enough. After having played over the farce, which was acted by the Yazoo squad at the last session, affecting to believe that an appropriation has been made by the Act of March 1803, for their especial benefit, they pray that Congress will be pleased to give them—what? That to which they assert they are entitled?—By no means—an eighth or a tenth part of it, if we may credit them, has been already appropriated to their use by law. From a knowledge of the memorialists and those whom they represent, can you believe for a moment that if they had the least faith in the volume of argument (I am sorry to profane the word) which they have presented to the House to prove the goodness of their title; can you believe that under such an impression they would accept a paltry compromise of two shillings in the pound—much less that to obtain it they would descend so low. Sir, when these men talk about public faith and national honour, they remind me of the appeals of the unprincipled gamester, and veteran usurer, to the honour of the thoughtless spendthrift, whilst in reality they are addressing themselves to his vices and his folly.

I have confined myself on this occasion principally to the question of notice, because it has been made an engine to play upon the generous feelings of many, and not because I deem it material to the question of title. It is not my intention to travel over the ground which I occupied at the last session on the following important points: that Georgia had no right to make the sale; that even if she had, the contract being laid in corruption and fraud, was null and void, *ab initio;* that consequently the question of notice was not material to the question of title, in the hands of third persons; since the original grant being obtained by bribery and fraud, no right could rest under it; and that the grantees of 1795 could not sell a greater or better title than they themselves possessed: and that even if these positions were as false as they are indisputably true, the present case presented a monstrous anomaly to which the ordinary and narrow maxims of municipal jurisprudence ought not, and cannot be applied. It is from the great first principles, to which the patriots of Georgia so gloriously appealed, that we must look for aid in such extremity. Yes, extreme cases, like this, call for extreme remedies. They bid defiance to palliatives, and it is only from the knife or the actual cautery, that you can expect relief. There is no cure short of extirpation. Attorneys and Judges do not decide the fate of Empires.

The right of the State of Georgia to sell, (although I do not propose to go largely into that question) is denied by your own statute book, by turning to which you will find, that so far from being able to transfer to others the right of extinguishing Indian title to land, she has not been able to exercise it for her own benefit. It is only through the agency of the United States that she can obtain the extinguishment of Indian title to the soil within her limits, much less could she delegate it to a few Yazoo men. But, as has been repeatedly stated on former discussions of this subject, even if the question of right on the part of Georgia to sell, and on the part of the grantees to take, be conceded, it cannot be controverted that the fraudulent and corrupt attempt of the Legislature of 1795 to betray the interest of those who had confided in them, was *ipso facto,* void; that no right could be vested by it in the instigators and participators of the fraud, and that these could not convey to others a better title than they themselves possessed. If the authority were worth any thing, I myself would cite that of the memorialists themselves and of the committee of claims in support of this position. It is allowed by these authorities that the title of the purchasers at second and third hand, is diminished in the ratio which five millions bear to the whole territory, which they modestly admit to contain thirty-five millions of acres, although there is the best reason to believe it to be nearer fifty. Now, Sir, they have not condescended to explain to us by what legerdemain it comes to pass that a title to thirty-five millions of acres (to take their own statement) is depreciated in their hands so fearfully as to quantity, is reduced to one seventh of its value, whilst the quality of the title, to that seventh is proportionately raised. Plain honest men would reason very differently. A man of this stamp would argue somewhat in this way: if the corrupt and cor-

rupting grantees of 1795 sold a claim to thirty-five millions
of acres to third persons, surely those persons would have
the same title to the whole of the property which they had
purchased, that they could pretend to set up to any part of
it. It would never occur to such a man, that whilst as to
quality these persons had bought a better title than the
vendors themselves had to sell, yet by some unintelligible
process, this better title was in quantity and of course in
value, wasted in their hands to one seventh part of its original worth: in other words, was seven times worse and at
the same time better, than the title of the original grantees.
Discoveries such as these have been reserved for the profound legal learning of the agents of the New England
Mississippi Land Company, and the ingenuity of the committee of claims! What, Sir, would you say to a pretender to
your estate, who, after laying claim to the whole of it, and
writing a volume of argument (if I may so abuse the term,
as to apply it to the sophisticated trash which I hold in my
hand) in support of his pretensions, should make it the
ground work of a proposal to receive a seventh or a tenth
part of what he declared him[self] legally and equitably
entitled to, and should at the same time affirm that you
were bound in honour to accede to his modest, considerate,
and generous proposition? Would you not scout him from
your presence as a swindler and as a disturber of the peace
of society, or would you be trepanned by his artifice, or
bullied by his effrontery out of your property?

The government of the United States, on a former
occasion, did not, indeed, ask in this firm and decided
manner. But those were hard, unconstitutional times, which
ought never to be drawn into precedent. The first year that I
had the honour of a seat in this House, an Act was passed

of a nature not altogether unlike the one now proposed. I allude to the case of the Connecticut reserve, by which the Nation were swindled out of some three or four millions of acres of land, which, like other bad titles, had fallen into the hands of innocent purchasers. Where I advert to the applicants by whom we were then beset, I find that among them was one of the very persons who style themselves agents of the New England Mississippi Land Company, who seems to have an unfortunate knack at buying bad titles. His gigantic grasp embraces with one hand the shores of Lake Erie and stretches with the other to the bay of Mobile. Millions of acres are easily digested by such stomachs. Goaded by avarice, they buy only to sell, and sell only to buy. The retail trade of fraud and imposture yields too small and slow a profit to gratify their cupidity. They buy and sell corruption in the gross, and a few millions more or less is hardly felt in the account. The deeper the play, the greater zest for the game and the stake which is set upon their throw, is nothing less than the patrimony of the people. Mr. Speaker, when I see the agency that has been employed on this occasion, I must own that it fills me with apprehension and alarm. This same agent is at the head of an executive department of our Government, subordinate indeed in rank and dignity, and in the ability required for its superintendence, but inferior to none in the influence attached to it. This officer, possessed of how many snug appointments and fat contracts, let the voluminous records on your table of the mere names, and dates, and sums declare, having an influence which is confined to no quarter of the Country, but pervading every part of the Union, with offices in his gift amongst the most lucrative, and at the same time the most laborious, or responsible, under the government, so tempting as to draw a member of the other House from his seat, and place him as a deputy at the feet of your applicant—this officer presents himself at your bar, at once a party and an advocate. Sir, when I see this tremendous patronage brought to bear upon us, I do confess that it strikes me with consternation and dismay. Is it come to this? Are Heads of Executive Departments of the Government to be brought into this House with all the influence and patronage attached to them, to extort from us now what was refused at the last session of Congress? I hope not, Sir, but if they are, and if the abominable villainy practised upon, and by, the Legislature of Georgia, in 1795, is now to be glossed over, I for one will ask what security they, by whom it shall be done, can offer for their reputations better than can be given for the character of that Legislature? I will pin myself upon this text and preach upon it as long as I have life. If no other reason can be adduced but a regard to our own fame, if it were only to rescue ourselves from this foul imputation, this weak and dishonourable compromise ought to receive a prompt and decisive rejection. Is the voice of patriotism lulled to rest? That we no longer hear the cry against an overbearing majority, determined to put down the Constitution, and deaf to every proposition of compromise? Such were the dire forebodings to which we have been heretofore compelled to listen. But if the enmity of such men be formidable, their friendship is deadly distinction, their touch pollution. What is the spirit against which we now struggle? Which we have vainly endeavoured to stifle? A monster generated by fraud, nursed in corruption, that in grim silence awaits his prey. It is the spirit of *Federalism!* That spirit which considers the many, as made only for a few, which sees in government nothing but a job, which is never so true to itself as when false to the nation. When I behold a certain party supporting and clinging to such a measure, almost to a man, I see men faithful only to their own principles; pursuing with steady step and untired zeal, the uniform tenor of their political life. But when I see associated with them in firm compact, others who once rallied under the standard of opposite principles, I am filled with apprehension and concern. Of what consequence is it that a man smiles in your face, holds out his hand, and declares himself the advocate of those political principles to which you also are attached, when you see him acting with your adversaries upon other principles, which the voice of the nation has put down, which I did hope were buried, never to rise again, in this section of the Globe? I speak of the plunder of the public property. Say what we will, the marrow and pith of this business will be found in the character of the great majority of its friends,—who stand, as they have before stood on this floor, the unblushing advocates of unblushing corruption. But this, it may be said, is idle declamation. We may be told, as we have been told before, that the squanderers of the public treasure are the guardians of the people against their worst enemies, themselves: that, to protect them from further dilapidation it is necessary to give the Cerberus of corruption, this many-headed dog of Hell a sop: that it is to your interest to pacify him:—and this sentiment is re-echoed by his yells. Good God, Sir! can you believe it, can any man believe it—is there a woman or child in the Country weak enough to credit it—that a set of speculators, out of pure regard for the public interest, are willing to sacrifice thirty millions of acres of land? That they press their offer to accept a seventh or a tenth of their claim, from motives of patriotism? Can

you believe that their love of Country has got the better of
their avarice, that their virtue is equal to such a sacrifice
at the shrine of the public welfare? Such men, I repeat it,
are formidable as enemies, but their friendship is fraught
with irresistible death. I fear indeed the *"Danaos et dona
ferentes."* But after the law in question shall have passed,
what security have you that the claimants will accede to
your terms of compromise?—That this is not a trap to obtain from Congress something like a recognition to their title
to be hereafter used against us? Sir, with all our wisdom, I
seriously doubt our ability to contend with the arts and
designs of the claimants, if they can once entangle us in
the net of our own Legislation. Let the Act of March, 1801,
of which already they have made so dexterous a use, be
remembered. They themselves have pointed out the course
which we ought to pursue. They have told us, that so long
as we refrain from Legislating on this subject, their case is
hopeless. Let us then persevere in a "wise and masterly
inactivity."

Whenever a bill shall be introduced in conformity to the
principles of the report, if such should unfortunately be the
decision of the House, I trust that some gentleman more
competent than myself will be ready to give it a more
effectual opposition. My weak health and want of preparation unfit me for the task. But, Sir, if this claim is to be
admitted, I hope we shall not fail to go the whole length of
our principle—that we shall not narrow down to five millions of acres a legal or equitable title to fifty. If Congress
shall determine to sanction this fraud upon the public, I
trust in God we shall have no more of the crimes and follies
of the former administration. For one, I promise that my
lips upon this subject shall be closed in eternal silence.—I

should disdain to prate about the petty larcenies of our predecessors, after having given my sanction to this atrocious public robbery. Their petty delinquencies will vanish before it, as the stars of the firmament fade at the effulgent approach of a summer's Sun.

DEBATE ON THE YAZOO CLAIMS
February 1, 1805

[Here Randolph heaps reproaches upon members of his own party for their advocacy of the Yazoo claims. The text is that of the manuscript in the hand of Randolph's secretary, in the Randolph papers at the University of Virginia.]

Mr. Randolph said, that, as well as his extreme indisposition, and excessive hoarseness would permit, he would lay before the House some observations on the various objections, which had been urged against the amendment of his worthy and respectable colleague (Mr. Clark), for such he was in every point of view. He complained of disingenuous and unfair practices on the part of some of his opponents. They had undertaken to argue upon a supposed admission of his friend and himself, that the Act of 1795 created a contract between the State of Georgia and the grantees therein named.

This is nothing less than begging, or rather a flagrant robbery, of the question. We deny that any contract has been, or could be made under such circumstances—that fraud is a basis on which a contract can be created. Gentlemen must drive into this morass of corruption, piles of stronger argument and sounder reasoning before they can build a Stadt House of a conclusion upon it. 'Tis a quagmire over which they cannot pass; and in their awkward attempts to get round it, they confess, even whilst they affect to deny its existence. Fraud has rendered it without bottom. The Act of 1795, is at once declaratory of that fraud, and the highest possible evidence of the fact. The claimants, and their advocates themselves concede it, when they cling to the report of the commissioners, by which it is expressly affirmed, and which explicitly declares that their title cannot be supported. And when they come into this House with that report in their hands, and whine and cringe for our bounty, do they not abandon all pretensions to title? Yes, the advocates of these claims are compelled to acknowledge the fraud, and yield the ground of contract. How else can they justify their own fraud and injustice in stripping fair contractors with a good title, of seven-eighths of their rightful, and *bona fide* purchase? This point cannot be kept too much in sight, nor too strongly insisted on.

The venerable gentleman from Pennsylvania (Mr. Findley) when he gave in his recantation of his last year's opinions on this subject, told you that General Washington's message had no reference to the fraudulence of the Act of 1795. He considered it as a caveat on behalf of the United States, who claimed a great part of the Territory in question. Be it so. Was that notice to subsequent purchasers or not? How will the gentleman reconcile this inconsistency? Within the disputed limits between the Federal Government and Georgia, five-sixths of this very New England Company's purchase were comprised, besides that valuable part of the Georgia Company's grant, contained in the fork of the Alabama and Tombigbee. The United States contended that the country west of the Chattahoochee, and south of a parallel of latitude which should intersect the mouth of the Yazoo river, never constituted a part of Georgia; that it was within the limits of the province of West Florida, from which being severed by the peace of 1783, it became vested in the Confederacy, and not in the State to which it happened to be contiguous. The far greater part of the grant to the Georgia Mississippi Company is embraced within these limits. The purchase of the New England Company is stated by themselves to have been made [by] that Company twelve months after the President's message: the gentleman from Pennsylvania himself considers this message as a formal annunciation of the adverse claim of the United States to the land in question, and in the same breath avers that the New England Company, subsequently purchasers of that very land were ignorant of any defect of title in the State of Georgia, or the grantees under her. How will he reconcile this?

The same gentleman has introduced into this debate the names of two persons; one of them, at that time a Judge of the Supreme Court of the United States, the other a Senator from the State of Georgia; who, he tells us, were deeply concerned in the transactions of 1795. Both these gentlemen are no more. Private character, always dear, always to be respected, seems almost to be canonized by the grave. When men go hence, their evil deeds should follow them, and, for me might sleep oblivious in their tomb. But if the mouldering ashes of the dead are to be raked up, let it not be for the furtherance of injustice. In every stage of this discussion, whilst I have kept my eye steadily fixed on the enormity of the Act of 1795, I have lost sight of the agents. Since, however, some of them have been mentioned, it may not be immaterial to notice the interest which they took in this business. It is too true, Sir, that the Senator in question was

one of the fathers of the Act of 1795. By the Assembly
which passed it, he was at the same session re-elected to the
Senate of the United States, for six years thereafter. It is
equally true, Mr. Speaker, that the notorious British treaty
was ratified by that Senator's casting vote. And as the
Yazoo speculation then carried through the British treaty,
now it seems that the adherents of that treaty are to drag
the Yazoo speculation out of the mire. The connection of
the two questions at that day is too notorious to be denied.
That very Senator, were he now here, would disdain to deny
it. With all his faults he was a man of some noble qualities.
Hypocrisy at least, was not in the catalogue of his vices.
The coupling together of the British treaty and the Yazoo
business cannot surely be unknown to the gentleman from
Pennsylvania. He was a member of the House of Representatives which voted for the appropriation for carrying
that treaty into effect, and is understood to have acted a
conspicuous part on the occasion. Can it be a matter of
surprise that the same Senate that ratified the British treaty
by the casting vote of one of the principal grantees of the
act of Georgia of 1795, should refuse to co-operate with the
House of Representatives in measures for obviating the mischief of that act? When you see this corruption extending
itself to the two great departments of Government, can you
wonder at the bitterness of its fruit? With their leaders in
the Legislature and on the judgment seat, well might the
host of corruption feel confident in their strength; even yet
they have scarcely laid aside their audacity.

A gentleman from Massachusetts (Dr. Eustis) has said
that the claimants from his state had no notice of the fraud,
that he *knows they had not*—I cannot have mistaken him,
for I took down the words. Sir, I would ask that gentleman,

whence arises the proverbial difficulty of proving a negative but from the difficulty of knowing one?

The facts which I am about to mention are derived from such a source, that I could almost pledge myself for their truth: when the agent of the Georgia Mississippi Company (under whom the New England Company claim) arrived in the Eastern States, he had great difficulty in disposing of his booty. The rumour of the fraud by which it was acquired had gone before him. People did not like to vest their money in the new Mississippi scheme. He accordingly applied to some leading men of wealth and intelligence, offering to some as high [as] 200,000 acres and others less, for which they were neither to pay money nor pass their paper, but were to stand on his books as purchasers at so much per acre. These were the decoy birds to bring ducks and geese into the net of speculation. On the faith of these persons, under the idea that men of their information would not risk such vast sums without some prospect of return—others resolved to venture, and gambled in this new land fund,—laid out their money in the Yazoo lottery and have drawn blanks. And these, Sir, are the innocent purchasers without price, who never paid a shilling, and never can be called upon for one; the vile panders of speculation: and in what do their dupes differ from the losers in any other gambling or usurious transaction. The premium was proportioned to the risk. As well may your buyers and sellers of stock, your bulls and your bears of the alley require indemnification for their losses at the hands of the nation.

The chairman of the Committee of Claims who brought in the report, under the lash of whose criticism we have all so often smarted that he is generally known as the pedagogue of the House, will give me leave on this subject to refer him to an authority. 'Tis one with which he is no doubt familiar and (however humble) well disposed to respect. The authority which I am about to cite is Dillworth's Spelling Book, and if it will be more grateful to the gentleman, not our common American edition, but the royal English Spelling Book. In one of the chapters of that useful elementary work it is related that two persons going into a shop on pretence of purchase—one of them stole a piece of goods and handed it to the other to conceal under his cloak. When challenged with the theft, he who stole it said he had it not, and he who had it said he did not take it. "Gentlemen," replied the honest tradesman, "what you say may be all very true, but at the same time, I know that between you I am robbed." And such precisely is our case. But I hope, Sir, we shall not permit the parties, whether original grantees who took it, or subsequent purchasers who have it, to make off with the public property.

The rigor of the Committee of Claims has passed into a proverb. It has more than once caused the justice of this House to be questioned. What then was our surprise on reading their report to find that they have discovered "equity" in the pretensions of these petitioners. Sir, when the war-worn soldier of the revolution or the desolate widow and famished offspring of him who sealed your Independence with his blood, ask at the door of that committee for bread, they receive the Statute of Limitation. On such occasions you hear of no "equity" in the case. Their claims have not the stamp and seal of iniquity. *"Summum jus"* is the measure dealt out to them. The equity of the committee is reserved for those claims which are branded with iniquity and stamped with infamy. This reminds me of the story of a poor distressed female in London, applying for admittance into the Magdalen Charity. Being asked who she was, her wretched tale was told in a few words—"I am poor, innocent, and friendless." "Unhappy girl," replied the Director, "your case does not come within the purview of this institution! Innocence has no admission here. This is a place of reception for prostitutes. You must go and qualify yourself before you can partake of our relief."

With equal discretion, the directors of the Committee of Claims suffer nothing to find support in their asylum but what is tainted with corruption, and stamped with fraud. Give it to these properties and they will give it "equity."

But we have been told that the United States gave even less for these lands than the price paid by the several companies of 1795. Admitting the fact (which is unquestionably false)—did Georgia sell to the Union for pounds, shillings and pence? Did North Carolina and Virginia in their Acts of cession of even more extensive countries, look to pecuniary profit? Are we become so grovelling that public spirit and the general good go for nothing? The money which we engaged to pay out of the proceeds of the lands, although more than double the amount paid by the four companies in 1795, constitutes but a small part even of the pecuniary consideration. We are, moreover, pledged to the extinguishment of the Indian title to an immense territory, within the present limits of Georgia—it has been whispered in my ear that the fate of the late treaty with the Greeks is to depend on the decision of this question; and as the British treaty and the Yazoo were made to stand or fall together in 1795, so the Greek treaty and the Yazoo are to stand or fall together in 1805. But those who hold out this threat to the members from Georgia should know them better; should be told that they are made of the sternest stuff of republicanism, and can neither be coaxed, or intimidated out of their principles. Of those who talk of the Western lands being acquired for nothing I would ask if that be an argument for throwing them away upon flagitious men? But were the toils, and dangers, and treasure of the revolution nothing? The bloody battles, the burning and devastation of the Southern and Western Countries? Was the expedition of the brave and intrepid Clark, which wants only a Polybius to rival the march of Thrasymene; were the exploits of this American Hannibal who secured the Western Country to you, nothing? Were your Indian wars and massacres, nothing?

This government, let me remind you, has acquired the confidence of the public by the disinterestedness of its measures. The repeal of the internal taxes is not the least conspicuous among them. How long will you retain that well earned confidence if you lavish on a band of speculators a landed capital whose annual interest is more than equivalent to the whole proceeds of those taxes? I will not go into petty details now, but I pledge myself that whoever makes the calculation will find the value of the land, together with the expense of extinguishing the Indian title at the rate of our last treaty in that quarter to yield a clear perpetual annuity equal to the receipt from the internal taxes. What would you say to a proposition to receive those taxes and mortgage them for the payment of the interest on a Yazoo stock? Do you wonder that we shrink from such a precipice? Shall a republican House of Representatives sanction this wanton waste of the public resources to nourish the bane of every Republic? Are you simple enough to believe that five millions will quiet them? Yes, as the tribute of the Roman world satisfied their barbarian enemies. You only whet their appetite to increase their means of extorting more. Like the Gauls after the sack of Rome, they will make their second attempt upon the capital before they have divided the plunder acquired in the first. When I see the formidable front displayed by this band of broken speculators I am irresistibly impelled to enquire what would have been their force if their attempt upon the Western Country of Georgia had not been baffled by the virtue and patriotism of that State? What is there in this Government that could have coped with them? Sir, you must have built another wing to your capitol, for the third branch of your Legislature. You would have had a Yazoo estate in your empire, not with a qualified negative, but an absolute veto on all your proceedings. Scarcely would they have left you the initiative.

I have said, and I repeat it, that the aspect in which this thing presents itself would, alone, determine me to resist it. In one of the petitioners I behold an Executive Officer, who receives and distributes a yearly revenue of 300,000 dollars, yielding scarcely any net profit to the Government. Offices in his disposal to the amount of 94,000 dollars, and contracts more lucrative making up the residue of that sum. A patronage limited only by the extent of our Country. Is this right? Is it even decent? Shall political power be made the engine of private interest? Shall such a suspicion tarnish your proceedings? How would you receive a petition from a President of the United States, if such a case can be supposed possible? Sir, I wish to see the same purity pervading every subordinate branch of administration, which I am persuaded exists in its great departments. Shall persons holding appointments under the great and good man who presides over our counsels, draw on the rich fund of his well earned reputation, to eke out their flimsy and scanty pretensions? Is the relation in which they stand to him to be made the cloak and cover of their dark designs? To the gentleman from New York (Mr. Root), who takes fire at every insinuation against his friend, I have only to observe on this subject, that what I dare to say I dare to justify. To the House, I will relate an incident how far I have lightly conceived or expressed an opinion to the prejudice of any man. I owe an apology to my informant for making public what he certainly did not authorize me to reveal. There is no reparation which can be offered by one gentleman and accepted by another that I shall not be ready to make him, but I feel myself already justified to him, since he sees the circumstances under which I act.

A few evenings since, a profitable contract for carrying the mail was offered to a friend of mine who is a member of this House. You must know, Sir, the person so often alluded to maintains a Jackall-face—not as you would suppose upon the offal of contract, but with the fairest prices in the shambles; and at night when honest men are abed, does this obscene animal prowl through the streets of this vast and desolate city, seeking whom he may tamper with— Well, Sir, when this worthy plenipotentiary has made his proposal in due form, the independent man to whom it was addressed saw at once its drift. "Tell your principal," said he, "that I will take his contract, but I shall vote against the Yazoo claims notwithstanding." Next day he was told that there had been some misunderstanding of the business, that he could not have the contract as it was previously bespoken by another.

Sir, I well recollect when first I had the honour of a seat in this House, we were then members of a small minority— a poor, forlorn hope—that this very petitioner appeared at

Philadelphia on behalf of another great Land Company on Lake Erie. He then told us, as an inducement to vote for the Connecticut reserve (as it was called), that if that measure failed it would ruin the republicans and the cause in that State. You, Sir, cannot have forgotten the reply he received—that we did not understand the republicanism that was to be paid for—that we feared it was not of the right sort, but spurious—and having maintained our principles through the ordeal of that day, shall we now abandon them to act with the men and upon the maxims which we then abjured? Shall we now condescend to means which we disdained to use in the most desperate crisis of our political fortune? This is indeed the age of monstrous coalitions . . . and this corruption has the quality of cementing the most inveterate enemies, personal as well as political. It has united in close concert those, of whom it has been said, not in the figurative language of prophecy, but in the sober narrative of History: "I have bruised thy head, and thou hast bruised my heel." Such is the description of persons who would present to the President of the United States an Act, to which, when he puts his hand, he signs a libel on his whole political life. But he will never tarnish the unsullied lustre of his fame; he will never sanction the monstrous position (for such it is—dress it up as you will) that a Legislator may sell his vote, and a right which cannot be divested will pass under such sale. Establish this doctrine, and there is an end of Representative Government; from that moment, Republicanism receives its death blow.

The feeble cry of "Virginian influence" and "ambitious leaders" is attempted to be raised. If such insinuations were worthy of reply, I might appeal to you, Mr. Speaker, for the fact that no man in this House, (yourself perhaps excepted) is oftener in a minority than I am. If by a leader, he meant one who speaks his opinions frankly and boldly—who claims something of that independence of which the gentleman from New York so loudly vaunts, who will not connive at public robbery—be the robbers whom they may; then the imputation may be just. Such is the nature of my ambition. But, in the common acceptation of words, nothing can be more false. In the coarse, but strong language of the proverb: " 'Tis the still sow that sucks the draff." No, Sir, we are not the leaders. *There* they sit, and well they know it, forcing down our throats the most obnoxious measures. Gentlemen may be silent, but they shall be dragged into public view. If they direct our counsels, at least let them answer for the result. We will not be responsible for their measures. If we do not hold the reins, we will not be accountable for the accidents which may befall the carriage.

But, Sir, I am a denunciator! Of whom? Of the gentlemen on my left? Not at all—but of those men, and their principles, whom the people themselves have denounced, on whom they have burnt their indelible curse deep and lasting as the lightning of Heaven. But you are told not to regard such idle declamation. I would remind the gentleman from New York that if to declaim be not to reason, so neither is it to be argumentative to be dull. Warmth is a creature of the heart, not of the head. A position in itself just can lose no part of its truth from the manner in which it is uttered, whether by the direst and most stupid special pleader, or bellowed with the lungs of Stentor. Are our opponents ashamed of their cause that they devolve its defence on the little ones by which we are beset?

Mr. Speaker, I had hoped that we should not be content to live upon the principal of our popularity—that we should go on to deserve the public confidence and the disapprobation of the gentleman over the way; but if every thing is to be reversed, if official influence is to become the hand maid of private interest, if the old system is to be revived with the old men—or any that can be picked up—I may deplore the defection but never will cease to stigmatize it. Never shall I hesitate between any minority far less that in which I now find myself, and such a majority as is opposed to us. I took my degrees, Sir, in this House, in a minority much smaller indeed, but of the same stamp. A majority whose every act bore the test of vigorous principle, and with them to the last I will exclaim *"fiat justitia ruat coelum."*

DEBATE ON MR. GREGG'S MOTION
March 5, 1806

[Randolph stated that this speech was the only one he ever prepared carefully in advance of delivery. In opposing Jefferson's plan for the purchase of West Florida from Spain (then dominated by Napoleon), Randolph severed himself permanently from the Jeffersonian Republicans. The manuscript of this speech, in Randolph's secretary's hand, is at the University of Virginia.]

Mr. Randolph said: I am extremely afraid, Sir, that so far as may depend on my acquaintance with details connected with the subject, I have very little right to address you, for, in truth, I have not yet seen the documents from the Treasury, which were called for some time ago, to direct the judgment of this House in the decision of the question now before you; and indeed, after what I have this day heard, I no longer require that document—or any other document—indeed, I do not know that I ever should have required it, to vote on the resolution of the gentleman from Pennsylvania. If I had entertained any doubts, they would have been removed by the style in which the friends of the resolution have this morning discussed it. I am perfectly aware that on entering upon this subject, we go into it manacled—hand-cuffed and tongue-tied; gentlemen know that our lips are sealed on subjects of momentous foreign relations which are indissolubly linked with the present question, and which would serve to throw a great light on it in every respect relevant to it. I will, however, endeavour to hobble over the subject as well as my fettered limbs and palsied tongue will enable me to do it.

I am not surprised to hear this resolution discussed by its friends as a war measure. They say (it is true) that it is not a war measure; but they defend it on principles that would justify none but war measures, and seem pleased with the idea that it may prove the forerunner of War. If war is necessary—if we have reached this point—let us have war! But while I have life, I will never consent to these incipient war measures, which, in their commencement, breathe nothing but peace, though they plunge us at last into war. It has been well observed by the gentleman from Pennsylvania behind me (Mr. J. Clay) that the situation of this nation in 1793 was in every respect different from that in which it finds itself in 1805. Let me ask too, if the situation of England is not since materially changed? Gentlemen who, it would appear from their language, have not got beyond the horn book of politics, talk of our ability to cope with the British navy, and tell us of the war of our revolution. What was the situation of Great Britain then? She was then contending for the empire of the British channel, barely

able to maintain a doubtful equality with her enemies, over
whom she never gained the superiority until Rodney's victory of the 12th of April. What is her present situation? The
combined fleets of France, Spain, and Holland are dissi-
pated; they no longer exist. I am not surprised to hear men
advocate these wild opinions, to see them goaded on by a
spirit of mercantile avarice, straining their feeble strength
to excite the nation to war, when they have reached this
stage of infatuation that we are over-matched for Great
Britain on the Ocean. It is mere waste of time to reason
with such persons. They do not deserve anything like serious
refutation. The proper arguments for such statesmen are a
strait waistcoat, a dark room, water, gruel, and depletion.

It has always appeared to me that there are three points
to be considered—and maturely considered—before we can
be prepared to vote for the resolution of the gentleman from
Pennsylvania. First, our ability to contend with Great
Britain for the question in dispute; Secondly, the policy of
such a contest; and Thirdly, in case both these shall be
settled affirmatively, the manner in which we can, with the
greatest effect, re-act upon, and annoy our adversary.

Now the gentleman from Massachusetts (Mr. Crowninshield) has settled at a single sweep, to use one of his
favourite expressions, not only that we are capable of contending with Great Britain on the Ocean, but that we are
actually her superior. Whence does the gentleman deduce
this inference? Because truly, at that time when Great
Britain was not mistress of the Ocean, when a North was
her Prime Minister and a Sandwich the first lord of her
admiralty, when she was governed by a counting house administration, privateers of this country trespassed on her
commerce. So did the cruisers of Dunkirk at that day Suf-

fren held the mastery of the Indian Seas. But what is the case now? Do gentlemen remember the capture of Cornwallis on land because De Grasse maintained the dominion of the ocean? To my mind, no position is more clear than that if we go to war with Great Britain, Charleston and Boston, the Chesapeake and the Hudson will be infested by British Squadrons. Will you call on the Count De Grasse to relieve them, or shall we apply to the Admiral Gravina or Admiral Villeneuve to raise the blockade?

But—you have not only a prospect of gathering glory, and what seems to the gentleman from Massachusetts much dearer, profit, by privateering; you will be able to make a conquest of Canada and Nova Scotia. Indeed? Then, Sir, we shall catch a Tartar. I confess, however, I have no desire to see the Senators and Representatives of the Canadian French, or of the tories and refugees of Nova Scotia sitting on this floor or that of the other House—to see them becoming members of the Union, and participating equally in our political rights. And on what other principle would the gentleman from Massachusetts be for incorporating those provinces with us? Or on what other principle could it be done under the Constitution? If the gentleman has no other bounty to offer us for going to war, than the incorporation of Canada and Nova Scotia with the United States, I am for remaining at peace. What is the question in dispute? The carrying trade. What part of it? The fair, the honest, and the useful trade that is engaged in carrying our own productions to foreign markets, and bringing back their productions in exchange? No, Sir—it is that carrying trade which covers enemy property, and carries the coffee, the sugar, and other West India products to the Mother Country. No, Sir— if this great agricultural nation is to be governed by Salem and Boston—New York and Philadelphia and Baltimore and Norfolk and Charleston, let gentlemen come out and say so: and let a committee of public safety be appointed from those towns to carry on the government. I, for one, will not mortgage my property and my liberty to carry on this trade. The nation said so seven years ago—I said so then—I say so now—It is not for the honest carrying trade of America, but for this mushroom, this fungus, of war— for a trade which as soon as the nations of Europe are at peace will no longer exist. It is for this that the spirit of avaricious traffic would plunge us into war. I am forcibly struck on this occasion by the recollection of a remark made by one of the ablest (if not the honestest) ministers that England ever produced. I mean Sir Robert Walpole, who said that the country gentlemen (poor meek souls!) came up every year to be sheared—that they lay mute and patient whilst their fleeces were taking off—but if he touched a single bristle of the commercial interest, the whole sty was in an uproar. It was indeed shearing the hog—great cry and little wool. But we are asked, are we willing to bend the neck to England: to submit to her outrages?

No, Sir, I answer that it will be time enough for us to tell gentlemen what we will do to vindicate the violation of our flag on the ocean, when they shall have told us what they have done in resentment of the violation of the actual territory of the U.S. Not your new-fangled country over the Mississippi, but the good old U.S.—part of Georgia, of the old thirteen states, where citizens have been taken, not from our ships, but from our actual territory. When gentlemen have taken the padlock from our mouths, I shall be ready to tell them what I will do, relative to our dispute with Britain, on the law of nations, on contraband, and such stuff.

I have another objection to this course of proceeding. Great Britain, when she sees it, will say: the American people have great cause of dissatisfaction with Spain. She will see, by the documents furnished by the President, that Spain has outraged our territory, pirated upon our commerce, and imprisoned our citizens. She will enquire what we have done. It is true she will receive no answer, but she must know what we have not done. She will see that we have not repelled these outrages, nor made any additions to our army and navy—nor even classed the Militia. No, Sir—not one of your militia generals in politics has marshalled a single brigade.

Although I have said it would be time enough to answer the question which gentlemen have put to me when they shall have answered mine, yet, as I do not like long prorogations, I will give them an answer now. I will never consent to go to war for that which I cannot protect. I deem it no sacrifice of dignity to say to the Leviathan of the deep: we are unable to contend with you in your own element, but if you come within our actual limits we will shed our last drop of blood in their defence. In such an event, I would feel, not reason, and obey an impulse which never has—which never can deceive me. France is at war with England. Suppose her power on the Continent of Europe no greater than it is on the ocean, how would she make her enemy feel it? There would be a perfect non-conductor between them. So with the United States and England—she scarcely presents to us a vulnerable point. Her commerce is now carried on for the most part in fleets—where in single ships they are stout and well armed—very different from the state of her trade during the American war, when her merchantmen became the prey of paltry privateers. Great Britain has been

too long at war with the three most powerful maritime nations of Europe not to have learnt how to protect her trade.
She can afford to convey it to all—she has eight hundred
ships in commission. The navies of her enemies are anni-
hilated. Thus, this war has presented the new and curious
political spectacle of a regular annual increase (and to an
immense amount) of her imports, and exports, and tonnage, and revenue, and all the insignia of accumulating
wealth, whilst in every former war, without exception, these
have suffered a greater or less diminution. And wherefore?
Because she has driven France and Spain and Holland from
the Ocean. Their marine is no more. I verily believe that
ten English ships of the line would not decline a meeting
with the combined fleets of those nations.

I forewarn the gentleman from Massachusetts, and his
constituents at Salem—that all their golden hopes are in
vain. I forewarn them of the exposure of their trade beyond
the Cape of Good Hope (or now doubling it) to capture and
confiscation—of their unprotected sea port towns, exposed
to contribution or bombardment. Are we to be Legislated
into war by a set of men, who, in six weeks from its commencement may be compelled to take refuge with us up in
the country? And for what? A mere fungus—a mushroom
production of war in Europe, which will disappear with the
first return of peace—an unfair trade. For is there a man
so credulous as to believe that we possess a capital not only
equal to what may be called our own proper trade, but large
enough also to transmit to the respective parent states the
vast and wealthy products of the French, Spanish, and
Dutch colonies? 'Tis beyond the belief of any rational being.

But this is not my only objection to entering upon this
naval warfare. I am averse to a naval war with any nation

whatever. I was opposed to the naval war of the last administration, and I am as ready to oppose a naval war of the
present administration, should they meditate such a measure. What? Shall this great Mammoth of the American
forest leave his native element and plunge into the water
in a mad contest with the Shark? Let him beware that his
proboscis is not bitten off in the engagement. Let him stay
on shore—and not be excited by the mussels and peri-
winkles on the strand, or political bears in a boat, to venture on the perils of the deep.

Gentlemen say: will you not protect your violated rights?
And I say: why take to water, where you can neither fight
nor swim? Look at France—see her vessels stealing from
port to port on her own coast—and remember that she is
the first military power of the Earth, and as a naval people,
second only to England. Take away the British navy, and
France tomorrow is the tyrant of the ocean.

This brings me to the second point. How far is it politic
in the United States to throw their weight into the scale of
France at this moment, from whatever motive, in view of
her gigantic ambition—to make her mistress of the sea and
land—to jeopardize the liberties of mankind? Sir, you may
help to crush Great Britain, you may assist in breaking
down her naval dominion, but you cannot succeed to it.
The iron sceptre of the ocean will pass into his hands who
wears the iron crown of the land. You may then expect a
new code of maritime law. Where will you look for redress?
I can tell the gentleman from Massachusetts that there is
nothing in his rule of three that will save us, even although
he should outdo himself and exceed the financial ingenuity
which he so memorably displayed on a recent occasion. No,
Sir, let the battle of Actium be once fought, and the whole

line of sea coast will be at the mercy of the conqueror. The Atlantic, deep and wide as it is, will prove just as good a barrier against his ambition if directed against you, as the Mediterranean to the power of the Caesars. Do I mean (when I say so) to crouch to the invader? No—I will meet him at the water's edge, and fight every inch of ground from thence to the mountains, from the mountains to the Mississippi. But after tamely submitting to an outrage on your domicile, will you bully and look big at an insult on your flag three thousand miles off?

But yet, sir, I have a more cogent reason against going to war for the honour of the flag in the narrow seas, or any other maritime punctilio. It springs from my attachment to the principles of the Government under which I live. I declare in the face of day, that this Government was not instituted for the purpose of offensive war. No—it was framed (to use its own language) for the common defence and the general welfare, which are inconsistent with offensive war. I call that offensive war which goes out of our jurisdiction and limits for the attainment or protection of objects not within those limits and that jurisdiction. As in 1798 I was opposed to this species of warfare, because I believed it would raze the constitution to its very foundation, so in 1806 am I opposed to it, and on the same grounds. No sooner do you put the Constitution to this use, to a test which it is by no means calculated to endure, than its incompetency to such purposes becomes manifest and apparent to all. I fear if you go into a foreign war for a circuitous, unfair foreign trade, you will come out without your Constitution. Have you not contractors enough in this House? Or do you want to be overrun and devoured by commissaries and all the vermin of contract? I fear, Sir, that what are called the energy men will rise up again—men who will burn the parchment. We shall be told that our Government is too free, or, as they would say, weak and inefficient. Much virtue, Sir, in terms. That we must give the President power to call forth the resources of the nation—that is, to filch the last shilling from our pockets, or to drain the last drop of blood from our veins. I am against giving this power to any man, be him who he may. The American people must either withhold this power, or resign their liberties. There is no other alternative. Nothing but the most imperious necessity will justify such a grant—and is there a powerful enemy at our doors?

You may begin with a first consul; from that chrysalis state he soon becomes an Emperor. You have your choice. It depends upon your election whether you will be a free, happy, and united people at home, or the light of your executive majesty shall beam across the Atlantic in one general blaze of the public liberty. For my part, I never will go to war but in self defence. I have no desire for conquests, no ambition to possess Nova Scotia. I hold the liberties of this people at a higher rate. Much more am I indisposed for war, when amongst the first means of carrying it on I see gentlemen propose the confiscation of debts due by Government to individuals. Does a *bona fide* creditor know who holds this paper? Dare any honest man ask himself the question? 'Tis hard to say whether such principles are more detestably dishonest than they are weak and foolish. What, Sir: will you go about with proposals for opening a loan in one hand, and a sponge for the national debt in the other? If on a late occasion you could not borrow at a less rate of interest than eight percent—when the Government avowed that they would pay to the last shilling of the public ability —at what price do you expect to raise money with an avowal of these nefarious opinions? God help you! if these are your ways and means of carrying on a war; if your finances are in the hands of such a Chancellor of the Exchequer!

Because a man can take an observation, and keep a log book and a reckoning, can navigate a cockboat to [the] West Indies or the East, shall he aspire to navigate the great vessel of State? To stand at the helm of public councils? *Ne sutor ultra crepidam.* What are you going to war for? For the carrying trade. Already you possess seven-eighths of it . . . you may go to war for the excrescence of the trade —and make peace at the expense of the Constitution. Your executive will lord it over you, and you must make the best terms with the conqueror that you can.

But the gentleman from Pennsylvania (Mr. Gregg) tells you that he is for acting in this as in all things, uninfluenced by the opinion of any minister whatever—foreign, or, I presume, domestic. On this point I am willing to meet the gentleman. I am unwilling to be dictated to by any minister at home or abroad. Is he willing to act on the same independent footing? I have before protested, and again protest against secret, irresponsible, over-ruling influence. The first question I asked when I saw the gentleman's resolution was: is this a measure of the cabinet? Not of an open, declared cabinet, but of an invisible, inscrutable, unconstitutional cabinet—without responsibility, unknown to the Constitution? I speak of backstairs influence—of men who bring messages to this House, which, although they do not appear on the journals, govern its decisions. Sir, the first question that I asked on the subject of British relations was: what is the opinion of the cabinet? What measures will they recommend to Congress? (Well knowing that whatever measures we might take, they must execute them—and therefore that we should have their opinion on the subject—my answer was [and from a cabinet minister too]: there is no longer any cabinet! Subsequent circumstances Sir, have given me a personal knowledge of the fact. It needs no commentary.)

But the gentleman has told you that you ought to go to war, if for nothing else, for the Fur Trade. Now, Sir, the people on whose support he seems to calculate, follow, let me tell him, a better business. And let me add, that whilst men are happy at home, reaping their own fields, the fruits of their labour and industry, there is little danger of their being induced to go sixteen or seventeen hundred miles in pursuit of beavers, raccoons, or opossums—much less of going to war for the privilege. They are better employed where they are.

This trade, Sir, may be important to Britain; to nations who have exhausted every resource of industry at home—bowed down by taxation and wretchedness. Let them, in God's Name, if they please, follow the Fur Trade. They may, for me, catch every beaver in North America. Yes, Sir, our people have a better occupation—a safe, profitable, honourable employment. Whilst they should be engaged in distant regions in hunting the beaver, they dread lest those whose natural prey they are, should begin to hunt *them*—should pillage their property, and assassinate their Constitution. Instead of these wild schemes, pay off your debt! Instead of prating about its confiscation, do not, I beseech you, expose at once your knavery and your folly. You have more lands than you know what to do with—you have lately paid fifteen millions for yet more. Go and work them, and cease to alarm the people with the cry of "Wolf," until they become deaf to your voice, or at least laugh at you.

Mr. Chairman, if I felt less regard for what I deem the best interests of this nation, than for my own reputation, I should not, on this day, have offered to address you; but would have waited to come out bedecked with flowers and bouquets of rhetoric in a set speech. But, Sir, I dreaded lest a tone might be given to the minds of the committee. They will pardon me, but I did fear, from all that I could see or hear, that they might be prejudiced by its advocates (under pretence of protecting our commerce) in favour of the ridiculous and preposterous project. I rose, Sir, for one, to plead guilty—to declare in the face of day that I will not go to war for this carrying trade. I will agree to pass for an idiot if this is not the public sentiment, and you will find it to your cost, begin the war when you will.

Gentlemen talk of 1793. They might as well go back to the Trojan War. What was your situation then? Then every heart beat high with sympathy for France—for Republican France! I am not prepared to say with my friend from Pennsylvania that we were all ready to draw our swords in her cause, but I affirm that we were prepared to have gone great lengths. I am not ashamed to pay this compliment to the hearts of the American people, even at the expense of their understandings. It was a noble and generous sentiment, which nations, like individuals, are never the worse for having felt. They were, I repeat it, ready to make great sacrifices for France. And why ready? Because she was fighting the battle of the human race against the combined enemies of their liberty; because she was performing the part which Great Britain now, in fact, sustains—forming the only bulwark against universal dominion. Knock away her navy, and where are you? Under the naval despotism of France, unchecked, and unqualified by any antagonizing

military power—at best but a change of masters. The tyrant
of the ocean, and the tyrant of the land is one and the same,
lord of all, and who shall say him nay, or wherefore dost
thou this thing? Give to the tiger the properties of the shark,
and there is no longer safety for the beasts of the forest or
the fishes of the sea. Where was this high anti-Britannic spirit
of the gentleman from Pennsylvania when his vote would
have put an end to the British Treaty, that pestilent source
of evil to this country? And at a time, too, when it was not
less the interest than the sentiment of this people to pull
down Great Britain and exalt France. *Then,* when the gentleman might have acted with effect, he could not screw his
courage to the sticking place. Then England was combined
in what has proved a feeble, inefficient coalition, but which
gave just cause of alarm to every friend of freedom. Now the
liberties of the human race are threatened by a single power,
more formidable than the coalesced world, to whose utmost
ambition, vast as it is, the naval force of Great Britain forms
the only obstacle.

I am perfectly sensible, and ashamed of the trespass I am
making on the patience of the committee—but as I know
not whether it will be in my power to trouble them again on
this subject, I must beg leave to continue my crude and
desultory observations. I am not ashamed to confess that
they are so.

At the commencement of this session, we received a
printed message from the President of the United States,
breathing a great deal of national horror and indignation at
the outrages which we had endured, particularly from Spain.
She was specially named and pointed at. She had pirated
upon your commerce, imprisoned your citizens, violated
your actual territory, invaded the very limits solemnly

established between the two nations by the Treaty of San Lorenzo. Some of the State Legislatures (among others, the very state on which the gentleman from Pennsylvania relies for support), sent forward resolutions, pledging their lives, their fortunes, and their sacred honour in support of any measures you might take in vindication of your injured rights. Well, Sir, what have you done? You have had resolutions laid upon your table, gone to some expense of printing and stationery—mere pen, ink, and paper, and that's all. Like true political quacks, you deal only in handbills and nostrums.

Sir, I blush to see the record of our proceedings. They resemble nothing but the advertisements for patent medicines. "Here you have the worm-destroying lozenges"; "There, Church's cough drops"; and to crown the whole, "Sloan's vegetable specific," an infallible remedy for all nervous disorders and vertigoes of brain-sick politicians: each man adjuring you to give his medicine only a fair trial. If, indeed, these wonder-working nostrums could perform but one half of what they promise, there is little danger of our dying a political death, at this time, at least. But Sir, in politics as in physics, the doctor is oftentimes the most dangerously diseased—and this I take to be our case at present.

But, Sir, why do I talk of Spain? There are no longer Pyrenees. There exists no such nation—no such being as a Spanish King or Minister. It is a mere juggle played off for the benefit of those who put the mechanism in motion. You know, Sir, that you have no differences with Spain—that she is the passive tool of a superior power, to whom, at this moment, you are crouching. Are your differences indeed with Spain? And where are you going to send your political panacea, resolutions and handbills excepted, your sole arcanum of Government—your King Cure All? To Madrid? No. You are not such quacks as not to know where the shoe pinches. To Paris. You know at least where the disease lies, and there you apply your remedy. When the nation anxiously demands the result of your deliberations, you hang your head and blush to tell. Your mouth is hermetically sealed. Your honour has received a wound, which must not take air. Gentlemen dare not come forward and avow their work, much less defend it in the presence of the nation. Give them all they ask—that Spain exists—and what then? After shrinking from the Spanish jackal do you presume to bully the British lion? But here the secret comes out. Britain is your rival in trade, and governed as you are by counting-house politicians; you would sacrifice the paramount interest of the country to wound that rival. For Spain and France you are carriers—and from good customers every indignity is to be endured. And what is the nature of this trade? Is it that carrying trade which sends abroad the flour, tobacco, cotton, beef, pork, fish, and lumber of this country, and brings back in return foreign articles necessary for our existence or comfort? No, Sir, 'tis a trade carried on, the Lord knows where, or by whom—now doubling Cape Horn, now the Cape of Good Hope. I do not say that there is no profit in it—for it would not then be pursued—but 'tis a trade that tends to assimilate our manners and Government to those of the most corrupt countries of Europe. Yes, Sir, and when a question of great national magnitude presents itself to you, causes those who now prate about national honour, and spirit, to pocket any insult—to consider it as a mere matter of debit and credit, a business of profit and loss, and nothing else.

The first thing that struck my mind when this resolution

was laid on the table, was *unde derivatur?* A question always put to us at school: whence comes it? Is this only the putative father of the bantling he is taxed to maintain, or indeed, the actual parent—the real progenitor of the child? Or is it the production of the Cabinet? But I knew you had no Cabinet—no system. I had seen dispatches relating to vital measures laid before you the day after your final decision on those measures—four weeks after they were received—not only their contents, but their very existence all that time unsuspected and unknown to men whom the people fondly believe assist with their wisdom and experience at every important deliberation. Do you believe that this system—or rather, this no system will do? I am free to answer, it will not. It cannot last. I am not so afraid of the fair, open, Constitutional, responsible influence of Government—but I shrink intuitively from this left-handed, invisible, irresponsible influence, which defies the touch, but pervades and decides every thing. Let the Executive come forward to the Legislature—let us see whilst we feel it. If we cannot rely upon its wisdom, is it any disparagement to the gentleman from Pennsylvania to say, that I cannot rely upon him? No, Sir, he has mistaken his talent. He is not the Palinurus on whose skill the nation at this trying moment can repose their confidence. I will have nothing to do with his paper—much less will I endorse it, and make myself responsible for its goodness. I will not put my name to it. I assert that there is no Cabinet, no system, no plan: that which I believe in one place, I shall never hesitate to say in another. This is no place—no time—for mincing our steps. The people have a right to know, they shall know, the state of our affairs—at least as far as I am at liberty to communicate them. I speak from personal knowledge: ten days ago there had been no consultation, there existed no opinion in your Executive department—at least, none that was avowed; on the contrary, there was an express disavowal of any opinion whatsoever on the great subject before you, and I have good reason for saying that none has been formed since.

Some time ago, a book was laid on our tables, which, like some other bantlings, did not bear the name of its father. Here I was taught to expect a solution of all doubts, an end to all our difficulties. If, Sir, I were the foe (as I trust I am the friend to this nation), I would exclaim, "Oh, that mine enemy would write a book!" At the very outset, in the very first page, I believe, there is a complete abandonment of the principle in dispute. Has any gentleman got the work? [It was handed by one of the members].

The first position taken is the broad principle of the unlimited freedom of trade between nations at peace, which the writer endeavors to extend to the trade between a neutral and a belligerent power, accompanied, however, by this acknowledgement: "But inasmuch as the trade of a neutral with a belligerent nation might in certain special cases affect the safety of its antagonist, usage founded on the principle of necessity had admitted a few exceptions to the general rule." Whence comes the doctrine of contraband blockade, and enemies' property? Now, Sir, for what does that celebrated pamphlet, *War in Disguise,* which is said to have been written under the eye of the British Prime Minister, contend—but this principle of necessity? And this is abandoned by this pamphleteer at the very threshold of the discussion. But, as this were not enough, he goes on to assign as a reason for not referring to the authority of the ancients, that "the great change which has taken place in the state of manners, in the maxims of war, and in the course of commerce, make it pretty certain"—what degree of certainty is this?)—"that either nothing will be found relating to the question, or nothing sufficiently applicable to deserve attention in deciding it." Here, Sir, is an apology of the writer for not disclosing the whole extent of his learning (which might have overwhelmed the reader). Is the admission that a change of circumstances "in the course of commerce" [justification for] a total change of the law of nations? What more could the most inveterate advocate of English usurpation demand? What else can they require to establish all, and even more than they contend for? Sir, there is a class of men—we know them very well—who, if you only permit them to lay the foundation, will build you up step by step, and brick by brick, very neat and showy, if not tenable, arguments. To detect them, 'tis only necessary to watch their [first] premises, where you will often find the point at issue totally surrendered, as in this case it is. Again —is the *mare liberum* anywhere asserted in this book? That free ships make free goods? No, Sir, the right of search is acknowledged. That enemies' property is lawful prize is sealed and delivered. And after abandoning these principles, what becomes of the doctrine that the mere shifting of the goods from one ship to another—the touching at another port—changes the property? Sir, give up this principle and there is an end of the question. You lie at the mercy of the conscience of a Court of Admiralty. Is Spanish sugar or French coffee made American property by the mere change of cargo, or even by the landing and payment of the duties? Does this operation effect a change of property? And when those duties are drawn back, and the sugars and coffee re-exported, are they not (as enemies' property) liable to seizure upon the principles of the *Examination of the British Doctrine,* etc.? And is there not reason to believe that this operation is performed in many, if not in most cases, to give a neutral aspect and colour to the merchandise?

I am not prepared, Sir, to be represented as willing to surrender important rights of this nation to a foreign Government. I have been told that this sentiment is already whispered in the dark by time servers and sycophants—but if your clerk dared to print them I would appeal to your journals. I would call for the reading of them, but that I know they are not for profane eyes to look upon. I confess that I am more ready to surrender to a naval power a square league of ocean than to a territorial one a square inch of land within our limits—and I am ready to meet the friends of the resolution on this ground at any time. Let them take off the injunction of secrecy. They dare not. They are ashamed and afraid to do it. They may give winks and nods, and pretend to be wise, but they dare not come out and tell the nation what they have done. Gentlemen may take votes, if they please, but I will never, from any motive short of self defence, enter upon war. I will never be instrumental to the ambitious schemes of Bonaparte, nor put into his hands what will enable him to wield the world: and on the very principle that I wished success to the French arms in 1793. And wherefore? Because the case is changed. Great Britain can ever again see the year 1760. Her continental influence has gone forever. Let who will be uppermost on the continent of Europe, she must find more than a counterpoise for her strength. Her race is run. She can only be formidable as a maritime power—and even as such, perhaps not long. Are you going to justify the acts of the last administration for which they have been deprived of the

Government at our instance? Are you going back to the ground of 1798–9? I ask any man who now advocates a rupture with England to assign a single reason for his opinion, that would not have justified a French war in 1798. If injury and insult abroad would have justified it, we had them in abundance then. But what did the Republicans say at that day? That under cover of a war with France, the Executive would be armed with a patronage and power which might enable it to master our liberties. They deprecated foreign war, and navies, and standing armies, and loans, and taxes. The delirium passed away: the good sense of the people triumphed and our differences were accommodated without a war. And what is there in the situation of England that invites [us] to war with her? 'Tis true, she does not deal so largely in perfectibility, but she supplies you with a much more useful commodity, with coarse woollens. With less profession, indeed, she occupies the place of France in 1793. She is the sole bulwark of the human race against universal dominion—no thanks to her for it. In protecting her own existence, she ensures theirs. I care not who stands in this situation, whether England or Bonaparte. I practise the doctrines now that I professed in 1798. Gentlemen may hunt up the journals if they please— I voted against all such projects under the administration of John Adams, and I will continue to do so under that of Thomas Jefferson. Are you not contented with being free and happy at home? Or will you surrender these blessings that your merchants may tread on Turkish and Persian carpets, and burn the perfumes of the East in their vaulted rooms?

Gentlemen say, " 'tis but an annual million lost, and even if it were five times that amount, what is it compared with your neutral rights?" Sir, let me tell them, a hundred millions will be but a drop in the bucket if once they launch without rudder or compass into this ocean of foreign warfare. Whom do they want to attack? England? They hope it is a popular thing and talk about Bunker Hill, and the gallant feats of our Revolution. But is Bunker's Hill to be the theatre of war? No, Sir, you have selected the ocean—and the object of attack is that very navy which prevented the combined fleets of France and Spain from levying contributions upon you in your own seas—that very navy which, in the famous war of 1798 stood between you and danger. Whilst the fleets of the enemy were pent up in Toulon, or pinioned in Brest, we performed wonders to be sure. But, Sir, if England had drawn off France, you would have told a very different tale. You would have struck no medals. This is not the sort of conflict that you are to count upon, if you go to war with Great Britain. *Quem Deus vult perdere prius dementat.*—And are you mad enough to take up the cudgels that have been struck from the nerveless hands of the three great maritime powers of Europe? Shall the planter mortgage his little crop and jeopardize the Constitution in support of commercial monopoly? In the vain hope of satisfying the insatiable greediness of trade? Administer the Constitution upon its own principles: for the general welfare and not for the benefit of a particular class of men. Do you meditate war for the possession of Baton Rouge or Mobile—places which your own laws declare to be within your limits? Is it even for the fair trade, that exchanges your surplus products for such foreign articles as you require? No, Sir, 'tis for a circuitous traffic, an *ignis fatuus.* And against whom? A nation from whom you have anything to fear?—I speak as to our liberties. No, Sir, a nation from whom you have nothing, or next to nothing, to fear—to the aggrandisement of one against which you have every thing to dread. I look to their ability and interest, not to their disposition. When you rely on that, the case is desperate. Is it to be inferred from all this, that I would yield to Great Britain? No, I would act toward her now as I was disposed to do toward France in 1798–9: treat with her, and for the same reason, on the same principles. Do I say I would treat with her? At this moment you have a negotiation pending with her Government. With her you have not tried negotiation and failed—totally failed, as you have done with Spain, or rather, France. And wherefore under such circumstances this hostile spirit to the one, and this (I won't say what) to the other?

But a great deal is said about the laws of nations. What is national law but national power guided by national interest? You yourselves acknowledge and practise upon this principle where you can, or where you dare—with the Indian tribes for instance. I might give another and more forcible illustration. Will the learned lumber of your libraries add a ship to your fleet, or a shilling to your revenue? Will it pay or maintain a single soldier? And will you preach and prate of violations of your neutral rights when you tamely and meanly submit to the violation of your territory? Will you collar the stealer of your sheep, and let him escape who has invaded the repose of your fireside—has insulted your wife and children under your own roof? This is the heroism of truck and traffic—the public spirit of sordid avarice. Great Britain violates your flag on the high seas. What is her situation? Contending not for the dismantling of Dunkirk, for Quebec, or Pondicherry, but for London and Westminster, for life; her enemy violating at will the territories of other nations—acquiring thereby a colossal power that threatens the very existence of her rival. But she has one vulnerable point to the arms of her adversary, which she covers with the ensigns of neutrality. She draws the neutral flag over the heel of Achilles. And can you ask that adversary to respect it, at the expense of her existence? And in favour of whom? An enemy that respects no neutral territory in Europe, and not even your own. I repeat that the insults of Spain towards this nation have been at the instigation of Frence: that there is no longer any Spain.

Well, Sir, because the French Government do not put this into the *Moniteur,* you choose to shut your eyes to it. None so blind as those who will not see. You shut your own eyes, and to blind those of other people you go into conclave, and slink out again, and say, "a great affair of state!" *C'est une grande affaire d'Etat!* It seems that your sensibility is entirely confined to the extremities. You may be pulled by the nose and ears, and never feel it; but let your strong box be attacked and you are all nerves: "Let us go to war!"

Sir, if they called upon me only for my little peculium to carry it on, perhaps I might give it: but my rights and liberties are involved in the grant, and I will never surrender them whilst I have life. The gentleman from Massachusetts (Mr. Crowninshield) is for sponging the debt. I can never consent to it. I will never bring the ways and means of fraudulent bankruptcy into your committee of supply. Confiscations and swindling shall never be found among my estimates, to meet the current expenditure of peace or war. No, Sir, I have said with the doors closed, and I say so when they are open: "pay the public debt." Get rid of that dead weight upon your Government, that cramp upon all your measures, and then you may put the world at defiance. So long as it hangs upon you, you must have revenue, and to have revenue you must have commerce, commerce, peace. And shall these nefarious schemes be advised for lightening the public burdens—will you resort to these low and pitiful shifts—dare even to mention these dishonest artifices—to eke out your expenses—when the public treasure is lavished on Turks and infidels, on singing boys and dancing girls, to furnish the means of bestiality to an African barbarian?

Gentlemen say that Great Britain will count upon our divisions. How! What does she know of them? Can they ever expect greater unanimity than prevailed at the last Presidential election? No Sir, 'tis the gentleman's own conscience that squeaks.

But if she cannot calculate upon your divisions, at least she will reckon upon your pusillanimity. She may well despise the resentment that cannot be excited to honourable battle on its own ground—the mere effusion of mercantile cupidity. Gentlemen talk of repealing the British Treaty. The gentleman from Pennsylvania should have thought of that before he voted to carry it into effect. And what is all this for? A point which Great Britain will not yield to Russia, you expect her to yield to you; Russia, indisputably the second power of continental Europe, with half a million hardy troops, with sixty sail of the line, thirty millions of subjects, a territory more extensive even than our own, Russia, Sir, whom it is not more the policy and the interest than the sentiment of that government to soothe and to conciliate; her sole hope of a diversion on the Continent; her only efficient ally. What this formidable power cannot obtain by fleets and armies, you will command by writ—with pot hooks and hangers. I am for no such policy.

True honour is always the same. Before you enter into a contest, public or private, be sure you have fortitude enough to go through with it. If you mean war, say so and prepare for it.

Look on the other side. Behold the respect in which France holds neutral rights on land. Observe her conduct in regard to the Franconian estates of the King of Prussia: I say nothing of the petty powers; of the Elector of Baden or the Swiss. I speak of a first rate Monarchy of Europe, and at a moment too, when its neutrality was the object, of all others, nearest to the heart of the French Emperor. If you make him monarch of the ocean, you may bid adieu to it forever. You may take your leave, Sir, of navigation; even of the Mississippi. What is the situation of New Orleans if attacked tomorrow? Filled with a discontented and repining people, whose language, manners, and religion all incline them to the invader? A dissatisfied people who despise the miserable governor you have set over them, whose honest prejudices, and basest passions alike take part against you? I draw my information from no dubious source [but] from a native American, an enlightened member of that odious and imbecile Government. You have official information that the town, and its dependencies are utterly defenceless, and untenable. Apprized of this, a firm belief that government would do something to put the place in a state of security alone has kept the American portion of that community quiet. You have held that post, and you now hold it, by the tenure of the naval predominance of England; yet you are for a British naval war.

There are now but two great commercial nations: Great Britain is one; we are the other. When you consider the many points of contact between our interests, you may be surprised that there has been so little collision. Sir, to the other belligerent nations of Europe, your navigation is a convenience—I might say, a necessity. If you do not carry for them, they must starve, at least for the luxuries of life, which custom has rendered almost indispensable. And if you cannot act with some degree of spirit towards those who are dependent upon you as carriers, do you reckon to brow-beat a jealous rival, who, the moment she lets slip the dogs of war, sweeps you at a blow from the ocean? And *cui bono?* For whose benefit? The planter? Nothing like it. The fair, honest, real American merchant? No, Sir. For renegades—today Americans, tomorrow Danes. Go to war when you will, the property now covered by the American, will then pass under the Danish, or some other neutral flag.

Gentlemen say that one English ship is worth three of ours; we shall therefore have the advantage in privateering. Did you ever know a nation get rich by privateering? This is stuff, Sir, for the nursery. Remember that your products are bulky—as has been stated—that they require a vast tonnage to transport them abroad, and that but two nations possess that tonnage. Take these carriers out of the market. What is the result? The manufacturers of England which, (to use the finishing touch of the gentleman's rhetoric) have received the finishing stroke of art, lie in a small comparative compass. The neutral trade can carry them. Your produce rots in the warehouse. You go to Statia or St. Thomas's and get a stupid blanket for a joe if you can raise one; double freight-charges and commission. Who receives the profit? The carrier. Who pays it? The consumer. All your produce that finds its way to England must bear the same accumulated charges, with this difference: that there the burden falls on the home price. I appeal to the experience of the last war, which has been so often cited. What then was the price of produce and of broad cloth?

But you are told: England will not make war; she has her hands full. Holland calculated in the same way in 1781. How did it turn out? You stand now in the place of Holland then, without her navy, unaided by the preponderating fleets of France and Spain, to say nothing of the Baltic powers. Do you want to take up the cudgels where these great maritime states have been forced to drop them? To meet Great Britain on the ocean and drive her off its face? If you are so far gone as this, every capital measure of your policy has hitherto been wrong. You should have nurtured the old, and devised new systems of taxation; have cherished your navy. Begin this business when you may, land taxes, stamp acts, window taxes, hearth monies, excise in all its modifications of vexation and oppression must precede, or follow after.

But, Sir, as French is the fashion of the day, I may be asked for my *projet*. I can readily tell gentlemen what I will not do. I will not propitiate any foreign nation with money. I will not launch into a naval war with Great Britain, although I am ready to meet her at the cow pens or on Bunker Hill. And for this plain reason: we are a great land animal and our business is on shore. I will send her no money, Sir, on any pretext whatsoever, much less on pretence of buying Labrador or Botany Bay, when my real object was to secure limits, which she formally acknowledged at the peace of 1783. I go further. I would (if anything) have laid an embargo. This would have got our own property home, and our adversary's into our power. If there is any wisdom left among us, the first step towards hostility will always be an embargo. In six months, all your mercantile megrims would vanish. As to us, although it would cut deep, we can stand it. Without such a precaution, go to war when you will, you go to the wall. As to debts, strike the balance tomorrow, and England is, I believe, in our debt.

I hope, Sir, to be excused for proceeding in this desultory course. I flatter myself I shall not have occasion to trouble you—I know not that I shall be able, certainly not willing, unless provoked, in self defence.

I ask your attention to the character of the inhabitants of that southern country on whom gentlemen rely for support of their measure. Who and what are they? A simple agricultural people, accustomed to travel in peace to market with the produce of their labour. Who takes it from us? Another people devoted to manufactures—our sole source of supply. I have seen some stuff in the newspapers about manufacturers in Saxony, and about a man who is no longer chief of a dominant faction. The greatest man whom I ever knew— the immortal author of the letters of Curtius—has remarked the proneness of cunning people to wrap up and disguise in well-selected phrases, doctrines too deformed and detestable to bear exposure in naked words; by a judicious choice of epithets to draw attention from lurking principle beneath, and perpetuate delusion. But a little while ago and any man might be proud to be considered the head of the Republican Party. Now it seems 'tis reproachful to be deemed the chief of a dominant faction. Mark the magic words! Head, Chief, Republican Party, Dominant Faction. But, as to these Saxon manufacturers, what became of their Dresden china? Why, the Prussian bayonets have broken all the pots, and you are content with Worcestershire or Staffordshire ware. There are some other fine manufacturers on the Continent, but no supply, except perhaps of linens, the article we can best dispense with. A few individuals Sir, may have a coat of Louviers cloth, or a service of Dresden china; but there is too little, and that little too dear to furnish the nation. You must depend on the fur trade in earnest, and wear buffalo hides and bear skins.

Can any man who understands Europe pretend to say that a particular foreign policy is now right, because it would have been expedient twenty or even ten years ago? Without abandoning all regard for common sense? Sir, it is the statesman's province to be guided by circumstances, to anticipate, to foresee them; to give them a course and a direction, to mould them to his purpose. It is the business of a computing house clerk to peer into the Day Book and Ledger to see no further than the spectacles on his nose, to feel not beyond the pen behind his ear, to chatter in coffee-houses, and be the oracle of clubs. From 1783 to 1793, and even later—(I don't stickle for dates)—France had a formidable marine; so had Holland; so had Spain. The two first [were] possessed of thriving manufacturers, and a flourishing commerce. Great Britain, tremblingly alive to her manufacturing interests and carrying trade, would have felt to the heart any measure calculated to favour her rivals in these pursuits. She would have yielded then to her fears and her jealousy alone. What is the case now? She lays an export duty on her manufacturers, and there ends the question.

If Georgia shall (from whatever cause) so completely monopolize the culture of cotton as to be able to lay an export duty of three percent upon it, besides taxing its cultivators in every other shape that human or infernal ingenuity can devise, is Pennsylvania likely to rival her and take away the trade?

But, Sir, it seems that we, who are opposed to this resolution, are men of no nerve, who trembled in the days of the British Treaty; cowards, I presume, in the reign of terror? Is this true? Hunt up the Journals; let our actions tell.

We pursue our old unshaken course. We care not for the nations of Europe, but make foreign relations bend to our political principles, and serve our country's interests. We have no wish to see another Actium or Pharsalia, or the lieutenants of a modern Alexander playing at piquet, or all-fours for the Empire of the world. 'Tis poor comfort to us to be told that France has too decided a taste for luxurious things to meddle with us; that Egypt is her object, or the coast of Barbary, and at the worst, we shall be the last devoured. We are enamoured with neither nation; we would play their own game upon them; use them for our interest and convenience. But with all my abhorrence of the British Government, I should not hesitate between Westminster Hall and a Middlesex jury, on the one hand, and the Wood of Vincennes and a file of grenadiers on the other. That jury trial which walked with Horne Tooke and Hardy through the flames of ministerial persecution is, I confess, more to my taste than the trial of the Duke d'Enghein.

Mr. Chairman: I am sensible of having detained the committee longer than I ought—certainly much longer than I intended. I am equally sensible of their politeness, and not less so, Sir, of patient attention. It is your own indulgence, Sir, badly requited indeed, to which you owe this persecution. I might offer another apology for these undigested, desultory remarks: my never having seen the treasury documents until I came into the House this morning. I have been stretched on a sick bed.

But when I behold the affairs of this nation, instead of being where I hoped—and the people believed they were—in the hands of responsible men, committed to Tom, Dick, and Harry—to the refuse of the retail trade of politics, I do feel—I cannot help feeling the most deep and serious concern. If the Executive Government would set forward and say, "Such is our plan; such is our opinion—and such our reasons in support of it;" but without a compass or solar star I will not launch into an ocean of unexplored measures which stand condemned by all the information to which I have access. The Constitution of the United States declares it to be the province and duty of the President to give to Congress, from time time, information of the State of the Union, and recommend to their consideration such measures as he shall deem expedient and necessary. Has he done it?

I know, Sir, that we may say and do say that we are independent; (would it were true)—as free to give a direction to the Executive as to receive it from him. He stands at the helm and must guide the vessel of State. Do what you will—foreign relations—every measure short of war—and even the course of hostilities depend upon him. You give him money to buy Florida, and he purchases Louisiana. You may furnish means; the application of those means rest with him. Let not the Master and Mate go below when the ship is in distress, and throw the responsibility upon the cook and the cabin boy. I said so when your doors were shut; I scorn to say less now that they are open.

Gentlemen may say what they please. They may put an insignificant individual to the ban of the Republic—I shall not alter my course. I blush with indignation at the misrepresentations which have gone forth in the public prints of our proceedings, public and private. Are the people of the United States, the real sovereigns of the country, unworthy of knowing what there is too much reason to believe has been communicated to the privileged spies of foreign governments? I think our citizens just as well entitled to know what has passed as the Marquis of Yurjo, who has bearded your President to his face, insulted your government within its own peculiar jurisdiction, and outraged all decency.

Do you mistake this diplomatic puppet for an automaton? He has orders for all he does. Take his instructions from his pocket tomorrow; they are signed Charles Maurice Talleyrand. Let the nation know what they have to depend upon. Be true to them and (trust me) they will prove true to themselves and to you. The people are honest! Now at home, at their ploughs—not dreaming what you are about. But the spirit of enquiry that has too long slept will be, must be, awakened. Let them begin to think, not to say, such and such things are proper because they have been done; but what has been done, and wherefore?—and all will be well.

SPEECH AGAINST WAR WITH ENGLAND
December 10, 1811

[These "remarks to the House of Representatives on foreign relations" are Randolph's passionate defiance of the War Hawks, then about to plunge the United States into the struggle against Britain. The text of this speech is taken from *The Annals of Congress,* Twelfth Congress, 1811–12, 441–55.]

The order of the day being called for, the Speaker observed that the gentleman from Virginia on the right of the Chair was entitled to the floor.

Mr. Randolph said that if any other gentleman had any observations to make on the question, he would feel obliged to him if he would offer them then; as he was much exhausted by the fatigues of the morning, and would be glad of a little time to recruit his wasted strength and spirits.

After a considerable pause—no gentleman having manifested a disposition to speak, Mr. Randolph rose:

He expressed his sense of the motive which had induced the gentleman from Tennessee (Mr. Grundy) to move the adjournment yesterday, and of the politeness of the House in granting it; at the same time declaring that in point of fact he had little cause to be thankful for the favor, well intended as he knew it to have been, since he felt himself even less capable of proceeding with his argument than he had been on the preceding day.

It was a question, as it had been presented to the House, of peace or war. In that light it had been argued; in no other light could he consider it, after the declarations made by members of the Committee of Foreign Relations. Without intending any disrespect to the Chair, he must be permitted to say, that if the decision yesterday was correct, that it was not in order to advance any arguments against the resolution, drawn from topics before other Committees of the House. The whole debate, nay, the report itself on which they were acting, was disorderly—since the increase of the military force was a subject at that time in agitation by the select Committee raised on that branch of the President's Message. But it was impossible that the discussion of a question broad as the wide ocean of our foreign concerns—

involving every consideration of interest, of right, of happiness, and of safety at home—touching, in every point, all that was dear to freemen, "their lives, their fortunes, and their sacred honour!"—could be tied down by the narrow rules of technical routine. The Committee of Foreign Relations had indeed decided that the subject of arming the militia (which he had pressed upon them as indispensable to the public security) did not come within the scope of their authority. On what ground, he had been and still was unable to see, they had felt themselves authorized (when that subject was before another Committee) to recommend the raising of standing armies, with a view (as had been declared) of immediate war—a war, not of defence but of conquest, of aggrandizement, of ambition; a war foreign to the interest of this country, to the interests of humanity itself.

He knew not how gentlemen, calling themselves Republicans, could advocate such a war. What was their doctrine in 1798–9, when the command of the army—that highest of all possible trusts in any Government, be the form what it may—was reposed in the bosom of the Father of his Country, the sanctuary of a nation's love, the only hope that never came in vain! When other worthies of the Revolution— Hamilton, Pinckney, and the younger Washington—men of tried patriotism, of approved conduct and valor, of untarnished honor, held subordinate positions under him! Republicans were then unwilling to trust a standing army, even to his hands who had given proof that he was above all human temptation. Where now is the Revolutionary hero to whom you are about to confide this sacred trust? To whom will you confide the charge of leading the flower of our youth to the Heights of Abraham? Will you find him in the person of an acquitted felon? What! then you were unwilling to vote an army where such men as had been named held high command! when Washington himself was at the head—did you then show such reluctance, feel such scruples; and are you now nothing loth, fearless of every consequence? Will you say that your provocations were less then than now? When your direct commerce was interdicted— your Ambassadors hooted with derision from the French Court—tribute demanded—actual war waged upon you!

Those who opposed the army then, were indeed denounced as the partisans of France, as the same men—some of them at least—are now held up as the advocates of England: those firm and undeviating Republicans who then dared, and now dare, to cling to the ark of the Constitution, to defend it even at the expense of their fame, rather than surrender themselves to the wild projects of mad ambition! There is a fatality attending plenitude of power. Soon or late, some mania seizes upon its possessors; they fall from the dizzy height through the giddiness of their own heads. Like a vast estate, heaped up by the labor and industry of one man, which seldom survives the third generation, power gained by patient assiduity, by a faithful and regular discharge of its attendant duties, soon gets above its own origin. Intoxicated with their own greatness, the Federal party fell. Will not the same causes produce the same effects now, as then? Sir, you may raise this army, you may build up this vast structure of patronage, this mighty apparatus of favoritism; but "lay not the flattering unction to your souls"— you will never live to enjoy the succession. You sign your political death warrant.

Mr. R. here adverted to the provocation to hostilities from shutting up the Mississippi by Spain in 1803—but more fully to the conduct of the House in 1805–6, under the strongest of all imaginable provocatives to war: the actual invasion of our country. He read various passages from the President's public Message of December 3, 1805:

"Our coasts have been infested and our harbors watched by private armed vessels; some of them without commissions, some with illegal commissions, others with those of legal form, but committing acts beyond the authority of their commissions." [These Mr. R. stated to have been Spanish and French corsairs, fitted out chiefly in the western ports of Cuba—the English cruisers complained of in the same Message having regular commissions and carrying their prizes into port for adjudication.] "They have captured in the very entrance of our harbors, as well as on the high seas, not only the vessels of our friends coming to trade with us, but our own also. They have carried them off under the pretence of legal adjudication, but not daring to approach a court of justice, they have plundered and sunk them by the way, or in obscure places, where no evidence could arise against them; maltreated the crews, and abandoned them in the open sea, or on desert shores, without food or covering."

"With Spain our negotiations for a settlement of differences have not had any satisfactory issue. Spoliations during the former war, for which she had formally acknowledged herself responsible, have been refused to be compensated but on conditions affecting other claims" [those for French spoliations carried into other ports] "in no wise connected with them. Yet the same practices are renewed in the present war, and are already of great amount. On the Mobile, our commerce passing through that river, continues to be obstructed by arbitrary duties, and vexatious searches. Propositions for adjusting amicably the boundaries of Louisiana have not been acceded to. While, however, the right is unsettled, we have avoided changing the state of things, by taking new posts or strengthening ourselves in the disputed territories, in the hope that the other Power would not, by a contrary conduct, oblige us to meet their example, and endanger conflicts of authority, the issue of which may not be easily controlled. But in this hope we have now reason to lessen our confidence. Inroads have been recently made into the Territories of Orleans and the Mississippi." [Bourbon county,

part of the State of Georgia, of the good old thirteen States!]
"Our citizens have been seized, and their property plundered, in
the very ports of the former which had actually been delivered
up by Spain, and this by the regular officers and soldiers of that
Government. I have, therefore, found it necessary to give orders
to our troops on that frontier, to be in readiness to protect our
citizens, and repel by arms any similar aggressions in future."

Mr. R. said, that, on the 6th of December, (three days
afterwards) a secret Message was received from the President, which was referred to a Committee of which it was his
fate to be Chairman. Its complexion might be gathered
from the report upon it, for the Message itself is not inserted
in the secret Journal since ordered to be printed. He read
the report:

"The Committee have beheld, with just indignation, the hostile
spirit manifested by the Court of Madrid towards the Government of the United States, in withholding the ratification of its
convention with us, although signed by its own Minister, under
the eye of his Sovereign, unless with alterations of its terms, affecting claims of the United States, which, by the express conditions of the instrument itself, were reserved for future discussion;
in piratical depredations upon our fair commerce; in obstructing
the navigation of the Mobile; in refusing to come to any fair and
amicable adjustment of the boundaries of Louisiana; and in a
daring violation, by persons acting under the authority of Spain,
and, no doubt, apprized of her sentiments and views of our un-
disputed limits, which she had solemnly recognized by her treaty.

"To a Government having interests distinct from those of its
people, and disregarding their welfare, here is ample cause for a
formal declaration of war on the part of the United States, and
such, did they obey the impulse of their feeling alone, is the
course which the Committee would not hesitate to recommend:
but to a Government identified with the citizens, too far removed
from the powerful nations of the earth for its safety to be endangered by their hostility, peace must always be desirable, so long
as it is compatible with the honor and interest of the community.

"Whilst the United States continue burdened with a debt which annually absorbs two-thirds of their revenue, and duties upon imports constitute the only resource from which that revenue can be raised, without resorting to systems of taxation not more ruinous and oppressive than they are uncertain and precarious, the best interests of the Union cry aloud for peace. When that debt shall have been discharged, and the resources of the nation thereby liberated, then may we rationally expect to raise, even in time of war, the supplies which our frugal institutions require, without recurring to the hateful, destructive expedient of loans: then, and not till then, may we bid defiance to the world. The present moment is peculiarly auspicious for his great and desirable work. Now, if ever, the national debt is to be paid by such financial arrangements as will accelerate its extinction, by reaping the rich harvest of neutrality, and thus providing for that diminution of revenue which experience teaches us to expect on the general pacification of Europe. And the Committee indulge a hope, that, in the changed aspect of affairs in that quarter, Spain will find motives for a just fulfilment of the stipulations with us, and an amicable settlement of limits, upon terms not more beneficial to the United States than advantageous to herself, securing to her an ample barrier on the side of Mexico, and to use the countries watered by the Mississippi, and to the eastward of it. But, whilst the Committee perceive, in the general uproar of Europe, a state of things peculiarly favourable to the peaceable pursuit of our best interests, they are neither insensible to the indignity which has been offered on the part of Spain, nor unwilling to repel similar outrage. On the subject of self defence, when the Territory of the United States is insulted, there can be but one opinion, whatever differences may exist on the question, whether that protection which a vessel finds in our harbors, shall be extended to her, by the nation, in the Indian or Chinese seas. Under this impression the Committee submit the following resolution; the annexed letter from the Secretary of War will explain why it is not more explicit.

"*Resolved,* That such number of troops (not exceeding _____) as the President of the United States shall deem sufficient to protect the Southern frontier of the United States, from Spanish inroads and insult, and to chastise the same, be immediately raised."

Mr. R. said, that, the peculiar situation of the frontier, at that time insulted, had alone induced the Committee to recommend the raising of regular troops. It was too remote from the population of the country for the militia to act, in repelling and chastising Spanish incursion. New Orleans and its dependencies were separated by a vast extent of wilderness from the settlements of the old United States; filled with a disloyal and turbulent people, alien to our institutions, language, and manners, and disaffected towards our Government. Little reliance could be placed upon them, and it was plain that if "it was the intention of Spain to advance on our possessions until she should be repulsed by an opposing force," that force must be a regular army, unless we were disposed to abandon all the country south of Tennessee. That if "the protection of our citizens and the spirit and the honor of our country required that force should be interposed," nothing remained but for the Legislature to grant the only practicable means, or to shrink from the most sacred of all its duties—to abandon the soil and its inhabitants to the tender mercy of hostile invaders.

Yet this report, moderate as it was, had been deemed of too strong a character by the House. It was rejected: and, at the motion of a gentleman from Massachusetts, (Mr. Bidwell), who had since taken a great fancy also to Canada, and marched off thither in advance of the Committee of Foreign Relations, "$2,000,000 were appropriated toward," (not in full of) "any extraordinary expense which might be incurred in the intercourse between the United States and foreign nations:" in other words, to buy off, at Paris, Spanish aggressions at home.

Was this fact given in evidence of our impartiality towards the belligerents? that to the insults and injuries and actual invasion of one of them we opposed not bullets, but dollars; that to Spanish invasion we opposed money, whilst for British aggression on the high seas we had arms; offensive war? But Spain was then shielded, as well as instigated, by a greater Power. Hence our respect for her. Had we at that time acted as we ought to have done in defence of rights, of the *natale solum* itself, we should (he felt confident) have avoided that series of insult, disgrace, and injury, which had been poured out upon us in long unbroken succession. We would not then raise a small regular force for a country where the militia could not act, to defend our own Territory; now, we are willing to levy a great army, for great it must be, to accomplish the proposed object, for a war of conquest and ambition—and this, too, at the very entrance of "the Northern Hive," of the strongest part of the Union.

An insinuation had fallen from the gentleman from Tennessee, (Mr. Grundy), that the late massacre of our brethren on the Wabash had been instigated by the British Government. Has the President given any such information? has the gentleman received any such, even informally, from any officer of this Government? Is it so believed by the Administration? He had cause to think the contrary to be the fact; that such was not their opinion. This insinuation was of the grossest kind—a presumption the most rash, the most unjustifiable. Show but good ground for it, he would give up the question at the threshold—he was ready to march to Canada. It was indeed well calculated to excite the feelings of the Western people particularly, who were not quite so tenderly attached to our red brethren as some modern philosophers; but it was destitute of any foundation, beyond mere surmise and suspicion. What would be thought if, without any proof whatsoever, a member should rise in his place and tell us that the massacre in Savannah, a massacre perpetrated by civilized savages, with French commissions in their pockets, was excited by the French Government? There was an easy and natural solution of the late transaction on the Wabash, in the well known character of the aboriginal savage of North America, without resorting to any such mere conjectural estimate. He was sorry to say that for this signal calamity and disgrace the House was, in part, at least, answerable. Session after session, their table had been piled up with Indian treaties, for which the appropriations had been voted as a matter of course, without examination. Advantage had been taken of the spirit of the Indians, broken by the war which ended in the Treaty of Greenville. Under the ascendency then acquired over them, they had been pent up by subsequent treaties into nooks, straightened in their quarters by a blind cupidity, seeking to extinguish their title to immense wildernesses for which, (possessing, as we do already, more land than we can sell or use), we shall not have occasion for half a century to come. It was our own thirst for territory, our own want of moderation, that had driven these sons of nature to desperation, of which we felt the effects.

Mr. R., although not personally acquainted with the late Colonel Daviess, felt, he was persuaded, as deep and serious regret for his loss as the gentleman from Tennessee himself. He knew him only through the representation of a friend of the deceased, (Mr. Rowan), sometime a member of that House; a man who, for native force of intellect, manliness of character, and high sense of honor, was not inferior to any that had ever sat there. With him he sympathized in the severest calamity that could befall a man of his cast of character. Would to God they were both then on the floor!

From his personal knowledge of the one, he felt confident that he would have his support—and he believed (judging of him from the representation of their common friend), of the other also.

He could but smile at the liberality of the gentleman, in giving Canada to New York, in order to strengthen the northern balance of power, while at the same time he forewarned her that the Western scale must preponderate. Mr. R. said he could almost fancy that he saw the Capitol in motion towards the falls of Ohio—after a short sojourn taking its flight to the Mississippi, and finally alighting on Darien; which, when the gentleman's dreams are realized, will be a most eligible seat of Government for the new Republic (or Empire) of the two Americas! But it seemed that "in 1808 we talked and acted foolishly," and to give some colour of consistency to that folly, we must now commit a greater. Really, he could not conceive of a weaker reason offered in support of a present measure, than the justification of a former folly. He hoped we should act a wiser part—take warning by our follies, since we had become sensible of them, and resolve to talk and act foolishly no more. It was indeed high time to give over such preposterous language and proceedings.

This war of conquest, a war for the acquisition of territory and subjects, is to be a new commentary on the doctrine that Republics are destitute of ambition—that they are addicted to peace, wedded to the happiness and safety of the great body of their people. But it seems this is to be a holiday campaign—there is to be no expense of blood, or treasure, on our part—Canada is to conquer herself—she is to be subdued by the principles of fraternity. The people of that country are first to be seduced from their allegiance, and converted into traitors, as preparatory to the making them good citizens. Although he must acknowledge that some of our flaming patriots were thus manufactured, he did not think the process would hold good with a whole community. It was a dangerous experiment. We were to succeed in the French mode by the system of fraternization—all is French! but how dreadfully it might be retorted on the Southern and Western slaveholding States. He detested this subornation of treason. No—if he must have them, let them fall by the valor of our arms, by fair, legitimate conquest; not become the victims of treacherous seduction.

He was not surprised at the war spirit which was manifesting itself in gentlemen from the South. In the year 1805–6, in a struggle for the carrying trade of belligerent colonial produce, this country has most unwisely been brought into collision with the great Powers of Europe. By a series of most impolitic and ruinous measures, utterly incomprehensible to every rational, sober-minded man, the Southern planters, by their own votes, had succeeded in knocking down the price of cotton to seven cents, and of tobacco (a few choice crops excepted) to nothing—and in raising the price of blankets, (of which a few would not be amiss in a Canadian campaign), coarse woollens, and every article of first necessity, three or four hundred percent. And now that, by our own acts, we have brought ourselves into this unprecedented condition, we must get out of it in any way but by an acknowledgement of our own want of wisdom and forecast. But is war the true remedy? Who will profit by it? Speculators—a few lucky merchants who draw prizes in the lottery—commissaries and contractors. Who must suffer by it? The people. It is their blood, their taxes, that must flow to support it.

But gentlemen avowed that they would not go to war for

the carrying trade—that is, for any other but the direct export and import trade—that which carries our native products abroad, and brings back the return cargo; and yet they stickle for our commercial rights, and will go to war for them! He wished to know, in point of principle, what difference gentlemen could point out between the abandonment of this or of that maritime right? Do gentlemen assume the lofty port and tone of chivalrous redressers of maritime wrongs, and declare their readiness to surrender every other maritime right, provided they may remain unmolested in the exercise of the humble privilege of carrying their own produce abroad, and bringing back a return cargo? Do you make this declaration to the enemy at the outset? Do you state the minimum with which you will be contented, and put it in her power to close with your proposals at her option; give her the basis of a treaty ruinous and disgraceful beyond example and expression? and this, too, after having turned up your noses in disdain at the treaties of Mr. Jay and Mr. Monroe! Will you say to England, "end the war when you please; give us the direct trade in our own produce; we are content"? But what will the merchants of Salem, and Boston, and New York, and Philadelphia, and Baltimore, the men of Marblehead and Cape Cod, say to this? Will they join in a war professing to have for its object what they would consider (and justly too) as the sacrifice of their maritime rights, yet affecting to be a war for the protection of commerce?

He was gratified to find gentlemen acknowledging the demoralizing and destructive consequences of the non-importation law—confessing the truth of all that its opponents foretold when it was enacted. And will you plunge yourselves in war, because you have passed a foolish and ruinous law and are ashamed to repeal it! "But our good friend, the

French Emperor, stands in the way of its repeal," and as we cannot go too far in making sacrifices to him who has given such demonstration of his love for the Americans, we must in point of fact become parties to his war. "Who can be so cruel as to refuse him this favor?" His imagination shrunk from the miseries of such a connexion. He called upon the House to reflect whether they were not about to abandon all reclamation for the unparalleled outrages, "insults and injuries," of the French Government, to give up our claim for plundered millions; and asked what reparation or atonement they could expect to obtain in hours of future dalliance, after they should have made a tender of their person to this great deflowerer of the virginity of Republics. We had by our own wise (he would not say *wise-acre*) measures, so increased the trade and wealth of Montreal and Quebec, that at last we began to cast a wistful eye at Canada. Having done so much towards its improvement by the exercise of "our restrictive energies," we began to think the laborer worthy of his hire, and to put in claim for our portion. Suppose it ours; are we any nearer to our point? As his Minister said to the King of Epirus, "may we not as well take our bottle of wine before as after this exploit?" Go! march to Canada! leave the broad bosom of the Chesapeake and her hundred tributary rivers—the whole line of seacoast from Machias to St. Mary's unprotected! You have taken Quebec—have you conquered England? Will you seek for the deep foundations of her power in the frozen deserts of Labrador?

> "Her march is on the mountain wave,
> Her home is on the deep!"

Will you call upon her to leave your ports and harbors untouched, only just 'til you can return from Canada to defend them? The coast is to be left defenceless, whilst men of the interior are revelling in conquest and spoil. But grant for a moment, for mere argument's sake, that in Canada you touched the sinews of her strength, instead of removing a clog upon her resources—an encumbrance, but one, which, from a spirit of honor, she will vigorously defend. In what situation would you then place some of the best men of the nation? As Chatham and Burke, and the whole band of her patriots, prayed for her defeat in 1776, so must some of the truest friends to their country deprecate the success of our arms against the only Power that holds in check the arch-enemy of mankind.

Mr. R. declared, that the Committee had outstripped the Executive. In designating the Power against whom this force was to be employed—as had most unadvisedly been done in the preamble or manifesto with which the resolutions were prefaced—they had not consulted the views of the Executive; that designation was equivalent to an abandonment of all our claims on the French Government. No sooner was the report laid on the table, than the vultures were flocking round their prey, the carcass of a great Military Establishment—men of trained reputation, of broken fortunes (if they ever had any) and of battered constitutions, "choice spirits, tired of the dull pursuits of civil life," were seeking after agencies and commissions; willing to doze in gross stupidity over the public fire; to light the public candle at both ends. Honorable men undoubtedly there were, ready to serve their country; but what man of spirit, or of self-respect, would accept a commission in the present Army?

The gentleman from Tennessee (Mr. Grundy) had addressed himself, yesterday, exclusively to the "Republicans of this House". Mr. R. knew not whether he might consider himself as entitled to any part of the benefit of the honorable gentleman's discourse. It belonged not, however, to that gentleman to decide. If we must have an exposition of the doctrines of Republicanism, he should receive it from the fathers of the church, and not from the junior apprentices of the law. He should appeal to his worthy friends from Carolina, (Messrs. Macon and Stanford), "men with whom he had measured his strength," by whose side he had fought during the reign of terror, for it was indeed an hour of corruption, of oppression, of pollution. It was not at all to his taste, that sort of Republicanism which was supported on this side of the Atlantic by the father of the sedition law, John Adams, and by Peter Porcupine on the other. Republicanism! of John Adams! of William Cobbett! *Par nobile fratrum,* now united as in 1798, whom the cruel walls of Newgate alone keep from flying to each other's embrace— but whom, in sentiment, it is impossible to divide! Gallant crusaders in the holy cause of Republicanism! Such "Republicanism does indeed mean anything or nothing".

Our people will not submit to be taxed for this war of conquest and dominion. The Government of the United States was not calculated to wage offensive foreign war—it was instituted for the common defence and general welfare; and whosoever should embark it in a war of offence, would put it to a test which it was by no means calculated to endure. Make it out that Great Britain had instigated the Indians on the late occasion, and he was ready for battle; but not for dominion. He was unwilling, however, under present circumstances, to take Canada at the risk of the Constitution—to embark in a common cause with France and be dragged at the wheels of the car of some Burr or Bonaparte. For a gentleman from Tennessee or Gennessee, or Lake Champlain, there may be some prospect of advantage. Their hemp would bear a great price by the exclusion of foreign supply. In that too, the great importers were deeply interested. The upper country on the Hudson and the Lakes would be enriched by the supplies for the troops, which they alone could furnish. They would have the exclusive market: to say nothing of the increased preponderance from the acquisition of Canada and that section of the Union, which the Southern and Western States had already felt so severely in the apportionment bill.

Mr. R. adverted to the defenceless state of our seaports, and particularly of the Chesapeake. A single spot only, on both shores, might be considered in tolerable security— from the nature of the port and the strength of the population—and that spot unhappily governed the whole State of Maryland. His friend, the late Governor of Maryland, (Mr. Lloyd), at the very time he was bringing his warlike resolutions before the Legislature of the State, was liable, on any night, to be taken out of his bed and carried off with his family, by the most contemptible picaroon. Such was the situation of many a family in Maryland and lower Virginia.

Mr. R. dwelt on the danger arising from the black population. He said he would touch this subject as tenderly as possible—it was with reluctance that he touched it at all— but in cases of great emergency, the State physician must not be deterred by a sickly, hysterical humanity, from probing the wound of his patient—he must not be withheld by a fastidious and mistaken humanity from representing his true situation to his friends, or even to the sick man himself, where the occasion called for it. What was the situation of the slaveholding States? During the war of the Revolution, so **fixed** were their habits of subordination, that when the whole Southern country was overrun by the enemy, who invited them to desert, no fear was ever entertained of an insurrection of the slaves. During the war of seven years, with our country in possession of the enemy, no such danger was ever apprehended. But should we therefore be unobservant spectators of the progress of society within the last twenty years—of the silent but powerful change wrought by time and chance, upon its composition and temper? When the fountains of the great deep of abomination were broken up, even the poor slaves had not escaped the general deluge. The French Revolution had polluted even them. Nay, there had not been wanting men in that House, witness their Legislative *Legendre,* the butcher who once held a seat there, to preach upon that floor these imprescriptible rights to a crowded audience of blacks in the galleries—teaching them that they are equal to their masters; in other words, advising them to cut their throats. Similar doctrines were disseminated by pedlars from New England and elsewhere, throughout the Southern country—and masters had been found so infatuated, as by their lives and conversation, by a general contempt of order, morality, and religion, unthinkingly to cherish these seeds of self-destruction to them and their families. What was the consequence? Within the last ten years, repeated alarms of insurrection among the slaves— some of them awful indeed. From the spreading of this infernal doctrine, the whole Southern country had been thrown into a state of insecurity. Men dead to the operation of moral causes, had taken away from the poor slave his habits of loyalty and obedience to his master, which lightened his servitude by a double operation; beguiling his own cares and disarming his master's suspicions and severity; and now, like true empirics in politics, you are called upon to trust to the mere physical strength of the fetter which holds him in bondage. You have deprived him of all moral restraint; you have tempted him to eat of the fruit of the tree of knowledge, just enough to perfect him in wickedness; you have opened his eyes to his nakedness; you have armed his nature against the hand that has fed, that has clothed him, that has cherished him in sickness; that hand, which, before he became a pupil of your school, he had been accustomed to press with respectful affection. You have done all this —and then show him the gibbet and the wheel as incentives to a sullen, repugnant, obedience. God forbid, Sir, that the Southern States should ever see an enemy on their shores, with these infernal principles of French fraternity in the van! While talking of taking Canada, some of us were shuddering for our own safety at home. He spoke from facts, when he said that the night-bell never tolled for fire in Richmond that the mother did not hug her infant more closely to her bosom. He had been a witness of some of the alarms in the capital of Virginia.

How had we shown our sympathy with the patriots of Spain, or with her American provinces? By seizing on one of them, her claim to which we had formerly respected, as soon as the parent country was embroiled at home. Was it thus we yielded them assistance against the arch-fiend who is grasping at the sceptre of the civilized world? The object of France is as much Spanish America as Old Spain herself. Much as he hated a standing army he could almost find it in his heart to vote one, could it be sent to the assistance of the Spanish patriots.

Mr. R. then proceeded to notice the unjust and illiberal imputation of British attachments, against certain characters in this country, sometimes insinuated in that House, but openly avowed out of it. Against whom were these charges brought? Against men, who in the war of the Revolution were in the councils of the nation, or fighting the battles of your country. And by whom were they made? By runaways, chiefly from the British dominions, since the breaking out of the French troubles. He indignantly said—it is insufferable. It cannot be borne. It must, and ought, with severity, be put down in this House, and, out of it, to meet the lie direct. We have no fellow feeling for the suffering and oppressed Spaniards! Yet even them we do not reprobate. Strange! that we should have no objection to any people or Government, civilized or savage, in the whole world. The great Autocrat of all the Russias receives the homage of our high consideration. The Bey of Algiers and his Divan of Pirates are very civil, good sort of people, with whom we find no difficulty in maintaining the relations of peace and amity—"Turks, Jews, and Infidels"; Mellimelli, or the Little Turtle; Barbarians and savages of every clime and colour are welcome to our arms. With chiefs of banditti, negro or mulatto, we can treat and can trade. Name, however, but England, and all our antipathies are up in arms against her. Against whom? Against those whose blood runs in our veins, in common with whom we claim Shakespeare, and Newton, and Chatham, for our countrymen; whose form of government is the freest on earth, our own only excepted; from whom every valuable principle of our own institutions has been borrowed—representation, jury trial, voting the supplies, writ of habeas corpus—our whole civil and criminal jurisprudence—against our fellow Protestants identified in blood, in language, in religion with ourselves. In what school did the worthies of our land, the Washingtons, Henrys, Hancocks, Franklins, Rutledges of

America learn those principles of civil liberty which were
so nobly asserted by their wisdom and valor? And American
resistance to British usurpation had not been more warmly
cherished by these great men and their compatriots; not
more by Washington, Hancock, and Henry, than by Chatham and his illustrious associates in the British Parliament.
It ought to be remembered, too, that the heart of the English
people was with us. It was a selfish and corrupt Ministry,
and their servile tools, to whom we were not more opposed
than they were. He trusted that none such might ever exist
among us—for tools will never be wanting to subserve the
purposes, however ruinous or wicked, of Kings and Ministers
of State.

He acknowledged the influence of Shakespeare and Milton upon his imagination, of Locke upon his understanding,
of a Sidney upon his political principles, of a Chatham
upon qualities which, would to God! he possessed in common with that illustrious man—of a Tillotson, a Sherlock,
and a Porteus, upon his religion. This was a British influence
which he could never shake off. He allowed much to the just
and honest prejudices growing out of the Revolution. But
by whom had they been suppressed when they ran counter
to the interests of his country? By Washington. By whom,
would you listen to them, are they most keenly felt? By
felons escaped from the jails of Paris, Newgate, and Kil-
mainham, since the breaking out of the French Revolution
—who, in this abused and insulted country, have set up for
political teachers, and whose disciples give no other proof
of their progress in Republicanism, except a blind devotion
to the most ruthless military despotism that the world ever
saw. These are the patriots who scruple not to brand with
the epithet of tory the men (looking towards the seat of

Col. Stuart) by whose blood your liberties have been ce-
mented. These are they, who hold in so keen remembrance
the outrages of the British armies, from which many of them
were deserters. Ask these self-styled patriots where they
were during the American war, (for they are for the most
part old enough to have borne arms), and you strike them
dumb—their lips are closed in eternal silence. If it were
allowable to entertain partialities, every consideration of
blood, language, religion, and interest, would incline us
towards England; and yet, shall they be alone extended to
France and her ruler, whom we are bound to believe a
chastening God suffers as the scourge of a guilty world! On
all other nations he tramples—he holds them in contempt—
England alone he hates; he would, but he cannot despise
her—fear cannot despise. And shall we disparage our ancestors? Shall we bastardize ourselves by placing them even
below the brigands of St. Domingo? with whom Mr. Adams
had negotiated a sort of treaty, for which he ought to have
been and would have been impeached, if the people had not
previously passed sentence of disqualification for their service upon him. This antipathy to all that is English must be
French.

But the outrages and injuries of England—bred up in
the principles of the Revolution, he could never palliate,
much less defend them. He well remembered flying with his
mother, and her newborn child, from Arnold and Phillips—
and they had been driven by Tarleton and other British pan-
doors from pillar to post, while her husband was fighting
the battles of his country. The impression was indelible
on his memory—and yet, (like his worthy old neighbor,
who added seven buck shot to every cartridge at the battle
Guilford and drew a fine sight at his man), he must be con-

tent to be called a tory by a patriot of the last importation. Let us not get rid of one evil (supposing it to be possible) at the expense of a greater—*mutatis mutandis*. Suppose France in possession of the British naval power—and to her the Trident must pass should England be unable to wield it— what would be your condition? What would be the situation of your seaports and their seafaring inhabitants? Ask Hamburg, Lubec? Ask Savannah? What, Sir! when their privateers are pent up in our harbors by the British bull-dogs, when they receive at our hands every rite of hospitality, from which their enemy is excluded—when they capture within our own waters, interdicted to British armed ships, American vessels; when such is their deportment towards you, under such circumstances, what could you expect if they were the uncontrolled lords of the ocean? Had those privateers at Savannah borne British commissions—or had your shipments of cotton, tobacco, ashes, and what not, to London and Liverpool, been confiscated, and the proceeds poured into the English Exchequer—my life upon it! you would never have listened to any miserable wire-drawn distinctions between "orders and decrees affecting our neutral rights," and "municipal decrees," confiscating in mass your whole property. You would have had instant war! The whole land would have blazed out in war.

And shall Republicans become the instruments of him who has effaced the title of Attila to the "Scourge of God!" Yet even Attila, in the falling fortunes of civilization, had, no doubt, his advocates, his tools, his minions, his parasites, in the very countries that he overran—sons of that soil whereon his horses trod; where grass could never after grow. If perfectly fresh, Mr. Randolph said, (instead of being as he was—his memory clouded, his intellect stupefied, his

strength and spirits exhausted), he could not give utterance
to that strong detestation which he felt towards (above all
other works of creation) such characters as Zingis, Tamer-
lane, Kubla-Khan, or Bonaparte. His instincts involuntarily
revolted at their bare idea. Malefactors of the human race,
who ground down man to a mere machine of their impious
and bloody ambition. Yet under all the accumulated wrongs
and insults and robberies of the last of these chieftains, are
we not in point of fact about to become a party to his views,
a partner in his wars?

But before this miserable force of ten thousand men was
raised to take Canada, he begged them to look at the state
of defence at home—to count the cost of the enterprise before it was set on foot, not when it might be too late—when
the best blood of the country should be spilt, and nought but
empty coffers left to pay the cost. Are the bounty lands to
be given in Canada? It might lessen his repugnance to that
part of the system, to granting these lands, not to those
miserable wretches who sell themselves to slavery for a few
dollars and a glass of gin, but in fact to the clerks in our
offices, some of whom, with an income of fifteen hundred or
two thousand dollars, lived at the rate of four or five thousand, and yet grew rich—who perhaps at that moment were
making out blank assignments for these land rights.

He would beseech the House, before they ran their heads
against this post, Quebec, to count the cost. His word for
it, Virginia planters would not be taxed to support such a
war—a war which must aggravate their present distresses;
in which they had not the remotest interest. Where is the
Montgomery, or even the Arnold, or the Burr, who is to
march to Point Levi?

He called upon those professing to be Republicans to

make good the promises held out by their Republican predecessors when they came into power—promises which for
years afterwards they had honestly, faithfully fulfilled. We
had vaunted of paying off the national debt, of retrenching
useless establishments; and yet had now become as infatuated with standing armies, loans, taxes, navies, and war,
as ever were the Essex Junto. What Republicanism is this?

Mr. Randolph apologized for his very desultory manner
of speaking. He regretted that his bodily indisposition had
obliged him to talk perhaps somewhat too wildly; yet he
trusted some method would be found in his madness.

SPEECH ON THE TREATY-MAKING POWER
January 10, 1816

[From his political eclipse during the war with England,
Randolph returned to Congress at the beginning of 1815,
to contend against the Bank of the United States, protective
tariffs, and internal improvements at national expense. "Although his early career had ended in the most conspicuous
failure yet known in American politics," Henry Adams
comments in his *History,* "he returned to the House, with
intelligence morbidly sharpened, to begin a second epoch of
his life with powers that gave him the position of equal
among men like Calhoun, Pinkney, and Webster."

President Madison had signed on July 3, 1815, a commercial treaty with Britain: discriminatory duties were abolished, and the United States was admitted to trade with the
East Indies. Enabling legislation was introduced into Congress in January 1816. Certain remarks by John C. Calhoun,
of South Carolina, and William Pinkney, of Maryland, implied that the House bill to put into effect this commercial

treaty, though advocated by them, was not strictly necessary
—since (in Randolph's phrase, when he replied to Calhoun
on January 9) "a treaty [in the view of Calhoun and Pink-
ney] . . . was paramount to law, and competent to repeal
existing laws."

In denying that a treaty may abrogate federal and state
statutes, Randolph raised a point of Constitutional interpretation which had troubled Jefferson, and has been much
debated, at intervals, to the present time. The speech which
follows—Randolph's reply to Pinkney—is a good specimen
of John Randolph's powers of logic.

This text occurs in *The Annals of Congress,* Fourteenth
Congress, 1815–16, 579–91.]

Mr. Randolph rose. He said he was certainly very far
from being among those, if any there were, who rejoiced in
the personal indisposition which deprived the House of the
very ingenious, correct, and, he might add, able argument
with which they had just been entertained. On the contrary,
Mr. R. said, he had listened to it with very great pleasure,
as a specimen of the powers of the human mind which he
was not often accustomed to witness, even in this honourable House. But, notwithstanding this display of eloquence,
he was disposed to return to an opinion which he had entertained when he first took his seat on Monday last, that this
question was swollen by the strange, not to say injudicious
management of it, to an importance which its real merits
do not deserve. I give up to the gentleman from Maryland,
said Mr. R.,—I am told he is from Maryland,—to his
utmost fury and indignation, those fanciful and fine-spun
theories which seem to interdict the Executive of the United
States from negotiating a commercial treaty, or any other

treaty whatsover, with any foreign Power. On this point, Sir, I agree with the gentleman altogether. I go with him the whole length, that it is competent to the President and Senate to negotiate a treaty of commerce, alliance, and subsidy, with any foreign Power, from the greatest potentate in Europe down to a Chickasaw chief. The honorable gentleman will excuse me when I rise to declare that, howsoever I have been gratified in the display which he has made of his abilities, in one respect he certainly has disappointed me. The honorable gentleman will excuse me when I say he has not met the question. The question, said Mr. R., is not the competency of the Executive to negotiate commercial or other treaties, but its competency, in doing so, to repeal existing laws of the land and enact other laws in their stead; in other words, the question is, the competency of the Executive to do by treaty that which can be done, as we contend, only by legislative acts. That is the question. If he understood the gentleman, Mr. R. said, he had declared that the bill before the House was not in execution of the treaty; that it contained no auxiliary enactments; that it was not necessary that the bill should pass at all; that it was a twin-brother of the treaty. If the gentleman had pursued his analogy with respect to laws and treaties, he would have found this second twin-brother worthy of being nurtured and brought to man's estate, instead of being treated as illegitimate and stifled in its birth; that this poor little twin, which came second-best in the world, had not that fair division of the patrimonial estate which our laws provide; that it was, in short, to be put out of the way, that the Presidential heir may inherit and enjoy the whole estate. If this bill were necessary, then, the gentleman had said that the President and Senate had been guilty of a tremendous usurpation. How far this view of the question might bear on the ultimate vote of the House, Mr. R. said, he could not say; but it would bear very hard upon the President if the vote should be today as it was yesterday. If the argument of the gentleman from Maryland were correct, unless his representations on this head should materially affect the vote of the House, that decision would bear hard on the President and Senate. But a few minutes before the gentleman had delivered his sentiments, the Senate themselves had, in open court, pleaded guilty to the charge of usurpation; for they had sent down to this House a bill, either something or nothing, which, if anything, had pronounced their usurpation. If the treaty were what the gentleman contended, *ipso facto* the law of the land, the bill which the Senate had sent down was mere surplusage. We do not deny, said Mr. R., that a treaty, the ratifications being exchanged, has existence without the sanction of this House— at least I do not deny it—and I am responsible for no man's opinions but my own—glad enough, at times, if I were irresponsible for them—but I do contend that a treaty does not deprive this House of one jot, one tittle, of its legislative and Constitutional authority. I am not, in the language of the learned doctor of laws in Padua, to Shylock: "take thou the pound of flesh, but not one jot of blood;" I am not for giving to the President and Senate the treaty-making power, and then denying to them the use of it; but I am for giving to them all the power, and all the influence, which they ought to have in the Government. Whilst the gentleman from Maryland was thinking on the responsibility of the President and Senate, why did he not reflect on our own? Go we not back to be pressed—I hope not to be oppressed —by laws of our own enaction? If the President and Senate go back to the community to receive their approbation or condemnation—I speak of the theory, of which I may say *odi et arceo,* for I have long lost my faith in theories, and in theorists too. If the President and Senate feel their accountability to the people, how much more are we amenable to them, when we return with the same responsibility, and at shorter periods, to our constituents? If there be any truth in the old adage that short accounts make long friends, we shall stand on as good footing with our neighbors as some Presidents who have retired to private life. Our responsibility is greater than that of the President and Senate. What is the responsibility of a man who is to retire after a service of eight or ten years to palaces which he has built with the plunder of his country; of a man who has enriched his relatives by a species of nepotism, and surrounded himself with a society of his own; who can be content to sit down with infamy in private life, provided his bags are swelled to distention, and his appetite pampered with delicacies which habit has made necessary to his enjoyment? But, granting the argument of the gentleman from Maryland, deeming of the responsibility of the President as he deems, we would make assurance doubly sure, and take a bond of fate for the correct discharge of the Executive functions in this respect. The gentleman from Maryland had said, that if the doctrine supported by the friends of this bill were sound, this Constitution was an anomaly in Government. It is so, Mr. R. said, and he was surprised to hear it found out today as if for the first time. It is an anomaly; happy for us that it is, and long might it continue so!

The gentleman from Maryland had said, if the sanction of this House became necessary to carry a treaty into effect, it was not only in their power, but it was their duty to pass a bill for that purpose. Mr. R. said he would grant the gentle-

man his position with a small modification; he would grant
it if the gentleman would add a proviso, that the provision
of said treaty did not betray the great interests, liberties, or
rights of the nation. The gentleman had put the case of a
definition of contraband by treaty, as being paramount to a
law of Congress encouraging the culture of the article declared to be contraband; a case which would, according to
his humble judgment, Mr. R. said, better suit a court of
admiralty than a legislative hall. But he ought, he added,
to be obliged to the honorable gentleman for having taken
into his argument an idea which Mr. R. had yesterday endeavoured to embody in his own; for, he said, taking the
very case the gentleman had put, there could not be a
stronger selected to prove that this general argument was
untenable.

Suppose the Executive were to make a treaty, in which
tobacco, rice, and cotton, were declared contraband of war
—to which he might add breadstuffs, butter, salt, beef,
onions, and notions of all sorts; would not this treaty require legislative enactment to carry it into effect? Or would
it, like a treaty of peace, require no intervention on the part
of this House? It would have that effect, perhaps, in a British
court of vice-admiralty at Halifax, Providence, or Bermuda;
but did the gentleman in his heart believe that such a treaty
could become the law of the land on the instant of its
promulgation? It could not stand: the breath, the tempest
of public indignation would, in an instant, sweep it to eter-
nity; it would go to the tomb of the Capulets. The gentleman demands of us, said Mr. R., to exorcise the treaty; to
question it, whether it brings with it "airs from Heaven or
blasts from Hell"; whether its "intents be wicked or charitable". The treaty, Mr. R. said, came to him in a most

agreeable shape; he was disposed to ratify it by legislation; and, if legislative enactment were not necessary, whence the bill which had passed to its third reading in this House, and whence the bill from the Senate? If a treaty were of that pervading force, that, like mercury, it searches the remotest parts of the Constitution, why the bill which in this House had progressed so far, and which he hoped would pass to the Senate, whatever imputation, according to the gentleman's argument, it might cast on the Executive of rank and tremendous usurpation.

For his part, Mr. R. said, he was extremely sorry that this should happen to be the only occasion which had come within his cognizance lately, in which, according to the illustration of the honorable gentleman from Maryland, the House had refused, like the clerk in the church, to make the appointed responses to the minister. Mr. R. said he was not one of those who would construe this occurrence into any imputation on the majority, any more than on the minority of the House; for it happened to be a two-edged sword—it cut as much upon the right hand as upon the left, and as much upon the left hand as upon the right. One side, he said, maintained its consistency because it cost them nothing, and the other side of the House maintained theirs for the same reason. We are each and all of us, said he, maintaining our consistency, and on the best possible terms—for it costs us nothing. The bill before us gives no power; it takes none away; it bestows no praise; it conveys no censure, except what may be inferred from the argument of the honorable gentleman. Mr. R. wished, he said, that in the future progress of their deliberations, the consistency of one side of the House might be equally maintained; he wished that the administration of Thomas Jefferson, of the first Congress assembled under his administration, might be maintained by the majority of this House of the present day—even if the minority should, for the sake of consistency, be obliged to take the other side, and load the country with debts, taxes, armies, and navies, and all the constituent elements of Federalism, under the name of Democracy. Yes, Mr. R. said, he wished that the consistency of one side might be maintained, even at the expense of consistency of the other —but, he believed, he was traveling a little out of the record. To return to the question.

Mr. R. said, he would suppose that this commercial treaty had stipulated that a duty, not exceeding a certain amount, should be imposed by the two contracting parties on certain manufactures, peculiar to ourselves only, and operating therefore on us exclusively. Could there be a doubt that this House would refuse to carry that treaty into effect by passing laws laying the necessary taxes, and would leave it to Great Britain, if she chose, to make it a cause of war with us? Have not this House the power, and would they not use it, of carrying such a treaty into effect; or, if it seems good to them, to refuse to carry it into effect, leaving it to the option of the other Party to make it a cause of war or not? But, the gentleman had said, grant these doctrines to be correct, and we are the most unfortunate people under the sun—we could have no treaties! Was there any fear, Mr. R. asked, was the theory of our Government so little understood, and the practice so much forgotten, that it could be supposed there would ever be wanting in this House a proper degree of deference (he would not say an improper degree of deference) to the wisdom and counsels of the Executive? Let us suppose it possible, however, said Mr. R. that we should be placed in this unfortunate situation; that it should not be in our power to make a commercial treaty with any people under the sun. I believe the sun would still shine as bright, and the grass grow as green as ever. Are we, Sir, to suppose, in this young country, that all diplomatic skill resides with us—and go abroad a-treaty-making as Hudibras and Don Quixote in quest of adventures, expecting to gain all the advantages and receive no blows in return? No two knights, Mr. R. said, ever were more woefully mistaken; but not more than we should be, entertaining notions equally absurd. No, said Mr. R., if we make a treaty with any people under the sun, we must give a *quid pro quo,* and must always expect to give more than we get. It had been, he said, a maxim in Great Britain, before the separation of the United States from that Government, and it was a maxim yet, that whatever she had acquired by the valor of her arms, she had lost by negotiation. The last treaty of Paris might form an exception to the general rule, but, like all exceptions, it would only prove the rule. The circumstance he had referred to grew out of the form of the Government of Great Britain. As the form of our Government is more popular than hers, our proceedings more public, and as we are equally liable to that state of faction which is the shadow of liberty and proves the substance to exist, until it shall be put down by the strong arm of military despotism— whatever we get abroad we may expect to pay for. We must pay, and dearly too, for any advantages we should obtain from those wily Kings and Ministers abroad, who glory in diplomacy, which is but another name for duplicity. After the treaty of 1783, he said, we sent Ministers abroad a-treaty-making with every Power that would treat with us, by way of trying our manhood—we had just come of age, taken our affairs into our own hands—he had known many young heirs try their skill in making bargains with their more wary neighbors, until they bargained away their whole estate. To such, perhaps, it would be no injurious restraint if they were debarred the treaty-making power until arrived at years of discretion. We shall get nothing at all from these foreign nations, he assured the House, without giving therefor a full equivalent.

The honorable gentleman from Maryland had stated, that if the President and Senate had not the power to make a commercial treaty, and that treaty when made did not instantly become the law of the land, then the President and Senate have the power to make no treaty—and yet the gentleman had furnished in the course of his own argument an instance in direct contradiction of this position—that is, a treaty of peace, which did not in any shape require the sanction of this House. The Treaty of Peace, then is an exception to the necessity of the intervention of this House to carry treaties into effect; and it might be said that a naked treaty of peace—"let there be peace, and there was peace" —was almost the only treaty which could be negotiated, that did not require the consent of this House. Under the old Confederation, however, it was said Congress had made an alliance with France. This, Mr. R. observed, was a strong case for the gentleman's argument—for it might be said, if the old Congress, confessedly inferior in power, possessed the right to make a treaty of alliance which had been near involving us in the vortex of the French Revolution, *a fortiori* the President and Senate now ought to have the power. He agreed to the force of this argument, if for President and Senate, the Government was substituted. This brought him, he said, to the old opprobium of legislation, that the question started is seldom the question run down—the question was, do the President and Senate possess the power, exclusive and independent of the legislative power, to bind the people in all cases whatsoever, and to make treaties paramount to all law? That was the point—that was the gist of the question—there the argument rubbed.

If, instead of a treaty of commerce, the treaty now under consideration had been a treaty of alliance and subsidy, could the troops have been raised or taxes levied without the intervention of the legislative authority of this House? Mr. R. said they could not; and he had understood the gentleman also to admit this. What, then, was the amount of difference between the gentleman and himself? It was this: that Mr. R. contended this treaty being, in his opinion, one requiring legislative enactment to carry it into effect, this House was to exercise its legislative power in this respect under a sound discretion, and a high responsibility for the public good. It was not, in Mr. R.'s opinion, a sound construction because it was competent to the President and Senate to make a treaty of peace, that they could repeal or modify a law laying a tax. Miserable indeed would be the condition of humanity, if the power to put an end to the calamities of war could not be entrusted to them; and, by the way, Mr. R. said he had no hesitation in saying, that, with all the pride, and consequence, and airs that the Government had given to itself, even in this Treaty of Peace— in that simple agreement—"let the conflict cease"—our adversary had got a fair and full equivalent, for she got full as much as she gave.

The President and Senate may restore the relations of peace, it had been argued. Might they therefore repeal all the laws of the land by treaty? But it seemed the President and Senate were controlled by public opinion, and that was a sufficient check—alluding, he supposed, to the press, the great battery of public opinion. Why, then, had it not been said in the Constitution: let there be a public opinion and all is safe; it is enough for us if the acts of our rulers may be freely canvassed. I believe, said Mr. R., that our rights and liberties are safe, but in a very different repository from that referred to—in the State Legislatures, in the bosom of the free yeomanry of the country, asserted by their muskets and their rifles, and never yielded unless cautiously and warily attacked, unless the ground be broken at a vast distance from the sentinels of public liberty, and the approach secretly made.

Was the sanction of the House necessary to carry this treaty into effect? It was, or it was not; if it was, the President and Senate had been guilty, it was said, of gross usurpation. But the gentleman from Maryland had acknowledged that as there are treaties which are self-executory, there are others which require legislative enactment, and which the aid of the House is required to carry into effect. A treaty of peace, by merely restoring the relations of peace and amity, Mr. R. said, did execute itself. But was it so with a treaty stipulating that duties should be taken off or laid on, or both? The analogy between a treaty restoring the relations of peace between this country and another, and other treaties, cannot be brought in aid of a treaty which is not self-executory—which does not require legislative enactment to carry it into effect, as proven by the vote of this House yesterday, and the vote of the Senate today, [referring to the bill passed by the Senate declaring the effect of the treaty]. Mr. R. said he could conceive a case in which even a treaty restoring the relations of peace and amity between the United States and another nation, might be received in this House as a breach of national confidence, which the House would not endure. As he liked to bring every case which he presented to this House as near the reality as could be, to liken it to something which had happened, or was very likely to happen, he would take a case which might have happened between the United States and France. It was well known, Mr. R. said, that a very large description of people in the United States, at the breaking out of the French Revolution, had been anxious to plunge the United States into a war with Great Britain and her allies; and it was contended that the public faith was pledged to guarantee the safety of the French West India Islands, etc. The demand of our aid has been made in a much more sacred name than that of a sugar island—in the name of the imprescriptible rights of mankind; the liberty of the world was said to be in jeopardy; the tyrants of the world, it was said, had conspired against liberty, and we ought no longer to withhold our aid. Mr. R. said he hoped no member of this House, nor the most worthless scribbler out of it, would understand him as imputing censure to those who felt thus ardently. By the wisdom of that man who alone, at that juncture, could have held the reins of empire, who alone could have reined in the public madness, by his wisdom we have been saved from being involved in the vortex of that tremendous comet, which

> —From his horrid hair
> Shook pestilence and war.

Every patriot, not the pseudo-patriot, not he who wishes to ride on the surface of the billow inflated by his own breath —every real patriot approved and honored his conduct. Suppose, instead of standing in opposition to the feelings of the

day, reversing the old adage: *Quicquid delirant reges, plec-
tuntur Achivi*—suppose General Washington had let slip
the dogs of war, hallooed them on, and engaged in that war
which was terminated by the truce of Amiens—or suppose
General Washington, as was the fact not long after, had
been removed from the councils of his country, and succeeded by a gentleman of different political opinions, and
·that the first act of the new President had been to patch up
a treaty of alliance with the allies, Great Britain particularly
—such a treaty as would inevitably, whilst it kept peace
with England, have produced war with France; would the
people of America have endured this? Mr. R. did not think
they would. Such was his opinion of the public sentiment of
hatred to Great Britain and predilection to republican
France, which then existed, that he believed this House, instead of carrying the treaty into effect, would have been
made the means of compelling peace with France, and re-
newing the war with Great Britain. He would take another
precedent, however, from a Government, the constitution
of which was not anomalous—a case anterior to the Revolution which, according to the fond idea of British jurists,
had fixed the liberty of England on an imperishable foundation; he would take a case from the most corrupt reign
of the most corrupt family that perhaps God ever permitted
to afflict the world—a case from the days of the Stuarts.
He averred it as a fact, and all history would bear him out
in it, that the last of the Stuarts lost his throne in the consequence of his subserviency to a foreign Power, which foreign Power was the object of the suspicion, deadly hatred,
and fear of the nation he governed. He did aver that the
Dutch wars of Charles II—that base and rotten policy laid
open more than a century after that wily man thought the

evidence of it buried below the caverns of the deep, would have lost him his crown, if he had continued to reign. James II was little else than the successor in form of Charles II; and James II lost his crown as Charles II would, in the end, have lost his, by making treaties against the wishes of the people, with a foreign Power most obnoxious and hateful to the British nation, etc. If such was the case in England, how much more strong is the argument that in this country the President and Senate should never make any treaty, particularly one which requires legislative enactment to carry it into effect, without the previous or subsequent consent of this body.

Mr. R. said he would trespass on the Committee only by a few other remarks. He was, he hoped it was unnecessary to say, no drawcansir. He was for peace and good will among men. He understood the honorable gentleman from Maryland, when dwelling on the effect of the power of impeachment, which he (Mr. R.) believed would have as much effect on great delinquents as a feather or a flake of snow on the impenetrable hide of a rhinoceros—he understood the gentleman to say, in allusion to a remark that the power of impeachment had been tried and found wanting, that the fact did not necessarily imply—as the honorable gentleman on whom it was tried would have said, it was a *non sequitur* to urge that the power of impeachment was nugatory. I grant it, said Mr. R. As little versed as I am in dialectics, as little of a logician or methodist in argument as I am, I am willing to admit that it does not follow, because a felon is acquitted, the law is inefficient—because the acquittal may have arisen from a defect in the evidence, in the law, or in the administration of the law; it may have arisen from another cause, which I would be the meanest and

basest of mankind to admit, or it might have arisen from
the defect of talent in the prosecuting attorney; and that is
one of the crying sins of this nation which calls loudly for
reform. Daily and hourly are felons acquitted because they
can give heavy fees to lawyers of great abilities who know
how to make the worst appear the better reason, in the
courts at least—while the Commonwealth is content to
have its business let out to the lowest bidder, and its judicial
business is managed, I will not say in the same manner, but
not always well. I do aver that I should be wanting in respect
for the gentleman with whom I was associated on that occasion if I admitted that the innuendo, if I am to understand
it as such, of the honorable gentleman had any application
to them. I have not the slightest indisposition to admit that
it may have application to one, but I believe I see in my eye
a much more substantial reason for the acquittal in the case
alluded to than the want of ability with which the prosecution was conducted. Mr. R. saw in the ability of the defence
of the accused at least as probable a cause of the acquittal
as the one which had been mentioned. But, it was really
paying to the highest court in this nation, a very poor compliment. What, Sir! our most potent, grave, and reverend
signiors—our very noble and approved good masters—if
the doctrine of the gentleman be correct, that, what they
approve, we must ratify—what, Sir! the Senate, on the
evidence of at least fifty witnesses not capable of making up
an opinion on a question presented to them! The acquittal
in that case was referable, not to the want of ability, on the
part of some of the gentlemen at least. Let us look back,
said he; one of those gentlemen has since filled the office of
Secretary of the Treasury. What, Sir! a man placed at the
head of the Treasury not capable of conducting an ordinary

prosecution in a court of justice? I will never admit an insinuation of that sort to wound the fame of one of my colleagues on that occasion. Another one is now a judge of the Supreme Court, civil and criminal, of the State of Maryland. Was he not capable of summing up the law and evidence in such a case? I will not admit it. Another of the managers of the impeachment has since illustrated the government of Georgia. He has displayed an independence which does him honor with all feeling and independent men. Was he not capable of speaking to an ordinary case before a court? I cannot admit it. No; the acquittal took place because the Constitution requires, and wisely, as in the case of a treaty, the assent of two-thirds of the court to the condemnation of the accused; and the assent of that two-thirds was not found in the case of impeachment alluded to, while it never has been and never will be found wanting to the ratification of any treaty which the President may negotiate. Mr. R. said he had received a lesson on that subject which it was not necessary now to repeat. He meant not to tell the secrets of his prison-house. In the year 1800, he received a lesson which, if he was not better, he trusted he should be wiser for, to his dying day, touching the nature of the initiatory and ratifying branches in relation to treaties.

One word more, Mr. R. said, and he had done. He wished he had followed the example of the honorable gentleman from Maryland in one respect, incapable as he was of following him in any other. He wished that he too had taken his leave, and sat down when he found his strength exhausted. He had thought it better, however, to finish what he had to say at once, and then to dinner with what appetite we may.

The gentleman had made one statement he wished to

notice; that the treaty was a treaty or no treaty; that the ratifications being exchanged, it was law or no law. It is a law in those respects not requiring the intervention of Congress, but it requires legislative provisions because it requires duties to be lowered or raised, which is equivalent to requiring an appropriation or the imposition of taxes— powers acknowledged to belong exclusively to Congress. What faith, the gentleman asked, could be put by foreign Powers in compacts with this Government, if a treaty may be rendered void, after its ratifications are exchanged, by the refusal of this House to act on it? There was the widest difference between the possession of power, and the expediency of expressing it. Suppose a treaty should have received every possible sanction—that of this House included—we still have at any time a right to break it off, without consulting the other party, and go to war. A nation puts faith in other nations, not because of this or that form of Government, this or that check, of this or that balance in the operations of a Government, but according to its conviction of the disposition of other nations to maintain their faith. By that criterion, by that standard of character, ours is at least as good as sterling, and, he believed, a carat better. Great Britain put faith in us for the same reason we put faith in her—tempering our faith—for though scepticism be damnable heresy in religion, it is sometimes otherwise in politics—tempering it with a proper degree of distrust on both sides. If we put faith in a single individual at the head of a Government, as in the case of treaties with European Powers, how much more reason have they to put faith in the guarantee afforded by the pledge of every branch of a Government like ours, representing the whole people of the United States? Before the Prince Regent in England can violate a treaty, and make war, he must be supported by a vote of credit from the House of Commons; this is some restraint on him; but we have made treaties with the despots of every clime and colour, from the lily and rose of the North to the jet black of Africa; and yet we are under no sort of doubt that these high contracting parties will adhere to their faith as long as they feel it their interest to do so. It, then, at last turned out, that foreign nations had nothing at all to do with this question; that whether the ratifications are exchanged properly or improperly, was an affair between us at home, with which foreign Powers could not be permitted to meddle; and, Mr. R. said, if he was asked for a just cause of war, he could figure to himself none better than an attempt by any foreign Power at intervention in our affairs. This treaty of commerce gave us leave to trade to the East Indies, and to touch at St. Helena. In that shape it came to the United States, and was ratified here by both Governments. How? In the shape in which it came? No. The very lowest grade of diplomatic functionary—he spoke of his office only—put his finger on one article and said: beware of St. Helena. A Minister of Great Britain can take a treaty and make a nose of wax or any thing else he pleases of it; but the House of Representatives of the United States are to have no word in it. He asked, whether it was competent to a British Minister after a treaty had been solemnly signed under the eye of his own master, materially to alter the provisions of a treaty?—and the alteration was a material one, because the comfort and refreshment of touching at St. Helena was a matter of some consequence in an East India voyage. It was of little consequence to us, who should be soon dismissed to a good hotel and smoking table; but to the poor scorbutic seaworn sailor, it was of great value.

Was it safer for this House to exercise a controlling power on the acts of the President and Senate, so as to meet the coming disease; or that it should be entirely restrained from interfering, and the President and Senate go on making treaties until an extreme case, when the people would interfere and correct the procedure? Mr. R. said he was no Jacobin; he hoped it was unnecessary to say that. He was no man for a Government of mobs, but of order, law, and religion; but, he said, there are points beyond which the people cannot be restrained; or should we rather let the President and Senate go on, provided they can find a Bey of Algiers to treat with; provided they can find a place to stand on until they make this sweeping treaty-making power a fulcrum to move the Constitution from its orbit?

Mr. R. concluded by observing that the Senate had sent a bill to this House; a bill which he considered as yielding the question, and on which it would perhaps be best to act in preference to that now before the House.

SPEECH ON THE GREEK CAUSE
January 24, 1824

[In January, 1824, Daniel Webster proposed that the House of Representatives pass a resolution expressing sympathy for the Greeks in their war of independence; he also desired to send American agents to Greece. Clay and other leading men of the House strongly endorsed Webster's general proposal. To this, Randolph replied in three speeches, maintaining that the United States should not rush into European entanglements; his remarks on such questions are rather in the tone of Washington, whom Randolph much admired.

The remarks which follow are Randolph's principal speech on the Greek question. The text is that of *The Annals of Congress,* Eighteenth Congress, 1823–24, 1181–90.]

Mr. Randolph rose, and said, that it was, to him, a subject of unfeigned regret, that the very few unpremeditated words into which, a few days since, he had been so suddenly and unexpectedly betrayed, should, in the opinion of those for whose judgment he had a much greater deference than for his own, have begot a necessity for some further illustration. He could, with most serious and unaffected sincerity, assure the Committee, that, whenever he was so unfortunate as to be under the necessity of trespassing on their attention, the pain which it gave them to listen was not greater than that which he felt in addressing them; and he hoped that that consideration would secure a respectful attention to the little—the very little, that he had to say.

Sir, said Mr. R., the resolution before you, if we are to take the word of the honorable gentleman that moved it, is, in itself, almost nothing—a speck in the political horizon: but, Sir, no man knows better than the honorable mover, that it is from clouds of that portent in the moral and political as well as in the natural atmosphere, that storms, the most disastrous in their consequences, usually proceed. The resolution, in itself, is nothing, when compared with the consequences which it involves. It appears to me that the bearings and consequences of the measure proposed by this resolution have not yet been traced to their utmost extent; nor, by any means, Mr. R. said, did he intend to undertake the task. But he would give the Committee, as succinctly as he could, some of the views in which it presented itself to him.

It is with serious concern and alarm that I have heard
doctrines broached in this debate, fraught with consequences more disastrous to the best interests of this people,
than any that I have ever heard advanced during the five
and twenty years since I have been honored with a seat on
this floor. They imply, to my apprehension, a total and
fundamental change of the policy pursued by this Government, *ab urbe condita*—from the foundation of the Republic, to the present day. Are we, Sir, to go on a crusade, in
another hemisphere, for the propagation of two objects as
dear and delightful to my heart as to that of any gentleman
in this, or in any other assembly—Liberty and Religion—
and, in the name of those Holy words—by this powerful
spell, is this nation to be conjured and beguiled out of the
high way of Heaven—out of its present comparatively
happy state, into all the disastrous conflicts arising from the
policy of European Powers, with all the consequences which
flow from them? Liberty and Religion, Sir! Things that are
yet dear, in spite of all the mischief that has been perpetrated in their name. I believe that nothing similar to this
proposition is to be found in modern history, unless in the
famous decree of the French National Assembly, which
brought combined Europe against them, with its united
strength, and, after repeated struggles, finally effected the
downfall of the French power. Sir, I am wrong—there is another example of like doctrine; and you find it among that
strange and peculiar people—in that mysterious book,
which is of the highest authority with them, (for it is at once
their gospel and their law), the Koran, which enjoins it to be
the duty of all good Moslems to propagate its doctrines at
the point of the sword; by the edge of the scimitar. The character of that people is a peculiar one; they differ from every

other race. It has been said, here, that it is four hundred years since they encamped in Europe. Sir, they were encamped, where we now find them, before this country was discovered, and their title to the country which they occupy is at least as good as ours. They hold their possessions there by the same title by which all other countries are held: possession obtained, at first, by a successful employment of force, confirmed by time, by usage, by prescription—the best of all possible titles. Their policy has been, not tortuous, like that of other States of Europe, but straight forward; they have invariably appealed to the sword, and they hold by the sword. The Russ had, indeed, said Mr. R., made great encroachments on their empire, but the ground had been contested inch by inch; and the acquisitions of Russia, on the side of Christian Europe—Livonia, Ingria, Courland—Finland to the Gulf of Bothnia—Poland —had been greater than she had made of the Mahometans. And, in consequence of this straight forward policy to which he had before referred, this peculiar people could boast of being the only one of the powers of continental Europe whose capital had never been insulted by the presence of a foreign military force. It was a curious fact, well worthy of attention, that Constantinople was the only capital in continental Europe—for Moscow was the true capital of Russia —that had never been in possession of an enemy. It is indeed true, that the Empress Catherine did inscribe over the gate of one of the cities that she won in the Crimea, (Cherson, I think), "Road to Byzantium", but, Sir, it has proved—perhaps too low a word for the subject—but a stumpy road for Russia. Who, at that day, would have been believed had he foretold to that august (for so she was) and illustrious woman, that her Cossacks of the Ukraine, and of the Don, would have been encamped in Paris before they reached Constantinople? Who would have been believed if he had foretold that a French invading force, such as the world never saw before, and, I trust, will never again see—would lay Moscow itself in ashes? These are considerations worthy of attention before we embark in the project proposed by this resolution, the consequences of which no human eye can divine.

I would respectfully ask the gentleman from Massachusetts, whether, in his very able and masterly argument—and he has said all that I supposed could be said upon the subject, and more than could have been said by any man in favor of his resolution—whether he himself has not furnished an answer to his speech—(I had not the happiness myself to hear his speech, but a friend has read it to me)—in one of the arguments in that speech? Towards the conclusion, I think, of his speech, the gentleman lays down, from Puffendorff, in reference to the honeyed words and pious professions of the Holy Alliance, that these are all surplusage, because nations are always supposed to be ready to do what justice and national law require. Well, Sir, if this be so, why may not the Greeks presume—why are they not, on this principle, bound to presume that this Government is disposed to do all, in reference to them, that they ought to do, without any formal resolutions to that affect? I ask the gentleman from Massachusetts whether the doctrine of Puffendorf does not apply as strongly to the resolution as to the declaration of the Allies—that is, if the resolution of the gentleman be indeed that "almost nothing" he would have us suppose—if there be not something behind this nothing which divides this House (not *horizontally,* as the gentleman has somewhat quaintly said, but *vertically*), into two unequal parties, one the advocate of a splendid system of crusades, the other the friends of peace and harmony, the advocates of a *fireside policy;* for, as has truly been said, as long as all is right at the fireside, there cannot be much wrong elsewhere—whether, he repeated, does not the doctrine of Puffendorf apply as well to the words of the resolution as to the words of the Holy Alliance?

But, Sir, we have already done more than this. The President of the United States, the only organ of communication which the people have seen fit to establish between us and foreign Powers, has already expressed all, in reference to Greece, that the resolution goes to express. *Actum est*—it is done—it is finished—there is an end. Not, said Mr. R., that he would have the House to infer that he meant to express any opinion as to the policy of such a declaration. The practice of responding to Presidential Addresses and Messages had gone out for now these two or three and twenty years.

Mr. R. then went on to say he had thought if the great master of political philosophy could arise from the dead, or had his valuable life been spared 'til now, he would not only have been relieved from all his terrors on the subject of a regicide peace, but also have witnessed a return of the age of chivalry, and the banishment of calculation even from the estimates of statesmen which that great man could never have foreseen; for the proposition now under consideration was that something new under the sun which Solomon himself never dreamed of. Is this all? No, Sir, if this was all, I should not have thrown myself upon your attention. But this is not all. Cases have already been stated, to which the principles of the resolution equally apply as to that of the Greeks. In addition to those already put, I will take the case of Canada, if you will. It is known to every body that discontents have for some time existed in the Canadian Provinces, with the mother country and the measures of its Government. Suppose the people of the British colonies to the North of us undertake to throw off the yoke—I will not put the case of Jamaica, because they, unhappily, are slaveholders. Are you ready to stake the peace, and welfare, and the resources of this nation in support of Canadian independence? Your doctrine goes that length—you cannot stop short of it. Where, in that case, will be the assistance of Great Britain, already referred to in debate as being the only spot in the world in which liberty resides except our country?

After some other observations, Mr. R. adduced another people—in valorous achievement and daring spirit on a footing with these Greeks themselves—and who have achieved their independence from a bondage far heavier than that of the Greeks to the Turks. How is it, Sir, that we have never sent an Envoy to our sister Republic of Haiti? Here is a case that fits—a case beyond dispute. It is not that of a people who have "almost," (aye, Sir! *almost,* but not *altogether*) who have *almost* but perfectly achieved their independence. To attempt to show that these cases are equally within the range of the principle of the resolution, would be to show a disrespect to the intellects of those around me. The man who cannot pursue the inference would not recognize my picture, though like the Dutchman's painting, were written under it, *"This* is the man, *that* the horse".

There was another remark that fell from the gentleman from Massachusetts, of which, Mr. R. said, he should speak, as he always should speak of any thing from that gentleman with all the personal respect which may be consistent with freedom of discussion. Among other cases forcibly put by the gentleman from Massachusetts, why he would embark in this incipient crusade against Mussulmen, he stated this as one—that they hold human beings as property. Ah, Sir, said Mr. R., and what says the Constitution of the United States on this point? unless, indeed, that instrument is wholly to be regarded as a mere useless parchment, worthy to be burnt, as was once actually proposed. Does not that Constitution give its sanction to the holding of human beings as property? Sir, I am not going to discuss the abstract question of liberty or slavery, or any other abstract question. I go for matters of fact. But I would ask gentlemen in this House, who have the misfortune to reside on the wrong side of a certain parallel of latitude, to take this question seriously into consideration—whether the Government of the United States is prepared to say that the act of holding human beings as property is sufficient to place the party so offending under the ban of its high and mighty displeasure?

Sir, the objections to this resolution accumulate as I proceed—*vires acqirit eundo.* If I should attempt to go through with a statement of them all, and had strength to sustain me, I should do what I promised I would not do— I should worry and exhaust the patience of this Committee.

Sir, what are we now asked to do? To stimulate the Executive to the creation of embassies. And what then? That we, or our friends, may fill them. Sir, the sending ambassadors abroad is one of the great prerogatives, if you will, of our Executive authority; and we are, I repeat, about to stimulate the President to the creation of a new, and I must be permitted to say, an unnecessary embassy—a diplomatic agency to Greece—that we, or our friends, may profit by it.

For, Sir, it is a matter of notoriety that all these good things are reserved for men who either have been, or are, *de facto,* members of this, or of the other, House. No doubt we shall be able to find some learned Theban, or some other Boeotian, willing to undertake this mission—perfectly willing to live upon the resources of the people, rather than his own. But then recurs the old-fashioned question, *Cui bono?* His own, undoubtedly, but surely not that of this nation.

But, it is urged, that we have sent and received Ministers from revolutionary France. True, we have; but what was revolutionary France? Our own ancient and very good ally; a substantive Power, if any such exist on the continent of Europe, whose independent existence no one could doubt or dispute, unless, indeed, the disciples of Berkeley, who deny that there is any such thing as matter. But, Sir, have the United States always received the Ministers that are sent to them from foreign Powers? How long did the person who was appointed diplomatic agent here from Spain (Don Onis) linger in your antechambers before he was acknowledged? And is it said that the situation of Greece approaches more nearly to independence than that of Spain when Don Onis came here as her Minister? Sir, let these Greeks send a Minister to us, and then we will deliberate on the question whether we will accredit him or not. If, indeed, there was a Minister of Greece knocking at the door of the President's antechamber for admittance, and that admittance was denied, the question of Grecian independence would be more legitimately before us; but I greatly doubt if even that case would be sufficient to call for the interference of this House.

But, Mr. R. said, there was one aspect of this question which, to him it appeared, ought to be conclusive on the minds of all, viz: that Russia, whose designs on Turkey have been unremittingly prosecuted ever since the days of Peter the Great for more than a century; that Russia, allied to the Greeks in religious faith—identified in that respect; that Russia, unassailable territorially, and dividing with us (according to the gentleman from Massachusetts) the dread and apprehension of the Allied Powers—even Russia, in "juxtaposition" (to use the words of the resolution) to Turkey—even Russia dare not move. But we, who are separated first by the Atlantic Ocean, and then have to traverse the Mediterranean Sea to arrive at the seat of conflict—we, at the distance of five thousand miles, are to interfere in this quarrel. To what purpose? To the advantage solely of this very colossal Power which has been held up as the great object of our dread, and of whom it is difficult to say whether it is more to be dreaded for its physical force, or its detestable principle.

Permit me, Sir, to ask why, in the selection of an enemy to the doctrines of our Government, and a party to those advanced by the Holy Alliance, we should fix on Turkey? She, at least, forms no party to that alliance; and I venture to say, that for the last century, her conduct, in reference to her neighbors, has been much more Christian than that of the "Most Christian," "Most Catholic," or "Most Faithful" Majesties of Europe—for she has not interfered, as we propose to do, in the internal affairs of other nations.

But, Sir, we have not done. Not satisfied with attempting to support the Greeks, one world, like that of Pyrrhus or Alexander, is not sufficient for us. We have yet another world for exploits: we are to operate in a country distant from us eighty degrees of latitude, and only accessible by a circumnavigation of the globe, and to subdue which we must

cover the Pacific with our ships, and the tops of the Andes
with our soldiers. Do gentlemen seriously reflect on the work
they have cut out for us? Why, Sir, these projects of ambition surpass those of Bonaparte himself!

It has once been said, of the dominions of the King of
Spain—thank God! it can no longer be said—that the sun
never set upon them. Sir, the sun never sets on ambition like
this: they who have once felt its scorpion sting are never
satisfied with a limit less than a circle, of our planet. I have
heard, Sir, the late coruscation in the heavens attempted to
be accounted for by the return of the lunar cycle, the moon
having got back into the same relative position in which she
was nineteen years ago. However this may be, I am afraid,
Sir, that she exerts too potent an influence over our legislation, or will have done so, if we agree to adopt the resolution
on your table. I think about once in seven or eight years, for
that seems to be the term of our political cycle, we may
calculate upon beholding some redoubted champion—like
him who prances into Westminster Hall, armed *cap-à-pie,*
like Sir Somebody Dimock at the coronation of the British
King, challenging all who dispute the title of the Sovereign
to the Crown—coming into this House, mounted on some
magnificent project such as this. But, Sir, I never expected
that, of all the places in the world, (except Salem), a proposition like this should have come from Boston!

Sir, I am afraid, that, along with some most excellent
attributes and qualities—the love of liberty, jury trial, the
writ of habeas corpus, and all the blessings of free government, that we have derived from our Anglo-Saxon ancestors
—we have got not a little of their John Bull, or rather, John
Bull Dog spirit—their readiness to fight for anybody, and on
any occasion. Sir, England has been for centuries the game

cock of Europe. It is impossible to specify the wars in which she has been engaged for contrary purposes; and she will, with great pleasure, see us take off her shoulders the labor of preserving the balance of power. We find her fighting, now, for the Queen of Hungary—then, for her inveterate foe, the King of Prussia—now at war for the restoration of the Bourbons—and now on the eve of war with them for the liberties of Spain. These lines on the subject were never more applicable than they have now become—

> "Now Europe's balanced—neither side prevails;
> For nothing's left in either of the scales."

If we pursue the same policy, we must travel the same road, and endure the same burdens under which England now groans. But, Mr. R. said, glorious as such a design might be, a President of the United States would, in his apprehension, occupy a prouder place in history, who, when he retires from office, can say to the people who elected him, "I leave you without a debt," than if he had fought as many pitched battles as Caesar, or achieved as many naval victories as Nelson. And what is debt? In an individual, it is slavery. It is slavery of the worst sort, surpassing that of the West India Islands, for it enslaves the mind as well as it enslaves the body; and the creature who can be abject enough to incur and to submit to it, receives in that condition of his being an adequate punishment. Of course I speak of debt with the exception of unavoidable misfortune. I speak of debt caused by the mismanagement, by unwarrantable generosity, by being generous before being just. Mr. R. knew that this sentiment was ridiculed by Sheridan, whose lamentable end was the best commentary upon its truth. No, Sir. Let us abandon these projects. Let us say to those seven millions of Greeks: "We defended ourselves, when we were but three millions, against a Power in comparison to which the Turk is but as a lamb. Go and do thou likewise." And so with respect to the Governments of South America. If, after having achieved their independence, they have not valor to maintain it, I would not commit the safety and independence of this country in such a cause. I will, in both cases, pursue the same line of conduct which I have ever pursued from the day I took a seat in this House in '99; from which, without boasting, I challenge any gentleman to fix upon me any colorable charge of departure.

The condition of my strength, or rather, of my weakness, admonishes me to conclude; but I cannot sit down without remarking, that the state of the world is, at this moment, unexampled. We are now carrying on a piratical war against the maritime banditti of the West Indies. The buccaneers are revived. At what expense of life, of health, of treasure, that war is carried on, perhaps every member of this Committee knows better than I—but, Sir, to what may this resolution lead? To the investing those banditti, and the banditti of all the rest of the world, with formal commissions which the maritime courts of every country in Europe would be bound to respect—and I should not be surprised if some of the renegadoes, whom we have admitted to the privileges of citizens, or the yet more spurious offspring of our own soil, should take those commissions to cruise against our commerce. That such conduct would not be without example, the records of our courts will show.

It is not, then, the mere power of Turkey which you are to encounter, supposing that you stop short with the original resolution. But you do not—you go further—out of the frying pan into the fire—the amendment of the gentleman from South Carolina and the proposition of the gentleman from Kentucky, go still further—by adopting which, you will put the peace of the nation into peril—and for whom? For a people of whom we know almost as little as we do about the Greeks. Can any man in this House say what even is the state of society in Buenos Aires—its moral condition, etc.?

Let us adhere to the policy laid down by the second, as well as the first founder of our Republic—by him who was the Camillus, as well as the Romulus, of the infant state; to the policy of peace, commerce, and honest friendship with all nations, entangling alliances with none; for to entangling alliances you must come, if you once embark in projects such as this. And with all his British predilections, said Mr. R., he suspected he should, whenever that question should present itself, resist as strongly an alliance with Great Britain as with any other Power. We were sent here, he said, to attend the preservation of the peace of this country, and not to be ready, on all occasions, to go to war whenever any thing like what in common parlance is termed a "turn up" takes place in Europe.

These, Sir, are some of the views which I have taken of the subject. There are other views of it which I might take, but from which I abstain (I may be permitted to say) out of self-respect, as well as from respect for this Committee.

I can, however, assure the Committee, for one, that the public burdens on those whom I represent here, (though they are certainly better off than those to the North and the West of them—that is, 'til you come to the favored States, where the interest of the public debt is paid, and where almost all the public monies are disbursed), are greater than they can bear, because their private engagements are greater than they can discharge; and if this is not a self-evident proposition, I am at a loss to know what can be such. And this universal distress in the country has been the effect of freaks of legislation. I do not deny but there may be some who have drawn great prizes in the lottery, but that is not the case with the great mass of the nation. And what is this scheme but a lottery? If it should end in war, there will be more great prizes to be drawn; but it will be for me, and those whom I represent, to pay them. I have been acquainted with my constituents a long time to little purpose, and have greatly mistaken their disposition and present temper of mind, if they are in any such "melting mood." The freaks of legislation to which I have referred, the vast expenditures which begot the necessities for over-issues of paper money— that system, compared with which all the evils of Pandora's Box are blessings—have brought both England and America to this distress. The two cases are strictly parallel—they run on all fours—and, if this resolution be adopted, not merely similar, but yet more disastrous consequences will ensue.

I shall then, return to my constituents without the least alarm in regard to this question. Unless, indeed, I, and those who in this case think with me, have reason to fear that our constituents will award us merited censure for not having better supported the cause we advocate. Unless on this account, I cherish not the least doubt that when I, for one, go back to those that sent me here, I shall be greeted with their honest, open countenances, and gratulating hands. There has not been a question, since I have been a member of this House, on which my opinion has been more clear than on this—no, not even in the case of the sedition law.

What is our situation? We are absolutely combatting shadows. The gentlemen would have us to believe his resolution is all but nothing; yet again it is to prove omnipotent, and fills the whole globe with its influence. Either it is nothing, or it is something. If it is nothing, let us lay it on the table, and have done with it at once; but, if it is that something which it has been on the other hand represented to be, let us beware how we touch it. For my part, I would sooner put the shirt of Nessus on my back, than sanction these doctrines—doctrines such as I never heard from my boyhood 'til now. They go the whole length. If they prevail, there are no longer any Pyrenees—every bulwark and barrier of the Constitution is broken down; it is become *tabula rasa*—a *carte blanche,* for every one to scribble on it what he pleases.

SPEECH ON SURVEYS FOR ROADS AND CANALS
January 30, 1824

[Henry Adams considered this Randolph's most important speech. Attacking loose construction of the Constitution, here Randolph argues that the liberal interpretation of constitutional provisions to justify J. Q. Adams' program of internal improvements may be extended to the abolition of slavery. He concludes by predicting the possibility of civil war. The text is in the *Annals of Congress,* Eighteenth Congress, 1296–1311.]

Mr. Randolph, of Virginia, rose. He began by saying, that he very much feared that the indulgence extended to him by the Committee, a few days since, might induce them to think that he was, thereby, emboldened to throw himself upon their attention more frequently than was seemly or befitting, and that he should, on too many occasions, offer to their consideration the crude conceptions of his very feeble understanding. But, said he, I can, with the utmost sincerity, assure the Committee that they may lay aside all alarm on that subject; for I do not foresee, at this time, any further occasion, at the present session, when it will be necessary for me to trespass on their attention. I shall not again, unless some very unexpected case should arise, arouse in their breasts the feeling which such a trespass is well calculated to inspire.

During a not very short course of public life, Mr. R. said, he did not know that it ever had been his fortune to rise under as much embarrassment, or to address the House with as much repugnance, as he now felt. That repugnance, in part, grew out of the necessity that existed for his taking some notice, in the course of his observations, of the argument, if argument it might be called, of an honorable member of this House from Kentucky. And, although I have not the honor to know, personally, or even by name, a large portion of the members of this House, it is not necessary for me to indicate the cause of that repugnance. But this I may venture to promise the Committee, that, in my notice of the argument of that member, I shall show at least as much deference to it as he showed to the Message of the President of the United States of America, on returning a bill of a nature analogous to that now before us—I say at least *as much*—I should regret if not *more*.

With the argument of the President, however, Mr. R. said, he had nothing to do—he washed his hands of it—and would leave it to the triumph, the clemency, the mercy, of the honorable gentleman of Kentucky—if, indeed, to use his own language, amid the mass of words in which it was enveloped, he had been able to find it. His purpose, in regard to the argument of the gentleman from Kentucky, was to show that it lies in the compass of a nut-shell—that it turns on the meaning of one of the plainest words in the English language. He was happy to be able to agree with that gentleman in at least one particular, to wit: in the estimate the gentleman had formed of his own powers as a grammarian, philologer, and critic—particularly, as those powers had been displayed in the dissertation with which he had favored the Committee, on the interpretation of the word *establish*.

"Congress," says the Constitution, "shall have power to *establish* (*ergo,* says the gentleman, Congress shall have power to *construct!*) post roads."

One would suppose that if any thing could be considered as settled by precedent in legislation, the meaning of the words of the Constitution must, before this time, have been settled, by the uniform sense in which that power has been exercised, from the commencement of the Government to the present time. What is the fact? Your statute book is loaded with acts for the "establishment" of post roads— and the Postmaster General is besieged with petitions for the "establishment" of post offices. And yet, we are now gravely debating on what the word "establish" shall be held to mean! A curious predicament we are placed in—precisely the reverse of that of Moliere's citizen-turned-gentleman, who discovered, to his great surprise, that he had been talking "prose" all his life long without knowing it—a common case—it is just so with all prosers, and I hope I may not exemplify it in this instance. But, sir, *we* have been, for five-and-thirty years, establishing post roads, under the delusion that we were exercising a power specially conferred upon us by the Constitution, while we were, according to the suggestion of the gentleman from Kentucky, actually committing *treason,* by refusing, for so long a time, to carry into effect that very article of the Constitution!

To forbear the exercise of a power vested in us for the public good, not merely for our own aggrandizement, is, according to the argument of the gentleman from Kentucky, treachery to the Constitution! I, then, must have commenced my public life in treason, and in treason am I doomed to end it. One of the first votes that I ever had the honor to give, in this House, was a vote against the *establishment,* if gentlemen please, of a uniform system of bankruptcy—a power as unquestionably given to Congress, by the Constitution, as the power to lay a direct tax. But, sir, my treason did not end there. About two years after the establishment of this uniform system of bankruptcy, I was *particeps criminis,* with almost the unanimous voice of this House, in committing another act of treachery in repealing it; and Mr. Jefferson, the President of the United States, in the commencement of his career, consummated the treason by putting his signature to the act of repeal.

Miserable, indeed, would be the condition of every free people, if, in expounding the charter of their liberties, it were necessary to go back to the Anglo-Saxon, to Junius and Skinner, and other black letter etymologists. Not, sir, that I am very skillful in language: although I have learned from a certain Curate of Brentford, whose name will survive when the whole contemporaneous bench of bishops shall be buried in oblivion, that *words*—the counters of wise men, the money of fools—that it is by the dextrous cutting and shuffling of this pack that is derived one-half of the chicanery, and more than one-half of the profits, of the most lucrative profession in the world—and, sir, by this dextrous exchanging and substituting of words, we shall not be the first nation in the world which has been cajoled, if we are to be cajoled, out of our rights and liberties.

In the course of the observations which the gentleman from Kentucky saw fit to submit to the Committee, were some pathetic ejaculations on the subject of the sufferings of our brethren of the West. Sir, our brethren of the West have suffered, as our brethren throughout the United States, from the same cause, although with them the cause exists in an aggravated degree—from the acts of those to whom they have confided the power of legislation; by a departure—and we have all suffered from it—I hope no gentleman will understand me as wishing to make any invidious comparisons between different quarters of our country—by a departure from the industry, the simplicity, the economy, and the frugality of our ancestors. They have suffered from a greediness of gain, that has grasped at the shadow while it has lost the substance—from habits of indolence, of profusion, of extravagance—from an apery of foreign manners, and of foreign fashions—from a miserable attempt at the shabby genteel, which only serve to make our poverty more conspicuous. The way to remedy this state of suffering is to return to those habits of labor and industry from which we have thus departed.

But, we have been asked, if, by some convulsion of nature, this Government should be suddenly destroyed, and should pass away, "like the baseless fabric of a vision, and leave not a rack behind," what monument would remain of the benefits derived from it in the West—in other words, what have we done for the West? Sir, let me reverse the question. What have we *not* done for the West? Do gentlemen want monuments? Unless the art of printing should be lost, posterity will find them in your statute books, and in the journals of this House. They may find them in Indian treaties for the extinguishment of title to lands—in grants of land, the effects of which begin now to be felt in Ohio, Kentucky, and Tennessee, as they have long been severely felt in Maryland, Carolina, and Virginia; they will find them in laws granting every facility for the nominal payment—and, I might also say, for the sponging, of the debts due this Government, by purchasers of the public lands—in the grants, which cannot be found in the older States, for the establishment of schools, and for other great objects of public concernment, for which nothing has been given to the States of the East. In a word, they would find them in the millions which this nation has disbursed, and is now disbursing, for the acquisition of the navigation of the Mississippi, and for the purchase of Louisiana. If these be nothing, then indeed we have done nothing for the West. It is true, sir, that these things were done when the names of more than *one* who now figure of this floor, had not been heard of out of their own parish. In a word, without speaking this in any invidious spirit, without the remotest intention of twitting our Western brethren with what we have done for them, I have stated some of the benefits conferred on the West, for the purpose of repressing the spirit of discontent, which, beginning at home, never fails to lay hold upon any external object with which it meets, as an excuse for complaining. I will not add, Mr. Chairman,—from Washington to Milledgeville—for *this* part of the country, what has been done?

With these few remarks, continued Mr. R., permit me now to recall the attention of the Committee to the original design of this Government. It grew out of the necessity, indispensable and unavoidable, in the circumstances of this country, of some general power, capable of regulating foreign commerce. Sir, I am old enough to remember the origin of this Government; and, though I was too young to participate in the transactions of that day, I have a perfect recollection of what was public sentiment on the subject. And I repeat, without fear of contradiction, that the proximate, as well as the remote cause of the existence of the Federal Government, was, the regulation of foreign commerce. Not to particularize all the difficulties which grew out of the conflicting laws of the States, I refer to but one, arising from Virginia taxing an article which Maryland then made duty-free—and to that very policy may be attributed, in a great degree, the rapid growth and prosperity of the town of Baltimore. If the old Congress had possessed the power of laying a duty of ten per cent *ad valorem* on imports, this Constitution would never have been called into existence.

But, we are told that, along with the regulation of foreign commerce, the States have yielded to the General Government, in as broad terms, the regulation of domestic commerce—I mean, the commerce among the several States, and that the same power is possessed by Congress over the one as over the other. It is rather unfortunate for this argument, that, if it applies to the extent to which the power to regulate foreign commerce has been carried by Congress, they may prohibit altogether this domestic commerce, as they have heretofore, under the other power, prohibited foreign commerce.

But why put extreme cases? This Government cannot go on one day without a mutual understanding and deference between the State and General Governments. This Government is the breath of the nostrils of the States. Gentlemen

may say what they please of the preamble to the Constitution; but this Constitution is not the work of the amalga-
mated population of the then existing confederacy, but the
offspring of the States; and however high we may carry our
heads, and strut and fret our hour, "dressed in a little brief
authority," it is in the power of the States to extinguish this
Government at a blow. They have only to refuse to send
members to the other branch of the Legislature, or to
appoint Electors of President and Vice President, and the
thing is done. I hope gentlemen will not understand me as
seeking for reflections of this kind—but, like Falstaff's rebellion—I mean Worcester's rebellion, they lay in my way,
and I found them.

But, we are asked, what if little Delaware should erect
her back, or New Jersey, and should undertake to stop the
transportation of the United States mail? It would be something very like the attempt virtually made by another State
during the late war, or an attempt to stop the transit of the
United States troops through the territory of a State. And
this brings me to another branch of the subject, on which, in
my discursive way, I mean to touch.

I recollect once to have heard, from a gentleman of
Kentucky, the power to re-charter the old Bank of the
United States called a "vagrant power," seeking through the
different clauses of the Constitution where to fix itself; but,
like a man in Kentucky seeking for his land, found the
ground shingled over with warrants! Now, *this* vagrant
power, (of making roads and canals), after being whipped
from parish to parish, is at last seeking a settlement under
the war-making power. And under this power to make war,
sir, what may we not do? Quarter troops upon you; burn
your house, sir, or mine; burn your own ships and your navy

yards, that the enemy may not have the pleasure of doing it. But would any man contend that, in time of peace, all the incidents to the war-making power take effect? I have always understood that *inter arma silent leges*—and a man might as well bring an action against the hero of New Orleans—yes, sir, the hero of New Orleans, if I may call him so—by an action of trespass *quare clausum fregit,* when he marched down to the beach, and gave the enemy a foretaste of what he gave them thereafter—a man might as well do that, as, in time of peace, sustain the power of the same hero —not, sir, that I impute the assumption of it to him—of doing all the things which he might rightfully do in a time of war. When, Mr. R. said, he considered this war-making power, and the money-raising power, and suffered himself to reflect on the length to which they go, he felt ready to acknowledge that, in yielding these, the States have yielded every thing. The last words of Patrick Henry on this subject, though uttered five-and-twenty years ago, were now ringing in his ears. If gentlemen will come fairly out and tell us, you have given us the power of the purse and of the sword, and these two enable us to take whatever else we may want, we shall understand them. Thank God, however, *that* has not *yet* become the construction of the Constitution.

I am sorry to say—because I should be the last man in the world to disturb the repose of a venerable man, to whom I wish a quiet end of his honorable life—that all the difficulties under which we have labored and now labor on this subject have grown out of a fatal admission by one of the late Presidents of the United States—an admission which runs counter to the tenor of his whole political life, and is expressly contradicted by one of the most luminous and able State papers that ever was written—an admission which gave a sanction to the principle that this Government had the power to charter the present colossal Bank of the United States. Sir, that act, and one other which I will not name, bring forcibly home to my mind a train of melancholy reflections on the miserable state of our mortal being:

> In life's last scene, what prodigies surprise,
> Fears of the brave, and follies of the wise!
> From Marlb'rough's eyes the streams of dotage flow,
> And Swift expires a driv'ler and a show.

Such is the state of the case, sir. It is miserable to think of it—and we have nothing left to us but to weep over it.

We have been told, sir, by my friend from New Jersey, over the way, that the framers of the Constitution foresaw the raising up of some new sects, which were to construe the powers of the Government differently from their intention; and, therefore, the clause granting a general power to make all laws that might be necessary and proper to carry the granted powers into effect, was inserted in that Constitution. Yes, such a sect did arise some twenty odd years ago—and, unfortunately, I had the honor to be a member of that church. From the commencement of the Government to this day, differences have arisen between the two great parties in this nation—one consisting of the disciples of Mr. Hamilton, the Secretary of the Treasury, and another party who believed that, in their construction of the Constitution, those to whom they opposed themselves exceeded the just limit of its legitimate authority—and I pray gentlemen to take into their most serious consideration the fact that, on this very question of construction, this sect, which the framers of the Constitution foresaw might arise, did arise in their might, and put down the construction of the Constitution according to the Hamiltonian version. But did we at that day dream that a new sect would arise after them, which would so far transcend Alexander Hamilton and his disciples, as they out-went Thomas Jefferson, James Madison, and John Taylor, of Caroline? This is the deplorable fact: such is now the actual state of things in this land; and it is not a subject so much of demonstration as it is self-evident—it speaks to the senses, so that every one may understand it. On the occasion of that great strife, Mr. Jefferson, then Vice President of the United States, drew, and sent to Kentucky, to be moved by the eminent and worthy man who was afterwards his Attorney-General, those celebrated resolutions, generally called the *Kentucky Resolutions.* These were followed by another set of resolutions, which were called *John Taylor's Resolutions,* but which we now, by the public declaration of Mr. Taylor, under his own hand, know were drawn up by Mr. Madison. These gave rise to that very able and masterly Report of the Massachusetts General Court, sustaining the constitutionality of the Alien and Sedition laws. Yes, sir, it was a very able report—and here permit me to say I have not heard a shadow of an argument on this floor—and I do not expect to hear it, because it is unsusceptible of it—as forcible, as strong, in support of the power now claimed for this House, as is the argument of the Legislature of Massachusetts in support of the Alien and Sedition laws—and I say that if you can *enact* this bill, you can *re-enact* the Alien and Sedition laws—not, sir, that I am at all afraid of their re-enactment now—they who burnt their fingers with the Sedition law have learnt lessons from experience, and so have those who have had their example before their eyes. For, we learn from high authority here, that, notwithstanding the representations of "venal and hireling presses" to the contrary, the country is in great distress—by which we are to understand that means have been taken to use the press here, like the bayonet beyond the water, for the support of *legitimate* authority. No, sir, I am not afraid of the enactment of the Sedition law; there is now no occasion to defend ourselves, by such a measure, against the idle bark of every unnecessary cur in the Republic. But, I recollect when this vagrant power was first detected by this new sect, like an insect feeling for the soft, pulpy parts of the body politic, &c.

I remember to have heard it said, elsewhere, that "when gentlemen talked of precedent, they forgot they were not in Westminster Hall." Whatever trespass I may be guilty of upon the attention of the Committee, one thing I will promise them, and will faithfully perform my promise—I will dole out to them no political metaphysics. Sir, I unlearned metaphysics almost as early as Fontenelle, and he tells us, I think, it was at nine years old. I shall say nothing about that word *municipal*. I am almost as sick of it as honest Jack Falstaff was of "security"—it has been like ratsbane in my mouth, ever since the late Ruler of France took shelter under that word, to pocket our money, and incarcerate our persons, with the most profound respect for our *neutral* rights. I have done with the word *municipal* ever since that day. Let us come to the plain, common-sense construction of the Constitution. Sir, we live under a government of a peculiar structure, to which the doctrines of the European writers on civil polity do not apply—and when gentlemen get up and quote Vattel, as applicable to the powers of the Congress of the United States, I should as soon have expected them to quote Aristotle or the Koran. Our government is not like the consolidated monarchies of the Old World—it is a solar system, an *imperium in imperio:* and, when the question is about the one or the other, what belongs to the *imperium* and what to the *imperio,* we gain nothing by referring to Vattel. He treats of an integral government, a compact structure—*totus teres atque rotundus.* But ours is a system composed of two distinct governments —the one general in its nature, the other internal. Now, sir, a government may be admirable for external, and yet execrable for internal purposes. And when the question of power in the Government arises, this is the problem which every honest man has to work. The powers of Government are divided, in our system, between the General and State Governments, except some powers, which the people have very wisely retained to themselves. With these exceptions, all the power is divided between the two Governments. The given power will not lie, unless, as in the case of direct taxes, the power is specifically given—and even then the States have a concurrent power. The question for every honest man to ask himself, is, to which of these two divisions of Government does the power in contest belong? And while I am on the subject of assumed power, permit me to say that, if my strength allows me, I shall be compelled to state some acts of assumption and usurpation on the part of the States, as well as on the part of the General Government; not that I at all agree with the gentleman from New York, (Mr. Storrs), that the danger of this Government is from the State Governments; nor can I imitate, while I greatly admire the generosity with which that gentleman, a Representative from the largest State in the Union, would shear her of her strength—to do what? To preserve this Union? No. To reduce her to a level, by possibility, with the smallest State

in the Union. And this, sir, reminds me of one other of the
nothings we have done for the Western country. We have,
among other nothings, given them, in case of an election of
a President coming into this House, nine votes out of twenty-
four. We have erected them, as soon as their numbers would
render it possible, under the law, into independent States,
and thus given them, in the other branch of the Legislature,
a voice to weigh down the voice, or counterpoise it, of New
York or Pennsylvania. These are among the nothings we
have done for them. This, then, is the problem we have to
settle: does this power of internal improvement belong to
the General or to the State Governments, or is it a concurrent power? Gentlemen say we have power, by the Constitution, to establish post roads, and, having established post
roads, we should be much obliged to you to allow us, therefore, the power to construct the roads and canals into the
bargain. If I had the physical strength, I could easily demon-
strate to the Committee that, supposing the power to exist
on our part—of all the powers that can be exercised by this
House, there is no power that would be more susceptible of
abuse than this very power. Figure to yourself, a committee
of this House determining on some road, and giving out the
contracts to the members of both Houses of Congress, or to
their friends, &c. Sir, if I had strength I could show to this
Committee that the Asiatic plunder of Leadenhall Street has
not been more corrupting to the British Government than
the exercise of such a power as this would prove to us.

The gentleman from New York says, that Congress possesses the power to coin money, and asks if that does not
involve a jurisdiction over the whole subject of money? It
does, sir; and yet I would, by-the-by, correct one mistake
into which that gentleman alone has not fallen. In what does

that power consist? In designating the metal, determining the rate of alloy, fixing the weight, directing the impress, and declaring the value of the coin—not in the mechanical act of coining. And if all our coin were struck by Watt & Bolton, at Birmingham, the coinage would be as much an act of sovereignty, if it had due weight, and the proper assay, &c., as if it were coined at the Mint in Philadelphia. But, sir, under this power what have we done? We have erected a bank, which will not redeem the notes of its branches, and the States are deluged with spurious bank paper, while, with this base currency throughout the land, debtors are bound to pay in specie. Sir, the bank note table in New York, in which they do not deign to name the banks of Kentucky, is a politico-economical curiosity; and, instead of one currency of uniform value, we have a thousand different kinds of base money, by ringing the changes upon which, we hear the profits which brokers, and shavers, and stock-jobbers levy on the honest industry of the nation. I said, that this Government, if put to the test—a test it is by no means calculated to endure—as a Government for the management of the internal concerns of this country, is one of the worst that can be conceived—which is determined by the fact, that it is a Government not having a party feeling and common interest with the governed. I know that we are told—and it is the first time that the doctrine has been openly avowed—that, upon the responsibility of this House to the people, by means of the elective franchise, depends all the security of the people of the United States against the abuse of the powers of this Government. But, sir, how shall a man from Mackinaw, or the Yellow Stone River, respond to the sentiments of the people who live in New Hampshire? It is as great a mockery—a greater mockery than it was to talk to these colonies about their virtual representation in the British Parliament. I have no hesitation in saying that the liberties of the Colonies were safer in the custody of the British Parliament than they will be in any portion of this country, if all the powers of the States, as well as those of the General Government, are devolved on this House; and in this opinion I am borne out, and more than borne out, by the authority of Patrick Henry himself.

But the gentleman from New York, and some others who have spoken on this occasion, say, What! shall we be startled by a shadow? Shall we recoil from taking a power clearly within—(what?)—our reach? Shall we not clutch the sceptre—the airdrawn sceptre, that invites our hand, because of the fears and alarms of the gentleman from Virginia? Sir, if I cannot give reason to the Committee, they shall at least have authority. Thomas Jefferson, then in the vigor of his intellect, was one of the persons who denied the existence of such powers. James Madison was another. He, in that masterly and unrivalled report in the Legislature of Virginia, which is worthy to be the textbook of every American statesman, has settled this question. For me to attempt to add any thing to the arguments of that paper, would be to attempt to gild refined gold—to paint the lily—to throw a perfume on the violet—to smooth the ice, or add another hue unto the rainbow—in every aspect of it, wasteful and ridiculous excess. Neither will I hold up my farthing rushlight to the blaze of that meridian sun. But, sir, I cannot but deplore, and to my dying day I shall deplore—my heart aches when I think of it—that the hand which erected that monument of political wisdom, should have signed the act to incorporate the present Bank of the United States.

It was not a matter of conjecture, merely, but of fact,

Mr. R. said, of notoriety—that there does exist on this subject an honest difference of opinion among enlightened men; that not one or two, but many States in the Union see with great concern and alarm the encroachments of the General Government on their authority. They feel that they have given up the power of the purse and the sword, and enabled men, with the purse in one hand and the sword in the other, to rifle them of all that they hold dear. Among the reveries of that strange and most extraordinary man, the late Ruler of France, while he was dying, inch by inch, among the rats of St. Helena, he expressed the thought, that, if instead of Elba, he had chosen Corsica as the place of his retreat, when he was driven by the Allies out of France, he would have been enabled, from the bravery and devotion of the people, and the mountainous passes of the country, &c., to hold it against the combined Powers of Europe—as if a man who could not keep France could keep any thing else. And we too, sir, now begin to perceive what we have surrendered—that, having given up the power of the purse and the sword, every thing else is at the mercy and forbearance of the General Government. We did believe there were some parchment barriers—no! what is worth all the parchment barriers in the world—that there was, in the powers of the States, some counterpoise to the power of this body; but, if this bill passes, we can believe so no longer.

I have mentioned Bonaparte—and, perhaps history cannot afford another example of such a sire, and of such a fall. We see him giving law in the Kremlin, in the ancient palace of the Muscovite Czars—in three years we see him in the island of St. Helena, enduring—I will not say what. With that example of humiliation before me, it costs me nothing to endure the triumph of the gentleman from Pennsylvania,

(Mr. Hemphill), who tells us that a new era is approaching
—(not the era of good feeling, I am afraid, for that has
come already)—in which all Presidential squeamishness is
to be at an end—when this Government shall enter on a
new course, and we are to take a new latitude and departure.
With this example before me, I must recall the recollection
of three-and-twenty years ago, when that gentleman, who
is the father of the present bill, was upholding, or, rather,
endeavoring to uphold, the wreck and remnant of that system of policy which its triumphant adversaries had cloven
down. I remember his exertions in regard to what has been
called the Midnight Judiciary. Sir, at that time, I stood, in
relation to this House, and to that gentleman, in a station
very different from that which I now sustain, or ever expect
—or, if I know myself, would ever wish, to occupy again.
If that era arrives, to which the hopes, and wishes of the
gentleman seem to aspire, it is a pity we have not some
Dryden to celebrate its advent. Another *Astraea redux* will
be hailed—and we shall once more listen to the strain:

Jam redit et Virgo, redeunt Saturnia Regna.

Sir, if this bill passes, we shall not only have a Midnight,
but a Daylight, and Starlight Judiciary bill. You will have
what one of—I was going to say, (I must not call him so,
but I will—I know not what else to call him), the most
violent Federalist I ever heard, once said, we ought to have:
federal justices of the peace. For, you are told, that all the
power that is claimed for Congress over roads, is a conservative power—that if robberies, (except of the mail), or
murders, are committed, or contracts are made on a road
belonging to the United States, they will fall under the
cognizance, and jurisdiction, of the State Government. Sir,

I am no lawyer; but this is the first time that I ever heard that the effects of contracts were limited to the place of signature. I always have heard that they were, in their nature, transitive. But, sir, suppose the power to be conservative only—and suppose some breach is made in the road, or any other injury done to it, are you not to punish that injury? And, if any thing of a trespass is committed on this road, are you to haul a man all the way from the extreme verge of the largest States in the Union—for he must be tried in the Federal Court, and not in a court of the State—to answer for having thrown a pebble in the road? And then, if aggrieved by the decision of the Court, is he to be left to the remedy of coming here, to the Supreme Court, for his appeal?

But, sir, it is said we have a right to establish post offices and post roads, and we have a right to regulate commerce between the several States; and it is argued that "to regulate" commerce, is to prescribe the way in which it shall be carried on—which gives, by a *liberal* construction, the power to *construct* the way; that is, the roads and canals on which it is to be carried! Sir, since the days of that unfortunate man of the German coast, whose name was originally Fyerstein, Anglicised to Firestone, but got, by translation, from that to Flint, and from Flint to Pierre-a-Fusil, and from Pierre-a-Fusil to Peter Gun—never was greater violence done to the English language, than by the construction, that, under the power to prescribe the way in which commerce shall be carried on, we have the right to construct the way on which it is to be carried. Are gentlemen aware of the colossal power they are giving to the General Government? Sir, I am afraid, that that ingenious gentleman, Mr. Macadam, will have to give up his title to the distinction of the

Colossus of Roads, and surrender it to some gentlemen of this Committee, if they succeed in their efforts on this occasion. If, indeed, we have the power which is contended for by gentlemen under that clause of the Constitution which relates to the regulation of commerce among the several States, we may, under the same power, *prohibit,* altogether, the commerce between the States, or any portion of the States—or we may declare that it shall be carried on only in a particular way, by a particular road, or through a particular canal; or we may say to the people of a particular district, you shall only carry your produce to market through *our* canals, or over our roads, and then, by tolls, imposed upon them, we may acquire power to extend the same blessings and privileges to other districts of the country. Nay, we may go further. We may take it into our heads: Have we not the power to provide and maintain a navy? What is more necessary to a navy than seamen? And the great nursery of our seamen is (besides fisheries) the coasting trade—we may take it into our heads, that those monstrous lumbering wagons that now traverse the country between Philadelphia and Pittsburgh, stand in the way of the raising of seamen, and may declare that no communication shall be held between these points but coastwise; we may specify some particular article in which alone trade shall be carried on. And, sir, if, contrary to all expectation, the ascendency of Virginia, in the General Government, should again be established, it may be declared that coal shall be carried in no other way that coastwise, &c. Sir, there is no end to the purposes that may be effected under such constructions of power. I here beg of gentlemen to recollect—I particularly call upon the very few members of this House, who happen to be interested in the navigation of the river on which I reside, (the Roanoke), to say, whether, after we have, with many efforts and a great expense, with the loss of at least half of our capital, effected the navigation of that river, it would be competent to this Government to seize upon our feeders, to assume jurisdiction of Lake Drummond, &c., and, for the accomplishment of some wild scheme—not more preposterous and ridiculous than some others I could name—drain the waters of that lake into the Atlantic Ocean, and abolish our canal? If we should chance to encounter the displeasure of the Government, under these constructions of power, they may say to every wagoner in North Carolina, you shall not carry on any commerce across the Virginia line, in wagons or carts, because I have some other object to answer, by a suppression of that trade. Are gentlemen prepared for this?

There is one other power which may be exercised, in case the power now contended for be conceded, to which I ask the attention of every gentleman who happens to stand in the same unfortunate predicament with myself—of every man who has the misfortune to be, and to have been born, a slaveholder. If Congress possesses the power to do what is proposed by this bill, they may not only enact a Sedition law—for there is precedent—but they may emancipate every slave in the United States—and with stronger color of reason than they can exercise the power now contended for. And where will they find the power? They may follow the example of the gentlemen who have preceded me, and hook the power upon the first loop they find in the Constitution; they might take the preamble—perhaps the war-making power—or they might take a greater sweep, and say, with some gentlemen, that it is not to be found in this or that of the granted powers, but results from all of them—

which is not only a dangerous, but *the most* dangerous doctrine. Is it not demonstrable that slave labor is the dearest in the world—and that the existence of a large body of slaves is a source of danger? Suppose we are at war with a foreign Power, and freedom should be offered them by Congress as an inducement to them to take a part in it—or suppose the country not at war, at every turn of this Federal machine, at every successive census, that interest will find itself governed by another and increasing power, which is bound to it neither by any common tie of interest or feeling. And, if ever the time shall arrive, as assuredly it has arrived elsewhere, and, in all probability, may arrive here, that a coalition of knavery and fanaticism shall, for any purpose, be got up on this floor, I ask gentlemen, who stand in the same predicament as I do, to look well to what they are now doing—to the colossal power with which they are now arming this Government. The power to do what I allude to is, I aver, more honestly inferrible from the war-making power, than the power we are now about to exercise. Let them look forward to the time when such a question shall arise, and tremble with me at the thought that that question is to be decided by a majority of the votes of this House, of whom not one possesses the slightest tie of common interest or of common feeling with us.

When, on a late occasion, it was proposed to this House to give a grant of some ninety pounds, lawful money, to rock the cradle of declining age, to smooth the pillow of an ancient gentlewoman, the mother of a race of heroes—a race to whom some of us seem to have a constitutional and instinctive antipathy—we have been met with a cry of danger to the Constitution! of danger to the liberties of the country! But, when it is proposed to draw the last shilling from the pockets of honest industry, to be laid out, as from the very nature of the thing it must be laid out in jobs, and contracts, and corruption—and if you will trace the execution of all your projects—the Rip Rap, or others, you will find the process is the same in all—you are told that in making roads and digging canals, and spending millions upon them, you are promoting the honor, and interest, and grandeur of the country! And this, Mr. Chairman, for fear that the States, which are all clamorous, burdening your table with daily petitions, to get you to extend your post routes through all the States and Territories, should undertake to stop the passage of the United States mail! Why, sir, if we suppose a case like this, we may suppose a universal madness seizing on the whole population of the country, and argue from that supposition.

And this brings me to notice an admission, as it has been called, of my worldly colleague, of the power of altering post roads, after they are established. I cannot understand this as gentlemen appear to do, and I know that my colleague is not correctly so understood. Sir, in the State, one of whose representatives I am, I don't know a single post route that has not been changed from what it was when established as a post road by the statute. Why, sir, you will not, at this moment, on the mail route from the capital of the United States to the capital of Virginia, travel for the first twenty miles on a single inch of the road as it existed when that mail route was first established. What follows from the doctrine of gentlemen on this subject? Why, that if Virginia should do what she ought to do—make a good road between the two points referred to—the mail is yet to continue to go, as now, plunging through the worse than Serbonian bogs between the Neabsco and Chapawamsic, and we shall do it, because it is treason—not by the Constitution of the United States, to be sure, but about as pretty a case of constructive treason as a latitudinarian judge could desire to see on a Summer's day, to alter a post road. From the doctrines now advanced on this floor, it follows, that every mile that a post route is changed, whether for the better or worse, the powers of Government are impugned; and (*nullum tempus occurrit regi*) we do not know what a mass of criminality may not have been incurred, and very innocently incurred, because never, 'til now, had our people a preceptor learned enough to instruct them in the true meaning of the word "establish."

After a short pause, Mr. R. said: It is to me a matter of painful reflection how utterly inadequate I feel myself to say *what* I intended to have said, and still more *as* I intended to say it. But, before I sit down, permit me to put it to the candor even of those members of this House who differ from me respecting the constitutionality of the power now claimed, to say what there is in the state of this nation, at this particular juncture, that calls for the immediate exercise of this power, supposing it to be possessed.

The honorable gentleman from Delaware tells us we have power to purchase stock, and thus promote objects of internal improvement, where they are commenced by the States or by individual enterprise. Sir, if we have money to spare, let me advise the gentleman, who is Chairman of the Committee of Ways and Means, to begin with buying our own stock. We can do nothing better with our money than buy our own bonds. I have known many speculators leave their own debts unpaid to purchase the property of others; but I never knew one of them to come to good. Let us discharge our war debt, and no longer put off the payment of it by shuffling evasions, under pretence of a change of stock. Individuals, not inferior to any in the country, and some of the great States, too, also entertain serious doubts of the power of Congress to pass this bill. I should wish, in the course of future discussion, that some gentleman would show the urgency of the occasion to make the plunge at this moment. Are there not already causes enough of jealousy and discord existing among us? Is this the most auspicious time to set up a new construction of the Constitution? Is this the most auspicious time for the exercise of the assumption of a power which the gentleman from New York, with his usual perspicacity, so clearly sees we possess, but which Thomas Jefferson, and James Madison, and others of at least equal authority with the gentleman from New York, as clearly see we do not possess? Is this a time to increase those jealousies between different quarters of the country already sufficiently apparent?

I intended, said Mr. R., to have managed this subject in a different manner; but the exhaustion of both bodily and mental powers calls on me to do what I ought to have done long ago—to draw these remarks to a close. But it is too late in the day for me to speak for reputation. Whatever is to be the fate of this bill—whether this splendid project shall or shall not go into operation now, or be reserved for the new reign, the approach of which is hailed with so much pleasure, my place must be either in the obscurity of private life, or in the thankless and profitless employment of attempting to uphold the rights of the States, and of the people, so long as I can stand—more especially the rights of my native State, the land of my sires, which, although I be among the least worthy or least favored of her sons, and although she may allot to me a step-son's portion—I will uphold, so long as I live.

Let us, then, I repeat, Mr. Chairman, pay our debts, personal and public; let us leave the profits of labor in the pockets of the people, to rid them of that private embarrassment under which they so extensively suffer, and apply every shilling of the revenue, not indispensable to the exigencies of the Government, to the faithful discharge of the public debt, before we engage in any new schemes of lavish expenditure. Sir, we have already paid more interest on the three per cent stock, than the amount of the whole principal of that debt at nominal par.

Should this bill pass, one more measure only requires to be consummated; and then we, who belong to that unfortunate portion of this Confederacy which is south of Mason and Dixon's line, and east of the Allegheny Mountains, have to make up our mind to perish like so many mice in a receiver of mephitic gas, under the experiments of a set of new political chemists; or we must resort to the measures which we first opposed to British aggressions and usurpations—to maintain that independence which the valor of our fathers acquired, but which is every day sliding from under our feet. I beseech all those gentlemen who come from that portion of the Union to take into serious consideration, whether they are not, by the passage of this bill, precipitately, at least without urgent occasion, now arming the General Government with powers hitherto unknown—under which we shall become, what the miserable proprietors of Jamaica and Barbadoes are to their English mortgagees, mere stewards— sentinels—managers of slave labor—we ourselves retaining, on a footing with the slave of the West Indies, just enough of the product of our estates to support life, while all the profits go with the course of the Gulf Stream. Sir, this is a state of things that cannot last. If it shall continue with accumulated pressure, we must oppose to it associations, and every other means short of actual insurrection. We must begin to construe the Constitution like those who treat it as a bill of indictment, in which they are anxious to pick a flaw—we shall keep on the windward side of treason—but we must combine to resist, and that effectually, these encroachments, or the little upon which we now barely subsist will be taken from us. With these observations, Mr. R. abandoned the question to its fate.

SPEECH ON EXECUTIVE POWERS
March 30, 1826

[This famous piece of invective against the administration of John Quincy Adams was provoked by the proposal of Henry Clay, as secretary of state, to send commissioners of the United States to the "Panama Congress," a convention of the new Latin-American republics. Randolph, who had taken his seat in the Senate only a few days before, assailed the administration for acting without the consent of Congress. The ridicule which Randolph heaped upon Clay, in this speech—particularly his reference to Adams and Clay as Blifil and Black George, the Puritan and the blackleg in coalition—so wounded the secretary of state that he called Randolph out; and their celebrated duel followed.

The text is in the *Register of Debates in Congress,* Nineteenth Congress, 1825–26, 389–406.]

Mr. Randolph rose, and said: I rise, sir, for the purpose of making an apology to the gentleman from North Carolina, for an unintentional word, ['never'] uttered, involuntarily, whilst he was speaking, although I was happy to see that it caused any thing rather than embarrassment to him. I rise, also, for the purpose of expressing to that gentleman my hearty thanks for having called up his motion, and for having relieved the Senate from that embarrassment, under which we have labored so long as that motion was nailed to that table. The unavoidable absence of the gentleman from North Carolina prevented its being taken up and disposed of; and the subject was thus put out of the reach, even of the Committee of Foreign Affairs, and is, therefore, not embraced in their report. And, whilst I am making my acknowledgments to the gentleman from North Carolina, I will make one more, in which, I believe, sir, another, and not the least member of this body, may participate with me, as an almost equal sharer in the obligation. The gentleman from North Carolina has steered his ship into action with a manliness and decision, a frankness and promptitude, a fearless intrepidity, that scorns all compromise with the foe, the common enemy of every true friend of his country; that will relieve, certainly, one, and, I believe, more than one, of this body from some part of the odium which has hitherto been borne almost exclusively by *two*. He forcibly reminded me of that gallant man, (was he not our countryman by birth, sir?) Hallowell, who so gallantly took the lead in the SWIFTSURE, at the battle of the Nile—the most brilliant and sublime naval conquest—the most important, whether in reference to itself or its consequence, that was ever won by man; when the brave but unfortunate Culloden, the leading ship, got around; when Trowbridge, for the first time, performed an important but unwilling service, in marking, as a beacon, the channel to the rest of the fleet. I am glad to find that the gentleman from North Carolina has spoken to this House with the plainness that belongs to him, not only as a Southern man, but, emphatically, as a Planter; it belongs to him as a slave-holder; it belongs to him as one who is not bound to electioneer and to curry favor with the driver of his carriage, or the brusher of his shoes, lest, when he shall have driven him to the polls, the one may dismount from his coach-box, or the other lay down his shoe-brush, and annihilate the master's vote at the next election; lest his servant may give him warning that he may no longer consider him as *his* "help," and go as a spy into the family of his enemy, if he shall have one, to tell, not only what he may have seen and heard, but what he never saw and never heard, in the family of his master. Master! did I say? No, sir, *"his gentleman."* This *delator* and champion of universal suffrage owns no master—he claims the mastery over you. I thank the gentleman from North Carolina—most sincerely and heartily do I thank him. I trust that it will turn out in the end—whether our adversaries be born to consume the fruits of the earth—*fruges consumere nati*—whether or not they belong to the caterpillars of the Treasury or of the Law; that, of us, it may be truly said, *nos numerus sumus;* that our name, too, is Legion: for, sir, we belong to the cause and the party of the People; we do claim to belong to the majority of this *nation?* No, sir, I acknowledge no nation—of this Confederate Republic. For I, too, disclaim any master, save that ancient Commonwealth whose feeble and unprofitable servant I am. The President himself has confessed that he does not possess the suffrage of the majority, or the confidence enjoyed by his predecessors. He is even desirous of a new trial. He shall have one, and no thanks to him for it. God send him a good deliverance from the majority; and God send us, the majority, a good deliverance from him.

Having thus, sir, disburthened myself of some of the feelings that have been excited by the gallant and fearless bearing of the gentleman from North Carolina, allow me to go
on and question some of his positions.

One of them is the durability of the Constitution. With
him and with Father Paul (of the Constitution of Venice) I
say *"esto perpetua:"* but I do not believe it will be perpetual.
I am speaking now of what Burke would call high matter.
I am not speaking to the groundlings, to the tyros and junior
apprentices; but to the grey-headed men of this nation, one
of whom, I bless God for it, I see is now stepping forward
as he stepped forward in 1799, to save the Republic. I speak
of William B. Giles. I speak to grey heads; heads grown
grey, not in the "receipt of custom" at the Treasury, of the
People's money; not to heads grown grey in iniquity and
intrigue; not to heads grown grey in pacing Pennsylvania
Avenue; not grown grey in wearing out their shoes at
levees; not to heads grown grey, (to use the words of the
immortal Miss Edgeworth, the glory and the champion of
her lovely sex and wretched country) in ploughing the Four
Acres. Am I understood? There is a little Court, sir, of the
"CASTLE" of Dublin, called the Four Acres; and there, back-
wards and forwards, do the miserable attendants and satel-
lites of power walk, each waiting his turn to receive the light
of the great man's countenance; hoping the sunshine; dread-
ing the cloudy brow. Spencer has well described the sweets
of his life,* and technically it is called ploughing the Four

---

* Full little knowest thou that hast not try'd
  What Hell it is in suing long to bide,
  To lose good days, that might be better spent,
  To waste long nights, in pensive discontent;

Acres. Now, when a certain character, in one of her incomparable novels, Sir Ulic—I have forgot his name, but he was a McSycophant; courtier, placeman, pensioner, and parasite—upbraided that kind, good-hearted, wrong-headed old man, King Corny, with his wretched system of ploughing, the King of the Black Islands ("every inch a King") replied, that there was one system of ploughing worse even than his; and that was ploughing the Four Acres. This was a settler to the McSycophant.

Sir, I shall not detain the Senate long. We are now making an experiment which has *"never"* yet succeeded in any region or quarter of the earth, at any time from the deluge to this day. With regard to the antediluvian times, history is not very full; but there is no proof that it has ever succeeded, even before the flood; one thing, however, we do know, that it has never succeeded *since* the flood; and, as there is no proof of its having succeeded before the flood; as, *de non apparentibus et non existentibus eadum est ratio;* it is good logic to infer, that it never has succeeded, and never can succeed any where. In fact the *onus probandi* lies on them that take up the other side of the question: for although *post hoc ergo propter hoc* be not good logic—yet when we find the same consequences generally following the same events, it requires nothing short of the skepticism of Mr. Hume, to deny that there is no connection between the one

---

To speed to-day, to be put back to-morrow,
To feed on Hope, to pine with Fear and Sorrow;
To have thy Prince's Grace, yet want *his* Peers;
To have thy asking, yet wait many years;
To *fret thy soul with Crosses and with Cares,*
To *eat thy heart thro' Comfortless Despairs;*
To *fawn,* to *crouch,* to *wait,* to *ride,* to *run,*
To *spend,* to *give,* to *want,* to *be undone.*

and the other; whatever, metaphysically speaking, there may be of *necessary* connexion between cause and effect. I say, then, that we are here making an experiment which has never succeeded in any time or country; and which, as God shall judge me at the great and final day, I do in my heart believe will here fail; because I see and feel that it is now failing. It is an infirmity of my nature—it is constitutional —it was born with me—it has caused the misery (if you will) of my life—it is an infirmity of my nature to have an obstinate constitutional preference of *the true* over the *agreeable;* and I am satisfied, that if I had an only son, or what is dearer, an only daughter—which God forbid! I say God forbid! for she might bring her father's grey hairs with sorrow to the grave; she might break my heart—but worse than that—what! Can any thing be worse than that? Yes, sir, I might break hers. I should be more sharp-sighted to her foible than any one else.

Sir, as much as they talk of filial ingratitude, how, sharper than the serpent's tooth, it is to have a thankless child—how much more does it run counter to all the great instincts of our nature, planted for good and wise purposes in our bosoms—not in our heads, but in our hearts—by the Author of all good—that the mother should be unkind to the babe that milks her; the father cruel to his own child. They are well called unnatural parents: for it is a well known law of nature, that the stream of succession and of inheritance, whether of property or affection, is in the descending line. I say, in my conscience and in my heart I believe, that this experiment will fail—if it should not fail, blessed be the Author of all Good for snatching this People as a brand from the burning which has consumed as stubble all the nations—all the fruitless trees of the earth; which before us have been cut down and cast into the fire. Why cumbereth it the ground; why cumbereth it? Cut it down—cut it down. I believe that it will fail; but, sir, if it does not fail, its success will be owing to the resistance of the usurpation of one man by a power which was not unsuccessful in resisting another man of the same name, and of the same race. And why is it that I think it will fail? Sir, with Father Paul, I may wish it to be perpetual, *esto perpetua,* but I cannot believe that it will be so. I do not believe that a free republican Government is compatible with the apery of European fashions and manners—is compatible with the apery of the European luxury and habits; but if it were, I do not know that it is entirely incompatible with what I have in my hand—a base and baseless paper system of diplomacy, and a hardly better paper system of exchange. I speak of paper money under whatever form it may exist; whether in the shape of the old continental Spanish milled dollar, printed on paper, or in the promise to pay, which promise is never intended to be redeemed—of the sound significant [a word] for the thing signified, [dollars]—of the emblem, multiplied at will, for the reality, which has an actual, if not a fixed, value: for there is, and can be no unchangeable standard of value—it is worse than shadow for substance: for shadow implies *some* substance; while promises to pay *dollars,* imply neither ability nor inclination to pay cents.

I have another objection to make to the proposition advanced by the gentleman from North Carolina, towards whom I feel no unfriendly sentiment or wish; it is this: I hope that he will pardon me, and I hope for the pardon of the Senate—at least I feel that *you,* sir, ought to pardon me —it is this: the unreasonableness of the gentleman from

North Carolina, in attempting, at this time of day, to alter the form of our Government, *"as established by the practice under the Constitution."* Now, sir the practice under the Constitution was settled, in the two first instances, in this way: That the Vice President succeed the President. At that time the President opened Parliament (or Congress) by a speech from the throne; but, since that time, the practice has been settled another way. Since the revolution of 1801, the practice has been settled, that the Secretary of State shall succeed the President; hence it is that the Secretaryship of State has been the apple of discord under all administrations succeeding that of Mr. Jefferson. It was the bone of contention between Mr. Gallatin and Mr. Robert Smith. There are more here besides myself [looking at Mr. Macon] that know it. It has been the apple of discord, aye, and of *concord* too, sir, since—it has been the favorite post and position of every bad, ambitious man, whether apostate federalist or apostate republican, who wishes to get into the Presidency, *per fas aut per nefas—rem quocunquo modo, rem— recte si possis—"honestly if they may; corruptly if they must."* It has been that which Archimedes wanted to move the world; πυστω (*pou sto*) "a place to stand upon;" aye, and to live upon too, sir; and with the lever of patronage to move *our* little world. Now, sir, the gentleman from North Carolina is so extremely unreasonable as to wish—he will bear with my reproof, I hope—as to wish to break the lineal succession of *our* monarchs, and to reduce us to something like the barbarism of Russia, where they haven't yet perfected themselves in the A B C of legitimacy; a regular indefeasible succession of tyrants; although they claim the head of the Table of the Holy Alliance—where there is hardly one instance of the lineal heir succeeding to the

throne without regicide and parricide, (which the case implies) from the time when Muscovy first became an European power—from the time of Peter Alexiovitch, (or
Alexiowitz, as I was taught in my youth to call him) who
was the slayer of his son, and who transmitted his power to
Catherine, the Livonian peasant girl, first his strumpet, then
his Chamberlain's; then an Empress; whom I have heard
more than once confounded with her namesake, Catherine,
Princess of Anhalt, the second of that name, who, by the
murder of her husband, Peter 3rd, usurped the throne. With
some "variation of the mode, not of the measure," it is the
case in this our day of Constantine Caesarovitch—which
means, I believe, Fitz-Caesar—as it was with his father,
Paul Petrovitch, and with *his* father, Peter, the son of somebody—nobody knows who—who went before Paul, not by
the same instrument; no, sir. In the case of Peter, the red-hot
poker—the actual cauterie—supplied the place of the new
Pahlen-tie of the twisted cravat—*a la Pichegru*—and it was
only the day after the news arrived of the deliverance of the
world from the autocracy of Alexander the Deliverer—as
well as I remember the date—I know that it was on the 9th
of February—three days before the unavoidable departure
of my colleague, that I endeavored, and, as I then thought,
not without some show of success, to impress the Senate
with the important bearing of the recent event at Tagan-
rock (recent as to us) upon the new, wild, dangerous, and,
as I fear, fatal policy, now, for the first time, if not announced, attempted to be practised upon by this rash and
feeble Administration. Elizabeth and Burleigh were cautious
and powerful. The Stuarts and the Buckinghams profligate,
feeble, and rash. It was then that I forewarned the Senate
that the red-hot poker of some Orloff the Balafre, or Orloff,

the other FAVORITE—(it was a regular household appointment of Catherine la Grande—somewhat irregularly filled
occasionally—*a la Cossaque.*) It was on that day that I
suggested to the Senate that the poker or the bowstring of
a Zuboff, or the something else of somebody else—some
other Russian or Russian-in-*off*—the instrument and the
mute nearest at hand in the Caprean styles of tyranny and
lust—was ready to despatch this new successor of the TSARS
—of the Constantines—of the Byzantine Caesars.

But, sir, I, the common libeller of great and good men,
did injustice to both these legitimates; to St. Nicholas and to
Caesarovitch. I thought too ill of one of them, and too well
of the other. I thought that Commodus would "show fight."
But, sir, let us not despair of the Russian. In spite of Montesquieu's sneer, he *"can feel"* for a brother, at least, even
although he be not flayed alive; except now and then, under
the autocracy of the knout. He has not, indeed, yet learned
"to make Revolutions with Rose Water"—that is the political philosopher's stone, which is set in the womb of time,
to be brought forth by some modern *Accoucheur*-reformer.
But he shows signs of capability that are quite encouraging.
He cannot, indeed, redeem his paper, neither can the Bank
of *Kentucky* redeem his paper; but the red-hot poker is replaced by a box of sweet-meats—the bowstring by a medal
hung around the neck—the badge, not of Death, but of
idiocy and cowardice. Commodus is brave no where, but in
the arena, with kittens, and puppy dogs, and women, for
his antagonists; a *veritable* master Thomas Nero—see Ho-
garth's progress of cruelty. An Ukase, backed by a hobby-
horse, or a medal, and a box of sweet-meats; *goody goodies,*
as the overgrown children say, is the full consideration paid,
had, and received, for the surrender of the autocratical

crown of the largest Empire in the world, and some say the most powerful—of the proud eminence of the Empire of Europe. How vastly amiable and sentimental! An Ukase now does what was formerly done with a red-hot poker, or a bowstring; an Ukase, with a most affectionate fraternal letter, a box of sweet-meats, a hobby-horse, or a medal— as we, in our barbarous slave-holding country, do, sometimes, hang a quarter of a dollar round a child's neck to keep it in good humor—all *cooled,* however, with the ideal of a few real adherents to legitimacy—in the persons of the guards of the Empire, faithful among the faithless—to make the charm firm and good. Would the gentleman from North Carolina reduce us to worse than this Russian barbarism? Will he contend, that even Judas was not entitled to the thirty pieces of silver—to the consideration money?

This is the first Administration that has openly run the principle of patronage against that of patriotism—that has unblushingly avowed, aye, and executed its purpose, of buying us up with our own money. Sir, there is honor among thieves—shall it be wanting then among the chief captains of our Administration? I hope not, sir. Let Judas have his thirty pieces of silver, whatever disposition he may choose to make of them hereafter—whether they shall go to buy a potter's field, in which to inter this miserable Constitution of ours, crucified between two gentlemen, suffering for "conscience sake," under the burthen of the two first officers of this Government—forced upon one of them by the terms of the Constitution, against its spirit and his own, which is grieved that the question cannot be submitted to the People —or, whether he shall do that justice to himself, which the finisher of the law is not, as yet, permitted to do for him, is quite immaterial. Judas, having done the work, ("it is fin-

ished!" No, sir, it is not finished:) was, on the principle
that the laborer is worthy of his hire, entitled to all that they
who employ him to do the work could give as wages; he was,
at least, entitled to what they had stipulated to give, even at
the eleventh hour; and, whatever promises may have been
máde to him, it is the bounden duty of the promiser to see
that they are made good to the promisee. The gentleman
from North Carolina must not complain that they are working in their vocation—" 'Tis my vocation, Hal! 'tis your vocation." Be it our vocation, sir, to call them to a more
suitable vocation. I, sir, have no personal resentments
against these unhappy People; these unfortunate gentlemen,
as they say of every man who is unmasked—I disclaim all
personal feelings. My resentments are entirely political—
they are for my country's enemies, not mine. Sir, let these
unhappy persons retire to the obscurity that becomes their
imbecility, and befits their shame, and they shall never hear
from me the language of sarcasm or reproach. I should as
soon think of setting out to Paris, to scald the vermin that
annoyed me there near two years ago—to have the fleas
catched, cracked, or boiled, in revenge, or, in experiment, to
ascertain whether or not they are lobsters. Sir, I would not
"d___n even *their* souls," if they had them. I should surely
be put into the Institute, for my devotion to science, and the
cause of humanity.

This Panama mission, is no new thing, as I shall now proceed to show: "January 20th, 1824. House of Representatives. On the motion of Mr. *Webster,* the House resolved
itself into a Committee of the Whole, on the state of the
Union, Mr. *Taylor* in the chair." It was well understood,
that our present Minister to Mexico—to the Government,
I presume, of Mexico—(I don't say *near* Mexico, because

a man who is at a town must certainly be more than near to
it)—was to offer a string of resolutions, and did offer them;
but Mr. *Clay,* who was then Speaker of the House of Representatives, and who could not make a motion except in
Committee of the Whole, by the rules of the House, anticipated Mr. *Poinsett* by moving this resolution, Mr. *Webster*
having first enabled him to do so, by moving for the Committee, whereupon Mr. *Taylor* was called to the chair.

[Here, a member of the Senate apprised Mr. R. that a
lady, for whom he feels much respect, as he does for the
whole class of ladies, was in the House. It was not Mrs.
_____, for whose character Mr. R. feels peculiar admira-
tion and reverence. Mr. R. said, "I cannot help it, sir; I shall
and must go on and do my duty at every hazard, however
unpleasant or invidious it may be." Then, checking himself, he smiled, and asked, "Is Mrs. T. also in the House?"]

*"Resolved by the Senate and House of Representatives of
the United States of America in Congress assembled,* That
the People of these States would not see, without serious
inquietude, any forcible interposition, by the Allied Powers
of Europe, in behalf of Spain, to reduce to their former subjection those parts of the Continent of America which have
proclaimed and established for themselves, respectively,
Independent Governments, and which have been solemnly
recognized by the United States."

"The Committee of the Whole having resumed the consideration of the resolution recommending an appropriation
to defray the expense of a mission to Greece, Mr. *Poinsett,*
of South Carolina, rose, and addressed the House, in a
speech of some length, which he concluded by moving the
following amendment:

"Resolved, That this House view with deep interest the

heroic struggle of the Greeks to elevate themselves to the rank of a free and independent nation; and to unite with the President in the sentiment he has expressed in their favor; in sympathy for their sufferings, in interest in their welfare, and in ardent wishes for their success.

"*Resolved,* That this House concur in the sentiments expressed by the President, in relation to this hemisphere, and would view any attempt to oppress or control the free government of America, South of us, by the Allied Powers of Europe, as dangerous to the peace and happiness of the United States; and that such measures as may be deemed expedient to protect them from the attacks of any power, other than that of Spain alone, and unassisted, will meet its cordial support."

[The latter resolution was withdrawn by Mr. P. in consequence of a resolution to a similar effect having been laid upon the table by the Speaker.]

I shall not read more. I say now, sir, that the House went into Committee of the Whole, on motion of Mr. *Webster*—that Mr. *Taylor* was in the chair—(I beg your attention to the names)—that Mr. *Poinsett* had resolutions to offer on the subjects of South America and Greece, in which he was anticipated by the then Speaker, now Secretary of State. I am speaking from the record—from the book. Is my date noted?—January 20, 1824. I must remark, (in passing) that a proposition was brought forward by Mr. *Webster,* at that very identical time, if my memory don't deceive me, in reference to interference of the United States in behalf of Greece. The *"nation?"*—no, sir, the United States, the People of the United States, can never forget the zeal, with which the present Secretary of State then hovered over the resolution—aye, and over the personal and political character of the mover, (Mr. *Webster*)—with all the tender anxiety of a parent hen with her one chicken. There was full as much bustle, and the object of at least equal value; for, little things are great to little men. We all know the gentleman, (Mr. *Bartlett*) from New Hampshire—Portsmouth, New Hampshire!—unfortunate Portsmouth!—*haud ignara mali, miseris succurrere disco*—thrice unhappy Portsmouth—*infelix Dido*—she who stands again almost alone, as in the days of John Langdon, for our rights—how was she treated on that occasion, and by a former Representative of Portsmouth too, as well as by his new ally—in defence of what? In defence of the proposition of Mr. *Webster,* and of his political character, as a federalist of the true Boston stamp; and by whom? By the then Speaker, now Secretary of State.

Now, sir, I do not pretend to be a man of more than ordinary sagacity. I never pretended to be able to see farther into a millstone than other People, and not so far as those that look through the eye—but I did, immediately after this transaction, write a letter to a friend, which letter, with its postmark and date, can now be produced, stating that, according to my view of things, an alliance, offensive and defensive, had been got up between old Massachusetts and Kentucky—between the frost of January, and young, blythe, buxom, and blooming May—the eldest daughter of Virginia—young Kentucky—not so young, however, as not to make a prudent match, and sell her charms for their full value. I had been an eye and ear witness of the billing and cooing between the old sinner and the young saint, and I had no doubt that the consummation would, in a *decent* time, be effected. I wrote that letter then, in the month of January, 1824; and therefore, when I came here in the month of

December, 1824, on my return from Europe, I wanted no
ghost to tell me about the future movements of certain *"dis-*
tinguished public characters," and consequently of the evolutions of the forces, whether the heavy phalanxes, or active
legions, under their command. I wanted nobody to tell me,
what I thought it required not more than half an eye to see.
I put myself, therefore, calmly into winter quarters, at
Dowson's No. 2, and hybernated very quietly during the
session, taking no part in what was done, legislatively or
otherwise. Almost the only time that I took a part, I was
acting, like the rest, a very selfish part; I was taking care
of number *one;* and having put number ONE *rectus in curia,*
I left number two and number three and four to play out the
game, and to divide the spoil in the ratio that they might
deem equitable—to have "a settlement upon equitable principles"—not at the Treasury—such accounts could never
pass there—but on the new-fashioned principles—"equitable principles"—by which accounts of anomalous character, without voucher or law, except the act of settlement, are
cast and paid out of our money—the People's money. Here
were the knowing ones addling their pates, and cudgelling
their brains, and wearing out their shoes, and wasting their
money, their whole *per diem,* some of them in hackhire,
driving from one end of that interminable and desolate city
to the other, intriguing about the Presidency; trying, perhaps, to make some dirty bargain for the Presidency, when
the question was settled as far back as in January, 1824.
I have not proof positive, but I think I have what the lawyers
call a *negative pregnant,* that this election was not conducted as it ought to have been conducted—that it was
managed, not conducted at all. The great Mr. Pitt once said
in his place in Parliament, that if any man, gentle or simple,

should put the direct question to him, whether or not a corrupt influence was used in elections there and exercised "through the means of patronage, over both Houses of Parliament?"—aye, and over the body of the People too, and over the press—he should laugh in such gentleman's or simpleton's face, and say, "Sir it is not so."

[Here ends Mr. R.'s revision of these remarks. What follows is furnished from the notes taken by the reporter for *Gales and Seaton's Register of Debates in Congress.*]

I intend, sir, to have gone into some other considerations more at length. I must reserve them for a future time. I believe that they have vital warmth in them sufficient to preserve their animation 'til that time shall arrive. I believe they will stand a Russian frost.

Now, sir, the election being over, about which I shall say nothing—I bring no sort of innuendo against great men— great let me call them, since they have conquered me, my constituents, my People—and so, having conquered that People, that is the affair of that People—I deal with them only as the half Representative of the State of Virginia— but there are some curious coincidences, sir, in regard to this matter. Not only do we find one of these gentlemen, almost the avowed confidential organ of the Executive and Manager of the House of Commons—I beg pardon—the House of Representatives; another, in the Secretaryship of State; a third, in the Speaker's chair; but we find the fourth Minister to Mexico. Now, sir, what better could be done for a gentleman, avowedly well qualified for the mission, than to make him some reparation for this cruel decollation of his motion? The reparation was due to him—it has been made. At that time—I mean in 1824—I took something of an active part in the House of Representatives; I was forced on in the Greek question, and we put the Greeks on the shelf, mover and all—*pro hac vice* I mean. But at that time the mover of this resolution, which I have just read, about South America, says, in reply to the gentleman from Virginia, to whom it does not become me to allude if I could possibly avoid it, that, when the discussion should come up, he pledged himself to show, I don't know how many fine things; and the gentleman said he had been too long acquainted with his promises to rely on them, and he looked for performance—which never came from that day to this—for that resolution has never been called up—it slept—it took a dose of Turkish opium—a dose from the Levant, brought in a Greek ship—it fell sound asleep and has not waked from that day to this—did I say from that day to this? Yes, sir. It waked up like the man in the Arabian Nights Entertainments, who having fallen asleep a groom, waked up in the palace of the Grand Vizier, with the Vizier's daughter for his wife—it waked up in the Department of State—while the friendly genius who had metamorphosed him, had put the bridegroom in a place not to be named before gentlemen, much more before ladies.

So much for the Presidential question, out of the House; now, one word of coming in. Sir, it was on that very occasion—[Here Mr. Hayne said something, in a low voice, to Mr. R.]—I beg pardon, I must go on. Well, sir, this alliance between the East and the West being consummated by a new species of Congress—not the Congress between the sexes, but a different one—this alliance being consummated, do you wonder that the President of the United States should, from his new ally, learn to play at the political game of brag? The gentleman from North Carolina complains of the President coming here with a plan of his powers: he imitated the wise man at Rome, who *could* jump thirty leagues at a leap, but took care not to go through it there— they buried the hatchet, and with it, the pledges they had given to prove each other to be—what, I shan't say.

Sir, in what book is it—you know better than I—in what parliamentary debate was it, that, upon a certain union between Lord Sandwich, one of the most corrupt and profligate of men in all the relations of life, and the sanctimonious, puritanical Lord Mansfield, and the other ministerial leaders—on what occasion was it, that Junius said, after Lord Chatham had said it before him, that it reminded him of the union between Blifil and Black George? I, who am no professional man, but only a planter: I, whose reading has not gone very deep into black letter, though I do know some little of that too: I do believe there is more wisdom— after the Bible, Shakespeare, and Milton—I do believe, that in *Don Quixote, Gil Blas,* and *Tom Jones,* there is contained a greater body of wisdom than is to be found in the same number of pages in the whole collection of English and foreign literature. I might have added to them, the famous *Thousand and One Nights:* for, though they are fabulous, they are human nature, sir. It is true it is Eastern literature, but it is the same thing that Fielding served up—it is human nature. I remember very well, one of the numerous heroes of *Gil Blas,* the son of Coscolina, our old friend Scipio—I recollect very well, an adventure that befell him. Towards the close of that inimitable and immortal romance, Scipio is called on to tell the story of his life. He begins by saying that he—it is a remarkable coincidence—he was born to indigence, ignorance—and, sir, the son of Coscolina might have kept up the alliteration, by adding, to impudence; and that, if he had been the author of his own being—if he had

been consulted on the occasion, he would have been a
grandee of the first class. Who doubts it? Who doubts Scipio
or any one else, when he says he should wish to have been
born of a good family, to a good estate, and to have been
brought up in good habits, and with the manners and principles of a gentleman? Who doubts it? It was Scipio's misfortune that he was not; and I would take even Scipio's
evidence in this case, or any other man's. Among other
adventures that befell the son of Coscolina, he entered into
the service of a certain Don Abel, who carried him to
Seville, in Andalusia; and, on a certain occasion, coming
home with very bad luck from a card table—*that* will sour
the temper even of the mildest—I have seen ladies themselves not bear heavy losses at cards very well—he gave
Scipio a box on the ear, because he had not done something
which he had not ordered him to do, but which it was the
part of a good servant to have done, without being ordered.
Scipio goes to tell his story to a bravo, and tells him that his
master is going to leave Seville, and that, as soon as the vessel runs down the Guadalquiver, he shall leave him. If this
is your plan of revenge, says the bravo, your honor is gone
forever—not only do this, but rob him—take his strong
box with you. Scipio, at that time, had not conceived the
atrocious idea of adding robbery to breach of trust; but he
agreed to the proposition. But, as they were descending the
stair-case, the bravo—strong as Hercules, to carry off other
men's goods—with the strong box on his shoulders, they
are met by Don Abel. The bravo puts down the coffer, and
takes to his heels, and Scipio awaits the issue of his master's
wrath. He can tell his story and put a face on the matter.
What are you doing with my coffer? I am going to take it
to the ship. Who told you to do so? Nobody. What is the

name of the ship? I don't know; but, having a tongue in my head, I can inquire. Why did you carry my coffer off? Did you not chastise me the other day for not having done something without being ordered? Did not I know you were about to embark, and was it not my duty to see your luggage safe on board the ship? Abel's reply was, "My good friend, go about your business. I never play with those who sometimes have a card too many, and sometimes a card too few."

It shall be my business to prove, at a future time, that this is the predicament in which our present Ministry stand; whereas, on a certain occasion, they had a card too few, on another, they had a card too many, or *e converso*. I believe I can prove it both ways. I, like Don Abel, am ready to bid them go their ways in peace, and to determine that they shall never play again, with the Power and the money of the people that I represent, with my leave. I say I will prove, if the Senate will have the patience to listen to me—I will prove to their satisfaction that the President has Jonathan-Russelled himself. I have as good a right to coin compound verbs as other people. I say the President of the United States has Jonathan-Russelled himself—has shown that, in the execution of a great public trust, he has done that which has damned Jonathan Russell to everlasting infamy, and enabled him to put his foot on Russell—to clap an extinguisher on him. If I don't prove it—it is a pledge that shall be redeemed—not like the pledge about the navigation of the Mississippi—not like the pledge about this Spanish American resolution—it shall be redeemed, or I will sit down infamous and contented for the rest of my life. And how, sir, has he Jonathan-Russelled himself? He has done it by the aid and instrumentality of this very new ally. I shall

not say which is Blifil and which is Black George. I do not
draw my pictures in such a way as to render it necessary to
write under them, "this is a man, this is a horse." I say this
new ally has been the means of Jonathan-Russelling him;
and for what? Sir, we hear a great deal about the infirmity of
certain constitutions—not paper constitutions—we hear a
great deal of Constitutional infirmity—seven years is too
long for some of us to wait; and if the President can be disposed of at the end of three years, then, being Jonathan-
Russelled, may they not, by some new turning up of trumps,
expect to succeed him? I shall suggest to my good friend
from Missouri, whether there is not in fact a Trojan horse
within the walls of the capital—no, not of the Capital, but
of the Executive Palace. I would suggest to him whether
there is not an enemy in the camp, who, if I should fail in
blowing any body sky high, will put them—below not only
the sky, but the ground—bury them. But, whatever the motive may have been, the fact is as I have stated it, that there
is a discrepancy in the communications of the Executive to
Congress; and I will state another thing when I come to it.
It is, that I do believe—though I do not pledge myself to
prove—but I will pledge myself to make out a very strong
case, such as would satisfy a jury in the county of Charlotte
—and I would put myself on that jury, and be tried by God
and my country—I then say, sir, that there is strong reason
to believe that these South American communications, which
have been laid before us, were manufactured here at Washington, if not by the pens, under the eye of our own Ministers, to subserve their purposes. Sir, though in one respect,
I am like the great Earl of Warwick the King-maker, and a
little unlike him in unmaking one King—though between
two hawks I can tell which flies the higher pitch—between

two dogs, which has the deeper mouth—between two horses, which bears him best—between two blades, which hath the better temper—between two girls, which hath the merrier eye—yet, in matters of law, I am like the unlearned Earl Goodlack. One thing has my attention been turned to— language—words—the counters of wise men, the money of fools—that machine and material with which the lawyer, the priest, the doctor, the charlatan of every sort and kind, pick the pocket and put the fetters upon the planter and upon the slaveholder. It is by a dexterous cutting and shuffling of this pack that the business is done. They who can shuffle the whole pack, are often quite ignorant of any foreign language, even of their own, and, in their attempts to write and talk finely, they only betray their poverty, like the fine ladies in the *Vicar of Wakefield,* by their outrageous attempts to be very genteel. The first thing that struck me in these documents was, how wonderfully these Spaniards must have improved in English in their short residence in the United States. It reminded me of a remark in one of Scott's novels, in the part about old Elspeth of the Craigburnfoot: "Aye," says old Edie, "she's a well educate woman; and an' she win to her English, as I hae heard her do at an orra time, she may come to fickle us a'."

These Spaniards have got to their English, and we are all fickled. But I shall be told—not as I have been told—but as I am prepared to be told—because I have kept this thing locked up to bring it out here in this Senate—I shall be told that these English letters were translations from the Spanish, made in the office of the Secretary of State. I hope not—I should be sorry to see any such tokens of affinity, and consanguinity, and good understanding; but they have the footprints and the flesh-marks of the style of that office, as I shall show on a future occasion. I cannot show it now—it would be unreasonable—but show it I will, and in a manner that shall satisfy any honest jury on the South side of Mason and Dixon's line—any honest jury—and I will bring the presumptions so strong, that he must possess more than Christian charity (which covereth all things) who will deny that there exists strong presumptive evidence—and, sir, against the honor of a man, as against the honor of a lady, strong presumptive evidence is a fatal thing—it is always fatal when that presumptive evidence cannot be cleared up and done away. Do you read the letters of these South American Missionaries over again, and compare them with the tone of the messages and letters which we have received— put them in columns, one against the other, and mark the similitude. My suspicious temper may have carried me too far—If it has, I beg pardon—but I will show enough—not a handkerchief—not to justify the jealousy of Othello—yet I believe that the jealousy might have been pardoned to the noble Moor, certainly by me, had he not been a black man; but the idea to me is so revolting of that connexion, that I never can read that play with any sort of pleasure—see it acted I never could.

Now, sir, John Quincy Adams coming to power under these inauspicious circumstances, and with these suspicious allies and connexions, has determined to become the apostle of liberty, of universal liberty, as his father was, about the time of the formation of the Constitution, known to be the apostle of monarchy. It is no secret—I was in New York when he first took his seat as Vice President. I recollect— for I was a school boy at the time, attending the lobby of Congress, when I ought to have been at school—I remember the manner in which my brother was spurned by the coachman of the then Vice President, for coming too near the arms blazoned on the scutcheon of the Vice-Regal carriage. Perhaps I may have some of this old animosity rankling in my heart, and, coming from a race who are never known to forsake a friend or forgive a foe—I am taught to forgive my enemies and I do from the bottom of my heart, most sincerely, as I hope to be forgiven; but it is *my* enemies—not the enemies of my country: for, if they come here in the shape of the English, it is my duty to kill them; if they come here in a worse shape—wolves in sheep's clothing—it is my duty and my business to tear the sheep skin from their backs, and, as Windham said to Pitt, open the bosom, and expose beneath the ruffled shirt the filthy dowlas. This language was used in the House of Commons, where they talk and act like men—where they eat and drink like men, and do other things like men—not like Master Bettys. Adams determined to take warning by his father's errors, but in attempting the perpendicular he bent as much the other way. Who would believe that Adams, the son of the sedition-law President, who held office under his father—what, up to Dec. 6, 1807, was the undeviating, staunch adherent to the opposition to Jefferson's Administration, then almost gone—who would believe he had selected for his pattern, the celebrated Anacharsis Cloots, "orator of the human race." As Anacharsis was the orator of the human race, Adams was determined to be the President of the human race, when I am not willing that he should be President of my name and race; but he is, and must be, 'til the third day of March, eighteen hundred and—I forget when. He has come out with a speech and a message, and with a doctrine that goes to take the whole human family under his special protection. Now, sir, who made him his brother's keeper? Who gave him, the President of the United States, the custody of the liberties, or the rights, or the interests of South America, or any other America, save only the United States of America, or any other country under the sun? He has put himself, we know, into the way, and I say God send him a safe deliverance, and God send the country a safe deliverance from his policy—from his policy. Sir, it is well known to you, that, up to the period of getting this message from Adams, I was the champion here of his rights as a co-ordinate branch of the Government. I was the person who rose immediately after the gentleman from New York, and protested against our opening the doors, for reasons with which I will not trouble the Senate. On that question of a call on the Executive, for other information than the treaties, &c., I said, the President is a co-ordinate branch of this Government, and is entitled to all possible respect from us. It is his duty to lay before us information on which we must act—if he does not give us sufficient information, it is not our business to ask more—I never will ask for more, and to be given confidentially, &c. [Mr. R. here briefly adverted to the history of the resolutions in the secret session.] I did maintain the rights of the President, but from the moment he sent us this message—from that moment, did my tone and manner to him change. From that moment was I an altered man, and I am afraid, not altered for the better. [Here Mr. R. read the Executive Message, of the 16th February, as follows:]

"In answer to the two resolutions of the Senate, of the 15th instant, marked (Excutive,) and which I have received, I state, respectfully, that all the communications from me to the Senate, relating to the Congress at Panama, have been made, like all other communications upon Executive business, in *confidence,* and none of them in compliance with a resolution of the Senate requiring them confidentially. Believing that the established usage of free confidential communications between the Executive and the Senate, ought, for the public interest, to be preserved unimpaired, I deem it my indispensable duty to leave to the Senate itself the decision of a question."

Sir, if he would leave to the Senate the decision of the question, I would agree with him; but the evil genius of the American House of Stuart prevailed—he goes on to say, that the question "involves a departure, hitherto, so far as I am informed, without example, from that usage, and upon *the motives for which,* not being informed of them, I do not feel myself competent to decide."

If this had been persecuted for a libel, what jury would have failed to have found a verdict on such an innuendo? that we were breaking up from our own usages, to gratify personal spleen? I say nothing about our *movements,* because he was not informed of them; the innuendo was, that our *motives* were black and bad. That moment did I put, like Hannibal, my hand on the altar, and swear eternal enmity against him and his, politically. From that moment I would do any thing within the limits of the Constitution and the law: for, as Chatham said of Wilkes, I would not, in the person of the worst of men, violate those sanctions and privileges which are the safeguard of the rights and liberties of the best;—but, within the limits of the Constitution and the law, if I don't carry on the war, whether in the Peninsula or any where else, it shall be for want of resources.

[Mr. R. went on to speak of the motions to which this message of the President's had given rise; one of which described the nature and character of the message.]

To the resolution, said he, I objected. I said, I would have
all the nakedness of the Greek statue; I would even take off
the skin, that the muscles might be developed, and that we
might have the naked fact.

[After further observations on the resolutions moved in
conclave on this subject, Mr. R. repeated what he had then
said, in reference to the message of the President.]

Who made him a judge of our usages? Who constituted
him? He has been a professor, I understand—I wish he had
left off the pedagogue when he got into the Executive Chair.
Who made him the *censor morum* of this body? Will any
one answer this question? Yes or no? Who? Name the person. Above all, who made him the searcher of hearts, and
gave him the right, by an innuendo black as hell, to blacken
our motives? Blacken our motives—I did not say that then
—I was more under self command; I did not use such strong
language—I said if he could borrow the eye of Omniscience
himself; and look into every bosom here—if he could look
into that most awful, calamitous, and tremendous of all
possible gulfs, the naked unveiled human heart—stripped
of all its coverings of self love—exposed naked as to the
eye of God—I said if he could do that, he was not, as President of the United States, entitled to pass upon our motives,
although he saw and knew them to be bad. I said, if he had
converted us to the Catholic Religion, and was our Father
Confessor, and every man in this House at the footstool of
the confessional had confessed a bad motive to him, by the
laws of his church, as by this Constitution, above the law
and above the church, he, as President of the United States,
could not pass on our motives, though we had with our own
lips told him our motives, and confessed they were bad. I
said this then, and I say it now. Here I plant my foot—here

I fling defiance right into his teeth, before the American People. Here I throw the gauntlet to him and the bravest of his compeers, to come forward and defend these miserable dirty lines: "involving a departure, hitherto, so far as I am informed, without example, from that usage, and upon the motives for which, not being informed of them, I do not feel myself competent to decide"! Amiable modesty! I wonder we did not, all at once, fall in love with him; and agree—*una voce,* to publish our proceedings—except myself—for I quitted the Senate ten minutes before the vote was taken. I saw what was to follow—I knew the thing would not be done at all, or would be done unanimously. Therefore, in spite of the remonstrances of friends, I went away, not fearing that any one would doubt what my vote would have been, if I had stayed. After twenty-six hours' exertion, it was time to give in. I was defeated, horse, foot, and dragoons—cut up—and clean broke down—by the coalition of Blifil and Black George—by the combination, unheard of 'til then, of the puritan with the black-leg.

Having disposed of this subject, I shall say one word more, and sit down. I said, on the subject already adverted to, let the Senate take a dignified stand—don't let them say, we sent to you for that thing, you sent us this; therefore, we shall not go any further—we shall stop. Let them behave like Romans, like Conscript Fathers. I am sorry I was prevailed on to withdraw my motion, even to make way for that of the gentleman from Portsmouth, New Hampshire. But she once went with us—we rode through the equinoctial gale together—Portsmouth overcame the first Adams, and Portsmouth, New Hampshire, I trust, will overcome the second. I should not have made this allusion but for a toast I heard lately of from a friend of mine—"Those who fell with the first Adams rise with the second." Very true—*c'est vrai.* Agreed—they who fell under the wrath and desperation of the first Adams—the dust and ashes men—have risen too. I saw one of them this morning. We too have risen, and the strife is to come. North Carolina has started forth boldly and manfully, like the fine fellow at the battle of the Nile—I believe he was an American—he led the van, and I humbly follow in the wake. It is skirmishing with the light armed troops—with the Voltigeurs—I hope we shall here form of phalanx, a legion—I hope to see, not only Hector in the field, but Troilus, and a host of worthies with him. If not, we too shall have to sing *Fuit Ilium*—we too shall have to sing, *Where the Capitol Stood, There Grows the Harvest.* We must put our shoulders to the wheel—having put our hand to the plow, we must not fall back. How men can find time to be sick I can't conceive—I must be dead before I could refrain at a call like this.

I never write out speeches. I am glad I am singular in that respect. But I would not lose those that have been published, and those that are about to be published very soon, (on the Panama Mission), for all the books that have been written in defence of Constitutions—that on the British Constitution (De Lolme) included. We poor narrow-minded wretches believed that it was not our business to go on a crusade to Terra del Fuego, to prevent somebody making a settlement where man cannot live, or to the North Pole. Our business is to attend to the interests and rights of the American Confederacy here. Like Hector's wife, who was found spinning amongst her maids, we did believe that the care of our household was our main concern. The card-table has gone out of fashion now—even lotteries are denounced—I don't mean such a one as that granted to

Jefferson by the Legislature of Virginia—I should have voted for that bill if I had been there—horse-racing and billiards are no longer in vogue—all these having been discarded, what is got up in their place? The same meddling, obtrusive, intrusive, restless, self-dissatisfied spirit shows itself in another way. The ennui breaks out in a new place —the *tedium vitae* appears in Sunday Schools, Missionary Societies, subscriptions to Colonization Societies—taking care of the Sandwich Islanders, free negroes, and God knows who. It is the same spirit which drove men from home to the card-table, to the billiard table, and the horse race. It is a matter of fact, that a gentleman told me, that, going to visit a very pious lady and gentleman in Virginia, the little negroes were so ragged as to be obliged to hide for shame, and the women of the family were employed in making pantaloons and jackets for the free negroes at Liberia. Whenever any of these Ministers, male or female, come to me with their complaints and petitions for aid, I never can forget Gil Blas and Señor Manuel Ordonez, who got rich and lived comfortably by administering the funds of the poor. If we cannot get here an account of the money we vote by appropriation, I should like to see a settlement of the accounts of the Otaheitans. I should like to see the vouchers of the expenditures for these Sandwich Islanders, and these Liberian people—I am afraid we should have to settle them on equitable principles—they would never pass the Treasury. When I cannot get an account from my own steward, as a private man; when, as a public man, I do not know what has become of the millions of the People's money; should I not be the veriest ass that ever existed, to expect a proper application of money when there is half the diameter of the globe between me and the applicant? I hold out this as a hint to all benevolent gentlemen and ladies, whose good hearts are imposed on for the support of sturdy beggars, who would rather beg than work. Begging is gone out of fashion for one's self—it is for some miserable establishment—we must convert the Catholics at Panama—we must convert the Jews—"Give me the money, my dear madam, and I will see it properly applied." We are now doing in this country, what has been done in every country under the sun—as the old cheats wear out, new ones spring up. As the old Faro Banks wear out, Banks of Discount spring up. When, in Virginia, we had billiard tables, and cards, and races, and not half the population we now have, I could produce you two honest men where we can now show one. We have no Faro Bank, no billiard table—we have hardly a race—we have got too good to run races—but we are not too good to embezzle the money entrusted to us, or to do any thing that is covered up under the garment of Religion. Hypocrisy is the only sin that walks abroad that cannot be discerned, except by the eye of God alone; yet, when you see a man's whole conduct at variance with his religious profession, you will not be defective in charity alone if you do not come to the conclusion that, like Manuel Ordonez, he is pretty much of a cheat.

I find, sir, that the regular speech I had been preparing for the Senate, has not arrived at its due term of parturition. But, in due time, I trust it will make its appearance. I will trespass no longer on the time and patience of the Senate—but there is more behind—come out it shall—redeem the pledge I will—I will show that this Panama Mission is a Kentucky cuckoo's egg, laid in a Spanish American nest. I will show that the President of the United States and his Ministers have Jonathan-Russelled the Congress of the

United States—that he has held one language at one time, on the same subject, to one House of Congress, while to another House he has held a different language on the same subject. I will not bring it here in notes. I will have the letters printed in parallel passages, that they may be compared with the style of the Department of State—whether the Department of State be, in this case, the President of the United States, or whether it be the officer who presides over that Department, it will show sufficient to satisfy any man of common penetration that these things were manufactured here, and that this Don Salazar, or whatever he is, had just as much hand in it as the Grand Inquisitor had in the commission with which Don Raphael and broker Ambrose de Lamela, in company with Gil Blas, made a visit to the Jew, and rifled his coffers. I will prove to any man—they may write what Spanish they please—carry it to an indifferent translator, and there shall be no similarity in style, grammatical construction, or any thing else, between the letter they write, and the letter which it is alleged they have written, and which has been translated and sent to us. Why were not the originals sent? Is the name of the translator given? No. They are not sent as purporting to be translations.

This is a strange world. The man who is whistling over the furrow, at the time he is turning in corn to give bread to his wife and family, knows no more of what is doing here than a man in South America. He does not know that they who never did plant corn, or never shall plant corn again, are to take the best part of his crop. He does not know, while his horses are poor because he cannot afford to keep them fat, that horses are driven in this City that are fed out of his crib—he does not know this, because you get the money from him *tarifically*—he is *tarified,* as we say in Virginia. He is taxed for all the real necessaries of life—and how does his money go? I wish he could come here to see. If every man in the United States could spend one day in Washington—if every woman could spend one hour here— and God forbid that my wife or daughter should spend more —then you would have salvation for the Republic. It must be some special interposition of Providence, though work- ing by secondary causes, that will snatch this nation from the downhill progress it is making, not merely to bankruptcy, but to perdition. We may flatter ourselves as long as we please, and think, and talk, and brag, and boast, in fourth of July orations and others, of being the most enlightened People under the sun—we may be all that and yet be radi- cally ignorant. We are going the road that has ruined nations before us—we are copying, as far as we are able, the worst parts of the British system, leaving out the best— and who are we, that we should be exempt from the law which the Author of the being of all mankind has imposed on them? What is the history of man, and what is he? The young lady who thinks so highly of her Philander, her Werther, her Sylvio, who will go with him to a certain point —who will go with him to the bottom of the garden, and listen to the nightingale and the mocking-bird, and talk sweet sentiment—but if she goes so far as that she is lost— she had much better go to her grandmama, and not Philan- der. So it is with a nation—the man who says, this is but a trifle—a peccadillo—I was absent for a few days from the Senate, but none will think of it—*c'est le premier pas qui coute*—the moment a man leaves the path of religion or virtue—the moment he takes Paley and the Jesuits to ascer- tain how far he may go on the borderline of villainy without overstepping it—that man, or woman, is lost. Our situation is awful beyond conception—we are in a state of utter ignorance of ourselves, and perhaps I may be supposed at this time worrying the patience of the Senate, when they would rather I should take my seat. It is my duty to leave nothing undone that I may lawfully do, to pull down this Administration. I see it, and only wait 'til the third of March, 1829—this month three years—and, if the People do not step in to correct the procedure, I am much mistaken if I ever take their part again—and why, sir? I do not think the honor of a daughter is to be preserved at the expense of bars and bolts: for, where the mind is polluted, what care I who has the worthless possession of the body? He who goes out *animo furandi,* is a thief, whether he exacts a purse or not. So it is with a nation. They who, from indifference, or with their eyes open, persist in hugging the traitor to their bosom, deserve to be insulted with different messages than this; they deserve to be slaves, with no other music to soothe them but the clank of the chains which they have put on themselves and given to their offspring.

SPEECH ON AMENDMENT OF THE CONSTITUTION
April 3, 1826

[A proposal to limit election to the Presidency to two terms —defeated in 1826, and not adopted, of course, until President Truman's administration—provoked this short speech, in which Randolph forcibly expressed his opposition to tinkering with constitutions. It is printed in *Register of Debates in Congress,* Nineteenth Congress, 1825–26, 407.]

The engrossed joint resolution proposing to amend the Constitution of the United States, so as to render any person ineligible for the Presidency after a second term, was read for the third time, and the question stated on its passage.

Mr. Randolph said, he hoped he should not be called on to vote on the resolution now: for, if so, he should be obliged to vote against it. He was opposed to all amendments of the Constitution, of every sort and kind, and he hoped he should not be called on now, to vote on this. He would vote to restore the Constitution to what it was, because, in stopping up one hole we made two. He should therefore move to lay the resolution on the table, at least 'til tomorrow.

Mr. Dickerson objected to laying the resolution on the table, unless the gentleman from Virginia wanted time to examine into its merits—and was about to add some remarks, when he was reminded by the Chair, that the motion now pending, to lay the resolution on the table, did not admit of debate, and Mr. D. took his seat.

Mr. Randolph then rose and said: I will tell the gentleman at once—it is unreasonable, after having spoken an hour and thirty-five minutes, to speak again today—I will tell him at once, in my plain, old-fashioned, outright, downright, and I hope, upright manner, that I am against all amendments of the Constitution that are nugatory; they are therefore hurtful. I believe the Constitution to be better now, than it would be with this amendment. I believe that we have got this thing on the very footing of security: this is my firm belief. Your tenure now is copyhold—with a *fine certain,* and that fine is the public indignation against any man who would attempt to break the custom of the manor. You are not obliged to resort to title deeds, in which the lawyers can and will find a flaw—it is equal to freehold or better. I put up no fences against usurpation, made up of paper or parchment. Power is the only thing that limits power. This thing will go back again to the blue book, and the articles of the Constitution *are* so numerous, that nobody now knows what the Constitution is. A Constitution which the People every day exercise by serving as jurors, as magistrates, by electing their Representatives, by claiming the privilege of the writ of habeas corpus,—this is a free Constitution; but a Constitution on paper, which leads us to inquire what is the Constitution—this is a Constitution which some quibbling lawyer, or quibbling planter, or merchants, or artisan, makes the paper speak in order to curry favor with People in power. I am for *ne quid nimis*— for the doctrine of doing nothing—for a wise and masterly inactivity about the Constitution. I am almost glad the gentleman objected to my motion, because I shall be able to supply what I just now omitted to say.

We altered the Constitution to guard against that scoundrel Aaron Burr, though not greater than him, who, after that event, formed the union of honest men of all parties. We altered the Constitution to guard against Aaron Burr —we altered it, and what sort of an alteration was it? It did guard against him; against whom there was no necessity to take any precaution at all, for he was *civiliter mortuus*— he was politically dead; but in this general resurrection of the dead; in this gathering together of the dry bones, I do not see why he may not be dug up and placed in office as well as some other people. The true evil consists, not in the Constitution—I am no worshipper of this Constitution —I think it was made by men, and at an evil time, when the great laxity of the old system had begot a great itch for an energetic government. But suppose every time that a man was to meet with a dishonest man, he went home and took a dose of calomel; it is the alternative of his constitution—

how long would his constitution stand? Every time any thing happens in this House or the other House, to disappoint this wish or that wish, take a little more of the blue pill—of the blue book, [holding up a copy of the Constitution, bound in blue paper]. I would put the Constitution back to where it was, because every alteration made in it—except the amendments at the end—I am not sure they do any good—I wish these amendments and provisions *ex abundanti cautela* were not in the Constitution—it is their being there which has given a color to the claims and usurpation under the Constitution. If I run a fence around my field, leaving down so many panels, I might as well have no fence at all: So it is with these cautions on the Constitution—The moment any thing happens, call in the doctor and give a little more medicine. We have now got the thing on a safe footing; and because it is so, I don't want it any better. I hold my land under the order of the King in council, and perhaps that is the reason that Orders in Council did not appear so terrible to me as they did to other people, and that I was not in favor of going to war about them. Do you think I would surrender this title to take another from the War Office, engrossed on the fairest parchment that ever came from that office? If my title were originally bad, it is now good by prescription—the best possible title.

The moment this resolution shall not pass, what is the innuendo then? Sir, the resolution is not going to pass—and if it does not, where are you? Just where you were. It is as bad to say, you will go into jail to be let out again; why not stay out? You go into the Constitution that it may be amended; why not amend it before you go into it?—that would be the part of wise men. I will vote for no alteration of the Constitution that does not take away some power from the General Government specifically to give it to the States.

The States have usurped one power from the General Government, which I should be willing to take from them, that is, the banking power. I would take it from the States—but it should be on the condition that it is taken from the General Government also. I shall not agree that you shall do it when the States shall not. The Constitution is just as safe in that behalf—the third election of any President—as the Rock of Gibraltar; and it would be just as wise in the British Government, instead of looking at home to their paupers and misery, to place the whole of their care on Gibraltar. It would be just as wise, as in their wisdom, instead of going to Ireland, they take care of the New Zealanders, the Otaheitans, and the Sandwich Islanders. If the question is pressed, vote against it I will.

SPEECH ON RETRENCHMENT AND REFORM
February 1, 1828

[Although generally, in 1828, Randolph's talents had sunk to their nadir, this rambling speech—a defense of his own conduct in the House of Representatives during the session, and an assault upon the Adams administration—displays Randolph's old evocative power and his learning. Later Randolph revised these remarks in the House and published them, with extensive notes, in a pamphlet dedicated to his constituents. The present text, that of the pamphlet, is taken from the Appendix to Powhatan Bouldin's *Home Reminiscences of John Randolph of Roanoke*. (Bouldin's own notes are omitted.)]

Mr. Randolph rose and said:

I cannot make the promise which the gentleman who has just taken his seat (Mr. Everett) made at the outset of his address, but I will make a promise of a different nature, and one which I trust it will be in my power to perform—I shall not say with more good faith than the gentleman from Massachusetts, but more to the letter—ay, sir, and more to the spirit too. I shall not, as the gentleman said he would do, act in mere self-defence. I shall carry the war into Africa. *Delenda est Carthago!* I shall not be content with mere parrying; no, sir, if I can, so help me God, I will thrust also, because my right arm is nerved by the cause of the people and of my country. I listened to the gentleman with pleasure —I mean to the general course of his remarks, with a single exception, and to that part of his speech I listened with the utmost loathing and disgust. But disgust is too feeble a term. I heard him with horror introduce the case of the Queen of France*—and in answer to what? To a handbill, a placard, an electioneering firebrand. And in the presence of whom? Of those who never ought to be present in a theatre where men contend for victory and empire. Sir, they have no more business there than they have in a field of battle of another sort. Women, indeed, are wanted in the camp; but women of a very different description. What maiden, nay, what matron, could hear the gentleman without covering her face with her hands, and rushing out of the House? But for some of the remarks of the gentleman from Massachusetts, in allusion to newspaper publications, I should have begun in at least as low a key and as temperate a mood as he did. To that key I will now pitch my voice.

---

* "The Devil himself will not eat a woman."—Shakespeare

I have been absent from the House for several days. I requested my colleague (Mr. Alexander) to state the cause of that absence, which he did. Yet even this could not be reported correctly. As this may be the last act of public duty which I shall be able to perform, at least during the present session, and as I have given up myself a sacrifice to its performance, I respectfully ask the House to give their attention to what I have now to say.

I understand that during my absence I have been replied to by various gentlemen (some of whom I have not the honor to know by person) on different sides of the House in a manner which I do not doubt was perfectly satisfactory, at least to the speakers themselves. I certainly do not wish to disturb their self-complacency—*de minimis non curat*—whether of persons or of things. The gentleman from Ohio (Mr. Vance), with that blunt plainness and candor which I am told belong to him, and which I admire in proportion as they are rare qualities in these time-serving days—I like him the better for his surly honesty—I hope he will take no offence at the term, for I can assure him that none is intended—charged me in my absence (so my friends have informed me) with what I believe he would not hesitate to have charged to my face, and to which I have no objection, but I must except to the authority on which he relied, for I protest against any gentleman's producing—as proof of what I have at any time said—a newspaper, or anything purporting to be a register of debates, unless I endorse it, and become answerable for it, and more especially remarks drawn from the debates of another body, which, in regard to me, are particularly unfaithful. I shall show to the House not such matter as the gentleman from Massachusetts stirred, to the offence of every moral sense, of every moral

being. I do not pretend to impose my standard of delicacy
and propriety upon the gentleman, who will no doubt measure by his own—*de gustibus non est disputandum*—and it
is not for me to interfere with the gentleman's tastes,
whether in literature, morals or religion. I shall refer to a
matter of recent notoriety, that will test the correctness of
these reports.

In the debate on the motion of the gentleman from South
Carolina (Mr. Hamilton), respecting a picture of the battle
of New Orleans, I did state, as distinctly as I could articulate, that I had seen a monument erected to the memory of
Andre, the British spy, in Westminster Abbey; that it was
mutilated, the head of General Washington, and arm (I
think) of Andre having been broken off, the General's, most
probably, by some Tory boy, from the neighboring school
of Westminster, and that of Andre probably by some Whig
boy in retaliation. The name of Hamilton did not escape my
lips. I thought, indeed, of Hamilton, but it was of a living
Hamilton—the gentleman from South Carolina. But then
parliamentary usage does not permit us to speak of one
another by name. Now, sir, I can show you, on the same
authority, which was relied on by the gentleman from Ohio
—although I acknowledge that the reports of that paper, so
far at least as I am concerned, have generally been more accurate this year than I have for a long time known them to
be before—that I am represented as saying that the monuments in Westminster Abbey were mutilated in the same
manner as the *tombs* of Hamilton and Washington had been
mutilated here. The word *tomb* never escaped my lips on
that occasion. This would have been a palpable falsehood.
Where is the tomb of Washington? There is no such thing
in this country, nor have I ever heard that a tomb has been

erected to the memory of Hamilton; but I suppose that the next thing we shall hear will be, that the Quarterly, or some other impartial Review, comes out and observes with a sneer, that as Roger Sherman said the vote was the monument, so a gentleman from Virginia had by a speech in Congress built up a tomb for Washington—a "constructive" tomb—that existed nowhere but in his eccentric imagination. Sir, the tombs of Washington and of Hamilton might stand anywhere in this country unenclosed; they might, indeed, be liable to injury from the beasts of the field, or from some invidious foreigner, but the hand of no American would ever mutilate them.

In the course of another debate, it seems that I rendered to a gentleman from New York (Mr. Storrs) the homage which his abilities deserved; and God forbid that the time should ever arrive when I refuse to do justice to an adversary, when I shall disparage any merit because it is found in the person of an opponent. When that time shall arrive, may I receive mercy from that fountain of it, to which alone we all must look if we hope for forgiveness hereafter. I said that I would not, *like him,* pronounce a palinodia, neither am I now going to pronounce a palinodia in respect to the gentleman from New York. I shall not take back one jot of praise bestowed upon him. With whatever views he introduced it, the doctrine has always been mine—the strict subordination of the military to the civil authority—Scripture is Scripture, by whom, or for whatever purpose it may be quoted. I know nothing of the private habits of that gentleman (Mr. Storrs), but I know that he has too much good taste not to agree with me that time may be much better spent than in reading the documents piled up there. Yet in the report of that debate, I was represented as saying that, like the gentleman from New York, I did not—what? pronounce a palinodia? No, not at all; but that, like him, I did not read the documents. Sir, nobody reads the documents, for this plain reason, that no man *can* read them, and, if he could, he could hardly be worse employed. Sir, with a few exceptions, the documents are printed that they may be printed, not that they may be read.

And now, sir, comes another charge about the miserable oppressed inhabitants of Ireland. This subject has been mentioned to me by no gentleman on the other side, except a member from Maryland, from the Eastern Shore of Maryland (Mr. Kerr), who is not only by the courtesy of this House, but in fact a gentleman. He, in Committee on the Rules and Orders of the House, expressed to me his astonishment, that what I said on that occasion could have been so much misunderstood and misrepresented, that he heard me most distinctly. I now call on any member, who understood me differently at the time, to rise in his place and say so. [Here Mr. Randolph paused for a reply. None being given, and some friends having said across the seats that no member could or would say that he had understood Mr. Randolph as he had been misrepresented, Mr. Randolph went on.] Without meaning to plead to; that is, without meaning to admit, the jurisdiction of the press in the extent which it arrogates to itself, I am perfectly sensible that no man is above public opinion. God forbid that any man in this country shall ever be able to brave it. That is what our great adversary has, with characteristic audacity, attempted to do, sorely to his cost and that of his less bold compeer— now braving, now truckling to it—bullying and backing out —all in character. I regret that any one should have supposed me capable of uttering such sentiments. So far from it, I have been the steady, firm, constant and strenuous advocate to the best of my poor ability of the oppressed people of Ireland. And why? For the reason I stated on a former occasion: they fought our battles, sir. I have known and esteemed many of them. Some of them have been—they are dead—others are now living among my warmest friends and best neighbors. In the course of a not uneventful life I have seen many things, but I have yet to see that *rara avis in terris* (I have seen a black swan) an Irish Tory. I have known Tories of every description; yes, sir, some even in Virginia—even we had a few of them during the Revolution, but too few to give us any trouble or alarm—but I never have yet seen an Irish Tory, or the man who had seen one.

Sir, I don't read the newspapers—I don't read gentlemen's speeches, and then come her to answer them. But I am extremely pleased, nay, flattered, in the highest degree, at being told by my friends that the gentleman from Ohio attributed in his speech so much to my efforts in bringing the administration to its present lank and lean condition. The gentleman could not have pleased me better—I only fear that with all his bluntness and frankness the gentleman was not quite sincere, and was only adorning me with fillets and garlands, like the priests of the sacrifice of yore, previous to knocking me, and with me the party whom he strives to wound through my sides, on the head. He was pleased to place me at the head of what has been denominated the opposition party in this House; but at its head, or that of any other party in this House, he will never find me, for reasons which I could state, but which are wholly unnecessary. Times are, indeed, changed with the gentleman and his friends when they hold this language concerning me. But a little while ago, and the friends of the administration, nay, the members of the administration, affected to consider me as one of their firmest props. They could not, indeed, vote for me—they were men too nice in their principles for that; but considering the great benefit which they derived from my opposition, they could not (except for the honor of the country) regret my reelection. Amiable and excellent men! But they now sing to a very different gamut.

If any gentleman will bring against me any allegation, from a clean and reputable source, I will do one of two things—I will either deny it, or admit and defend it upon my views and principles. Sir, it seems I committed a great offence in not voting for the admission of the new States into the Union, and especially of Ohio. Yet, if the thing were to do over again, I should act precisely in the same manner, and past experience would teach me I was right. What were the new States? Vast deserts of woods, inhabited by the Aborigines, to whom, if we come to the question of right, they did of right belong; and it was a question whether sound policy would dictate that we ought, by creating these States, to encourage sparse settlements, and thereby to weaken our frontier. I thought this was bad policy. Not that I am in favor of a very dense population. I am against the rabble of your great cities, but I am equally opposed to having a land without inhabitants. But, sir, I had other reasons —*graviora manent*. Does the gentleman from Ohio, with all his laudable prejudice and partiality towards his own State, think that I, as a Virginian, feeling at least equal prejudice and partiality to my native land with that which he feels for his State, would lend my sanction to an act on the part of Virginia, which beggars every instance of fatuity and folly extant in the history of nations? Why, sir, the Knight of La

Mancha himself, or poor old Lear in the play, never was guilty of a grosser act of fatuity than was the State of Virginia when she committed that suicidal deed—the surrendering of her immense territory beyond the river Ohio, upon the express condition of excluding her own citizens from its benefit, when the country (yielded for the common good of the confederacy) should come to be settled. Yes, sir, it was an act of suicide—of political suicide—the effects of which she has felt, and will continue to feel, so long as she has any political existence at all. This was one of the most amiable and philanthropic acts of legislation, which, however good in point of intention, lead to the most disastrous and ruinous consequences. Can the gentleman from Ohio conceive that I, a Virginian, could further this cut-throat policy? I thought the Ohio a well defined natural boundary, and that we ought not to weaken by extending our frontier. The late war verified my foresight. Whom have I injured? The native savages and the trees, or the States that have been drained of their population to fill out Ohio? I offered no wrong to the people of Ohio, for there were then none to injure. They have gone there, or have been born since. This was "the head and front of my offending;" and if the gentleman has his apparatus ready, I am prepared to undergo any form of execution which his humanity will allow him to inflict, or which even his justice may award.

Smarting under the injurious election of a President against the will of the people, by the votes of Louisiana and Missouri balancing those of Pennsylvania and Virginia in this House, I spoke of ourselves as the only people so over-wise as to acquire provinces, not that we might govern them, but that they might give law to us.

And, sir, I have always held, and shall forever hold it to

be the height of injustice (and of folly, too, on the part of the old States), that thirty or forty thousand persons, who so long as they remained in Pennsylvania or Virginia, were represented in the Senate, only as the rest of the Pennsylvanians and Virginians should, by emigrating to one of the geographical diagrams beyond the Ohio or the Mississippi, acquire, *ipso facto,* an equipollent vote in the other House of Congress with the millions that they left behind at home. In case of the old States, necessity gave this privilege to Rhode Island, &c.; they were coordinate States—free, sovereign and independent—and as such, *ex vi termini,* equal to the largest; but here it was a gratuitous boon, at the expense of the original members of the confederacy—not called for by justice or equity.

Sir, do not understand me as wishing to establish injurious or degrading distinctions between the old and the new States, to the disadvantage of these last. Some such already exist, which I would willingly do away. No, sir, my objection was to the admission of such States (whether south or north of the Ohio, east or west of the Mississippi) into the Union, and, by consequence, to a full participation of power in the Senate with the oldest and largest members of the confederacy, before they had acquired a sufficient population that might entitle them to it, and before that population had settled down into that degree of consistency and assimilation which is necessary to the formation of a body politic. The rapidity with which these new States fill up, would have retarded their full participation in the power of their co-states but a very short time. And in that short interval the safety of the other States (witness the vote of Missouri for President) required such a precaution on their part. If I

had been an emigrant myself to one of these new States—
and I have near and dear connexions in some of them—I
could not have murmured against the denial to forty or fifty
thousand new settlers (although I had been one of them)
of a voice in the Senate, potential as New York's, with a
million and a half of people.

The gentleman from Massachusetts cannot expect that I
shall follow him through his elaborate detail of the diplomatic expenses of this government with which he came
prepared. The House, however, will permit me to observe
that there was a hiatus—*valde deflendus,* I do not doubt,
but certainly not deeply lamented by me—a *hiatus* which
embraces the whole period of the administration of Mr.
Jefferson. I am not going into the question of these expenses;
I will stir no such matter—demands which have dogged the
doors of the treasury so long, and so perseveringly, as that
they have been at length allowed, some from motives of
policy, others to get rid of importunate and sturdy beggars,
although they were disallowed under Mr. Jefferson's administration. But, sir, if every claim that gets through this
House, or is allowed by this government, after years of
importunity (some of them of thirty years standing), is for
that reason considered by the gentleman as a just claim, and
fit to be drawn into precedent, my notions of justice and of
sound precedent differ greatly from his. I, too, am as much
opposed as he can be to what is truly called the prodigality
of parsimony. The gentleman thinks that the salaries of our
foreign ministers are too low, and therefore they must be
eked out by these allowances from the contingent fund—
out of what is called the secret service money. The gentleman is right as to the existence of such a fund. It was

appointed, and perhaps properly, for Washington was to be the first charged with its disbursement. But our early Presidents always made it a point of honor to return this fund untouched. They said to the nation, you trusted me with your purse—I have had no occasion to use it—here it is—count the money—there is as much by tale and as much by weight as I received from you. But was it ever dreamed that such a fund was to be put into the hands of a President of the United States, to furnish him with the means of rewarding his favorites? No, sir; it was to pay those waiters and chambermaids, and eaves-droppers, and parasites, and panders, that the gentleman told us of on the other side of the water—and there it might be all very right and proper —but not here, because we flatter ourselves that the state of morals in this country is such as to save us from any such necessity. No gentleman would understand him as speaking of the sums which had been placed at the disposal of different Presidents, to a vast amount, for the purpose of negotiating with the Barbary Powers, &c., but of that amount set apart and generally known as *secret service money*. Mr. Jefferson used a small portion of this fund one year, the last of his administration, to pay some expense in relation to Burr's conspiracy, which was not allowed at the treasury.

With regard to the old billiard table, which is said to have cost some fifty dollars, it is a subject that I should never have mentioned. I consider that game as a healthy, manly, rational mode of exercise, when the weather is such as to confine us within doors. I shall certainly never join in any cant or clamor against it. I look upon it as a suitable piece of furniture in the house of any gentleman who can afford it, where it is allowed by law, as it is here and throughout the State of Maryland, as well as many other States. It is a fit subject for taxation, but I should be sorry if we were to proscribe that manly and innocent amusement.* If I have any objection to that item, it is that such a pitiful article should have been bought. I would have given him one that cost five hundred dollars, and I would have voted the appropriation with cheerfulness. My objection to such a charge is, that it is a shabby affair, and looks too much like a sneaking attempt to propitiate, by the cheapness of the thing, popular displeasure. The attempt to keep the thing

---

* It would be matter of curious inquiry to ascertain how it has come to pass that in proportion as we in Virginia have proscribed or abandoned the cheerful exercises and amusements of our fathers, we have become less amiable and moral as a people. When I was a young man, no gentleman was ashamed of playing a game of billiards or of cards. There was much less gaming then than now. Men then drank and played in public, from a spirit of society, as well as the love for both inherent in human nature. Publicity is the great restraint upon individuals as well as government. The *"hells"* of London and the styes of Capreæ and the *Parc aux Cerfs* attest this. Publicity represses excess, until the man is sunk in the beast and every restraint of shame thrown off. Formerly, friends had it in their power to restrain the votaries of chance or of the bottle; but now their incurable ruin, in mind, body, and estate, gives the first notice of their devotion to play or drink. Solitary intoxication on ardent spirits is the substitute for the wine table; and in some den of thieves, some cellar or some garret, the unhappy youth is stripped of his property, with no witness of the fairness of the game but his desperate and profligate undoers.

In Virginia we are, and I trust shall ever be, alive to States rights. But have the people no rights as against the Assembly? All oppression commences under specious pretexts. I have wondered that no rural, or rather rustic, Hampden has been found to withstand the petty tyranny which has as good a right to take away his wife's looking-glass or frying pan as his billiard table. By what authority is this thing done? Under color of law, I know, but a law in the teeth of all the principles of free government.

The principle of what is called the dueling law—it ought to be called the perjury law—is yet more detestable. I am no advocate of dueling; but it may be put down by something worse. Bad as it is, it is better than dirking and gouging; and they are hardly worse than calling names and bandying

out of sight only makes the matter still worse. I do not charge the gentleman from North Carolina with any such intention, but this seems to me to be too small a matter. I would strike at higher game.

The gentleman from Massachusetts says that Franklin received a higher compensation than Mr. Adams did, and other ministers of these times. He did, sir, and what was the answer which that shrewd and sensible man gave (for poor

---

insults, if so bad. The oath prescribed by the dueling law is in the teeth of every principle of free government, of the act for establishing religious freedom, and would justify any test, religious or political, even an oath of belief in transubstantiation.

We are a merry-making, kind-hearted, hospitable people, fond of *"junketting"* (as the old President of the Court of Appeals used to say); and no one, as the men of Caroline county and Essex can testify, liked "junketting" (*"soberly"* as Lady Grace says) better than Edmund Pendleton. Yes, the Mansfield of Virginia, whom he resembled in the polished suavity of his manners, his unrivalled professional learning and abilities, and the retention of his faculties unimpaired to a very advanced old age. There is another splendid example of the same rare qualities in the first judicial officer of the United States. Who is fonder of a game of billiards, or any other innocent amusement, than the Chief Justice? Yes, I regret, nay, deplore, the change from our old and innocent pastimes and holidays to the present state of listless *ennui* or prowling rapacity. In proportion as we have approached puritanical preciseness and gloomy austerity, so have we retrograded in morals.

I do not indeed carry the matter quite so far as an acquaintance of mine, who has a knack of "hitching into rhyme," and who, among other good advice, says:

> "Hence, if you have a son, I would advise,
> (Lest his fair prospects you, perchance, may spoil)
> If you would wish him in the State to rise,
> Instead of GROTIUS, let him study HOYLE.
> And if his native genius should betray
> A turn for petty tricks, indulge the bent;
> It may do service at some future day;
> A dextrous CUT may rule a great event,
> And a stock'd PACK may make a President."

Richard had always an eye to the main chance) when his accounts were scrutinized into, and his receipts were deemed exorbitant! It was this, sir: "Thou shalt not muzzle the ox that treadeth out the corn." The very answer that I myself gave in Morrison's Hotel, in Dublin, to a *squireen* and an *agent*. For a description of these varieties of the plagues of Ireland, see Miss Edgeworth—delightful, ingenious, charming, sensible, witty, inimitable, though not unimitated Miss Edgeworth. When describing the misery of the South and West of Ireland, that I had lately traveled over, I was asked, "And what would you do, pray, sir, for the relief of Ireland?" with an air that none but Miss Edgeworth can describe, and that no one that has not been in Ireland can conceive. My reply was, "I would unmuzzle the ox that treadeth out the corn;" and I had like to have got myself into a sad scrape by it, as any one who has been in Ireland will readily understand. Yes, sir, I was disposed to give to the houseless, naked, shivering, half-starved Irish laborer something like a fair portion of the product of his toil, of the produce of the land on which he breathes, but does not live; to put victuals into his stomach, clothes upon his back, and something like a house over his head, instead of the wretched pig-sty that is now his only habitation—shelter, it is none; and this was just the last remedy that an Irish agent, or middle man, or tytheproctor, or absentee, would prescribe or submit to.

But to return. "These salaries are too small." I cannot agree with the gentleman. There is one touchstone of such a question—it is the avidity with which those situations are sought— I will not say by members of this House—we are hardly deemed of sufficient rank to fill them. A receivership or inspectorship of the LAND OFFICE must do for us; ay, even for such of us as, by our single vote, have made a President. Sir, the generous steed by whose voice the son of Hystaspes was elevated to the throne of Persia, was better recompensed, as he deserved to be, than the venal asses whose braying has given a ruler to seven millions of freemen, and to a domain far surpassing in power as well as extent of the GREAT KING—the GRAND MONARQUE of antiquity! So long as these foreign missions are sought with avidity—so long as members of Congress, and not of this House only, or chiefly, will bow, and cringe, and duck, and fawn, and get out of the way at a pinching vote, or lend a helping hand at a pinching vote, to obtain these places, I never will consent to enlarge the salary attached to them. Small as the gentleman tells us those salaries are, I will take it on me to say, that they are three times as great as they are now managed, as the net proceeds of his estate, made by any planter on the Roanoke. But then we are told that they live at St. Petersburg and London, and that living there is very expensive. Well, sir, who sent them there? Who pressed them to go there? Were they impressed there like D'Auterive's slave? Were they taken, like a freeborn Englishman, by a press-gang, on Tower Hill, knocked down, hand-cuffed, chucked on board of a tender, and told that they must take the pay and rations which his Majesty was pleased to allow? No such thing, sir. I will now quit this subject, and say only this, that our minister (Mr. Adams) was paid for a *constructive* journey—that, I think, is the phrase, which means neither more nor less than a journey which was never performed.

[Here Mr. Everett made a gesture of dissent.]

The gentleman shakes his head. Sir, we shall see more of this hereafter, but I will reason only hypothetically. If the gentleman in question, while he remained at St. Petersburg, could make the journey imputed to him, it beats the famous journey from Mexico to Tacubaya, as far as some distance, however small, exceeds no distance whatsoever. If a gentleman from Washington goes to Georgetown or to Alexandria; yes, sir, to Bladensburg, I will acknowledge that he performs, at least in some sense, a sort of journey. But not if he remains in this city, and never stirs out of it. However, I will not now press this matter further—others will do more justice to it—*de minimis non curat.*

Paulo majora canamus: there was one remark which I took down while the gentleman was speaking, and which I cannot pass over. Who that gentleman was, described by the member from Massachusetts, who proposed to him that if he would move to raise these salaries that gentleman would join with him and support him, I cannot conjecture or divine. Be he who he may, I will venture to say thus much: He is some gentleman who expects to be sent upon a mission himself, and, with great forecast and prudence, he was calculating to throw upon the present administration beforehand all the odium of the increase of the salary which he hoped to finger. I am disposed to be more just to the gentleman and to the administration, because I believe that he will get full as much as he may deserve; and they have full as much weight as they can carry, without adding to it another feather.

I am afraid that I may be charged with some want of continuity, but what I have to say is at least as relevant; ay, and as pertinent too to the subject before the House as the handbill which the gentleman read, 'til *his* delicacy would permit him to read no further, though I must confess I thought that he had already gone so far that there was no *Ultima Thule* beyond. Sir, the gentleman might have spared himself this last exertion of his delicacy, and even have read to the end. There could be nothing more gross behind than what we had already heard, and were to hear, in the case of the ill-fated Queen of France. The gentleman, with much gravity, with some dexterity, and with great plausibility, but against certain principles which I have held in this House, *ab ovo,* and whch I shall continue to hold, *usque ad mala,* 'til I leave the feast, spoke of the headlong commencement of the opposition before the administration could give reasonable cause of discontent. I have now no *palinodi*a to sing or to chant upon that subject. I drew from that fountain, which never failed an observing and sagacious man, and which even the simple and inexperienced (and I among the rest) may drink at—it is nature and human life. I saw distinctly, from the beginning, that if we permitted this administration—if we listened to those who cried to us, "Wait, wait, there is a lion in the path" (and, sir, there always is a lion in the path to the sluggard and the dastard), and which cry was seconded no doubt by many who wished to know how the land lay before they ran for a port—on which side victory would incline before they sounded *their* horn of triumph. If we had thus waited, the situation of the country would have been very different from what it is now. Sir, there was a great race to be run—if you will permit me to draw an illustration from a sport to which I have been much addicted—one in which all the gentlemen in Virginia, when we had gentlemen in Virginia, delighted, and of which I am yet very fond—I mean from the turf—and it must be lost or won, as the greatest race in this country was won—I mean the race on Long Island, which I saw, and that was by running every inch of the ground—by going off at score— by following the policy of Purdy. Purdy, sir, was a man of sound sense and practical knowledge—a man of common sense I mean, and worth a thousand of your old and practised statesmen and "premature" gentlemen who never arrive at maturity—and who, meaning to side with the next administration in case of our success, were, nevertheless, resolved to get all they could in the meantime out of this. Sir, to one of these trimming gentry, it is worse than death to force him to take sides before a clear indication of victory; and hence the cry of its being "premature" to stir the question of the next Presidential election. If we had set off one session later, we should not have had ground enough left to run upon, to overtake, and pass, and beat them, before they would have passed the winning post and pocketed the stakes. Such would have been the effect if we had delayed our push, and I know no one who would have enjoyed the result and chuckled at our folly with more hearty glee than one of these same old and practised gentlemen.

[Here something was said which the reporter did not hear, and to which Mr. Everett was understood to reply, that he had not stated it as his sentiment, but as a fact.]

I beg the gentleman's pardon: I never was misrepresented by him, and I never will misrepresent him unless I misunderstand him. But I wonder it never occurred to the gentleman from Massachusetts what could be the cause why such a hue and cry should be raised against an administration so very able (permit me in this, however, to differ from the gentleman—*de gustibus non est*); what, I say, could have been the cause why Actæon and all his hounds, or, rather, why the dogs of war were let slip against this wise and able and virtuous and loving administration; these patterns of political friendship and consistency; and have continued to pursue them, 'til they lie panting and gasping for breath on the highway—until they realize the beautiful fable of the hare and many friends. The cause of all this is to be found in the manner in which they came into power—the cause of this "premature" opposition lies there, and there mainly. I would defy all the public presses in the world to have brought them to this pass, had there not been a taint of original sin in their body politic, and which cleaves to them even as the sin of our first parents taints our fallen nature and cleaveth to us all. The gentleman refers to those who compose the party called the opposition, and says it is formed of very discordant materials. True, sir; but what are the materials of the party which upholds the administration; nay, of the administration itself? Are they perfectly homogeneous? I know one of them, who has been raised to a higher station than most men in this country. Was that because he opposed, or because he espoused, the election of the present chief magistrate?

Let me ask the gentleman from Massachusetts what could cause the old Republican party in New England—the worthy successors of John Langdon—to be now found acting with us? They know—but perhaps some in this House do not know—they know that the southern interest is as much their ally in protecting them against an overweening oligarchy at home, as England is the natural ally of Portugal against the power of Spain and France; and though they left us for a time, yet now apprehending danger, and seeing through the artifices of their betrayer, they have returned to us their old, natural, and approved allies. Have not the administration as well as the opposition ways and means and funds in their hands to obtain influence and buy success? Have they not the whole of the great mass of patronage in their hands? But the gentleman says, that so far from taking care of their adherents, they have been too liberal in bestowing this upon their enemies. But it is easy to account for this. An ancient apothegm tells us that it is better to judge between two of your enemies than between two of your friends. In the one case you are almost sure by your decision to make a friend, and in the other to lose one. Now, sir, our able and practised statesmen know that by giving a loaf and a fish to an enemy they make a friend, when by giving them to one of their friends they might disoblige another, who might think his claims disparaged—and that, sir, is the whole secret of their neglecting their friends.

Permit me, sir, again to ask, how comes it that this administration are brought into their present very curious and unprecedented predicament? How happens it that they alone, of all the administrations which have been in this country, find themselves in the minority in each House of Congress— *"palsied by the will of their constituents"*— when the very worst of their predecessors kept a majority 'til midnight on the third or fourth of March, whichever you please to call it? Ay, sir, under the administration to which I allude, there were none of these compunctious visitings of nature at the attacks made on private character. We had no chapter of Lamentations then on the ravaging and desolating war on the fair fame of all the wise and virtuous and good of our land. The notorious Peter Porcupine, since even better known as William Cobbett, was the especial protege of that administration. I heard them say, I do not mean the head of that administration, but one of its leaders, that he was the greatest man in the world; and I do not know that, in point of sheer natural endowment, he was so very far wrong. Yes, sir, it was that very Cobbett, who, if the late publications may be trusted, now says that Mr. Adams has fifteen hundred slaves in Virginia. Was there any slander too vile, too base for that man to fabricate? I remember well the nicknames under which we passed—yes, sir, I can proudly say *we,* although the humblest in the ranks: Mr. Gallatin was CITOYEN GUILLOTINE, with *le petit fenêtre national* at his back. The caricature then, as well as now, constituted no small part of the munitions of political war. The pencil and the graver (they had no want of *tools* of any sort) lent their aid to the pen and the ballad and the military band of music. "Down with the French!" (that is, the best man of our country), was the cry. My excellent and able colleague, Mr. Nicholas—one of the purest and most pious of men, who afterwards removed to the State of New York, and was a model of Republican virtue and simplicity, that might have adorned the best days of Sparta or of Rome—he, sir, having the misfortune to lose an eye, was held up to ridicule as *Polyphemus.** You are shocked at this, sir; but let me tell you that it was only a little innocent, harmless, Federal wit —and the author was the especial protege of "government" and its adherents. All chuckled over the Porcupine. To that

---

* He also was described as CITIZEN NICOLAI. General Sumter, of South Carolina, a veteran of the Revolution, covered with honorable wounds and scars, was, by some of the myrmidons of the administration, forced from his seat in the CIRCUS, compelled to stand up, his hat taken from his head, and his hands forcibly made to clap, when Mr. Adams entered the theatre, and "HAIL COLUMBIA!" was struck up by the band. This stern old Republican was thus involuntarily compelled to join in the incense to the idol of the day. He yet lives to read, I hope, this mention of him by an old friend.

My venerable friend, Mr. Macon, told me, within twenty-four hours past, that the only time in his life that he ever drew a knife was in the play-house, when our party (myself especially) was insulted by the military.

They used to play the Rogue's March under the windows of the house where he and Nicholas and Gallatin lodged! So much for THE REIGN OF TERROR! as it was justly styled by the Republicans of that day.

party the present incumbent then belonged—and another member of this pure administration; and these two Sedition Law, black-cockade heroes, are recommended by the "ANTI-JACKSON Convention" to Virginia for her President and Vice President! They have not even the merit of an early conversion. They are true Swiss of State—*point d'argent, point de Suisse.* My venerable friend from North Carolina was Monsieur Maçon, with a cedilla under the ç, to mark him the more for a Frenchman. I forget the cognomen of the learned gentleman from Louisiana (Mr. Livingston): I know that he was never spared. I remember well my own: I wish, sir, it was applicable now, for I was then a *boy.* Every sanctuary was then invaded. As to Mr. Jefferson, every epithet of vituperation was exhausted upon him. He was an atheist, a Frenchman; we were all atheists and traitors; our names and cause associated with the cannibals and the cannibalism of the revolutionary tribunal, and with all the atrocities, the most atrocious and revolting of which has this day been presented to the House by the chaste imagination of the gentleman from Massachusetts. Yes, sir, then, as now, a group of horrors was pressed upon the public imagination, to prop the sinking cause of a desperate administration. Religion and order were to be subverted, the national debt to be sponged, and the country to be drenched in its best blood by Mr. Jefferson and his Jacobin adherents. Even good men, and not unwise men, were brought to believe this. Mr. Jefferson was elected; and we know what followed. But this, it may be said, was not done by our own people; it was done by foreign hirelings, mercenaries. Sir, it is not only of this description of persons that I speak. It was done in the glorious days of the Sedition Law and the black cockade, when we found in General Shee and his legion protection against the Praetorian bands of the administration. These brave fellows were many of them Irish or German, and most of them of Irish or German parentage, chiefly from the Northern Liberties, then the stronghold of Republicanism; and therefore branded with the opprobrious name of the Faubourg St. Antoine, the most Jacobin quarter of Paris.

At the very time that the act noted by the gentleman from Massachusetts was passed (May, 1800), when Professor Cooper was escorted to jail, a victim of the Sedition Law, the New York election then, as of late, rung the knell of the departing administration. Sir, when the gentleman favored us with his opinion of this present stupendous administration, I imagine he drew it from a comparison with some of the administrations which preceded it. In comparison with some of these, even this administration is great: for we have seen the least of all possible things—the poorest of all poor creatures that ever was manufactured into a head of a department (and that's a bold word), a member of a former administration—almost a satire on the name. This personage, as I have very lately learned, in imitation of another great man from the same state, took some liberties in public with my name, when he had the Atlantic for a barrier, the Summer before last. Like his great friend, his courage shows itself three thousand miles off. It is in the ratio of the square of the distance of his adversary. Sir, I should like to have seen how he would have looked, if on finishing his harangue, he had found me at his elbow. I think I can conceive how he would have *felt*.*

Sir, I have much to say, which neither my own weakness,

---

* "Mr. C. very humorously, and it is said very closely, mimicked Mr. Randolph in quoting some parts of Mr. R.'s speech."—*Salem Observer.* "O rare Ben!"

nor my regard to the politeness of this House, will permit me now to say. As I have exonerated the principal of that weighty affair of the billiard table, I also exonerate him and his lieutenant from every charge of collusion—*in the first instance;* and, if it is in order, I will state the reasons for my opinion. When the first alliance was patched up between the two great leaders of the East and West, neither of the high contracting parties had the promotion of the present incumbent at all in view. Sir, I speak knowingly as to one of these parties, and with the highest degree of moral probability of the other.* Can it be necessary that I prove this? The thing proves itself. The object was to bring in one of the parties to the compact, whom the constitution subsequently excluded, and, of course, to provide for the other. A gentleman, then of this House, was a candidate, who, to the last hour, cast

---

* After my arrival in Europe, I saw in the newspapers Mr. Webster's toast, given, if I forget not, on the fourth of July—"Henry Clay, the orator of the West," &c., &c. I quote from memory. N.B.—Mr. Clay was then the rival and declared enemy of Mr. Adams. Mr. Clay, in the debate on the Greek motion of Mr. Webster, and in the affair of Mr. Ichabod Bartlett (a name of omen), was ostentatious in his declarations of friendship and connection with Mr. Webster, whom he gratuitously assumed to have been assailed by the said Ichabod! that he might manifest his devotion to his new friend. I then looked upon Mr. Clay as laying an anchor to windward and eastward, and in fact offering his blandishment to New England in the person of Mr. Webster, while at the same time he proclaimed his strength in that quarter as the ally of Mr. Webster and the powerful party of which he is the leader and mouthpiece. If the maxim be true, *ars est celare artem,* then there lives not a less artful man upon earth than Mr. Clay. His system consists in soothing by flattery, or bullying—these constitute his whole stock in trade—and very often he applies both to the same person. The man of delicacy, to whom his coarse adulation is fulsome, and the man of unshaken firmness, when these two characteristics unite in the same person, cannot be operated on by him.

Mr. Webster and the rival of Chilly McIntosh were put on the A.B. Committee to run down Mr. Crawford. I too, though in Baltimore when Mr. Floyd (my colleague) moved to raise that Committee, was put upon it. I was not then the *political* friend or supporter of Mr. Crawford. His

many a longing, although not lingering, look, with out-stretched neck, towards Louisiana—*jugulo quœ sita negatur* —to discover whether or not he should be one upon the list. Sir, it is impossible that he could, in the first instance, have looked to the elevation of another, or have designed to promote the views of any man, but in subserviency to his own. Common sense forbids it. But all these calculations, however skillful, and Demoivre could not have made better, utterly failed. The partners had two strings to their bow— Mr. Crawford's death, or Mr. Clay's being ahead of Mr. Crawford, by getting the vote of Louisiana, or those votes in New York which were so strangely, and at the time unaccountably, given to Mr. Crawford. They took the field with a double percussion gun, and banged away, right and left; but, good marksmen as they were, both barrels missed. Louisiana refused to vote as obstinately as Mr. Crawford refused to die; and so the gentleman was excluded. It was then that Mr. Adams was first taken up, as a *pis aller,* which we planters of the South translate, *a hand plant.*

Sir, I have a right to know; I had a long while before an interview with the very great man; but not on that subject: no, Sir,—It was about business of this House—and he so far descended, or I should rather say of so very great a

---

political principles, on the United States Bank and some other questions, were to mine nearly, although not quite, as obnoxious as those of his competitors. I never took sides with him until he was persecuted. Mr. Macon and Mr. Floyd both know that, on my arrival from Baltimore, I peremptorily declared that I would not serve on that Committee. I believed it to be (as it was) a snare for me—a snare from which I providentially escaped. Mr. Webster's true character first developed itself to me then, as at the time I told Mr. Tazewell. At the earnest persuasion of Mr. Macon and entreaty of Mr. Floyd, I reluctantly agreed to serve. Mr. Floyd being taken violently ill and confined to his bed, I abandoned my seat in the Committee and went abroad for health.

man, condescended, as to electioneer even with me. He said
to me, among other things, "if you of the South will give
us of the West any other man than John Quincy Adams for
President, we will support him." Let any man deny this
who dare—but remember, he then expected to be a candidate before the House himself. "If you will give us any other
man!" Sir, the gentleman in question can have no disposition
to deny it. It was at a time when he and the present incumbent were publicly pitted against each other, and Mr. Adams
crowed defiance and clapped his wings against the Cock of
Kentucky. Sir, I know this to be a strong mode of expression.
I did not take it literally. I thought I understood the meaning
to be that Virginia, by her strenuous support of Mr. Crawford, would further the success of Mr. Adams. "Any other
man, sir, besides John Quincy Adams." Now, as neither Mr.
Crawford nor General Jackson in the end proved to be "any
other man," it follows clearly who any other man was, viz:
one other man—*id est,* myself (as a gentleman once said in
this House), "we will support him." But, sir, as soon as this
egomet was out of the question, we of the South lost all our
influence, and "we of the West" gave us of the South this
very John Quincy Adams for President, and received from
him the very office, which being held by him, we of the West
assigned as the cause of our support, considering it to be a
sort of reversionary interest in the presidency. (See the
letter to Mr. F. Brooke.) It was, indeed, "ratsbane in our
mouth," but we swallowed the arsenic.*

---

* It has been suggested to me since the above was spoken, by one who
ought to know a good deal of New York politics, and to whom it occurred while I was making this development, and in consequence of it,
that Mr. Adams, who could not be blind to the game that was playing
between Mr. C. and Mr. W., caused the vote which Mr. Crawford got in

Sir, a powerful party of New England was equally opposed to Mr. Adams, the high Federal party, or the Essex
junto, so-called—all the successors of the George Cabots,
and Caleb Strongs, and Stephen Higginsons—I should
rather say their representatives, and all their surviving co-
adjutors—were against him, with one exception, and that
was an honest man, of whom it was said in this House that
he ought to desire no other epitaph but that which might
truly be inscribed to his tomb: "Here lies the man who was
honored by the friendship of Washington, and the enmity
of his successor." Sir, who persecuted the name of Hamilton
while living, and followed him beyond the grave? The
father and the son. Who were the persecutors of Fisher
Ames, whose very grave was haunted as if by vampyres?
Both father and son. Who attempted to libel the present chief
justice, and procure his impeachment—making the seat of
John Smith, of Ohio, the peg to hang the impeachment on?
The son, I, as one of the grand jury, and my colleague, Mr.
Garnett,* were called upon by the chairman of the com-
mittee of the Senate in Smith's case (Mr. Adams) to testify

New York to be given to him, then no longer the most formidable opponent, for the express purpose of excluding Mr. Clay, from whom the
greatest danger was to be apprehended from the House, by ensuring Mr.
Crawford's return. Thus the *biters were bit,* and Messrs. C. and W. had
to make terms with Mr. A. who, in requital for the vote of Mr. C. and his
friends, graciously received them into favor. Yes, the allies completely
circumvented by this manœuvre on the part of Mr. A., had no other alternative than to go over to him, who, no doubt, nothing loth, met them
full half way.

Reader! Is there anything in Molière or Congreve surpassing this? Can
Scapin or Maskwell beat this?

* James M. Garnett, Esq., of the county of Essex, Virginia, a member
of the grand jury, and also of Congress during Mr. Jefferson's administration. Our friendship commenced soon after he took his seat in Congress,
and has continued uninterrupted by a single moment of coolness or aliena-

in that case. Sir, do you remember a committee, raised at the same time in this House, to inquire whether the failure of Burr's prosecution grew out of "the evidence, the law, or the administration of the law?" For my sins, I suppose, I was put upon that committee. The plain object was the impeachment of the judge who presided on the trial. This was one of the early oblations (the first was the writ of *habeas corpus*) of the present incumbent on the altar of his new political church. Who accused his former Federal associates in New England of a traitorous conspiracy with the British authorities in Canada to dismember the Union? The present incumbent. Yet all is forgiven him—Hamilton, Ames, Marshall, themselves accused of treason—all is forgiven; and these men, who one exception, now support him; and for what?

Sir, I will take the letter to the President of the Court of Appeals in Virginia, and on that letter, and on facts which are notorious as the sun at noonday, it must be established that there was a collusion, and a corrupt collusion, between the principals in this affair. I do not say the agreement was a written or even a verbal one—I know that the language of the poet is true—that men who "meet to do a damned deed" cannot bring even themselves to speak of it in distinct terms —they cannot call a spade a spade—but eke out their unholy purpose with dark hints, and innuendoes, and signs, and shrugs, where more is meant than meets the ear. Sir, this person was willing to take any man who would secure

---

tion during three-and-twenty years, and very trying times, political and otherwise. I take a pride in naming this gentleman among my steady, uniform, and unwavering friends. In Congress he never said an unwise thing, or gave a bad vote. He has kept the faith from 1799, when he supported the doctrines of Madison's famous report made at the session of the Virginia Assembly, of which he was a member. He came into Congress in 1805, and left it March 4, 1809.

the end that he had in view. He takes office under Mr. Adams, and that very office, too, which had been declared to be in the line of safe precedents—that very office which decided his preference of Mr. Adams. Sir, are we children? Are we babies? Can't we make out apple-pie, without spelling and putting the letters together—a-p, ap, p-l-e, ple, apple, p-i-e, pie, apple-pie? Sir, the fact can never be got over, and it is this fact which alone could make this administration to rock and totter to its base in spite of the indiscretion (to say no worse), in spite of all the indiscretions of its adversaries. For, sir, there never was a man who had so much cause as General Jackson has had to say, "Save me from my friends and I will take care of my enemies." Yes, sir, he could take care of his enemies—from them he never feared danger; but not of his friends—at least of some, whose vanity has prompted them to couple their obscure names with his—and it is because he did take care of his enemies, who were his country's enemies, and for other reasons which I could state, that his cause is now espoused by that grateful country. "But General Jackson is no statesman." Sir, I deny that there is any instance on record in history of a man not having military capacity being at the head of any government with advantage to that government, and with credit to himself. There is a great mistake on this subject. It is not those talents which enable a man to write books and make speeches that qualify him to preside over a government. The wittiest of poets has told us, that

> "All a Rhetorician's rules,
> Teach only how to name his tools."

We have seen Professors of Rhetoric who could no doubt descant fluently upon the use of these said tools; yet sharpen them to so wiry an edge as to cut their own fingers with these implements of their trade. Thomas à Becket was as brave a man as Henry the Second, and, indeed, a braver man—less infirm of purpose. And who were the Hildebrands and the rest of the Papal freebooters who achieved victory after victory over the proudest monarchs and states of Christendom? These men were brought up in a cloister perhaps, but they were endowed with that highest of all the gifts of heaven, the capacity to lead men, whether in the Senate or the field. Sir, it is one and the same faculty, and its successful display has always received, and ever will receive, the highest honors that man can bestow; and this will be the case do what you will, cant what you may, about military chieftains and military domination. So long as man is man, the victorious defender of his country will, and ought, to receive that country's suffrage for all that the forms of her government allow her to give.

A friend said to me, not long since, "Why, General Jackson can't write"—"admitted." (Pray, sir, can you tell me of any one that can write? for I protest I know nobody that can.) Then turning to my friend I said, "It is most true that General Jackson cannot write" (not that he can't write his name, or a letter, &c.), "because he has never been taught; but his competitor cannot write, because he was not teachable;" for he has had every advantage of education and study. Sir, the Duke of Marlborough, the greatest captain and negotiator of his age—which was the age of Louis XIV —and who may rank with the greatest men of any age; whose irresistible manners and address triumphed over every obstacle in council, as his military prowess and conduct did in the field—this great man could not even spell, and was notoriously ignorant of all that an undergraduate must know, but which it is not necessary for a man at the head of affairs to know at all. Would you have superseded him by some Scotch schoolmaster? Gentlemen forget that it is an able helmsman we want for the ship of State, and not a Professor of Navigation or Astronomy.

Sir, among the vulgar errors that ought to go into Sir Thomas Browne's book this ought not to be omitted: that learning and wisdom are not synonymous, or at all equivalent. Knowledge and wisdom, as one of our most delightful poets sings:

> "Knowledge and wisdom, far from being one,
> Have oft times no connexion—knowledge dwells
> In heads replete with thoughts of other men;
> Wisdom, in minds attentive to their own.
> Knowledge is proud that he has learned so much;
> Wisdom is humble that he knows no more.
> Books are not seldom talismans and spells,
> By which the magic art of shrewder wits
> Holds the unthinking multitude enchained."

And not books only, sir—speeches are not less deceptive. I not only consider the want of what is called learning not to be a disqualification for the commander in chief in civil or military life, but I do consider the possession of too much learning to be of most mischievous consequence to such a character; who is to draw from the cabinet of his own sagacious mind, and to make the learning of others, or whatever other qualities they may possess, subservient to his more enlarged and vigorous views. Such a man was Cromwell— such a man was Washington.* Not learned, but wise. Their

---

* Washington had a plain English education, and mathematics enough to qualify him for a land surveyor.

understandings were not clouded or cramped, but had fair play. Their errors were the errors of men, not of school boys and pedants. So far from the want of what is called education being a very strong objection to a man at the head of affairs, over-education constitutes a still stronger objection. [In the case of a lady it is fatal. Heaven defend me from an over-educated, accomplished lady. Yes, accomplished indeed, for she is *finished* for all the duties of a wife, or mother, or mistress of a family.] We hear much of military usurpation —of military despotism—of the sword of a conqueror—of Caesar, and Cromwell, and Bonaparte. What little I know of Roman history has been gathered chiefly from the surviving letters of the great men of that day—of Cicero especially—and I freely confess that, if I had then lived, and had been compelled to take sides, I must, though very reluctantly, have sided with Caesar, rather than have taken Pompey for my master. It was the interest of the house of Stuart—and they were long enough in power to do it—to blacken the character of Cromwell—that great, and, I must add, bad man. But, sir, the devil himself is not so black as he is sometimes painted. And who would not rather have obeyed Cromwell than that self-styled Parliament, which obtained a title too indecent for me to name, but by which it is familiarly known and mentioned in all the historians from that day to this? Cromwell fell under a temptation, perhaps too strong for the nature of man to resist—but he was an angel of light to either of the Stuarts—the one whom he brought to the block, or his son, a yet worse man, the blackest and foulest of miscreants that ever polluted a throne. It has been the policy of the house of Stuart and their successors—it is the policy of kings to vilify and blacken the memory and character of Cromwell. But the cloud is rolling away. We no longer consider Hume as deserving of the slightest credit. Cromwell was "guiltless of his country's blood." His was a bloodless usurpation. To doubt his sincerity at the outset, from his subsequent fall, would be madness—religious fervor was the prevailing temper and fashion of the times. Cromwell was no more of a fanatic than Charles the First, and not so much of a hypocrite. It was not in his nature to have signed the attainder of such a friend as Lord Strafford, whom Charles meanly and selfishly and basely and cruelly and cowardly repaid for his loyalty to him by an ignominious death—a death deserved, indeed, by Strafford, for his treason to his country, but not at the hands of his faithless, perfidious master. Cromwell was an usurper, 'tis granted; but he had scarcely any choice left him. His sway was every way preferable to that miserable corpse of a Parliament that he turned out, as a gentleman would turn off a drunken butler and his fellows; or the pensioned tyrant that succeeded him—a dissolute, depraved bigot and hypocrite, who was outwardly a Protestant, and at heart a Papist. He lived and died one, while pretending to be a son of the church of England; aye, and swore to it, and died a perjured man. If I must have a master, give me one whom I can respect, rather than a knot of knavish attorneys. Bonaparte was a bad man; but I would rather have had Bonaparte than such a set of corrupt, intriguing, public plunderers as he turned adrift.* The Senate of Rome—the Parliament of England—"the councils of elders and of

---

* The Directory and the Councils (the first especially), we are told by high authority, were known familiarly in Paris by the appellation of *"Les Gueux plumes."* It was then and there probably that a late President of the United States acquired the first rudiments of his taste for *etiquette* and *costume,* which has since displayed itself so pitiably.

youngsters"—the Legislature of France—all made themselves first odious and then contemptible; and then comes an usurper; and this is the natural end of a corrupt civil government.

There is a class of men who possess great learning, combined with inveterate professional habits, and who are *ipso facto,* or perhaps I should rather say, *ipsis factis,* for I must speak accurately, as I speak before a professor, disqualified for any but secondary parts anywhere—even in the cabinet. Cardinal Richelieu was what? A priest. Yes, but what a priest! Oxenstierna was a chancellor. He it was who sent his son abroad to see—*quam parva sapienta regitur mundus*—with how little wisdom this world is governed. This administration seemed to have thought that even less than that little would do for us. The gentleman called it a strong, an able cabinet—second to none but Washington's first cabinet. I could hardly look at him for blushing. What! Sir, is Gallatin at the head of the treasury?—Madison in the department of State? The mind of an accomplished and acute dialectician, of an able lawyer, or, if you please, of a great physician, may, by the long continuance of one pursuit—of one train of ideas—have its habits so inveterately fixed, as effectually to disqualify the possessor for the command of the councils of a country. He may, nevertheless, make an admirable chief of a bureau—an excellent man of details, which the chief ought never to be. A man may be capable of making an able and ingenious argument on·any subject within the sphere of his knowledge; but every now and then the master sophist will start, as I have seen him start, at the monstrous conclusions to which his own artificial reasoning had brought himself. But this was a man of more than ordinary natural candor and fairness of mind. Sir, by words

and figures you may prove just what you please; but it often
and most generally is the fact, that in proportion as a proposition is logically or mathematically true, so is it politically
and commonsensically (or rather nonsensically) false. The
talent which enables a man to write a book or make a
speech, has no more relation to the leading of an army or a
Senate than it has to the dressing of a dinner. The talent
which fits a man for either office is the talent for the management of men—a mere dialectician never had, and never
will have it; each requires the same degree of courage,
though of different kinds. The very highest degree of moral
courage is required for the duties of government. I have
been amused when I have seen some dialecticians, after asserting their words—"the counters of wise men, the money
of fools"—after they had laid down their premises, and
drawn, step by step, their deductions,* sit down, completely
satisfied, as if the conclusions to which they had brought
themselves were really the truth—as if it were irrefragably
true. But wait until another cause is called, or 'til another
court sits—'til the bystanders and jury have had time to
forget both argument and conclusion, and they will make
you just as good an argument on the other side, and arrive
with the same complacency at a directly opposite conclusion,

---

* A caterpillar comes to a fence; he crawls to the bottom of the ditch
and over the fence, some of his hundred feet always in contact with the
subject upon which he moves. A gallant horseman at a flying leap clears
both ditch and fence. "Stop!" says the caterpillar, "you are too flighty, you
want connection and continuity; it took me an hour to get over; you can't
be as sure as I am, who have never quitted the subject, that you have
overcome the difficulty and are fairly over the fence." "Thou miserable
reptile," replies our fox-hunter, "if, like you, I crawled over the earth
slowly and painfully, should I ever catch a fox, or be anything more than
a wretched caterpillar?" N.B.—He did not say, "of the law."

and triumphantly demand your assent to this new truth. Sir, it is their business—I do not blame them. I only say that such a habit of mind unfits men for action, for decision. They want a client to decide for them which side to take; and the really great man performs that office. This habit unfits them for government in the first degree. The talent for government lies in these two things—sagacity to perceive, and decision to act. Genuine statesmen were never made such by mere training—*nascunter non fiunt*—education will form good business men. The maxim (*nascitur non fit*) is as true of statesmen as it is of poets. Let a house be on fire, you will soon see in that confusion who has the talent to command. Let a ship be in danger at sea, and ordinary subordination destroyed, and you will immediately make the same discovery. The ascendancy of mind and of character exists and rises as naturally and as inevitably, where there is free play for it, as material bodies find their level by gravitation. Thus a great logician, like a certain animal, oscillating between the hay on different sides of him, wants some power from without, before he can decide from which bundle to make a trial. Who believes that Washington could write as good a book or report as Jefferson, or make as able a speech as Hamilton? Who is there that believes that Cromwell would have made as good a judge as Lord Hale? No, sir; these learned and accomplished men find their proper place under those who are fitted to command, and to command them among the rest. Such a man as Washington will say to a Jefferson, do you become my Secretary of State; to Hamilton, do you take charge of my purse, or that of the nation, which is the same thing; and to Knox, do you be my master of the horse. All history shows this; but great logicians and great scholars are for that very reason unfit to be rulers.

Would Hannibal have crossed the Alps when there were no roads—with elephants—in the face of hardy mountaineers—and have carried terror to the very gates of Rome if his youth had been spent in poring over books? Would he have been able to maintain himself on the resources of his own genius for sixteen years in Italy, in spite of faction and treachery in the Senate of Carthage if he had been deep in conic sections and fluxions, and the differential calculus—to say nothing of botany, and mineralogy, and chemistry? "Are you not ashamed," said a philosopher, to one who was born to rule; "are you not ashamed to play so well upon the flute?" Sir, it was well put. There is much which it becomes a secondary man to know—much that it is necessary for him to know that a first rate man ought to be ashamed to know. No head was ever clear and sound that was stuffed with book learning. You might as well attempt to fatten and strengthen a man by stuffing him with every variety and the greatest quantity of food. After all, the chief must draw upon his subalterns for much that he does not know, and cannot perform himself. My friend, William R. Johnson, has many a groom that can clean and dress a race horse, and ride him too, better than he can. But what of that? Sir, we are, in the European sense of the term, not a military people. We have no business for an army—it hangs as a dead weight upon the nation—officers and all. All that we hear of it is through pamphlets, indicating a spirit that, if I was at the head of affairs, I should very speedily put down. A state of things that never could have grown up under a man of decision of character at the head of the State or the department —a man possessing the *spirit of command*—that truest of all tests of a chief, whether military or civil. Who rescued Braddock when he was fighting—*secundum artem*—and his men were dropping around him on every side? It was a Virginia militia major. He asserted in that crisis the place which properly belonged to him, and which he afterwards filled in the manner we all know.

Sir, I may, without any mock modesty, acknowledge what I feel, that I have made an unsuccessful reply to the gentleman from Massachusetts. There are some objects which I could have wished to have touched upon before I sit down now and forever. I had the materials in my possession when I came to the House this morning, but I am disabled by physical weakness from the most advantageous use of them.

What shall we say to a gentleman, in this House or out of it, occupying a prominent station, and filling a large space in the eye of his native State, who should, with all the adroitness of a practised advocate, gloss over the acknowledged encroachments of the men in power upon their fair construction of the Constitution, and then present the appalling picture, glaring and flaming, in his deepest colors, of a bloody military tyrant—a raw-head and bloody-bones—so that we cannot sleep in our beds; who should conjure up all the images that can scare children, or frighten old women —I mean very old women, sir—and who offers this wretched caricature—this vile daub, where brick-dust stands for blood, like Peter Porcupine's BLOODY BUOY, as a reason for his and our support in Virginia, of a man in whom he has no confidence, whom he *damns with faint praise*—and who, moreover—tell it not in Gath! had zealously and elaborately (I cannot say ably) justified every one of these very atrocious and bloody deeds? Yes, sir, on paper—not in the heat of debate, in the transports of a speech, but—as the author of the Richmond Anathema full well knew—and knew that we, too, knew—deliberately and officially. Who instituted

the festival of Santa Victoria on the 8th of January in
honor of General Jackson, and of Mrs. Jackson too? The
present incumbent—when Mr. Crawford was the great object of dread. If we did not know that lawyers never see
but one side of a case—that on which they are retained,
and that they fondly hope that the jury will see with their
eyes—what should we say of such a man? His client having
no character, he attacks defendant's character upon a string
of charges, in every one of which (supposing them to be
true) his client was self-avowed *particeps criminis*—having
defended, adopted, and made each and every one of them
his own. Sir, such a man may be a great lawyer (although
this is but a poor specimen of his skill in that line), or a
great mathematician, or chemist; but of a man guilty of such
glaring absurdity it may be fearlessly pronounced that, in
the management of his own concerns and in the affairs of
men, he has not "right good common sense." And here, sir,
we come to that great and all-important distinction which
the profane vulgar—whether they be the great vulgar or the
small—too often overlook; and which I have lamely, I fear,
endeavored to press upon the House—I mean the distinction
between knowledge and learning on the one hand, and
sense and judgment on the other. And there lies the great
defect of the gentleman in question. I have heard it said of
him, by those who know, and love him well, that "he can
argue either side of a question, whether of law, of policy, or
of constitutional construction, with great ingenuity and
force; but he wants that sagacity in political affairs, which
first discerns the proper *end,* and then adopts the most
appropriate *means:* and he is deficient in that knowledge of
mankind, which would enable another (much his inferior)
to perceive that his honest disinterestedness is played upon

by those who are conscious that he prides himself upon it. *It is the lever by which he is on all occasions to be moved.* It is his pride—an honest and honorable pride, which makes him delight to throw himself into minorities, because he enjoys more self-gratification from manifesting his independence of popular opinion—than he could derive from anything in the gift of the people. His late production—the Adams Convention manifesto, is the feeblest production of the day. The reason is, *his head and heart did not go together.*"

This picture is drawn by the hand of a friend. As we have had billiard tables and chess boards introduced into this debate, I hope I may be allowed to borrow an illustration from this last game. One of these arguing machines reminds me of the bishop at chess. The black or white bishop (I use the term not in reference to the color of the piece, but of that of the square he stands upon) is a serviceable piece enough in his way; but he labors under this defect; that moving in the diagonal only, he can never get off his original color. His clerical character is indelible.* He can scour away all over *just one-half* of the board; but his adversary may be on the next square, and perfectly safe from his attack. To be safe from the bishop, you have only to move upon any one of the thirty-two squares that are forbidden ground to him. But not so the irregular knight, who, at successive leaps, can cover every square upon the board, to whose *check* the king can interpose no guard, but must move or die. Even the poor pawn has a privilege which the bishop has not; for he can elude his mitred adversary by moving from a white square to a black one, and finally reach the highest honors of the

---

* As Horne Tooke found to his cost.

game. So even a poor peasant of sense may instruct the philosopher, as the shepherd did, who drew all his notions of men and things from nature. It is in vain to turn over musty folios, and to double down dog's ears; it does very well in its place—in a lawyer's office or a *bureau*—I am forced to use the word for want of a better; but it will not supply the place of that which books never gave, and never can give— of sagacity, judgment, and experience. Who would make the better leader in a period of great public emergency—old Roger Sherman, or a certain very learned gentleman from New York, whom we once had here, who knew everything in the world for which man has no occasion, and nothing in the world for which man has occasion? The people, who are always unsophisticated—and though they may occasionally be misled, are always right in their feelings, and always judge correctly in the long run—have taken up this thing. It is a notorious fact that in Virginia, in the county courts, where men are admitted to sit as judges, who are not of the legal profession—plain planters, who have no pretensions to be considered as lawyers—the decisions are much seldomer reversed than in those courts where a barrister presides—his reasons may be more plausible, but his decisions will be oftener wrong. Yes, sir, the people have decided upon this thing.

On my return home last March I passed by Prince Edward Court-house. It was court day. I had been abroad during the recess of Congress, and I had not seen my constituents for two years. They crowded around me, and many of them said, "Now we expect that you will explain to us how it is that we are to vote for General Jackson." They, as well as myself, had had objections to General Jackson, although I always said in regard to him, *"that I could put my finger upon his public services*—that he had strong claims upon his country, while his competitors, and the predecessor of the successful one, had never rendered any for which they had not been amply paid, and some of them greatly overpaid." My objections to General Jackson were greatly diminished by a personal acquaintance with him when he was last in the Senate. But to my constituents. Singling out one of them, a steady old planter, and staunch Republican friend, I asked him, "When you have a faithless, worthless overseer, in whom you could place no confidence, and have resolved to dismiss him, did you ever change your mind, because, for no matter what reason, you could not get the man that you preferred to every other? or have you been satisfied to turn him off, and employ the best man that you could get?" Sir, a word to the wise is enough. They were entirely satisfied, and in a few weeks we were, as we are, unanimous for Jackson.

I will suppose a case: I will suppose that the late convulsive struggles of the administration may so far succeed as they shall be able to renew their lease for another four years. Now if a majority of this House can't get along with such a minority hanging on their rear, cutting off supplies, and beating up their quarters, what will be the situation of the administration then? Sir, what is it now? *"Palsied by the will of their constituents."* Did anybody ever hear of a victory obtained by the Executive power while a decided majority of the Legislature was against it? I know of no such victory, but one—and that was the parricidal victory of the younger Pitt over the constitution of England; and he gained that only by the impenetrable obstinacy of the king, which then gave indications of the disease that was lurking in his constitution, and afterwards so unhappily became manifest.

The king was an honest man, and a much abler man than he ever had credit for. But he was incurably obstinate. He had just lost the colonies. No matter—he would risk the Crown of England itself, and retire to his hereditary States in Germany rather than yield; and, but for a bare-faced coalition, he would have so retired, and have supplied a most important defect in the act of settlement—the separation of Hanover from England, But the corrupt bargain of Lord North and Mr. Fox, to share office between them, disgusted the people—they took side even against their own liberties. But here the coalition is not on the side of the people's rights, but against them. Mr. Pitt (the Crown rather) triumphed. Knaves cried Hosanna: fools repeated the cry. England recovered by that elasticity which belongs to free institutions, and Mr. Pitt attained a degree of power that enabled him to plunge her into the mad vortex of war with Revolutionary France. Nine hundred millions of debt; taxes, in amount, in degree, in mode, unheard of; pauperism, misery, in all possible forms of wretchedness; attest the greatness of the heaven-born minister, who did not weather the storm, but was whelmed beneath it, leaving his country to that Providence whom it pleased to rescue her in her utmost need, by inflicting madness on her great unrelenting enemy, and sending this modern Nebuchadnezzar to grass. Mr. Pitt is as strong an instance of my purpose as I could have wanted. He was a rhetorician, a speech maker; a man of words, and good words too, at will; a dexterous debater; and if he had continued to ride the Western circuit, he might have been an eminent wrangler at the bar, and, in due time, a Chief Justice or Lord Chancellor. But, for the sins of England, he was made Prime Minister, and at five-and-twenty, too. Mr. Pitt no more saw what was ahead of him, than the pauper in the parish work-house. He no more dreamed, when the war began, to what point he would be able to push his system, if system it may be called, than any clerk in his office. He did not even foresee the stoppage of the Bank, which he was compelled to resort to in the fourth year of the war. If he had foreseen it, the war would never have been made. Indeed, Mr. Pitt did not foresee even the war—for in the preceding year, I think, he held out the promise of a long peace to the faithful Commons.

The productive powers of a people like the English, where property is perfectly secure and left free to act, and where the industrious classes are shut out from almost any participation in public affairs, is incredible, is almost without a limit. Two individuals discovered each a mine, more precious and productive than Guanaxuato or Potosi, that furnished the means for his prodigality, that astonished even Mr. Pitt. These were Sir Richard Arkwright and Mr. Watt —the spinning machine and the steam engine. And this imbecile and blundering Minister has been complimented with what is due to the unrivalled ingenuity and industry of his countrymen.* So, sir, in like manner this young Hercules

---

* Mr. Madison (I speak it without the slightest disrespect to that eminent man) is a still stronger case in point than Mr. Pitt. Except Mr. Jefferson and Mr. Jay, as Secretary of State—(and as Mr. Jay is mentioned, I cannot omit my poor tribute to the example of consummate dignity which this great and good man has set to every other great man in retirement. He has been withdrawn from public life too long—yet even here his error leans to virtue's side—about thirty years. Who sees, or has seen, his name in a newspaper? *O si sic omnes!*)—he had not perhaps his equal in our country—his superior nowhere—a profound thinker, a powerful reasoner, "with tongue or pen"—a great civilian, reminding one of his prototype, John Selden; to whose "MARE CLAUSUM" no man was better fitted than Mr. Madison to have opposed a MARE LIBERUM. Yet, advanced to the helm of affairs, how consummate his ignorance of men,

of America, who if we can keep him from being strangled in the cradle by the serpents of corruption, must grow to gigantic strength and stature; every improvement which he makes, in spite of the misrule of his governors, these very modestly arrogate to themselves.

We have been told, officially, that the President wished the great question to have been referred back to the people, if, by the forms of the Constitution, this could be done. If I were the friend, as I am the undisguised enemy of this administration, I would say to them, you may be innocent,

---

let his selections for great offices, civil and military, tell. I will enumerate a few just as they occur to me, beginning with his cabinet.

Secretary of State—Robert Smith.

Secretary of the Treasury—George W. Campbell; also Minister to St. Petersburg.

Secretary of War—Dr. Eustis.

Secretary of the Navy—Paul Hamilton and Benjamin W. Crowninshield, the Master Slender—no, the Master Silence of Ministers of State. Shakespeare himself could go no lower. It is the thorough base of human nature. He seems to us to have drawn Robert Shallow, Esquire, and his cousin Slender, as the comparative and superlative degree of fatuity; and when we believe that he has sounded his lowest note, as if reveling in the exuberance of his power, he produces Silence as the *ne plus ultra* of inanity and imbecility. Mr. Madison has, in this one instance, outdone Shakespeare himself—he gives us the real man whom the bard only drew.

Attorney General—Richard Rush; not being fit for Comptroller, he is selected to preside over the treasury! and by the Richmond Adams Convention for Vice President!

Commander in the Northwest—William Hull.

Commander in the Northeast—James Wilkinson and Wade Hampton.

Commander at Bladensburg—William Winder! assisted by "The Flying Cabinet," as Wilkinson had the insolence to designate them in his diagram of that famous route. In this memorable *disengagement* the GRAND ROLE was played by Mr. Attorney General, "for that time only," *without his hat.* We have no "Master of the Rolls" in our country; but like the witty authors of the Rolliad, for Sir Lloyd Kenyon, we might take as a motto for Mr. Rush, *"Jouez bien votre rôle."* And, verily, never did political adventurer make more of his parts than this solemn gentleman has done.

your intentions may be upright, but you have brought the country to that pass that you can't carry on the government. As gentlemen, possessing the least self-respect, you ought to retire—leave it—try another venue—you can't carry on the government without us, any more than we can act while everything in the Executive Government is against us. Sir, there are cases in which suspicion is equivalent to proof; and not only equal to it, but more than equal to the most damning proof. There is not a husband here who will not ratify this declaration—there may be suspicion so agonizing that it makes the wretch cry out for certainty as a relief from the most damning tortures. Such is the picture which the great master of the human heart presents to us in the person of the noble Moor—and Shakespeare seems to have known the heart of man as if himself had made it. Such suspicions, resting on no false suggestions of an Iago, but supported by a cloud of witnesses and a long array of facts and circumstances that no sophistry can shake, are entertained with respect to these gentlemen; and although they are making

---

Never were abilities so much below mediocrity so well rewarded; no, not when Caligula's horse was made Consul.

A few days ago I stumbled upon the following stanza of an unfinished poem on the Glories and Worthies of our Administration:

> "And as for R., his early locks of snow,
> Betray the frozen region that's below.
> Though Jove upon the race bestow'd some fire,
> The gift was all exhausted by the sire.
> A sage consum'd what thousands well might share,
> And ASHES! only, fell upon the heir!"

These lines are the only article of the growth, produce or manufacture of the country north of Patapsco, that I have knowingly used since the Tariff bill passed. They are by a witty son of a witty sire—as Burns sings, "a true gude fellow's get."

a convulsive effort to roll back the tide of public opinion, they can't allay the feeling; the suspicion rests upon the facts; and, do what they may, facts will not bend at their bidding. Admit it to be suspicion, it is equally fatal as regards them and the public service with the reality. Mr. R. would not go in pursuit of the *alibis* and *aliasses* of the accused—of the tubs, whether with false bottoms or double bottoms, thrown out to amuse the public. The whole conduct of the accused had displayed nothing of the calm dignity of innocence, but all the restlessness of conscious guilt. Every word of Mr. Clay's late pamphlet might be true, and yet the accused be guilty notwithstanding. Mr. R. would not now examine his inconsistent declarations to different persons and at different times and occasions. The secretary was not the first witness who had proved too much. "He who pleads his own cause," says the proverb, "generally has a fool for his client."*

---

* Mr. Clay took his seat in the House of Representatives in December, 1811; his first stride was from the door to the chair, where he commenced to play the dictator; he fixed his eyes on the presidency, and I, who had been twelve years in Congress, fixed mine upon him, and have kept them there ever since. Sulla said that he saw many a Marius in Caesar. So I, who had heard Mr. Clay for the first time in the Senate the year before, on the renewal of the charter of the Bank of the United States, was persuaded that he would not keep the faith. Without affecting an inferiority that I do not feel, I may be allowed to say, that my position as the guardian of the Constitution and country, against the assaults of a man goaded and blinded by his ambition, would have placed a dwarf on a level with a giant. He went to Europe, and returned a changed man.

And not Mr. Clay only. Mr. Monroe, the stern Mr. Monroe, for whom General Washington's administration was not Republican enough, comes back after four years spent in Paris, Madrid, and London, to settle points of *etiquette and invent coat patterns* for our foreign ministers, because, forsooth, they are not Franklin's. So that, like the king's fool, our envoys must have a party-colored coat to make up for their want of sense and dignity. *"Motley is your only wear."*

The gentleman from Massachusetts warned us, that if the individual we seek to elevate shall succeed, he will in his turn become the object of public pursuit, and that the same pack will be unkennelled at his heels that have run his rival down. It may be so. I have no hesitation to say, that if his conduct shall deserve it, and I live, I shall be one of that *pack;* because I maintain the interests of stockholders against presidents, directors, and cashiers. And here, sir, I beg leave to notice an objection urged, as I have heard, against me by the gentleman from Ohio (Mr. Vance). He says that I have been opposed to all Administrations. Sir, I deny it to be fact. I did oppose the elder Adams, because he attacked the liberty of the press and of the subject, because his opinions were at war with the genius of our institutions. He avowed them openly, and I liked him the better for his frankness. But I suppported for more than five years the administration of his successor. I did for it what I could —little enough, God knows. The first case in which I differed from that administration was the case of the Yazoo claims, which I thought a case of flagrant corruption! I do not mean, and I never did believe, that there was corruption in the president or his two secretaries; and it did not cause me to separate myself from them. I separated from that administration three years afterwards, with pain and sorrow, and not without some anger too; for I have no idea of that extreme of candor and meekness which denounces the measures of a government, as Bottom says in the play, "and will roar you as gently as any suckling dove." It is not my nature to do so; and it would be criminal and ridiculous in me, because it would be hypocrisy to affect it. When the former restrictive system was first commenced, I thought I saw what I now know I did then see—the fatal and ruinous consequences that would grow out of it. I told Mr. Jefferson, candidly and frankly, that if he expected support in a certain quarter and did not find it, he must not impute want of candor to me. I will not repeat what he told me on that occasion; it is unnecessary to say his language and conduct was that of a gentleman. I frankly laid before him the facts and reasons which rendered such an event inevitable. I will not repeat what he said: but he deplored it.

Sir, I know that he deplored it—for he told me so. And when some of the *ear-wigs,* that infest all great men, sought to curry favor with him by relating, after their manner, the hard and sharp things which I was said to have uttered on the floor of this House on that occasion, he coldly replied, that, to do Mr. R. justice, he had been full as explicit as severe in his presence.* But permit me to remind you, sir—for you were then too young to know much of these matters—that previously, but nearly at the time of my leaving that administration, a certain wise man from the East joined it, who soon after went off to Canada, under strong suspicion of felony; and this was soon followed by a certain gentleman's giving in his adhesion, who had before been violently opposed to it, and to all its best measures. Sir, I have not the least objection to its being said of me, that I separated myself from Mr. Jefferson, when Barnabas Bidwell and John Quincy Adams joined him.†

---

* How unlike the system of delators, and spies, and runners, from the Senate Chamber or Hall of the Representatives to the Secretary of State's office or house during a debate, in which that great man does not wish to be present in person.

† Never was an administration more brilliant than that of Mr. Jefferson's up to this period. We were indeed in the "full tide of successful experiment." Taxes repealed, the public debt amply provided for—both

Some allusion has been made to the discordant materials of the present opposition. They are somewhat discordant—at least they have been so. But are they more so than the adherents of the present administration, or the materials of the administration itself? I well remember almost the first propitiation (the first was the writ of *habeas corpus*) which he who is now the President of the United States made to Mr. Jefferson and his party. It was an attempt to run down the present chief justice. The right of John Smith to a seat in the Senate was made the peg to hang it on. I will tell the

---

principal and interest—sinecures abolished—Louisiana acquired—public confidence unbounded. We had all, and we wanted more than all. We played for eleven and lost the game, when we held ten in hand. From the junction of Bidwell and Adams, we may date that embargo of fifteen months that eclipsed the sun of our glory, and disastrous twilight shed on more than half the nation. Mr. Madison removed this *incubus,* of which we were tired, but ashamed to rid ourselves. The arrangement with Erskine followed. At the May session of 1809 the House of Representatives evaded a motion expressive of their approbation of the promptitude and frankness with which the President had concluded this arrangement. It was soon after disavowed by England.

Mr. Madison's first message to Congress was sent on Tuesday, May 23, 1809, announcing the arrangement with Erskine, and the consequent restoration of our intercourse with England from and "after the 10th day of June next." "On Friday, the 26th, a motion was made by Mr. Randolph, and seconded, that the House do come to the following resolution:

"*Resolved,* That the promptitude and frankness with which the President of the United States has met the overtures of the government of Great Britain towards a restoration of harmony and a free commercial intercourse between the two nations, receives the approbation of this House." Reports Journal, 1 Sess., 11 Congress, page 35.

Mr. Ezekiel Bacon, of Massachusetts, moved to amend (in order to defeat it), and Mr. John G. Jackson, of Virginia, moved the indefinite postponement of both the resolution and amendment. It is curious to pursue the fate of this resolution through page 39, when the House refused to resume the consideration of the unfinished business (which was Mr. Randolph's resolution)—pages 44, 45, 46—when the consideration of the resolution was carried by yeas 66, against nays 61 (a lean ma-

gentleman the whole reason why I have opposed the administration since that time, and may again, if, according to my judgment, they shall not consult the good of the country. It is, Sir, simply because I am for the interests of the stockholders—of whom I am one—as opposed to those of the President, Directors, and Cashiers; and I have the right of speaking my opinion, and shall exercise it, though it happen to be against the greatest and proudest names.

Sir, I am no judge of human motives: that is the attribute of the name which I will not take in vain—the attribute of Him who rules in heaven, or who becomes incarnate upon earth; motives free from alloy belonged to that Divine incarnation, and to Him only, of all that have borne the form of man. Mere man can claim no such exemption.

---

jority!)—all the decided friends of the administration voting in the minority, among them connexions of Mr. Madison himself—*e.g.,* John G. Jackson, Richard Cutts, who were nearly connected with him by marriage. See further, pages 48, 49, 54, when the motion for indefinite postponement being withdrawn by Mr. Jackson, was renewed by another member —pages 62, 63—when (May 31st) the resolution received the *go-by* by an adjournment.

When Mr. Randolph was asked by the late Mr. Bayard and some other friend "What he thought of the state of things?" He replied that "we must have war with England." "With France you mean," said they. (For then—our interdict—taken off England—was in force against France.) "No, with England. The vote of the House of Representatives, on the motion to approve the conduct of the President, assures me of that fact." And accordingly he wrote to his correspondent in Virginia to the same effect.

The embargo struck the first staggering blow on our agriculture, and *scuttled* our ships. The landed and navigating interests have never recovered from it. It is the *nidus,* the hot-bed rather, and the *fomes* too, of the manufacturing system and policy—fostered since by the war by double duties and by tariffs. What bounty on manufactures does the Harrisburg Convention propose that is equal to a total prohibition of exports?

I do not pretend that my own motives do not partake of their full share of the infirmity of our common nature—but, of those infirmities, neither avarice nor ambition form one iota in the composition of my present motives. Sir, what can the country do for me? Poor as I am—for I am much poorer than I have been—impoverished by unwise legislation—I still have nearly as much as I know how to use—more certainly than I have at all times made a good use of—and as for power what charm can it have for one like me? If power had been my object, I must have been less sagacious than my worst enemies have represented me to be (unless, indeed, those who would have kindly shut me up in bedlam) if I had not obtained it. I may appeal to all my friends to say whether there have not been times when I stood in such favor in the closet that there must have been something very

---

Virginia may thank herself. She is the author of her own undoing. Mercantile clamor induced her in an evil hour to commence the restrictive system. She laid embargoes, and at length made war for "Free Trade and Sailors' Rights." *Cui bono?* The Hartford nation, as Mr. J., their greatest, although unintentional benefactor, denominated them. *We* took the *credit, they* the *cash.*

"Which had the better bargain?" "Honest Congreve is a man after my own heart." The Hartford nation may sing now to an old tune—

> *"Populus me sibilat at mihi plaudo*
> *Ipse domi, simul ac nummos contemplor in arca."*

General reflections are always unjust, and therefore unwise. Mr. Randolph greatly respects many New England men, and many points in the New England character. He regrets the change at home, as well as there, from the original distinctive marks of the cavalier and the covenanter. New England has no longer her Samuel Adamses and her Roger Shermans. Virginia also seeks in vain for her Washingtons, and Randolphs, and Blands, and Lees, and Nelsons, and Henrys. But, at the worst, the character of a miser is far preferable to that of a spend-thrift. Even the cheat is not more contemptible than the bubble.

extravagant and unreasonable in my wishes if they might not *all* have been gratified. Was it office? What, sir, to drudge in your laboratories in the departments, or be at the tail of the *corps diplomatique* in Europe? Alas! sir, in my condition a cup of cold water would be more acceptable. What can the country give me that I do not possess in the confidence of such constituents as no man ever had before? I can retire to my patrimonial trees, where I may see the sun rise and set in peace. Sir, as I was returning the other evening from the capital, I saw—what has been a rare sight here this winter—the sun dipping its broad disk among the trees behind those Virginia hills, not allaying his glowing axle in the steep Atlantic stream; and I asked myself if, with this Book of Nature unrolled before me,* I was not the most foolish of men to be struggling and scuffling here in this heated and impure atmosphere, where the play is not worth the candle? But then the truth rushed upon my mind that I was vainly perhaps, but honestly, striving to uphold the liberties of the people who sent me here—yes, sir, for can those liberties coexist with corruption? At the very worst the question recurs,—Which will the more effectually destroy them?—collusion, bargain and corruption here, or a military despotism? When can that be established over us? Never, 'til the Congress has become odious and contempt-

---

> * "O how canst thou renounce the boundless store
> Of charms which Nature to her votary yields!
> The warbling woodland, the resounding shore,
> The pomp of groves and garniture of fields,
> And all that the genial ray of Morning gilds,
> And all that echoes to the song of Even,
> All that the mountain's sheltering bosom shields,
> *And all the dread magnificence of heaven,*
> O how canst thou renounce and hope to be forgiven?"

ible in the eyes of the people. I have learned, from the highest of all authority, that the first step towards putting on incorruption is the putting off corruption. That recollection nerves me in the present conflict, for I know, that if we are successful, I shall hold over the head of those who shall succeed the present incumbent a rod which they will not dare, even if they had the inclination, to disobey. They will tremble at the punishment of their predecessors. Sir, if we succeed, we shall restore the Constitution—we shall redress the injury done to the people—we shall regenerate the country. If the administration which ensues shall be as bad as the character of the opposing candidate [General Jackson] is represented by his bitterest foes to be, still I had rather it were in the seat of power than the present dynasty, because it will have been fairly elected. The fountain of its authority will not be poisoned at the source. But if we perish under the spasmodic struggles of those now in power to re-instate themselves on the throne, our fate will be a sacred one—and who would wish to survive it? There will be nothing left in the country worth any man's possession. If after such an appeal has been made to the people, and a majority has been brought into this and the other House of Congress, this administration shall be able to triumph, it will prove that there is a rottenness in our institutions which ought to render them unworthy of any man's regard.

Sir, my *church-yard cough* gives me the solemn warning, that whatever part I shall take in the chase, I may fail of being in at the death. I should think myself the basest and the meanest of men—I care not what the opinion of the world might be—I should know myself to be a scoundrel, and should not care who else knew it—if I could permit any motive, connected with division of the spoil, to mingle in this

matter with my poor but best exertions for the welfare of my
country. If gentlemen suppose that I am giving pledges they
are mistaken—I give none—they are entitled to none—and
I give none. I shall retire upon my resources—I will go back
to the bosom of my constituents—to such constituents as
man never had before, and never will have again—and I
shall receive from them the only reward that I ever looked
for, but the highest that man can receive—the universal expression of their approbation—of their thanks. I shall read
it in their beaming faces—I shall feel it in their gratulating
hands. The very children will climb around my knees to
welcome me. And I shall give up them and this? And for
what? For the heartless amusements and vapid pleasures
and tarnished honors of this abode of splendid misery, of
shabby splendor, for a clerkship in the War Office, or a
foreign mission, to dance attendance abroad instead of at
home, or even for a department itself? Sir, thirty years make
sad changes in man. When I first was honored with their
confidence I was a very young man, and my constituents
stood almost in parental relation to me, and I received from
them the indulgence of a beloved son. But the old patriarchs
of that day have been gathered to their fathers; some adults
remain, whom I look upon as my brethren: but the far
greater part were children—little children—or have come
into the world since my public life began. I know among
them grandfathers and men muster-free, who were boys at
school when I first took my seat in Congress. Time, the
mighty reformer and innovator, has silently and slowly, but
surely, changed the relation between us; and I now stand
to them *in loco parentis*—in the place of a father—and receive from them a truly filial reverence and regard. Yes, sir,
they are my children—who resent, with the quick love of
children, all my wrongs, real or supposed. Shall I not invoke

the blessings of a common Father upon them? Shall I deem any sacrifice too great for them? To them I shall return, if we are defeated, for all the consolation that awaits me on this side of the grave. I feel that I hang to existence but by a single hair—that the sword of Damocles is suspended over me.

If we succeed, we shall have given a new lease of life to the Constitution. But should we fail, I warn gentlemen not to pour out their regrets on General Jackson. He will be the first to disdain them. The object of our cause has been, not so much to raise Andrew Jackson to the Presidency—be his merits what they may—as the signal and condign punishment of those public servants on whom, if they be not guilty, the strongest suspicion of guilt must ever justly rest.

SPEECHES AT THE VIRGINIA CONVENTION OF 1829–30

[These speeches—among Randolph's strongest, and almost his last—are to be found only in a volume now rare, *Proceedings and Debates of the Virginia State Convention of 1829–1830*. Although all Randolph's remarks at the Convention deserve printing, space confines us here to one long speech, and three shorter. Other remarks by Randolph at the Convention are quoted in the text of this book.]

IN DEFENSE OF FREEHOLD SUFFRAGE

[It had been proposed that the suffrage be restricted to householders who paid a certain amount in taxes; Randolph here sets his face against such a qualification, which might exclude from the franchise poor freeholders who already enjoyed the suffrage. *Proceedings,* 346.]

Mr. Randolph said, that he rose simply to make a suggestion to the gentleman from Chesterfield, and one to the
Committee. I believe, said he, that I shall hardly be contradicted, when I state that the great moving cause, which led
to this Convention, has been the regulation of the Right of
Suffrage. After all the out-cry that has been raised on the
subject, judge my surprise, when I found that a proposition
coming from the Legislative Committee, and which extends
the Right of Suffrage almost *ad infinitum,* to many classes
of persons within the Commonwealth, contained a blow at
the elective franchise of the freeholder, the present sovereign of this land. We are met to extend the Right of
Suffrage; nobody can tell how far under the out-cry that it
is *too much* restricted, and the very first step we take, is to
restrict it *still further, quoad* the freeholder. Do gentlemen
suppose the freeholders will be blind to this? What becomes
of all the considerations of philanthropy of which we have
heard so much? What becomes of all the gentlemen's abstractions? Sir, the only good I ever knew these abstractions
to do, is to abstract money out of the pockets of one great
division of the country, to put it into the pockets of another,
a species of abstraction the least of all others to my taste.

Sir, I demand, as a freeholder, in behalf of the freeholders, on what plea you are to put them, and them only, to
the ban of this Convention. Other and larger classes of persons are selected to be drawn within the range of the elective privilege, while the poorer classes of the freeholders are
to be disfranchised. So, after all, this great and illustrious
Assembly are met to make war on the poorer classes of the
freeholders of the Commonwealth. You are not only to extend rights, but you are to take away the rights, the vested
rights, of a large and respectable, however they may be a

poor, class of your fellow-citizens. Sir, I will never consent to deprive the freeholder of his rights, however trivial in the view of assessors or patricians, his humble shed may appear. I saw this measure in the Legislative Committee, and I thought I saw, what I think I see now, (here Mr. R. pointed with his finger), a snake in the grass. I will never consent to be the agent in taking away from any man the Right of Suffrage he now enjoys.

On the Landed Interest
[*Proceedings,* 430]

Mr. Randolph said, he believed he was not singular in the opinion he was about to express, (though he might be the only member of the Convention, by whom it was uttered), of sincere gratification, on finding that the gentleman who had just taken his seat, was in favor of what he (Mr. R.) conceived to be the only safe ground, in this Commonwealth, for the Right of Suffrage—he meant *terra firma:* literally *firma:* The Land. The moment, said he, you quit the land, (I mean no pun), that moment you will find yourselves at sea: and without compass—without land-mark or polar star. I said that I considered it the only safe foundation IN THIS COMMONWEALTH. For whom are we to make a Constitution? For Holland? For Venice, (where there is no land)? For a country where the land is monopolized by a few? where it is locked up not only by entails, (I do not mean such as the English law would laugh at), but by marriage settlement, so that a large part of the people are necessarily excluded from the possession of it: but for a people emphatically agricultural; where land is in plenty, and where it is accessible to every exertion of honest industry. I will venture to say, that if one-half the time had been spent in honest labor, which has been spent in murmuring and getting up petitions, that the signers might be invested with that right, all-important at muster-rolls, at crossroads, and in this Convention, yet not worth three months' labor, the right would have been possessed and exercised long ago.

I will not go into the discussion; I rose merely to express my extreme satisfaction, that the gentleman who has just taken his seat is of opinion that we ought to abide in the land.

The amendment of the gentleman from Chesterfield, as proposed to be modified by the gentleman from Spottsylvania, is one which I do not exactly understand. So far as it depends on a landed qualification, (which is the great principle of our present Government), the proposition of the gentleman from Chesterfield, appears to be only an equitable modification of it, and to retain the great stable, solid qualification of land, which I view as the only sufficient evidence of permanent, common interest in, and attachment to, the Commonwealth.

I had thought that the experience of this Commonwealth and of the United States had read us such lessons on the subject of personal security, that we never should think of leaving real. As I am not sufficiently acquainted with the measure proposed by the gentleman from Spottsylvania, I respectfully move that the Committee do now rise.

The Committee rose accordingly, and the House adjourned

ON THE COUNTY COURTS

[*Proceedings,* 532–33. Here Randolph defends the aristocratic institution of the county courts—which the Convention proceeded to abolish. For an account of the Virginian county courts, see Charles S. Sydnor's *Gentlemen Freeholders* (University of North Carolina Press, 1952).]

Mr. Randolph said, that he hoped and trusted that the Committee would re-consider. He had never been more surprised in his life than on yesterday, when after the very slender vote their exertions had enabled them to obtain, he found *instanter,* a sudden change produced by the adoption of an amendment, which, to put the most fair construction upon it, was equivalent to striking out the whole of that which the Committee had determined to retain, and which was susceptible of a construction still more hostile to the existing system. Mr. R. said that he did not know any other thing which could have induced him, in the present pitiable condition of his frame, to throw himself upon the attention of the Committee. He had long considered the County Court System, and the freehold Suffrage, as the two main pillars in the ancient edifice of our State Constitution. In the course of my life I have repeatedly been called upon by various eminent men, to explain to them the system of Government in this Commonwealth; and I never knew a single individual of the number who was not struck with admiration at the structure of our County Court system. I have been asked, whether it was the effect of design, or of one of those fortunate combinations of circumstances, which enabled its framers "to snatch a grace beyond the reach of art." Whether it was design or chance, one thing is certain, that the plan has proved in practice to be one of the very best which the wit of man could have devised for this Commonwealth; preserving in the happiest manner, a just administration of our affairs, between the instability attendant upon

popular elections, and the corruption or oppression of
Executive patronage. It insures to us that the power of the
Commonwealth will always be in the hands of good and
lawful men. I never met an individual who cursed the
appointment of Jackson, or a Federalist, when Federalism
was uppermost, or a Republican, when it was downmost,
who did not express envy at this feature of our polity.
Virginia stands between Scylla and Charybdis. We must
have magistrates appointed by the people or by the Executive, (unless the present mode be continued). Suppose by
the people. Then, in a cause between a man of great influence, popularity, and power—and a poor man—he that is
poor will have no chance of justice. If they are appointed
by the Executive, it must be by recommendation:—but of
what sort? Such as prevails at Washington? (Thank God
no man ever dared to approach me for my name to one of
them). Recommendations obtained by cabal and intrigue?
—and after all, you must be doomed to instability—yes, to
utter instability. At present, the Government of each county
is in hands best fitted for it. The gentleman from Chesterfield, in enumerating so ably and clearly the Herculean
labours of their office, has truly said that they step in between the accused and the Commonwealth in all cases where
the crime is not so great as to be sent on to the higher courts.
Their mode of appointment may be an anomaly, but I
consider it the most valuable feature of the system.

If we abandon this, we must resort to infamous jobbers
and trading justices; who will foment instead of allaying
village quarrels. If you will strike the pettifogger out of
existence, you shall have my vote most heartily. It can be
done thus alone. But there are some (I speak, of course, of
those *out* of this House), who delight to excite clamour—

who long to suck blood—and raise popular commotion; who want to be judges and justices, because the people refuse them a livelihood as lawyers. I was pained and surprised at the description given by the gentleman from Loudoun, of drunken justices. I had thought there were none of such a description; but the testimony is given by a respectable gentleman—and in his county, the fact must be so. I bless God it is so no where else. Our justices are not so ignorant as he imagines—my confidence is infinitely greater in County Courts than in the Superior Courts. The bench of the latter is filled too often by lawyers who can't get a livelihood at the bar. I speak not of Judges in general. But the gentleman says that when he wants a pair of boots, he goes to a skillful bootmaker; but, Sir, when I want either boots or a Constitution, I will go to capable workmen, and not to cobblers.

Great stress has been laid on the opinion of Mr. Jefferson, by a gentleman not now in his place. Sir, the opinion of Mr. Jefferson comes strangely from him. He has gone beyond the Ganges into the uttermost East. But I have no hesitation to say, that on a subject like this, I have not much deference for the opinion of Mr. Jefferson. We all know he was very confident in his theories—but I am a practical man and have no confidence *a priori* in the theories of Mr. Jefferson, or of any other man under the sun.

Not an argument has been advanced against the County Courts, but would be equally good *a priori* against jury trial. What could have taught us its value but experience? *A priori,* it seems absurd to trust a dozen ploughmen—good and lawful of the vicinage I grant, but still ploughmen— with a point of law in criminal cases, without appeal—and in civil cases under circumstances almost equivalent. We

can hardly conceive any thing more ridiculous in theory—
yet we find none half so valuable in practice: So vain is it to
argue against fact. I once witnessed a contest of argument
against fact, and if it will relieve the oppression and *ennui* of
this debate, I will relate it: I saw one of the best and wor-
thiest men on a visit at some distance from home, urging his
lady to make preparation to ride, for "the sun was down."
His lady said, "the sun was not down." Her lord gravely replied, "the sun sets at half past six: it is now past that time."
(Every man's watch is right and his was in his hand.) The
company looked out of the window and saw the sun in all
his blaze of glory—but the sun ought to have been down, as
fleas ought to have been lobsters. The sun, however, was not
down, and fleas are not lobsters: whether it be because they
have not souls, I leave to St. Jerome and the Bishops to
settle.

We are not to be struck down by the authority of Mr.
Jefferson. Sir, if there be any point in which the authority of
Mr. Jefferson might be considered as valid, it is in the
mechanism of a plough. He once mathematically and geo-
metrically demonstrated the form of a mould-board which
should present the least resistance. His mould-board was
sent to Paris, to the *Savants*—it was exhibited to all the
visitors at the Garden of Plants. The *Savants* all declared
una voce that this was the best mould-board that had ever
been devised. They did not decree to Mr. Jefferson the
honours of Hermes Trismegistus, but they cast his mould-
board in plaster; and there it remains, an eternal proof that
this form of mould-board presents less resistance than any
other on the face of the earth. Some time after, an adversary
brought into Virginia the Carey plough; but it was such an

awkward, ill-looking thing, that it would not sell. At length, some one tried it, and though its mould-board was not that of least resistance, it beat Mr. Jefferson's plough as much as common sense will always beat theory and reveries. Now there is not in Virginia, I believe, one plough with the *mould-board of least resistance.* I have had some experience in its use, and find it the handsomest plough to draw I ever saw. So much for authority!

Sir, when we shall have given up County Courts, and jury trial, and Freehold Suffrage, there will be nothing in the Commonwealth worth attention to anyone of practical sense. The County Courts hold the just balance between popular mutability, (the opprobrium and danger of all popular systems), on the one hand, and Executive patronage on the other. I said before that there must be recommendation of some sort. *Quaere* then, which is better? that it shall be made openly by the justices when assembled, on notice, or by a private letter? Sir, I am for a strict adherence to the anchorage ground of the Constitution: it has hitherto kept the Commonwealth from swinging from its moorings; when it shall drag its anchors, or slip its cable, God knows what will become of the vessel of State. But my hand may not be wanting at the plough. If gentlemen succeeded in introducing the newest, theoretical, pure, defecated Jacobinism into this Commonwealth, I do upon my soul believe, they will have inflicted a deeper wound on Republican Government than it ever experienced before.

I wish I could have presented my thoughts in a manner more worthy of the subject and the occasion. The gentleman who has aspired to out-act Caesar in the Capitol, folds himself in his robe, and exclaims *et tu Brute!*

On King Numbers
[*Proceedings,* 312–21]

Mr. Randolph rose, and addressed the Committee as follows:

Mr. Chairman: It has been with great disappointment, and yet deeper regret, that I have perceived an invincible repugnance on the part of gentlemen representing here a large portion of the Commonwealth extending from Cape Henry to the Mountains, along the whole length of the North Carolina line, that portion of it in which my own district is situated, to take a share in this debate—a repugnance not resulting—I say so from my personal knowledge of many of them—not resulting from any want of ability, nor from the want of a just, modest, and manly confidence in the abilities they possess. I have looked to Norfolk; I have looked to Southampton; I have looked to Dinwiddie; I have looked to Brunswick, for the display of talent which I knew to exist; but, Sir, I have looked in vain.

And it is this circumstance only—I speak it with a sincerity I have too much self-respect to vouch for, which has induced me to overcome the insuperable aversion— (insuperable until now)—that I have felt, to attract towards myself the attention of the Committee.

As long as I have had my fixed opinions, I have been in the habit of considering the Constitution of Virginia, under which I have lived for more than half a century, with all its faults and failings, and with all the objections which practical men—not theorists and visionary speculators—have urged, or can urge against it, as the very best Constitution; not for Japan; not for China; not for New England; or for

Old England; but for this, our ancient Commonwealth of Virginia.

But, I am not such a bigot as to be unwilling, under any circumstances, however imperious, to change the Constitution under which I was born; I may say, certainly, under which I was brought up, and under which I had hoped to be carried to my grave. My principles on that subject are these: the grievance must first be clearly specified, and fully proved; it must be vital, or rather, deadly in its effect; its magnitude must be such as will justify prudent and reasonable men in taking the always delicate, often dangerous step, of making innovations in their fundamental law; and the remedy proposed must be reasonable and adequate to the end in view. When the grievance shall have been thus made out, I hold him to be not a loyal subject, but a political bigot, who would refuse to apply the suitable remedy.

But, I will not submit my case to a political physician, come his diploma from whence it may, who would at once prescribe all the medicines in the Pharmacopoeia, not only for the disease I now have, but for all the diseases of every possible kind I ever might have in future. These are my principles, and I am willing to carry them out; for, I will not hold any principles which I may not fairly carry out in practice.

Judge then, with what surprise and pain, I found that not one department of this Government—no, not one— Legislative, Executive, or Judicial—nor one branch of either, was left untouched by the spirit of *innovation*—(for I cannot call it reform). When even the Senate—yes, Sir, the Senate, which had so lately been swept by the besom of innovation—even the Senate had not gone untouched or unscathed. Many innovations are proposed to be made without any one practical grievance having been even suggested, much less shown.

Take that branch of the Government which was so thoroughly reformed in 1816, and even that is not untouched. Sir, who ever heard a whisper, *ab urbe condità* to this day, that the Senators of Virginia were too *youthful?* I never heard such a sentiment in my life. And in the House of Delegates, what men ever heard that the members—I speak of them, of course, in the aggregate—that the members were too young? Yet, even there, it is to be declared, that all men who might be elected to that body between the ages of twenty-one and twenty-four, are to be disfranchised; and as regards the Senate, all between the ages of twenty-one and thirty. Yes, Sir, not only the spring and seed-time, but the summer and harvest of life—that delightful season which neither you, Sir, nor I can ever recall—the dearest and the best portion of our lives; during this period of nine years, the very prime of human life, men are to be disfranchised. And for what? For a political megrim, a freak—no evil is suggested.

The case is certainly very rare that a man under thirty is elected a member of the Senate. It will then be said, there is no privation, and, therefore, no injury. But, Sir, there is a wide difference between a man's being not elected, and a fundamental law stamping a stigma upon him by which he is excluded from the noblest privilege to which no merit or exertion on his part can restore him. But, all this, I suppose, is in obedience to the all-prevailing principle that *vox populi, vox dei;* aye, Sir, the all-prevailing principles that Numbers, and Numbers alone, are to regulate all things in political society, in the very teeth of those abstract natural rights of man which constitute the only shadow of claim to exercise this monstrous tyranny.

With these general remarks, permit me to attempt—I am afraid it will prove an abortive attempt—to say something on the observations of other gentlemen, to which I have given the most profound attention I am capable of. Sir, I have no other preparation for this task than a most patient attention to what has been said here, and in the Committee of which I was a member, and deep, intense, and almost annihilating thought on the subjects before us. This is all the preparation that I have made. I cannot follow the example which has been set me. I cannot go into the history of my past life, or defend my political consistency here or elsewhere. I will not do this for this reason: I have always held it unwise to plead 'til I am arraigned, and arraigned before a tribunal having competent and ample jurisdiction. My political consistency requires no such defence. My claim to Republicanism rests on no patent taken out yesterday, or to be taken out tomorrow. My life itself is my only voucher, a life spent for thirty years in the service of the most grateful of constituents.

The gentleman from Augusta, who occupies so large a space, both in the time and in the eye of the House, has told us that he fought gallantly by the side of his noble friend from Chesterfield, so long as victory was possible, and that it was not until he was conquered, that he grounded his arms. The gentleman further told us that, finding his native country and his early friends on this side the mountain, on whose behalf he had waged that gallant war—he found he hesitated what part to take *now,* until his constituents, aye, Sir—and more than that, his property, on the other side— and he has taken his course accordingly. Well, Sir, and will he not allow, on our part, that some consideration is due to our constituents, although they happen to be our neighbours, or to *our property,* although we reside upon it? Are either or both less dear on that account?

But, Sir, I put it to the Committee, whether the gentleman is not mistaken in point of fact? Whether the victory *is* indeed won? Every one, to be sure, is the best judge whether he is beaten or not. But, I put it to the gentleman himself, whether, if he were now fighting along side of his noble friend from Chesterfield, the scale might not possibly turn the other way? No man, however, is compelled to fight after he feels himself vanquished.

—Sir, I mean no ill-timed pleasantry, either as it regards the place where it is uttered, the person to whom it refers, and least of all, as it respects him by whom the remark is made, when I say that in this prudent resolution of the gentleman from Augusta he could not have been exceeded in caution and forecast by a certain renowned Captain Dugald Dalgetty himself. Sir, the war being ended, he takes service on the other side: the sceptre having passed from Judah, the gentleman stretches out his arm from Richmond to Rockfish Gap to intercept and clutch it in its passage.

Among various other observations with which he favoured the Committee, he protested with great earnestness against opinions relating to the Federal Government or its administration being introduced here. Sir, the gentleman is too great a lawyer not to know that the Federal Government is *our* Government: it is the Government of Virginia—and if a man were disposed to shut his eyes to the Constitution, and the administration of the Federal Government, he could not do it: they would be forced open, Sir, by the interests, and feelings, aye, and by the passions too, which have existed, do exist, and will continue to exist, as long as Virginia herself shall have existence.

It is not the least of my regrets that one of the most inevitable consequences of these changes, if they shall take effect, will be totally to change all the politics of Virginia in reference to the Federal Government—(without considering the hands in which it may happen to be placed)—and I do confidently believe that the very greatest cause of them is to be found in the hope of producing that all-desired change. In many cases I know it to exist, of my own personal knowledge.

Sir, we can't shut our eyes to the Federal Government.

When in 1788, the Convention of Virginia adopted the Federal Government as a part of her Constitution, they effected a greater change in our Constitution than the wildest reformer now suggests to us. To estimate the amount of that change we must have reference to her interests and power at that day; if not, we may call *ourselves* Statesmen, but the world will apply to us a very different epithet. Among innumerable causes why I now oppose a change is my full recollection of the change which was then brought about. I have by experience learned that changes, even in the ordinary law of the land, do not always operate as the drawer of the bill, or the Legislative body, may have anticipated: and of all the things in the world, a Government, whether ready made to suit casual customers or made per order, is the very last that operates as its framers intended. Governments are like revolutions: you may put them in motion, but I defy you to control them after they are *in* motion.

Sir, if there is any one thing clearer than another, it is that the Federal Constitution intended that the State Governments should issue no paper money; and by giving the Federal Government power *"to coin money"* it was intended to insure the result that this should be a hard money Government. And what is it? It is a paper-money Government. If this be the result, in spite of all precautions to the contrary —(Sir, this is no time, as the late illustrious President of the Court of Appeals was wont to say, to mince words)—and these Governments have turned out to be two most corrupt paper-money Governments, and you could not prevent it. How can we except now to define and limit the operation of new and untried principles? For new and untried they are, and if God lends me strength, I will prove it.

I have very high authority—the authority of the gentleman from Augusta—to say that the Federal Government was intended to be charged only with the external relations of the country; but, by a strange transformation, it has become the regulator, (abandoning the Colonial trade by negligence, or incapacity, or both, and crippling all our other trade), it has become the regulator of the interior of the country: its roads, its canals, and, more than that, of its productive, or rather, its *unproductive* labour—for they have made it so.

Yet, with these facts staring us in the face, we are gravely told not to look at the Federal Government at all. And this in the Government of Virginia, where, to use a very homely phrase, but one that exactly suits the case: we can't take a step without breaking our shins over some Federal obstacle.

Sir, I can readily see a very strong motive for wishing to do away with all past distinctions in politics, to obliterate the memory of old as well as of recent events, and once more to come with something like equal chances into the political lottery.

Let me return to my illustration. What provision is there, Mr. Chairman, either in the Constitution of Virginia or the Constitution of the United States, which establishes it as a principle that the Commonwealth of Virginia should be the sole restraining and regulating power on the mad and unconstitutional usurpations of the Federal Government? There is no such provision in either:—yet in practice and in fact, the Commonwealth of Virginia has been, to my certain knowledge, for more than thirty years, the sole counterpoise and check on the usurpations of the Federal Government— so far as they have checked at all: I wish they had been checked more effectually.

For a long time, our brethren of the South, because we were the frontier state of the great Southern division of the Union, were dead to considerations to which they have, I fear, awaked too late. Virginia was left alone and unsupported, unless by the feeble aid of her distant offspring, Kentucky. It is because I am unwilling to give up this check or to diminish its force, that I am unwilling to pull down the edifice of our State Government from the garret to the cellar, aye, down to the foundation stone. I will not put in hazard this single good for all the benefits the warmest advocate of reform can hope to derive from the results of this body.

The gentleman from Augusta told us, yesterday, I believe, or the day before, or the day before that—I really do not remember which—that slaves have always been a subject of taxation in Virginia, and that a long while ago, neat cattle had also been taxed. In regard to these horned cattle, I think they have occupied full as much attention as they are entitled to in this debate. But, let it be remembered, that we were then not taxing the cattle *of the West,* for there was no

West, but a few scattered settlements beyond the mountain; and what we have been discussing was the proportion
of taxes paid by the East and the West. No sooner was an
interest in this subject established beyond the mountains,
than the tax was laid aside. At that time, Sir, the Commonwealth of Virginia was throughout, a slave-holding Commonwealth: (would to God she were so now). And is it
then so wonderful that slaves should have been a subject of
taxation? Yes, Sir: Virginia was then not only throughout, a
slave-holding, but a tobacco-planting Commonwealth. You
can't open the Statute Book—I mean one of the old Statute
Books, not those that have been defaced by the finger of
reform—and not see that tobacco was, in fact, the currency
as well as staple of the State. We paid our clerks' fees in
tobacco; verdicts were given in tobacco; and bonds were
executed payable in tobacco. That accounts for it all. While
a large portion of the State has ceased to be a slave-holding,
and a still larger portion has ceased to be a tobacco-planting
community, the burden has rested on the necks of a comparatively small, unhappy, and I will say it, a proscribed
caste in the community. Not that any such effect was intended, when all were tobacco-planters, taxes on slaves and
tobacco were fair and equal. But time, the greatest of innovators, has silently operated to produce this great and
grinding oppression. My nativity cast my lot there. I am
one of them. I participate in all their interests and feelings.
And if I had been told, until I had the evidence of fact to
prove it, that one of the great slave-holding and tobacco-
planting districts would lend itself to the support of the
report of the Legislative Committee, unmitigated, or—to
use a term for which I am indebted to the gentleman from
Spottsylvania—*unmollified,* or *undulcified* by anything to

give it a wholesome operation, I would not have believed it. Nothing but ocular and auricular demonstration would have made me believe it possible. For my part, I had not only, as the gentleman from Chesterfield has said, never have been born, but, being born, and grown up as I am, it were better for me that a mill-stone were hanged about my neck and I cast into the uttermost depths of the sea, than to return to my constituents after having given a naked vote for the report of the Committee.

Sir, when I speak of danger, from what quarter does it come? From whom? From the corn and oat growers on the Eastern Shore, the Rappahannock and the Pamunkey? From the fishermen on the Chesapeake? The pilots of Elizabeth City? No, Sir—from ourselves—from the great slave-holding and tobacco-planting districts of the State. I could not have brought myself to believe it—nothing could have persuaded me to believe, that the real danger which threatens this great interest should spring from those districts themselves. And, arrogant and presumptuous as it may appear in me, (these epithets have been applied to us by the gentleman from Augusta), I will risk any thing short of my eternal salvation on the fact that when the people of that region come to understand the real question, you will as soon force ratsbane down their throats as a Constitution with such a principle in it.

The gentleman from Augusta told us, yesterday, or the day before—I cannot be certain as to the precise day—with some appearance as if it were a grievance, that the people had interfered; and he asked if we are to be instructed out of our seats? I answer: yes. Such as cannot be instructed *in* their seats must be instructed *out* of their seats. He says the voices of the people from county meetings and crossroads and taverns will come here and interrupt the harmony of our deliberations.

I trust they will. Though the people have hitherto been supine, on this side the mountains, I trust they will take the matter into their own hands. I hope they are beginning to rouse from their torpor: and I know it. I will state one fact, to show that the current of public sentiment is fast setting in on our side. I do not say whether it was for or against us before. I have heard, not one, not ten, not fifty, (and when I say not fifty, I mean not less but more than that number), of intelligent men declare that, if by any possibility, they could have foreseen (poor innocents) that such were to be the results, they never would have voted for this Convention. In the mean while, not a single convert has been made from our cause; if there has, name the man. I could name ten, twenty, aye, fifty; and if I were to resort to documentary evidence, I could name more. So far am I from being one of those who wish to precipitate the question, I am glad, I rejoice in the prospect, that our Session will run into that of the Virginia Assembly. In politics, I am always for getting the last advices. You can never get at the true temper of the public mind 'til the occasion presents itself for decisive action.

I have made, and shall make, no disclaimer of having intended offence to any person or party in this body—and this for the same reason I before stated. I never will plead 'til I am arraigned by a competent tribunal, and the disclaimer would be misplaced. Gentlemen on all sides have spoken of the *intention* with which they are demanding power, (for the gentleman from Augusta lifted the veil and owned to us that power, and power alone, is the object he is in pursuit of). Sir, I mean no disrespect when I say, that however important it may be to themselves, to me it is a matter of perfect indifference—I speak in reference to the operation of their measures—whether their intents be wicked or charitable. I say, the demand which they make is such as ought to alarm every considerate and forethoughted man; and that there is nothing to mitigate that alarm in the stern, unrelenting, inexorable, remorseless cry which they raise for power, and their determination to listen to no compromise. One gentleman, indeed, has abated somewhat of his tone of triumph. Perhaps, the prospect of speedy enjoyment has claimed his exultation and sobered him down.

Mr. Chairman, since I have been here, the scene has recalled many old recollections. At one time I thought myself in the House of Representatives, listening to the debate on the Tariff; at another time, I imagined myself listening to the debate on the Missouri Question; and sometimes I fancied myself listening to both questions debated at once. Are we men? met to consult about the affairs of men? Or are we, in truth, a Robinhood Society discussing rights in the abstract? Have we no house over our heads? Do we forget that we are living under a Constitution which has shielded us for more than half a century?—that we are not a parcel of naked and forlorn savages on the shores of New Holland; and that the worst that can come is that we shall live under the same Constitution that we have lived under, freely and happily, for half a century? To their monstrous claims of power, we plead this prescription; but then we are told: *nullum tempus occurrit Regi.* King whom? King Numbers. And they will not listen to a prescription of fifty-four years—a period greater by four years than would secure a title to the best estate in the Commonwealth, unsupported by any other shadow of right. Nay, Sir, in this case, prescription operates *against* possession. They tell us it is only a case of long-continued, and therefore of aggravated, injustice. They say to us, in words the most courteous and soft— but I am not so soft as to swallow them—"we shall be—we will be—we must be your masters, and you shall submit." To whom do they hold this language? To dependents? weak, unprotected, and incapable of defence? Or is it to the great tobacco-growing and slave-holding interest, and to every other interest on this side the Ridge? "We are numbers, you have property." I am not so obtuse as to require any further explanation on this head. "We are numbers, you have property." Sir, I understand it perfectly.

Mr. Chairman, since the days of the French Revolution, when the Duke of Orleans, who was the richest subject not only in France but in all Europe, lent himself to the *mountain* party in the Convention, in the vain and weak hope of grasping political power, perhaps of mounting the throne— still slippery with the blood of the last incumbent—from that day to this, so great a degree of infatuation has not been shown by any individual as by the tobacco-grower and slave-holder of Virginia who shall lend his aid to rivet this yoke on the necks of his brethren, and on his own. Woe betide that man! Even the Duke of Orleans himself, profligate and reprobate as he was, would have halted in his course had he foreseen in the end, his property confiscated to the winds, and his head in the sack of the executioner.

I enter into no calculations of my own, for I have made none, nor shall I follow the example which has been set me. I leave that branch of the argument, if argument it can be called, of the gentleman from Augusta, to be answered by himself.

The gentleman told us, the day before yesterday, that in

fifteen minutes of the succeeding day, he would conclude all he had to say; and he then kept us two hours, not by the Shrewsbury clock, but by as good a watch as can be made in the city of London. *(Drawing out and opening his watch.)* As fifteen minutes are to two hours in the proportion of one to eight, such is the approximation to truth in the gentleman's calculations. If all the calculations and promises of the gentleman from Augusta, which he held out to gull us— I speak not of his intentions, but only of the effect that would have ensued—shall be no nearer the truth than these, where then should we be who trust them?

In the course of what I fear will be thought my very wearisome observations, I spoke of the Tariff Law. When the people of the United States threw off their allegiance to Great Britain, and established Republican Governments here, whether State or Federal, one discovery since made in politics had not yet entered into the head of any man in the Union, which, if not arrested by the good sense and patriotism of the country, will destroy all Republican Government as certainly and inevitably as time will one day destroy us. That discovery is this: that a bare majority—(the majority on the Tariff was, I believe, but two—my friend behind me [Mr. P. P. Barbour] tells me that I am right—and on one important branch of that law, that, I mean, which relates to cotton bagging, the majority was but one, and *that* consisted of the casting vote of the Speaker)—that a bare majority may oppress, harass, and plunder the minority at pleasure, but that it is their interest to keep up the minority to the highest possible point consistent with their subjugation, because, the larger that minority shall be, in proportion to the majority, by that same proportion are the profits of the majority enhanced, which they have extracted and ex-torted from the minority. And after all our exclamations against this crying oppression; after all our memorials and remonstrances; after all our irrefragable arguments against it—(I refer not to the share I had in them; I speak of the arguments of other gentlemen, and not of my own)—shall we in Virginia introduce this deadly principle into our own Government? and give power to a bare majority to tax us *ad libitum,* and that when the strongest temptation is at the same time held out to them to do it? It is now a great while since I learned from the philosopher of Malmesbury that a state of nature is a state of war; but if we sanction this principle, we shall prove that a state, not of nature, but of society, and of Constitutional Government, is a state of interminable war. And it will not stop here. Instructed by this most baneful, yes, and most baleful example, we shall next have one part of a county conspiring to throw their share of the burden of the levy upon the other part. Sir, if there is a destructive principle in politics, it is that which is maintained by the gentleman from Augusta.

But we are told we are to have a stay of execution. "We will give you time," say the gentlemen: "only give us a bond binding all your estate, secured by a deed of trust on all your slaves." Why, Sir, there is not a hard-hearted Shylock in the Commonwealth who will not, on such conditions, give you time. Are we so weak that, like the spend-thrift who runs to the usurer, we are willing to encounter this calamity because it is not to come upon us 'til the year 1856? a period not as long as some of us have been in public life? Sir, I would not consent to it if it were not to come 'til the year 2056! I am at war with the principle! Let me not be told that I am at war with the Bill of Rights. I subscribe to every word in the Bill of Rights. I need not show how this

can be. It has been better done already by the gentleman
from Spottsylvania (Mr. Stanard), to whom I feel personally indebted as a tobacco-planter and a slave-holder, for
the speech he has made. The Bill of Rights contains unmodified principles. The declarations it contains are our lights
and guides, but when we come to apply these great principles, we must modify them for use; we must set limitations
to their operation, and the enquiry then is *quousque?* How
far? It is a question not of principle but of degree. The very
moment this immaculate principle of theirs is touched, it
becomes what all principles are: materials in the hands of
men of sense, to be applied to the welfare of the Commonwealth. It is not an incantation. It is no Talisman. It is not
witchcraft. It is not a torpedo to benumb us. If the naked
principle of numbers only is to be followed, the requisites
for the Statesman fall far below what the gentleman from
Spottslyvania rated them at. He needs not the four rules of
arithmetic. No, Sir, a negro boy with a knife and a tally-
stick is a Statesman complete in this school. Sir, I do not
scoff, jeer or flout—(I use, I think, the very words of the
gentleman from Augusta; two of them certainly were employed by him)—at the principles of the Bill of Rights, and
so help me Heaven, I have not heard of any who did. But I
hold with one of the greatest masters of political philosophy,
that "no rational man ever did govern himself by abstractions and universals. I do not put abstract ideas wholly out
of any question, because I know well that under that name
I should dismiss principles; and that without the guide and
light of sound, well understood principles, all reasonings in
politics, as in every thing else, would be only a confused
jumble of particular facts and details, without the means of
drawing out any sort of theoretical or practical conclusion.

"A Statesman differs from a Professor in a University. The latter has only the general view of society; the former, the Statesman, has a number of circumstances to combine with those general ideas, and to take into his consideration. Circumstances are infinite, are infinitely combined, are variable and transient: he who does not take them into consideration is not erroneous, but stark mad—*dat operam ut cum ratione insanat*—he is metaphysically mad. A Statesman, never losing sight of principles, is to be guided by circumstances, and judging contrary to the exigencies of the moment, he may ruin his country forever."

Yes, Sir—and after that ruin has been effected, what a poor consolation is derived from being told, "I had not thought it". *Stulti est dixisse non putaram.* "Who would have thought it?" "Lord bless me! I never thought of such a thing, or I never would have voted for a Convention".

If there is any country on earth where circumstances have a more important bearing than in another, it is here, in Virginia. Nearly half the population are in bondage—yes, Sir, more than half in the country below the Ridge. And is this no circumstance? Yet, let me say with the gentleman from Accomac (Mr. Joynes), whose irresistible array of figures set all figures of speech at defiance, that if there were not a negro in Virginia, I would still contend for the principle in the amendment. And why? Because I will put it in the power of no man or set of men who ever lived, or who ever shall live, to tax me without my consent. It is wholly immaterial whether this is done without my having any representation at all, or, as it was done in the case of the Tariff Law, by a phalanx stern and inexorable who, being the majority, and having the power, prescribe to me the law that I shall obey. Sir, what was it to all the Southern interest that we came within two votes of defeating that iniquitous measure? Do not our adversaries, (for adversaries they are), know that they have the power? and that we must submit? Yes, Sir. This whole slave-holding country, the whole of it, from the Potomac to Mexico, was placed under the ban and anathema of a majority of two! And will you introduce such a principle into your own State Government? Sir, at some times during this debate I doubted if I were in my right mind. From the beginning of time 'til now, there is no case to be found of a rational and moral people subverting a Constitution under which they had lived for half a century—aye, for two centuries, by a majority of *one*. When revolutions have happened in other countries, it was the effect of a political storm, a Levanter, a tornado, to which all opposition was fruitless. But did any body ever hear of a revolution affecting the entire condition of one half of a great State being effected by a majority of one? Did it ever enter the head of the wildest visionary, from the days of Peter the Hermit to—a day I will not name—to accomplish a revolution by a majority of *one?* Sir, to change your constitution by such a majority is nothing more than to sound the tocsin for a civil war. It may be at first a war of words, a weaponless war, but it is one of those cases in which, as the lawyers tell us, fury supplies arms. Sir, this thing cannot be: it must not be. I was about to say, it *shall* not be. I tell gentlemen now, with the most perfect deliberation and calmness, that we cannot submit to this outrage on our rights. It surpasses that measure of submission and forebearance which is due from every member of an organized Government to that Government. And why do I so tell them? Sir, we are not a company of naked savages on the coast of New Holland, or Van Diemans Land. We have a Government; we have rights; and do you think that we shall tamely submit, and let you deprive us of our vested rights, and reduce us to bondage? Yes, vested rights! that we shall let you impose on us a yoke hardly lighter than that of the *villeins regardant* of the manor? We are now little better than the trustees of slave-labour for the nabobs of the East, and of the North (if there be any such persons in our country), and to the speculators of the West. They regulate our labour. Are we to have *two* masters? When every vein has been sluiced— when our whole system presents nothing but one pitiful enchymosis—are we to be patted and tapped to find yet another vein to breathe, not for the Federal Government, but for our own? Why, Sir, the richest man in Virginia, be that man who he may, would make a good bargain to make you a present of his estate, provided you give him a bond upon that estate allowing him to tax it as he pleases, and to spend the money as he pleases. It is of the very essence of property that none shall tax it but the owner himself, or one who has a common feeling and interest with him. It does not require a plain planter to tell an Assembly like this, more than half of whose members are gentlemen of the law, that no man may set his foot on your land without your permission but as a trespasser, and that he renders himself liable to an action for damages. This is of the very essence of property. But, he says, "thank you, for nothing, with all my heart, I don't mean to set my foot on your land, but, not owning one foot of land myself, I will stand here in the highway, which is as free to me as it is to you, and I will tax your land, not to your heart's content but to *mine,* and spend the proceeds as I please. I cannot enter upon it myself, but I will send the Sheriff of the county, and he shall enter upon it, and do what I cannot do in my own person."

Sir, is this to be endured? It is not to be endured. And unless I am ignorant of the character and feelings and—what is dearer to me than all—the prejudices of the people of the lower country, it will not be endured. You may as well adjourn *sine die*. We are too old birds to be taken with chaff, or else we are not old enough: I don't know which. We will not give up this question for the certainty, and far less for the hope, that the evil will be rectified in the other branch of the Legislature. We know, every body knows, that it is impossible. Why, Sir, the British House of Peers, which contains four hundred members, holding a vast property, much more now, it is true, than when Chatham said they were but as a drop in the ocean compared with the wealth of the Commons: If they, holding their seats for life, and receiving and transmitting them by hereditary descent, have never been able to resist the House of Commons in any measure on which that House chose to insist, do you believe that twenty-four gentlemen upstairs can resist one hundred and twenty below? especially when the one hundred and twenty represent their own districts, and are to go home with them to their common constituents? Sir, the case has never yet happened, I believe, when a Senator has been able to resist the united delegation from his district in the lower House.

Mr. Chairman, I am a practical man. I go for solid security, and I never will, knowingly, take any other. But, if the security on which I have relied is insufficient, and my property is in danger, it is better that I should know it in time, and I may prepare to meet the consequences while it is yet called today, than to rest on a security that is fallacious and deceptive. Sir, I would not give you a button for your mixed basis in the Senate. Give up this question, and I have

nothing more to lose. This is the entering wedge, and every
thing else must follow. We are told, indeed, that we must
rely on a restriction of the Right of Suffrage; but, gentlemen,
know, that after you shall have adopted the report of the
Select Committee, you can place no restriction upon it.
When this principle is in operation, the waters are out. It is
as if you would ask an industrious and sagacious Hollander*
that you may cut his dykes, provided you make your cut
only of a certain width. A rat hole will let in the ocean. Sir,
there is an end to the security of all property in the Commonwealth, and he will be unwise who shall not abandon the
ship to the underwriters. It is the first time in my life that I
ever heard of a Government which was to divorce property
from power. Yet this is seriously and soberly proposed to
us. Sir, I know it is practicable, but it can be done only by
a violent divulsion, as in France, but the moment you have
separated the two, that very moment property will go in
search of power, and power in search of property. "Male
and female created He them;" and the two sexes do not more
certainly, nor by a more unerring law, gravitate to each
other, than power and property. You can only cause them
to change hands. I could almost wish, indeed, for the ac-
commodation of the gentleman from Augusta, that God had
ordained it otherwise; but so it is, and so it is obliged to be.
It is of the nature of man. Man always has been in society—
we always find him in possession of property, and with a
certain appetite for it which leads him to seek it, if not *per
fas,* sometimes *per nefas;* and hence the need of laws to protect it, and to punish its invaders.

---

* Looking to the Chevalier Huygens, the Dutch Minister, who was
present.

But I am subjecting myself, I know, to a most serious reproach. It will be said that I am not a friend to the poor. Sir, the gentleman from Chesterfield and the gentleman from Spottsylvania have dealt with the "friends of the people" to my entire satisfaction. I wish to say a word now as to the "friends of the poor." Whenever I see a man, especially a rich man, endeavouring to rise and to acquire consequence in society by standing out as the especial champion of the poor, I am always reminded of an old acquaintance of mine, one Señor Manuel Ordonez, who made a comfortable living, and amassed an opulent fortune by administering the funds of the poor. Among the strange notions which have been broached since I have been on the political theatre, there is one which has lately seized the minds of men: that all things must be done for them by the Government, and that they are to do nothing for themselves. The Government is not only to attend to the great concerns which are its province, but it must step in and ease individuals of their natural and moral obligations. A more pernicious notion cannot prevail. Look at that ragged fellow staggering from the whiskey shop, and see that slattern who has gone there to reclaim him; where are their children? Running about, ragged, idle, ignorant, fit candidates for the penitentiary. Why is all this so? Ask the man and he will tell you, "Oh, the Government has undertaken to educate our children for us. It has given us a premium for idleness, and I now spend in liquor what I should otherwise be obliged to save to pay for their schooling. My neighbor there, that is so hard at work in his field yonder with his son, can't spare that boy to attend, except in the winter months, the school which he is taxed to support for mine. He has to scuffle hard to make both ends meet at the end of the year, and keep the wolf from the door. His children can't go to this school, yet he has to pay a part of the tax to maintain it." Sir, is it like friends of the poor to absolve them from what Nature, what God himself has made their first and most sacred duty? For the education of their children is the first and most obvious duty of every parent, and one which the worthless alone are ever known wholly to neglect.

Mr. Chairman, these will be deemed, I fear, unconnected thoughts; but they have been the aliment of my mind for years. Rumination and digestion can do no more; they are thoroughly concocted.

In the course of not a short or uneventful life, I have had correspondence with various persons in all parts of the Union, and I have seen gentlemen on their return from the North and East, as well as from the new States of the West; and I have never heard from any of them but one expression of opinion as it related to us in Virginia. It was in the sentiment, if not in the language of Virgil: Oh, fortunate, if we knew our own blessedness. They advise us with one voice, "Stick to what you have got; stick to your Constitution; stick to your Right of Suffrage. Don't give up your freehold representation. We have seen enough of the opposite system, and too much." I have received and seen letters breathing this spirit from men who dare not promulgate such a sentiment at home because it would only destroy their hopes of usefulness—from North Carolina, from South Carolina, from Georgia, from Alabama, from Pennsylvania, and from New York.

Sir, the day, come when it may, which sees this old and venerable fabric of ours scattered in ruins, and the mattock and the spade digging the foundation for a new political edifice, will be a day of jubilee to all those who have been, and who must be, in conflict with those principles which have given to Virginia her weight and consequence, both at home and abroad. If I understand aright the plans which are in agitation, I had sooner the day should arrive that must close my eyes forever, than witness their accomplishment. Yes, Sir, to this Constitution we owe all that we have preserved —(much I know is lost, and of great value)—but all that we have preserved from the wreck of our political fortunes. This is the mother which has reared all our great men. Well may she be called *magna mater virum*. She has, indeed, produced men, and mighty men.

But, I am told, that so far is this from being true, we have been living for fifty-four years under a Government which has no manner of authority, and is a mere usurpation at best. Yet, Sir, during that time, we have changed our Government; and I call the attention of this body to the manner in which that change was made. The Constitution of '88 was submitted to the people, and a Convention was called to ratify it, and what was that Convention? It was the old House of Burgesses with a nickname—the old House of Delegates, Sir, with a nickname—in which the same municipal divisions of the State were regarded—the same qualifications required—the same qualified freeholders were returned from the same districts and by the same sheriffs—and yet, by the waving of a magic wand, they were converted into a Convention in which Warwick was made equal with Culpeper, then by far the largest county in the State. Do not gentlemen see where the point of their own argument leads to? If it is a *sine qua non* of a legitimate Government that it must have the assent of a majority of the people told by the head, then is the Federal Government an usurpation to which the people *per capita*—King Numbers—has never given his assent.

It is now thought necessary to have another Convention, and what is it? It is nothing but the Senate of Virginia, elected from the same districts, by the same voters, and returned by the same sheriffs—many of them the self-same men; yet when multiplied by four, by talismanic touch they become a Convention. Yes, Sir. You can't trust the House of Delegates and Senate with your affairs, but you can trust a smaller body. You can't trust the whole, but you can trust a part. You can't trust the Senate, but you can trust the same men from the same districts if multiplied by four. Sir, are we men? Or are we children?

For my share, this is the first Convention in which I ever had a seat; and I trust in God it will be the last. I never had any taste for Conventions; or for new Constitutions made per order, or kept ready made to suit casual customers. I need not tell *you,* Sir, that I was not a member of the Staunton Convention. No, Sir, nor was I a member of the Harrisburg Convention—nor the Charlottesville Convention. No, Sir, nor the anti-Jackson Convention—though I had the honour (in very good company) of being put to the ban and anathema of that august Assembly—and when, to their very great surprise and alarm, we returned their fire, they scattered like a flock of wild geese.

Mr. Chairman, the wisest thing this body could do, would be to return to the people from whom they came, *re infecta.* I am very willing to lend my aid to any very small and moderate reforms which I can be made to believe that this our ancient Government requires. But, far better would it be that they were never made, and that our Constitution remained unchangeable like that of Lycurgus, than that we should break in upon the main pillars of the edifice.

Sir, I have exhausted myself, and tried you. I am physically unable to recall or to express the few thoughts I brought with me to this Assembly. Sir, that great master of the human heart, who seemed to know it as well as if he had made it, I mean Shakespeare—when he brings before our eyes an old and feeble monarch, not only deserted, but oppressed by his own pampered and ungrateful offspring, describes him as finding solace and succour, only in his discarded and disinherited child. If this, our venerable parent, must perish, deal the blow who will, it shall never be given by my hand. I will avert it if I can, and if I cannot, in the sincerity of my heart I declare, I am ready to perish with it. Yet, as the gentleman from Spottsylvania says, I am no candidate for martyrdom. I am too old a man to remove; my associations, my habits, and my property, nail me to the Commonwealth. But, were I a young man, I would, in case this monstrous tyranny shall be imposed upon us, do what a few years ago I should have thought parricidal. I would withdraw from your jurisdiction. I would not live under King Numbers. I would not be his steward, nor make him my taskmaster. I would obey the principle of self-preservation, a principle we find even in the brute creation, in flying from this mischief.

A Randolph Chronology

June 2, 1773. John Randolph born at Cawsons, Virginia, near the mouth of the Appomattox.

January 3, 1781. Flight of Mrs. Tucker and her children from the British under Arnold.

1787. Randolph at Princeton.

1788–89. Randolph at Columbia College.

1790–91. Randolph studies law under Edmund Randolph.

December, 1799. Randolph enters Congress.

December, 1801. Randolph assumes leadership of the majority in the House of Representatives.

January 29, 1805. Randolph commences his denunciation of the Yazoo scandal.

February 9, 1805. Randolph prosecutes Justice Chase.

December, 1805. Randolph quarrels with Jefferson and Madison over the projected purchase of Florida from France.

March 5, 1806. Randolph's speech against Gregg's Resolution.

April, 1806. Randolph denounces the Florida negotiations and the Yazoo men and breaks with the Jeffersonians.

May, 1807. Randolph foreman of the grand jury in the case of Aaron Burr.

December 10, 1811. Randolph's speech against war with England.

April, 1813. Randolph loses his seat in Congress.

April, 1815. Randolph regains his seat in the House.

January, 1816. Randolph attacks the Bank of the United States. He debates with Calhoun on the revenue bill.

February, 1820. Randolph opposes the Missouri Compromise.

March–November, 1822. Randolph's first visit to England.

January, 1824. Randolph speaks on the Greek question and against internal improvements.

April, 1824. Randolph opposes the tariff of 1824.

December 17, 1825. Randolph elected by the Virginia legislature to the Senate.

April, 1826. Randolph's speech on the Panama Mission and his consequent duel with Clay.

May–November, 1826. Randolph's third trip abroad, to England, Holland, and France.

January, 1827. Randolph defeated for the Senate.

April, 1827. Randolph elected to the House of Representatives.

1828. Randolph supports Jackson for the presidency.

March, 1829. Randolph retires from Congress.

December 30, 1829. Randolph's speech on change at the Virginia Convention.

May 1830–autumn, 1831. Randolph serves as minister to Russia.

February, 1833. Randolph denounces Jackson for his proclamation against South Carolina.

May 24, 1833. Randolph dies in Philadelphia.

A Select Bibliography

The following list consists of works cited in the text, books and articles touching directly upon Randolph, and the principal collections of manuscripts. It does not include standard histories of the United States, nor the latest editions of the papers of certain of Randolph's contemporaries—publication of some of these last not being complete in 1978.

Manuscripts

ELLIS-MUNFORD PAPERS. Duke University Library.

JAMES M. GARNETT PAPERS. Duke University Library.

NATHANIEL MACON PAPERS. North Carolina State Department of Archives and History.

JOHN P. MATTHEWS PAPERS. Duke University Library.

JOHN RANDOLPH LETTERS (copies). University of North Carolina Library.

JOHN RANDOLPH PAPERS. Virginia State Library (collected by William Cabell Bruce).

JOHN RANDOLPH PAPERS, AND ASSOCIATED PAPERS. Alderman Library, University of Virginia. (This is much the largest collection.)

RICHARD STANFORD PAPERS. North Carolina State Department of Archives and History.

JOHN TAYLOR PAPERS. Duke University Library.

HENRY ST. GEORGE TUCKER PAPERS. Duke University Library.

The Library of Congress possesses many of Randolph's early letters, and most of his correspondence with Monroe, Jackson, and other political leaders.

Other manuscripts may be found scattered across the country: the University of California, the Huntington Library, Yale University, the National Archives, the Missouri Historical Society, the Maine Historical Society, the Maryland Historical Society, the New York Historical Society, Princeton University, the New York Public Library, the University of Rochester, the Pennsylvania Historical Society, the Virginia Historical Society, Randolph-Macon Women's College, and Colonial Williamsburg, Inc. Probably some unexamined Randolph letters remain in private hands, though many have been destroyed; certainly many of those printed in the biographies by Garland and by Bruce can be found nowhere today.

An admirable guide to these papers exists: *The Papers of Randolph of Roanoke, a Preliminary Checklist of His Surviving Texts in Manuscript and in Print,* by William E. Stokes, Jr., and Francis L. Berkeley, Jr. (University of Virginia Library, 1950). This includes all of Randolph's letters, speeches, and other writings, whether printed or in manuscript, known to exist in 1950—with the exception of his speeches at the Virginia Convention of 1829–30, inadvertently omitted.

Newspapers

Niles' Weekly Register. Various dates.
Richmond Enquirer. 1804–33.
Virginia Argus. 1800–33.

Printed Documents

Abridgement of the Debates of Congress, 1797–1833. Compiled by Thomas Hart Benton. New York, 1860.
American State Papers. Class VIII: Public Lands, Vol. I. Washington, D.C., 1833.
Annals of Congress: Fifth Congress, First Session—Eighteenth Congress, First Session. Washington, D.C., 1851.
Proceedings and Debates of the Virginia State Convention of 1829–30. Richmond, 1830.
Register of Debates in Congress, 1824–37. Washington, D.C., 1825–37.

Periodical Articles

ANON. "The Grave of John Randolph." *Littell's Living Age,* XIV (October, 1846), 195.

ANON. "John Randolph's Case: Dr. Parrish's Deposition." *Littell's Living Age,* XV (October, 1847), 153–56.

BOULDIN, POWHATAN. "John Randolph of Roanoke: Recollections and Unpublished Letters," *Century Magazine,* LI (March, 1896), 712–18.

CAPERS, GERALD M. "A Reconsideration of John C. Calhoun's Transition from Nationalism to Nullification." *Journal of Southern History,* XIV (February, 1948), 34–48.

COLEMAN, MARY HALDANE. "Whittier on John Randolph of Roanoke." *New England Quarterly,* VIII (December, 1935), 551–54.

GREGORY, HORACE. "Our Writers and the Democratic Myth." *The Bookman,* LXXV (August, 1932), 377–82.

GRIGSBY, HUGH BLAIR. "The Library of John Randolph." *Southern Literary Messenger,* XX (February, 1854), 79–82.

HONEYWELL, ROY J. "President Jefferson and his Successor." *American Historical Review,* XLVI (October, 1940), 64–75.

KIRK, RUSSELL. "John Randolph of Roanoke on the Genius of Edmund Burke." *The Burke Newsletter,* IV (Fall, 1962), 167–69.

OGDEN, H. V. S. "The Decline of Lockian Political Authority in England." *American Historical Review,* XLVI (October, 1940), 21–44.

RANDOLPH, JOHN. "Pickings from a Portfolio of Autobiography: Two MSS. Letters of John Randolph." *Southern Literary Messenger,* XXIII (November, 1836), 379–85.

SANFORD, WILLIAM. "John Randolph of Roanoke." *Scott's Monthly Magazine,* II (August, 1866), 187–88.

TUCKER, NATHANIEL BEVERLEY. "Account of John Randolph." *Historical Magazine,* III (June, 1859), 187–88.

———. "Correspondence of Judge Tucker." *William and Mary College Quarterly Historical Magazine,* XII (October, 1903), 84–95.

———. "Garland's Life of Randolph." *Southern Quarterly Review,* IV (new ser.; July, 1851), 41–46.

———. "Manuscripts of John Randolph." *Southern Literary Messenger,* II (July, 1836), 461–64.

Books, Pamphlets, and Unpublished Dissertations

ADAMS, HENRY. *History of the United States of America during the Administrations of Jefferson and Madison.* 9 vols. New York, 1891–98.

———. *John Randolph.* Boston and New York, 1882.

———. *The Writings of Albert Gallatin.* 3 vols. Philadelphia, 1879.

ADAMS, JOHN. *Works.* Edited by C. F. Adams. 10 vols. Boston, 1851.

ADAMS, JOHN QUINCY. *Memoirs of John Quincy Adams.* Edited by Charles Francis Adams. 12 vols. Philadelphia, 1874–77.

———. *The Writings of John Quincy Adams.* Edited by W. C. Ford. 7 vols. New York, 1913–17.

AMBLER, CHARLES HENRY. *Sectionalism in Virginia from 1776 to 1861.* Chicago, 1910.

———. *Thomas Ritchie: A Study in Virginia Politics.* Richmond, 1913.

BALDWIN, JOSEPH GLOVER. *Party Leaders.* New York, 1855.

BEARD, CHARLES A. *The Economic Origins of Jeffersonian Democracy.* New York, 1915.

BECKER, CARL. *The Declaration of Independence: A Study in the History of Political Ideas.* New York, 1922.

BEMIS, SAMUEL FLAGG. *John Quincy Adams and the Foundations of American Foreign Policy.* New York, 1950.

———. *John Quincy Adams and the Union.* New York, 1956.

BENTON, THOMAS HART. *Thirty Years' View; or, a History of the Working of the American Government for Thirty Years, from 1820 to 1850.* 2 vols. New York, 1854.

BEVERIDGE, ALBERT J. *The Life of John Marshall.* 4 vols. Boston, 1916.

BLAND, THEODORICK. *The Bland Papers.* 2 vols. Edited by Campbell. Petersburg, Va., 1840–43.

BOULDIN, POWHATAN. *Home Reminiscences of John Randolph of Roanoke.* Richmond, 1837.

BOWERS, CLAUDE. *Jefferson in Power.* New York, 1937.

BRACKENBRIDGE, HUGH HENRY. *Modern Chivalry.* Edited by Claude Newlin. New York, 1937.

BRADFORD, GAMALIEL. *Damaged Souls.* New York, 1922.

BRANT, IRVING. *James Madison.* 6 vols. Indianapolis, 1941–61.

BROWNSON, ORESTES. *Orestes Brownson: Selected Essays.* Edited by Russell Kirk. Chicago, 1955.

—. *The Writings of James Monroe.* Edited by S. M. Hamilton. 7 vols. New York, 1898–1903.

ЗЕ, EUGENE TENBROECK. *The Social Philosophy of John Taylor of Caroline: A Study in Jeffersonian Democracy.* New York, 1939.

s, JOSEPH HOWARD. *Felix Grundy, Champion of Democracy.* University, La., 1940.

INGTON, VERNON L. *The Romantic Revolution in America, 1800–1860.* New York, 1927.

ON, JAMES. *Famous Americans of Recent Times.* Boston, 1867.

IPS, ULRICH B. *American Negro Slavery.* New York, 1918.

E, BENJ. PERLEY. *Perley's Reminiscences of Sixty Years in the National Metropolis.* 2 vols. Philadelphia, 1886.

I, JULIUS W. *The Expansionists of 1812.* New York, 1925.

CY, EDMUND. *Life of Josiah Quincy of Massachusetts.* Boston, 1867.

CY, JOSIAH. *Figures of the Past.* Boston, 1901.

OLPH, JOHN. *Letters of John Randolph to a Young Relative: Embracing a Series of Years, from Early Youth, to Mature Manhood.* Edited by Theodore Dudley. Philadelphia, 1834.

NEL, MRS. ST. JULIEN. *Life and Times of William Lowndes, of South Carolina, 1783–1822.* Boston, 1901.

RD, NORMAN K. *The Old Republicans: Southern Conservatism in the Age of Jackson.* New York, 1965.

, RICHARD. *John Randolph at Home and Abroad.* Philadelphia, 1828.

YANA, GEORGE. *Reason in Society.* New York, 1905.

ER, LEMUEL. *A Biography of John Randolph of Roanoke.* New York, 1844.

s, HENRY HARRISON. *John Taylor of Caroline: The Story of a Brilliant Leader in the Early Virginia State Rights School.* Richmond, 1932.

I, PAGE. *John Adams.* 2 vols. New York, 1963.

, AUGUST O. *The Political Theory of John C. Calhoun.* New York, 1951.

IS, PETER. *Edmund Burke and the Natural Law.* Foreword by Russell Kirk. Ann Arbor, Mich., 1958.

s, WILLIAM E., JR. "The Early Life of John Randolph of Roanoke, 1773–1794." Master's thesis, University of Virginia, 1950.

BRUCE, PHILIP A. *John Randolph* ("Library of Southern Literature," Vol. X). Atlanta, 1907.

———. *The Virginia Plutarch.* 2 vols. Chapel Hill, N.C., 1929.

BRUCE, WILLIAM CABELL. *Below the James.* Boston, 1937.

———. *John Randolph of Roanoke.* 2 vols. New York, 1922.

BURKE, EDMUND. *Works.* 8 vols. London, 1857.

CALHOUN, JOHN C. *Calhoun: Basic Documents.* Edited by John M. Anderson. State College, Pa., 1952.

———. *The Papers of John C. Calhoun.* 10 vols. Columbia, S.C., 1959–77.

———. *Works.* Edited by R. K. Crallé. 6 vols. New York, 1853–55.

CANAVAN, FRANCIS. *The Political Reason of Edmund Burke.* Durham, N.C., 1960.

CARPENTER, JESSE T. *The South as a Conscious Minority, 1789–1861.* New York, 1930.

CHAPMAN, GERALD W. *Edmund Burke: The Practical Imagination.* Cambridge, Mass., 1967.

CHINARD, GILBERT. *Thomas Jefferson: The Apostle of Americanism.* Boston, 1928.

COIT, MARGARET C. *John C. Calhoun, American Portrait.* Boston, 1950.

COLEMAN, MARY HALDANE. *St. George Tucker, Citizen of No Mean City.* Richmond, 1938.

CONWAY MONCURE DANIEL. *Omitted Chapters of History Disclosed in the Life and Papers of Edmund Randolph.* New York, 1888.

COOPER, JAMES FENIMORE. *The American Democrat.* Cooperstown, N.Y., 1837.

———. *Sketches in Switzerland.* 2 vols. New York, 1836.

COOPER, THOMAS. *Lectures on the Elements of Political Economy.* Columbia, S.C., 1826.

CRAIGHILL, ROBERT T. *The Virginia "Peerage"; or Sketches of Virginians Distinguished in Virginia's History.* Richmond, 1880.

DABNEY, RICHARD HEATH. *John Randolph: A Character Sketch.* Chicago, 1898.

DAVIDSON, DONALD. *The Attack on Leviathan: Regionalism and Nationalism in the United States.* Chapel Hill, N.C., 1938.

DAVIS, RICHARD BEALE. *Francis Walker Gilmer: Life and Learning in Jefferson's Virginia.* Richmond, 1939.

DODD, WILLIAM E. *The Cotton Kingdom: A Chronicle of the Old South.* New Haven, 1921.

———. *The Life of Nathaniel Macon.* Raleigh, 1903.

DUNLAP, O. A. "The Economic Ideas of John Taylor." Master's thesis, Duke University, 1934.

EATON, CLEMENT. *Freedom of Thought in the Old South.* Durham, N.C., 1940.

ECKENRODE, H. J. *The Randolphs.* Indianapolis, 1946.

FEILING, KEITH. *Sketches in Nineteenth Century Biography.* London, 1930.

FITZHUGH, GEORGE. *Sociology for the South.* Richmond, 1854.

GABRIEL, RALPH HENRY. *The Course of American Democratic Thought: An Intellectual History Since 1815.* New York, 1940.

GARLAND, HUGH A. *The Life of John Randolph of Roanoke.* 2 vols. New York, 1850.

GILMER, FRANCIS WALKER. *Sketches, Essays, and Translations.* Baltimore, 1828.

GREEN, FLETCHER M. *Constitutional Development in the South Atlantic States, 1776–1860.* Chapel Hill, N.C., 1930.

GRIGSBY, HUGH BLAIR. *Discourse on the Life and Character of the Hon. Littleton Waller Tazewell.* Norfolk, Va., 1860.

———. *The Virginia Convention of 1829–30.* Richmond, 1854.

HARRIS, CICERO W. *The Sectional Struggle: First Period.* Philadelphia, 1902.

HATCHER, WILLIAM B. *Edward Livingston, Jeffersonian Republican and Jacksonian Democrat.* University, La., 1940.

HAYNE, ROBERT Y., and WEBSTER, DANIEL. *The Several Speeches Made During the Debate in the Senate of the United States, on Mr. Foot's Resolution . . . by General Hayne and Mr. Webster.* Charleston, 1830.

HEARNSHAW, F. J. C., ed. *The Social and Political Ideas of Some Representative Thinkers of the Revolutionary Era.* London, 1931.

HESSELTINE, WILLIAM B. *A History of the South, 1607–1936.* New York, 1936.

HOFFMAN, ROSS, and LEVACK, PAUL. *Burke's Politics.* New York, 1949.

JACKSON, ANDREW. *The Correspondence of Andrew Jackson.* Edited by John Spencer Bassett. 7 vols. Washington, D.C., 1926–35.

JACOBS, JOHN RIPLEY. *Tarnished Warrior: Major-General James Wilkinson.* New York, 1938.

JEFFERSON, THOMAS. *The Commonplace Book of Thomas Jefferson.* Edited by Gilbert Chinard. Baltimore, 1927.

———. *The Complete Anas of Thomas* lin B. Sawvel. New York, 1903.

———. *Correspondence Between Thom* uel du Pont de Nemours. Boston, 191

———. *The Literary Bible of Thomas J Book.* Edited by Gilbert Chinard. Ba

———. *The Living Thoughts of Thoma* Dewey. New York, 1940.

———. *Notes on the State of Virginia.*

———. *The Writings of Thomas Jeffe* vols. Washington, D.C., 1904.

JENKINS, WILLIAM SUMNER. *Pro-Slaver* Chapel Hill, N.C., 1935.

JOHNSON, GERALD W. *America's Silver* Webster–Calhoun. New York, 1939

———. *Randolph of Roanoke: A Pol* 1929.

KENNEDY, JOHN PENDLETON. *Memoirs* 2 vols. Philadelphia, 1849–50.

KING, CHARLES R. *The Life and Cor* 5 vols. New York, 1898.

KIRK, RUSSELL. *The Conservative Mi* 1978.

KNAPP, SAMUEL LORENZO (Ignatius *Sketches of Public Characters.* Nev

LEGARÉ, HUGH SWINTON. *The Writing* Charleston, 1846.

LIPSKY, GEORGE A. *John Quincy Ada* New York, 1950.

LODGE, HENRY CABOT. *Daniel Webster.*

MACCUNN, JOHN. *The Political Philosop*

MADISON, JAMES. *The Writings of Jam* lard Hunt. 8 vols. New York, 1908

MALONE, DUMAS. *Jefferson and His 1* 62.

———. *The Public Life of Thomas C* ven, 1926.

MEIGS, WILLIAM M. *The Life of Joh* New York, 1917.

MONROE, JAMES. *Autobiography of Jan* Gerry Brown. Syracuse, N.Y., 195

MU

PAR

PAR

PAR

PHI

POO

PRA

QUI

QUI

RAN

RAV

RISJ

RUS

SAN

SAW

SIMI

SMI

SPAI

STAN

STO

————. "Randolph of Roanoke: A Virginia Portrait—The Early Career of John Randolph of Roanoke, 1773–1805." Doctoral dissertation, University of Virginia, 1955.

SYDNOR, CHARLES S. *The Development of Southern Sectionalism, 1819–1848*. University, La., 1948.

TAYLOR, JOHN, OF CAROLINE. *Arator*. Georgetown, S.C., 1814. Also edition with introduction by M. E. Bradford, Indianapolis, 1977.

————. *Construction Construed, and Constitutions Vindicated*. Richmond, 1820.

————. *Definition of Parties*. Philadelphia, 1794.

————. *An Inquiry into the Principle and Policy of the Government of the United States*. Washington, 1823.

THOMAS, E. S. *Reminiscences of the Last Sixty-Five Years, Commencing with the Battle of Lexington*. Hartford, 1840.

THOMAS, F. W. *John Randolph of Roanoke, and Other Sketches of Character, Including William Wirt*. Philadelphia, 1843.

TOCQUEVILLE, ALEXIS DE. *Democracy in America*. 2 vols. Edited by Phillips Bradley. New York, 1948.

TRENT, WILLIAM P. *Southern Statesmen of the Old Regime*. New York, 1897.

TUCKER, GEORGE. *The Life of Thomas Jefferson*. 2 vols. London, 1837.

TUCKER, ST. GEORGE. *A Dissertation on Slavery*. Philadelphia, 1796.

TURNER, FREDERICK JACKSON. *The Significance of Sections in American History*. New York, 1932.

TYLER, LYON G. *The Letters and Times of the Tylers*. 2 vols. Richmond, 1884.

WILTSE, CHARLES MAURICE. *John C. Calhoun*. 3 vols. Indianapolis, 1935, 1944, 1951.

WISE, JOHN S. *The End of an Era*. Boston and New York, 1899.

WOODFIN, MAUDE H. "Contemporary Opinion in Virginia of Thomas Jefferson," in *Essays in Honor of William E. Dodd* (edited by Avery Craven). Chicago, 1935.

Index

For convenience, this index is divided into two parts. The first portion includes names of persons and places, and titles of books mentioned; the second consists of the principal subjects touched upon. Books and authors mentioned only once by Randolph, and persons incidentally mentioned by him who otherwise remain obscure, generally are omitted from the index.

Index of Names and Titles

Index of Subjects

Page 46
Banks a scorge of the people

This book was linotype set in the Times Roman series of type. The face was designed to be used in the news columns of the *London Times*. The *Times* was seeking a type face that would be condensed enough to accommodate a substantial number of words per column without sacrificing readability and still have an attractive, contemporary appearance. This design was an immediate success. It is used in many periodicals throughout the world and is one of the most popular text faces presently in use for book work.

Book design by Design Center, Inc., Indianapolis, Indiana
Typography by Weimer Typesetting Co., Inc., Indianapolis, Indiana
Printed by Worzalla Publishing Co., Inc., Stevens Point, Wisconsin

BRUCE, PHILIP A. *John Randolph* ("Library of Southern Literature," Vol. X). Atlanta, 1907.

———. *The Virginia Plutarch.* 2 vols. Chapel Hill, N.C., 1929.

BRUCE, WILLIAM CABELL. *Below the James.* Boston, 1937.

———. *John Randolph of Roanoke.* 2 vols. New York, 1922.

BURKE, EDMUND. *Works.* 8 vols. London, 1857.

CALHOUN, JOHN C. *Calhoun: Basic Documents.* Edited by John M. Anderson. State College, Pa., 1952.

———. *The Papers of John C. Calhoun.* 10 vols. Columbia, S.C., 1959–77.

———. *Works.* Edited by R. K. Crallé. 6 vols. New York, 1853–55.

CANAVAN, FRANCIS. *The Political Reason of Edmund Burke.* Durham, N.C., 1960.

CARPENTER, JESSE T. *The South as a Conscious Minority, 1789–1861.* New York, 1930.

CHAPMAN, GERALD W. *Edmund Burke: The Practical Imagination.* Cambridge, Mass., 1967.

CHINARD, GILBERT. *Thomas Jefferson: The Apostle of Americanism.* Boston, 1928.

COIT, MARGARET C. *John C. Calhoun, American Portrait.* Boston, 1950.

COLEMAN, MARY HALDANE. *St. George Tucker, Citizen of No Mean City.* Richmond, 1938.

CONWAY MONCURE DANIEL. *Omitted Chapters of History Disclosed in the Life and Papers of Edmund Randolph.* New York, 1888.

COOPER, JAMES FENIMORE. *The American Democrat.* Cooperstown, N.Y., 1837.

———. *Sketches in Switzerland.* 2 vols. New York, 1836.

COOPER, THOMAS. *Lectures on the Elements of Political Economy.* Columbia, S.C., 1826.

CRAIGHILL, ROBERT T. *The Virginia "Peerage"; or Sketches of Virginians Distinguished in Virginia's History.* Richmond, 1880.

DABNEY, RICHARD HEATH. *John Randolph: A Character Sketch.* Chicago, 1898.

DAVIDSON, DONALD. *The Attack on Leviathan: Regionalism and Nationalism in the United States.* Chapel Hill, N.C., 1938.

DAVIS, RICHARD BEALE. *Francis Walker Gilmer: Life and Learning in Jefferson's Virginia.* Richmond, 1939.

DODD, WILLIAM E. *The Cotton Kingdom: A Chronicle of the Old South.* New Haven, 1921.

————. *The Life of Nathaniel Macon.* Raleigh, 1903.

DUNLAP, O. A. "The Economic Ideas of John Taylor." Master's thesis, Duke University, 1934.

EATON, CLEMENT. *Freedom of Thought in the Old South.* Durham, N.C., 1940.

ECKENRODE, H. J. *The Randolphs.* Indianapolis, 1946.

FEILING, KEITH. *Sketches in Nineteenth Century Biography.* London, 1930.

FITZHUGH, GEORGE. *Sociology for the South.* Richmond, 1854.

GABRIEL, RALPH HENRY. *The Course of American Democratic Thought: An Intellectual History Since 1815.* New York, 1940.

GARLAND, HUGH A. *The Life of John Randolph of Roanoke.* 2 vols. New York, 1850.

GILMER, FRANCIS WALKER. *Sketches, Essays, and Translations.* Baltimore, 1828.

GREEN, FLETCHER M. *Constitutional Development in the South Atlantic States, 1776–1860.* Chapel Hill, N.C., 1930.

GRIGSBY, HUGH BLAIR. *Discourse on the Life and Character of the Hon. Littleton Waller Tazewell.* Norfolk, Va., 1860.

————. *The Virginia Convention of 1829–30.* Richmond, 1854.

HARRIS, CICERO W. *The Sectional Struggle: First Period.* Philadelphia, 1902.

HATCHER, WILLIAM B. *Edward Livingston, Jeffersonian Republican and Jacksonian Democrat.* University, La., 1940.

HAYNE, ROBERT Y., and WEBSTER, DANIEL. *The Several Speeches Made During the Debate in the Senate of the United States, on Mr. Foot's Resolution . . . by General Hayne and Mr. Webster.* Charleston, 1830.

HEARNSHAW, F. J. C., ed. *The Social and Political Ideas of Some Representative Thinkers of the Revolutionary Era.* London, 1931.

HESSELTINE, WILLIAM B. *A History of the South, 1607–1936.* New York, 1936.

HOFFMAN, ROSS, and LEVACK, PAUL. *Burke's Politics.* New York, 1949.

JACKSON, ANDREW. *The Correspondence of Andrew Jackson.* Edited by John Spencer Bassett. 7 vols. Washington, D.C., 1926–35.

JACOBS, JOHN RIPLEY. *Tarnished Warrior: Major-General James Wilkinson.* New York, 1938.

JEFFERSON, THOMAS. *The Commonplace Book of Thomas Jefferson.* Edited by Gilbert Chinard. Baltimore, 1927.

————. *The Complete Anas of Thomas Jefferson.* Edited by Franklin B. Sawvel. New York, 1903.

————. *Correspondence Between Thomas Jefferson and Pierre Samuel du Pont de Nemours.* Boston, 1910.

————. *The Literary Bible of Thomas Jefferson: His Commonplace Book.* Edited by Gilbert Chinard. Baltimore, 1928.

————. *The Living Thoughts of Thomas Jefferson.* Edited by John Dewey. New York, 1940.

————. *Notes on the State of Virginia.* Philadelphia, 1787.

————. *The Writings of Thomas Jefferson.* Memorial edition. 20 vols. Washington, D.C., 1904.

JENKINS, WILLIAM SUMNER. *Pro-Slavery Thought in the Old South.* Chapel Hill, N.C., 1935.

JOHNSON, GERALD W. *America's Silver Age: The Statecraft of Clay–Webster–Calhoun.* New York, 1939.

————. *Randolph of Roanoke: A Political Fantastic.* New York, 1929.

KENNEDY, JOHN PENDLETON. *Memoirs of the Life of William Wirt.* 2 vols. Philadelphia, 1849–50.

KING, CHARLES R. *The Life and Correspondence of Rufus King.* 5 vols. New York, 1898.

KIRK, RUSSELL. *The Conservative Mind.* Sixth edition. Chicago, 1978.

KNAPP, SAMUEL LORENZO (Ignatius Loyola Robertson, pseud.). *Sketches of Public Characters.* New York, 1830.

LEGARÉ, HUGH SWINTON. *The Writings of Hugh Swinton Legaré.* Charleston, 1846.

LIPSKY, GEORGE A. *John Quincy Adams: His Theory and Ideas.* New York, 1950.

LODGE, HENRY CABOT. *Daniel Webster.* Boston, 1894.

MacCUNN, JOHN. *The Political Philosophy of Burke.* London, 1913.

MADISON, JAMES. *The Writings of James Madison.* Edited by Gaillard Hunt. 8 vols. New York, 1908.

MALONE, DUMAS. *Jefferson and His Time.* 3 vols. Boston, 1948–62.

————. *The Public Life of Thomas Cooper, 1783–1839.* New Haven, 1926.

MEIGS, WILLIAM M. *The Life of John Caldwell Calhoun.* 2 vols. New York, 1917.

MONROE, JAMES. *Autobiography of James Monroe.* Edited by Stuart Gerry Brown. Syracuse, N.Y., 1959.

———. *The Writings of James Monroe.* Edited by S. M. Hamilton. 7 vols. New York, 1898–1903.

MUDGE, EUGENE TENBROECK. *The Social Philosophy of John Taylor of Caroline: A Study in Jeffersonian Democracy.* New York, 1939.

PARKS, JOSEPH HOWARD. *Felix Grundy, Champion of Democracy.* University, La., 1940.

PARRINGTON, VERNON L. *The Romantic Revolution in America, 1800–1860.* New York, 1927.

PARTON, JAMES. *Famous Americans of Recent Times.* Boston, 1867.

PHILLIPS, ULRICH B. *American Negro Slavery.* New York, 1918.

POORE, BENJ. PERLEY. *Perley's Reminiscences of Sixty Years in the National Metropolis.* 2 vols. Philadelphia, 1886.

PRATT, JULIUS W. *The Expansionists of 1812.* New York, 1925.

QUINCY, EDMUND. *Life of Josiah Quincy of Massachusetts.* Boston, 1867.

QUINCY, JOSIAH. *Figures of the Past.* Boston, 1901.

RANDOLPH, JOHN. *Letters of John Randolph to a Young Relative: Embracing a Series of Years, from Early Youth, to Mature Manhood.* Edited by Theodore Dudley. Philadelphia, 1834.

RAVENEL, MRS. ST. JULIEN. *Life and Times of William Lowndes, of South Carolina, 1783–1822.* Boston, 1901.

RISJORD, NORMAN K. *The Old Republicans: Southern Conservatism in the Age of Jackson.* New York, 1965.

RUSH, RICHARD. *John Randolph at Home and Abroad.* Philadelphia, 1828.

SANTAYANA, GEORGE. *Reason in Society.* New York, 1905.

SAWYER, LEMUEL. *A Biography of John Randolph of Roanoke.* New York, 1844.

SIMMS, HENRY HARRISON. *John Taylor of Caroline: The Story of a Brilliant Leader in the Early Virginia State Rights School.* Richmond, 1932.

SMITH, PAGE. *John Adams.* 2 vols. New York, 1963.

SPAIN, AUGUST O. *The Political Theory of John C. Calhoun.* New York, 1951.

STANLIS, PETER. *Edmund Burke and the Natural Law.* Foreword by Russell Kirk. Ann Arbor, Mich., 1958.

STOKES, WILLIAM E., JR. "The Early Life of John Randolph of Roanoke, 1773–1794." Master's thesis, University of Virginia, 1950.